EDWARD LEAR THE LANDSCAPE ARTIST

Tours of Ireland and the English Lakes, 1835 & 1836

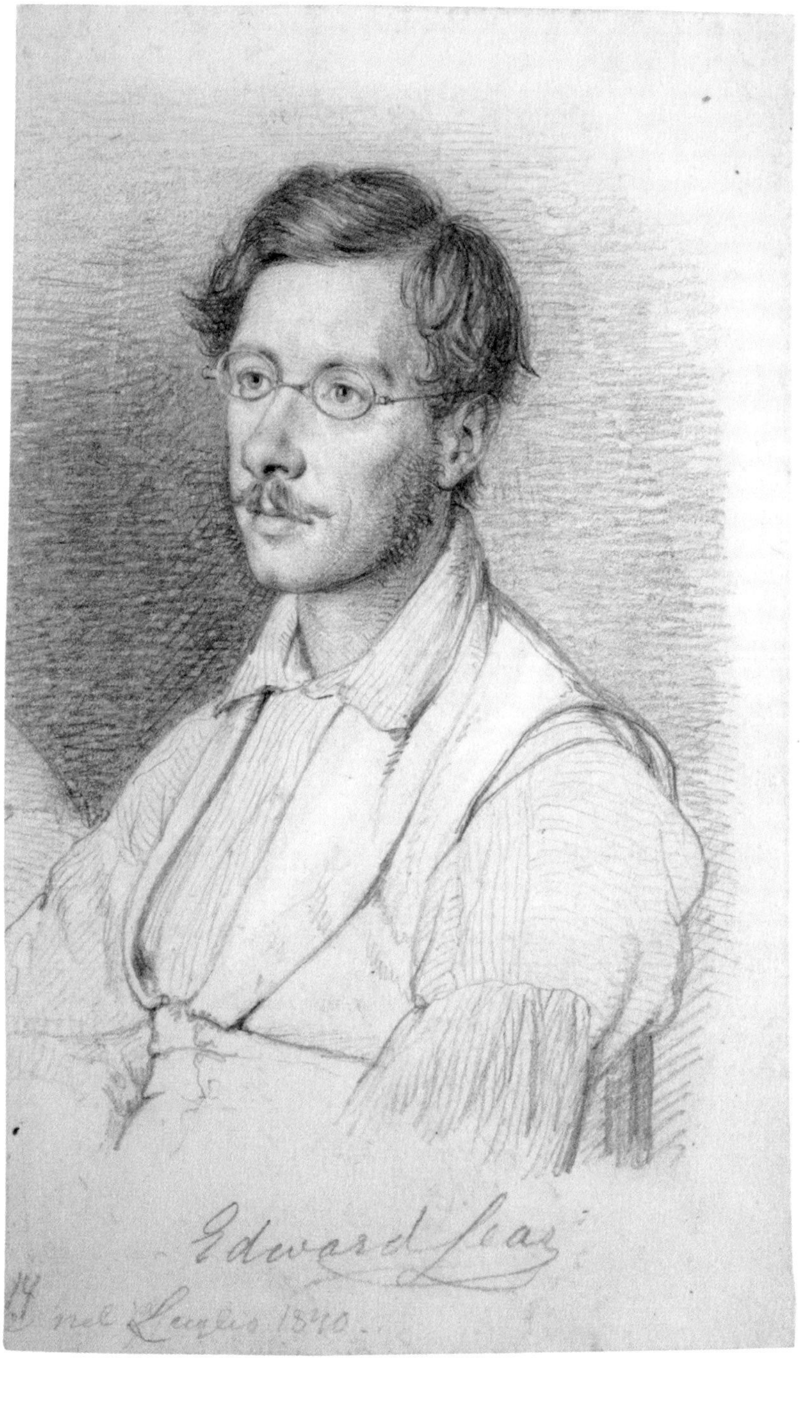
Edward Lear
1840

Edward Lear the Landscape Artist

Tours of Ireland and the English Lakes, 1835 & 1836

Charles Nugent

with an essay by
Michael Twyman

THE WORDSWORTH TRUST
GRASMERE 2009

Published by the Wordsworth Trust
Dove Cottage, Grasmere, Cumbria LA22 9SH

ISBN 978-1-905256-38-9

Designed by Stephen Hebron
Picture research by Amy Concannon
Set in Monotype Dante
Printed by Titus Wilson, Kendal

Frontispiece:
Edward Lear by Wilhelm Nicolai Marstrand, 1840,
pencil, 17.8 × 10.8 cm (National Portrait Gallery, London)

Assisted by grants from the
W.W. Spooner Charitable Trust
Northern Rock Foundation
Trusthouse Charitable Foundation
Westmorland Arts Trust

CONTENTS

PREFACE

The first exhibition at the Grasmere and Wordsworth Museum, *The Discovery of the Lake District 1750–1810: A Context for Wordsworth,* opened in May 1982. Curated by Robert Woof, it was to be the first of his rewarding co-operations with Peter Bicknell, architect and climber, whose special interest was the art and literature of mountain regions. The following year the roles of the artists, the tourists, and William Wordsworth were examined in the summer exhibition, *The Lake District Discovered 1810–1850*. This contained seventeen works by Edward Lear, including one belonging to Dove Cottage, 'The Pillar, Ennerdale', which had been gifted by Dr Charles Warren.

I discovered as a schoolboy Edward Lear's *Book of Nonsense*, but I remained unaware that he was a composer of songs, particularly with Tennyson's words, and an illustrator and landscape artist of rare originality. In the early 1960s I was encouraged by Mouse and William Spooner to study their collection of watercolours at Ashbrook in Ilkley. There for the first time I discovered Edward Lear the landscape artist: the drawing was of Skiddaw from Grange, inscribed 'Clouds Frizzled', and dated 22 September 1836. William, a lifetime collector of watercolours and no mean artist in his own right, patiently explained the technique to me, and provided a brief biography of Lear the traveller and topographer.

The W.W. Spooner Charitable Trust first became supporters of the Wordsworth Trust in 1996, when we assisted in the purchase of various sketch books and drawings. Robert Woof was aware that I owned one Lear drawing, and that in August 2003 I had purchased 'Honister from Near Buttermere', dated 27 September 1836. In November 2003 he was consulted by Christie's in advance of a sale to assist in identifying a series of seven Lake District views by Lear. With the assistance of the Art Fund the seven drawings were acquired, and we were successful two years later in securing at Sotheby's three further examples. Robert was now intent upon curating an exhibition dedicated to Lear's 1836 tour of the Lakes, and in September 2005 he, Stephen Hebron and I discussed the possibility of Spooner support for the Wordsworth exhibition programme. The Spooner Trust had never considered this type of sponsorship before, but it accorded well with our founder's passionate belief that great works of art should be displayed for the benefit and enjoyment of a wider public. Here I must express deep gratitude to my co-Trustees, who have always been generously supportive of our partnership with the Wordsworth Trust. We committed to co-operate in a programme of exhibitions and the detail was agreed with Robert before his passing in November 2005. Stephen discussed the Lear exhibition with Charles Nugent, who was enthusiastic and offered every support.

We have now reached the completion of a project for which the first seed was sown twenty-six years ago. It embraces all the virtues of teamwork, patient acquisition, diligent research and original scholarship. Robert would say that this is the Wordsworth Trust at its very best, punching above its weight in pursuit of excellence! The exhibition and catalogue are timely, coming three years in advance of the bicentenary of Edward Lear's birth in 1812, and, for the first time, exploring in detail his development as a landscape artist before he began his self imposed exile in July 1837 as a 'wandering painter – whose life's occupation is travelling for pictorial and topographical purposes'.

I and my fellow Trustees would like to thank Charles Nugent for his invaluable contribution as the exhibition curator, and we are deeply appreciative of his rigorous research and scholarship, which greatly enhances our understanding of Lear's development as a landscape artist. We are extremely grateful to Michael Twyman for providing a fascinating insight into the artist's development of his printmaking skills. We thank Amy Concannon, Exhibition and Publications Officer, Jeff Cowton, Curator of the Wordsworth Trust, and Alex Black for his photography. Their enthusiasm and dedication has contributed to a project completed with great professionalism. Michael McGregor, Director of the Wordsworth Trust, has offered generous support and encouragement with constructive advice at all times. Stephen Hebron has co-ordinated the project with a true generosity of spirit and has given us a catalogue of enduring beauty, designed with flair yet rich in scholarly content and illustration.

The partnership between the Spooner Trust and the Wordsworth Trust continues resolutely to advance research and scholarship and enlightened acquisition, supporting an innovatory and challenging exhibition programme.

Michael Broughton
Chairman, The W.W. Spooner Charitable Trust

FOREWORD

Edward Lear the Landscape Artist continues our series of exhibitions looking at the ways in which artists and writers depicted the Lake District in the eighteenth and nineteenth centuries. Edward Lear's later years, when he travelled widely around the Mediterranean and published his popular nonsense verse, have been well explored. This exhibition concentrates on his less well-known early career, and offers the first full account of his visit to Ireland in 1835 and extensive tour of Lancashire, Westmorland and Cumberland the following year.

I must first thank Charles Nugent, the curator of the exhibition and the author of this catalogue. The project has occupied him for the better part of two years, and it has been a great pleasure to work with such a generous and assiduous scholar. That his many discoveries can now be presented in an exhibition is thanks to the goodwill of several public institutions, and the kindness of an unusually large number of private owners, to all of whom the Trustees are most grateful.

I would also like to thank Michael Twyman, who has contributed a typically perceptive and authoritative essay on Lear as a lithographer, and Stephen Hebron, who has been involved in the exhibition since its inception and designed this catalogue. Among my colleagues in Grasmere I must particularly thank Jeff Cowton, Amy Concannon and Alex Black.

In mounting an exhibition of this kind, the Trust depends upon the generosity of its supporters, and we are very grateful to the Northern Rock Foundation for their continuing support of our exhibition programme, to the Westmorland Arts Trust, and to the Trusthouse Charitable Foundation. Above all, the Trustees would like to thank Michael Broughton and the W.W. Spooner Charitable Trust. In recent years they have enabled us to build up our own collection of Lake District drawings by Edward Lear, and in supporting this exhibition and catalogue have ensured that our fine art collection continues to benefit from the highest standards of research and scholarship.

Michael McGregor
Director, The Wordsworth Trust

ACKNOWLEDGEMENTS

Every scholar working on Lear is inevitably indebted to the pioneering and ongoing work of Vivien Noakes. From the inception of this project, she has generously shared her scholarship with me, even to the extent of lending me her research files for Lear's early years, as well as books from her extensive library. I am extremely grateful to her for all her help, as well as her hospitality on several visits; she is also a generous lender to the exhibition.

I am also indebted to other scholars who have worked on aspects of Lear's life, and in particular to Charles Lewsen, Clemency Fisher and Valerie Wadsworth.

In addition, I am personally and professionally indebted to Professor Michael Twyman, who has contributed an authoritative essay on Lear and lithography to this catalogue. I have benefited from lengthy interesting discussions on the subject of lithography in England with Professor Twyman, who has been prodigal with his knowledge, as well as generous with loans from his personal collection.

A larger proportion than usual of the loans to this exhibition comes from private collections, and there is no doubt that without the agreement of these owners the exhibition would never have taken the form that it has. I am delighted that the present Earl of Derby, the 19th, has viewed this Lear project of the early years of the third millenium with the same enlightened enthusiasm that his ancestor the 13th Earl treated his young artist protégé in the 1830s. Without the support of Lord Derby and of David Sekers, who together provide nearly a quarter of the Lear loans, this exhibition would have been considerably less impressive.

The majority of the works in the exhibition have appeared on the London art market in the last fifty years, and I am grateful to those dealers and auction house specialists who have facilitated my journeys in these often tortuous and arcane paths; with one exception, they have been receptive to and helped with my sometimes repeated enquiries. They include Claire Anderson, Noël Annesley, Philip Athill, John Baskett, Harriet Drummond, Venetia Harlow, Jeremy Howard, Lowell Libson, Lynda McLeod, Anthony Spink, Henry Wemyss, and Andrew Wyld.

Curators, librarians, museum administrators, art historians, conservators and independent scholars have been helpful with general or specific aspects relating to the exhibition; they include Martyn Anglesea, Heather Birchall, Peter Bower, David Cross, John Falconer, Melanie Gardner, Sue Gardner, Sarah Glenn, Colin Harrison, Peter Henderson, Matthew Hyde, Adrian James, Edward King, Emma McCarthy, Melinda McCurdy, Janet Martin, Michael Meredith, Hope Mayo, David Morris, Jane Roberts, John Martin Robinson, Angela Roche, Nick Rogers, Henrietta Ryan, Kim Sloan, Graeme Storey, Kirstin Waibel, Peter Whitehead and Scott Wilcox.

Private collectors and enthusiasts, owners or descendants of owners of the houses which Lear visited, and members of the Cumbrian cultural community have helped me enormously in my researches. They include Araminta,

Lady Aldington, Sir David Attenborough, Hal Bagot, Christopher Lennox-Boyd, Sir Mark Lennox-Boyd, Michael Broughton, Mary Burkett, Lord Chorley, Mikle Coker, Maldwin Drummond, Susan Dunn, Sir William Gladstone, Brian Hancock, Laurence Harwood, Lord Henley, Jocelyn Holland, Michael Hornby, Philip Howard, Cressida Inglewood, John Lee, Richard Lockett, Ian Lowe, Cecily Mason-Hornby, Francis Mason-Hornby, Diana Matthews, Katie Mawson, Susie Reynolds, Andrew Roberts, John Spedding, Jonathan Stanley, Lord Stanley of Alderly, Nick Stanley, Rupert Villiers-Smith and Charles Townley.

This exhibition brings together for the first time all of Lear's known drawings relating to his brief visit to Ireland in 1835. I am particularly grateful to Nicholas Tromans, who pointed out to me the importance of the meeting of the British Association for the Advancement of Science in Dublin in 1835, which Lear attended. In addition, a number of administrators, collectors, curators, historians and scholars in Ireland have helped me to break new ground in this little-researched aspect of Lear's early life. They include Helen Beaney, Paul Caffrey, Mary Davies, Desmond FitzGerald, Peter Harbison, Anne Hodge, Brian Lalor, Simon Lang and John Ross.

Lear's considerably longer trip round what was then Lancashire, Westmorland and Cumberland between August and the end of October 1836 has also never before been in the spotlight of scholarship, and I am grateful to those Lake District residents and Cumbrian topographical enthusiasts, walkers and runners alike, who have helped me largely to reconstruct Lear's journey. They include Richard Askwith, Michael Baron, Julian Cooper, Chris Jesty, Joss Naylor and David Unsworth.

The team at the Wordsworth Trust, Dove Cottage, Grasmere, is a group of very special individuals; without their dedication and enthusiasm, this exhibition would never have taken place. I am grateful to the previous Robert Woof Director of the Wordsworth Trust, David Wilson, who first asked me to take on this exhibition, and to the current holder of the post Michael McGregor, who has been supportive and enthusiastic throughout. Jeff Cowton, the Curator of the Wordsworth Trust, has been interested and helpful during the long gestation of this project. In addition, Alex Black, Carrie Taylor, Lucy Clarke and Paul Kleian have helped with general or specific aspects relating to the exhibition. The smooth organisation and administration of the exhibition is largely due to the ever cheerful and immensely efficient Amy Concannon, the Wordsworth Trust's Exhibitions and Publications Officer; she has endured my frequent telephone conversations and demands with patience and enthusiasm. Stephen Hebron, who at the start of the project was on the staff of the Wordsworth Trust and is now freelance, has dealt with a wayward author and designed a beautiful catalogue with his customary flair and professionalism.

Lastly, I would like to thank my wife Lulu, who has put up with the presence of the young Edward Lear in the house for the past two years, and the frequent sleepless nights and absences from home which this demanding addition to the family has entailed.

THE EARLY LIFE OF EDWARD LEAR

In 1861 Edward Lear published a new and enlarged edition of his *Book of Nonsense*. This, the third edition, was the first to bear Lear's name, and for a later reissue he included 'by way of preface' a condensed account of his life.[1] Of the years up to 1837 he wrote:

> Born in 1812 (12th May), I began to draw, for bread and cheese, about 1827, but only did uncommon queer shop sketches – selling them for prices varying from nine pence to four shillings: colouring prints, screens, fans: awhile making morbid disease drawings, for hospitals and certain doctors of physic. In 1831, through Mrs Wentworth, I became employed at the Zoological Society, and, in 1832, published 'The Family of Psittacidae', the first complete volume of coloured drawings of birds on so large a scale published in England. ... J. Gould's 'Indian Pheasants' were commenced at the same time, and after a little while he employed me to draw many of his birds of Europe, while I assisted Mrs Gould in all her drawings of foregrounds, as may be seen in a moment by any one who will glance at my drawings in G.'s European birds and the Toucans. From 1832 to 1836, when my health failed a good deal, I drew much at the Earl of Derby's; and a series of my drawings was published by Dr. Gray of the British Museum. ... I also lithographed many various detached subjects. ... In 1835 or '36, being in Ireland and the Lakes, I leaned more and more towards landscape, and when in 1837 it was found that my health was more affected by the climate month by month, I went abroad, wintering in Rome until 1841.[2]

The later life of Edward Lear is extremely well-documented. The diaries that he kept over a thirty-year period between 1858 and 1887 are preserved in the Houghton Library at Harvard University, and have been exhaustively studied. The letters that he wrote to Chichester Fortescue, Lord Carlingford, and Frances, Lady Waldegrave, begin in 1847 and are an invaluable source for the later period of Lear's career.[3] Sadly, however, this is not the case for the earlier years, in particular for those up to 1837, when, at the age of twenty-five, Lear left England to live on the Continent. Although he did return to England periodically in the years that followed, sometimes staying for long periods, he always returned to Europe, where he spent most of the rest of his life. The years up to 1837 can therefore be regarded as a distinct first part of his career.

None of the diaries for the years before 1858 survive, and only a handful of letters from his formative years. It seems that both Lear himself and his executor, Franklin Lushington, Lord Carlingford (1823–1901), are to blame. Lear wrote

1. The whole text (written in the form of a letter) is reproduced in the introduction to *Letters*, pp. xxvii–xxx.

2. Ibid., pp. xxvii–xxviii.

3. Published in 1907 as *Letters of Edward Lear* and in 1911 as *Later Letters of Edward Lear*. The originals are in the Somerset Record Office.

in 1871: 'for 12 or 13 years when at Knowsley, I kept a journal about everything and every body, but one day in 1840, I burnt the whole. It has all turned up again, for I copied all, or nearly all, in letters to my sister, and she preserved all those'.[4] These letters to his sister Ann (1790–1861), which date mostly from after 1837, were still in existence in the 1930s, when copies were made, but have since disappeared.[5] Although he did preserve nearly thirty years of diaries, which are now in the Houghton Library, Harvard University, Franklin Lushington is responsible for the remainder of the destruction. It may have been partly Victorian discretion, but it was probably more practicality, that led to the loss of this evidence, since, although Lear was one of twenty-one children, very few relatives survived him and none of them lived in England.

The rediscovery of part of the correspondence of Lear to the Drewitt family, who were childhood friends in Sussex, has shed a great deal more light on this early part of Lear's career. Fanny Drewitt married George Coombe in the early 1830s, and the content of Lear's letters to them both necessitated Vivien Noakes's rewriting of her 1968 biography of Lear, published in a revised edition in 2004. Those up to July 1837 are published in this catalogue in their entirety for the first time (see Appendix A, pp. 201–27).

Like many large middle-class families of the time, the Lears hovered above penury but maintained their respectability. Lear's father Jeremiah (1757–1833) was fertile even by the standards of the time in producing twenty-one children who survived to adulthood, but he did not have the means to provide for them, and when he decided to retire in 1827, the family had to split up. Lear set up house with his eldest sister Ann in Gray's Inn Road, London, and it was from this point that he dated his start in life. He was later to write of being 'at the age of 14 & a half … turned out into the world, *literally without a farthing* – & nought to look for a living but [my] own exertions';[6] since Ann seems to have inherited a small annuity from her grandmother, brother and sister were not utterly destitute, but Lear did need to begin to earn his own living. Up to this point, as a short-sighted and sickly child, he had been educated at home, mostly by Ann and another elder sister, Sarah; as part of this education, Lear had been taught to draw. A few drawings survive from this part of Lear's life; they are small, highly worked in pencil, and often derivative. Generally, they show the teenage artist at a level of proficiency barely above the standard of the average Regency drawing-room. His earliest surviving landscape drawing is of Peppering House, the Sussex home of the Drewitt family (fig. 1); it is a competent exercise in draughtsmanship, with formal shading and no attempt at colour.

As the pupil of amateurs, Lear felt the lack of proper training all his life, and indeed never became a really proficient figure draughtsman. However, his need to improve as an artist was always more than counterbalanced by his need to earn a living, and it seems that some time around 1828 Lear began to do this by drawing birds. There is no evidence one way or the other, but it has been suggested

4. *Letters*, p. xix.
5. Noakes 2006, p. [vii].
6. *Selected Letters*, p. 14.

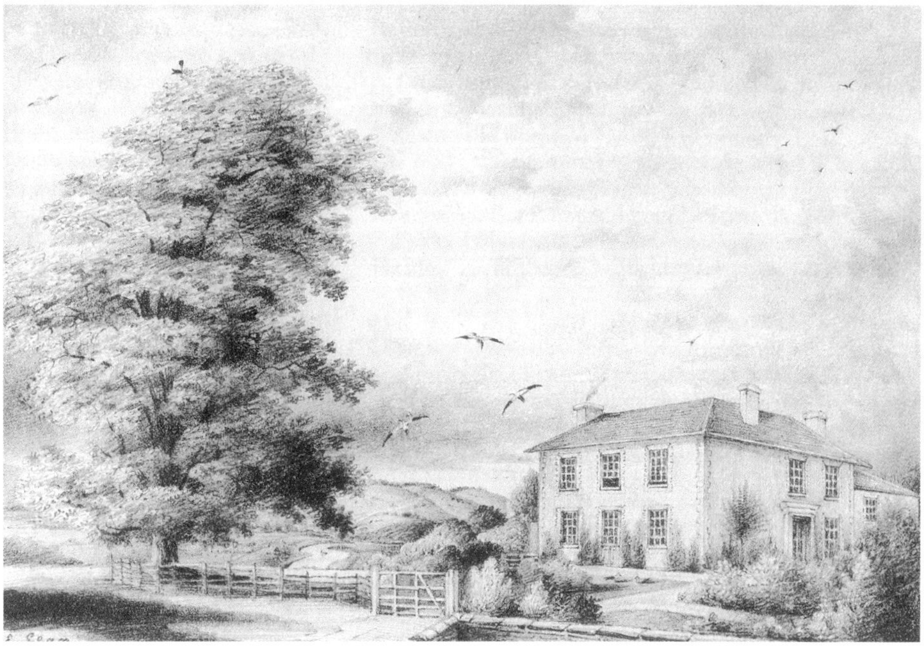

Fig. 1 Edward Lear, Peppering House, 1829, pencil, 12.8 × 19.1 cm (Private Collection).

that Lear served some sort of informal apprenticeship with Prideaux John Selby, whose *Illustrations of British Ornithology* was published in parts between 1821 and 1834.[7] Selby was a Northumberland squire, and Lear probably met him through Mrs Godfrey Wentworth, whom he certainly credits with his introduction to the newly formed Zoological Society.[8] This is not the place to go over Lear's contribution to the field of natural history, which has been done extensively by others,[9] but it is sufficient to say that, after his publication of *Illustrations of the Family of Psittacidae, or Parrots* in 1832, Lear, at the age of nineteen, had become a significant figure in the field of British bird illustration.

Although again there is no definite evidence, it is probable that Lear learnt the process of lithography from Charles Hullmandel (1789–1850), who was certainly a close friend by the early 1830s. Hullmandel had begun his career as an artist before becoming a lithographic printer. As is noted by Michael Twyman: 'It is no exaggeration to say that nearly every major improvement made to lithography in Britain in the first half of the 19th century, in terms of extending its modes of expression, stemmed from Hullmandel. … Hullmandel's improvements related primarily to those aspects of the process that concerned the artist, and in this respect they reflected his own interests and training. His attitudes were coloured by his early days as an artist and it is no coincidence that he called his book on lithography *The Art of Drawing on Stone*'.[10] Published in 1824, this volume, the title page of which is reproduced here (fig. 2, p. 4; see also cat. 4), was a

7. Noakes 1991, p. 33.
8. *Letters*, p. xxviii.
9. See in particular Fisher pp. 165–73 and Noakes 1985, pp. 208–10.
10. Twyman 1988, p. 68.

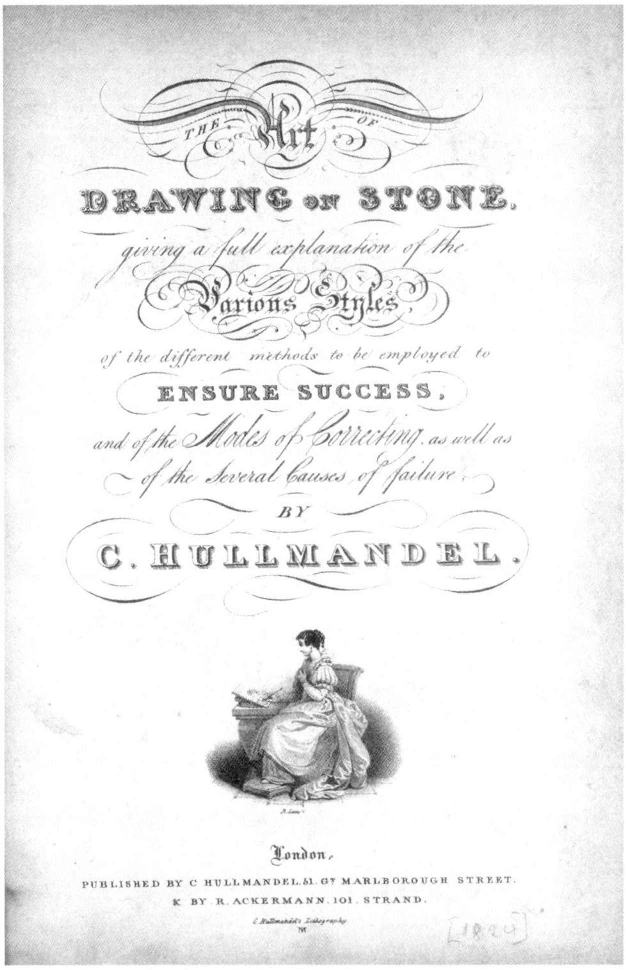

THE Art OF
DRAWING ON STONE,
giving a full explanation of the
Various Styles,
of the different methods to be employed to
ENSURE SUCCESS,
and of the Modes of Correcting, as well as
of the Several Causes of failure.
BY
C. HULLMANDEL.

London.
PUBLISHED BY C HULLMANDEL, 51. Gt MARLBOROUGH STREET.
& BY R. ACKERMANN. 101. STRAND.

Fig. 2 Title page of Charles Hullmandel's *The Art of Drawing on Stone*, 1824 (Private Collection).

detailed handbook for artists practising lithography, and is surely one with which Lear would have been intimately familiar. Hullmandel was a convivial and social man, who surrounded himself with artists, and gave parties at his London house (which was also his business premises), 49, Great Marlborough Street. The lithographic draughtsman, George Barnard, recorded: 'we had very pleasant conversaziones of artist, actors and musicians at Hullmandel's ... and the society of most of the Royal Academicians, such as Stanfield, Turner, Westall, Landseer, &c.'.[11] Such evenings must have been meat and drink for the young natural history illustrator dreaming of becoming a fully fledged artist. There is evidence that Lear was able to return the social favour and organise a bachelor party of his own in his lodgings (letter of 19 June 1835, see Appendix A, pp. 206), and that Hullmandel was among the guests.

One of the artists who worked most closely with Hullmandel was James Duffield Harding (1797–1863). Surprisingly, it does not appear that Lear knew Harding, but he did know his work as a lithographer, which began to appear in

11. Ibid., p. 46.

drawing books from the early 1820s. Lithographs such as those in *Hullmandel's Drawing Book for 1827* (cat. 2) and in *Elementary Art, or The Use of the Lead Pencil Advocated and Explained*, first published in 1834 (a second edition came out in 1838) (cat. 6), which culminated in the monumental *Sketches at Home and Abroad* (1836) (cat. 89), exercised a strong and persistent influence on Lear's lithographic and drawing style well into the 1840s.

A good source for our knowledge of both Hullmandel and Harding, as well as for Lear, is the autobiography of Daniel Fowler (1810–1894). Fowler was a pupil of Harding for three years from about 1831 to 1834; the drawings which Fowler brought back from his tour of Holland, the Rhine, Switzerland and Italy in 1834 and 1835 were one of the things that inspired Lear to go to Italy himself (see cat. 12). When Lear left for Europe in July 1837, Fowler travelled with him. Although they later parted company, and Fowler emigrated to Canada in 1843, they maintained their friendship by correspondence, and it is unfortunate that none of their letters survives. Late in life, Fowler began work on his autobiography, which survives partly in manuscript, and records in amazing detail the events of more than half a century earlier. Fowler is less than complimentary about Harding:

> If the size and weight of the brain is a true index of its intellectual force, then Harding must have been a man of unusual talent, for he could never find a hat large enough to fit him. He was not a genial man, and was without a spark of humour that I ever discovered. ... Harding's work was, however slightly, artificial and conventional. And I *must* add mechanical, if only from the too apparent perfection of handling. ... Harding was a man of energy, determination, perseverance, and those qualities, combined with such intelligence as he possessed are certain to carry a man upward, and he had forced his way from a somewhat lower station. ... Harding was an indefatigable worker. ... It was out of Harding's power to make another Harding, but he could make an artist of any man, provided that he had malleable material to work on'.[12]

The same unsympathetic seriousness of purpose was noted by others. Ruskin, who was briefly Harding's pupil in the 1840s, wrote to Samuel Prout, who had been displaced by Harding as the artist of the *Landscape Annual* in 1832 and had strong professional reasons for disliking him: 'if that man had but a soul he would make a great painter'.[13]

Of Lear and his early career Fowler recorded:

> Among the acquaintances whom I made at that time was Edward Lear, and with him it grew into a friendship – mostly kept up by correspondence – as long as he lived. He was truly a remarkable man. He was painter, musician, traveller, author, linguist, and humourist, not exactly the greatest in any of these departments, but an excellent second in them all. ... Left without father or mother, he was brought up under very straitened circumstances by an elder sister. His first attempts at

12. Smith, pp. 99–102.
13. Abbey *Travel*, vol. i, p. 37.

earning money were made in offering his little drawings for anything he could get to stage coach passengers in inn yards. Then he took to zoological drawings for publishers, and, while engaged in that work, came under the notice of Lord Derby, whose tastes lay in that direction. His lordship had him down to his country seat, Knowsley, near Liverpool, to make certain drawings for him, and while so employed he was given into the charge of the housekeeper. It was after this that he and I first came together. He must then have been about twenty. Tall, not handsome, and rather ungainly in figure, he was very agreeable and genial in manner. There indeed was partly the secret of his great success in life; he was all things to all people. ... He had had at that time a renewed summons to Knowsley and he could not determine from their mode of its expression whether he was invited as a guest at his lordship's table or as that of the housekeeper. ... Arrived at Knowsley – we had it all from himself – he took the safer part; he went below and presented himself to his old friend, but almost immediately Lord Derby was heard calling out from the head of the stairs leading to the lower regions 'Mister Lear, Mister Lear, come up here.' And up Lear went and from that moment took his place among the society which he was likely to find in his lordship's dining room, and which he kept with ease, all his life. [This episode is described in Lear's letter from Knowsley written on 24 June 1835, cat. 14.] He had already published a book on the parrott tribe. ... He had also made a beginning in landscape painting, with all promise. And thus it came to pass that Lord Derby, by himself and his friends, made up a purse for Lear that he might go to Italy and study painting at his leisure. There are not many to whom such a happy opportunity would fall, and perhaps there are *some* to whom its taking such a shape would not be *quite* acceptable, but Lear was perfectly free from all such scruples. His career was founded on patronage, and under that he was content to enter upon it. It was, too, more or less patronage all his days, but he proved himself worthy of it, if any man ever did.[14]

Even with the passing of nearly sixty years, Fowler's comments are very perceptive. Lear's career was indeed founded on patronage, and, quite simply, he needed the money. This is very clear in his relationship with the bird illustrator John Gould (1804–1881), who was some years Lear's senior. In 1824 Gould set himself up as a taxidermist in Windsor, and in 1827 became the first Curator and Preserver for the Zoological Society's new museum in Bruton Street, London. From the early 1830s he began to produce a series of increasingly ambitious lithographic publications on birds, many of them with Lear's help. Described by Duff Hart-Davis in a recent book on Audubon as 'industrious, cunning, equipped with a good business sense, if not entirely straightforward, ... neither a talented draughtsman nor a dedicated naturalist',[15] Gould was in many ways the very opposite of Lear, but he needed the younger artist's skills and services, and used them mercilessly in the early 1830s. Hart-Davis suggests that Gould brought Lear into his team in order to slow down the progress of a rival, and there is some truth in this; certainly, without Lear's contributions, Gould's publications would have been much less impressive.

14. Smith, pp. 103–4.
15. Duff Hart-Davis, *Audubon's Elephant* (London: Phoenix, 2003) p. 227.

Gould's first book, *A Century of Birds from the Himalaya Mountains*, came out in parts in 1830 and 1831. This was followed by the more lengthy and ambitious *The Birds of Europe*, which came out between 1832 and 1837; in the Preface to this book, Gould wrote that 'by far the greater number of the Plates of this work ... have been drawn and lithographed by Mrs Gould ... The remainder of the drawings have been made by Mr Lear, whose abilities as an artist are so generally acknowledged that any comments of my own are unnecessary'. Of the 449 plates in the five published volumes, sixty-eight are by Lear. At least Lear's contribution was acknowledged, which was not the case for his work on the toucans for Gould's *A Monograph of the Ramphastidae, or Family of Toucans*, published in 1833–5, where, although ten of the plates are signed by Lear, the lettering reads 'Drawn from nature and on stone by J. & E. Gould'. The extent of Lear's contribution to Gould's work is examined in detail by Vivien Noakes,[16] and Brian Reade is surely accurate in his asssessment: 'he committed himself to a long stretch of tedious and unprofitable second-fiddling'.[17]

While he was working for Gould, Lear was complimentary about him in letters to his friends. A letter to George Coombe written in April 1833 (cat. 5) goes into some detail about their business and personal relationship:

> John Gould—a man without any prospects or education, has by dint of a singularly active mind, good talents, & uncontrollable perseverance (not to say impudence backed by no little good luck—risen in the world beyond belief for the last ten years—John Gould who married a wife—which wife with a little of my instruction commenced lithography, & after publishing the Himalayan Birds—in helping her husband with a magnificent work on the birds of Europe, John Gould, I say, with whom I have always been by circumstances very much allied—as I do all the backgrounds to the European birds besides various touchings up ... which consequently brings me a good deal to his home ... Gould has always behaved in the most handsome & grateful manner to me ... now in March it came to his ears that I wanted to get rid of my Parrots ... so he came to me—& ... offered me £50 ... on condition that I would continentalize with him—& to pay my expenses there & back entirely ... I accepted his offer.

It is known that Gould visited the Continent in July and August 1833, and it seems likely, although there is no evidence apart from this letter, that Lear went with him. Later, in March 1836, Lear wrote to Fanny Coombe: 'Gould who is about to visit the Americas, & who has engaged to finish his work on European birds before he goes, has made me enter into a written engagement that I will do a certain number of birds before I work for any one else, & as he has always employed me & paid me well, I am bound ..... to pay some attention to him'. The following year, on 3 January 1837, Lear wrote that he was 'to go to Paris in three weeks time to make some drawings (Zoological) for Gould'. This visit was initially postponed by the illness and death of Lear's sister, and eventually took place at the end of April or beginning of May. The news of Lear's decision

16. Noakes 1985, pp. 208–9.
17. Reade, p. 26.

to move to Rome to study, which he was able to do because of a gift of money, relayed in the letter of 3 March (cat. 93) obviated the need to work for Gould any more, and it seems that Gould did not take kindly to this news; perhaps he tried to use the signed agreement of the previous year.

Whatever the case, in later life Lear only ever mentioned Gould in negative terms. Although they continued to exchange friendly letters in the early 1840s,[18] by the early 1860s Lear referred to him as 'hardly altered – kindly & coarse' (Diary, 1 March 1861) and the following month he is described as 'singularly vulgar & odious ... he is always so more or less' (Diary, 26 April 1861). In 1863, Lear wrote: 'he is always a hog ... as to how *such* a man could portray humming birds or anything refined' (Diary, 27 Nov. 1863). Much later, Lear wrote: 'About 1830 I think or earlier, perhaps 1828 – I went with [Gould] to Rotterdam, Berne, Berlin and other places, – but it was not a satisfactory journey; – and at Amsterdam we laid the foundation of many subsequent years of misery to me'.[19] When he heard of Gould's death in 1881, Lear wrote: 'He was one I never liked really, for in spite of a certain jollity & Bonhomie he was a harsh & violent man. At the Zoological G. at 33 Bruton St. at Hullmandel's ... ever the same, persevering, hard working toiler in his own (ornithological) line, but ever as unfeeling for those about him. In this earliest phase of this bird drawing, he owed everything to his excellent wife, – & to myself, without whose help in drawing he had done nothing.'[20]

In the late 1820s and early 1830s, Lear followed the route of most professional artists, and took on pupils. There are occasional references to these in the Drewitt/Coombe letters, such as that of 15 April 1837 (cat. 94), where he writes: '2 mornings in the week, I have had a class of pupils in Grosvenor Square of 6 or 8 – & it has been quite delightful.' This was not the experience of his friend Daniel Fowler, who wrote, 'Every teacher will have a parcel of young girls on his hands, who have not the remote idea what art means. ... [They have] as much comprehension of it as a parrot has of the speech it learns. This is the case with ninety nine out of a hundred young ladies who take it up as an accomplishment, so called, I suppose, because nothing is accomplished'.[21] A commonplace book, containing drawings by a Miss Fraser, a Lear pupil, and by Lear himself, which is dateable to between 1828 and 1832, was sold at Christie's in 1990, and is now in a private collection.[22] Lear also used his contacts in Sussex to make his earliest contribution to a topographical publication, a study of the nave of Arundel Church, which appeared in *The History and Antiquities of the Castle and Town of Arundel; including the Biography of its Earls, from the Conquest to the Present Time*, by the Rev. M.A. Tierney, F.S.A.; this was published in two volumes in 1834. This book is illustrated with numerous engravings, mostly of antiquities, with only one after Lear (fig. 3); with slightly awkward treatment of the perspective, it shows a view of the nave of the church looking back towards the organ from the altar.

18. *Selected Letters*, pp. 51–3 and 60–2.
19. Reade, p. 26. Unfortunately, the source for this quotation is not known.
20. Ibid.
21. Smith, pp. 122–3.
22. Noakes 1991, pp. 34–5.

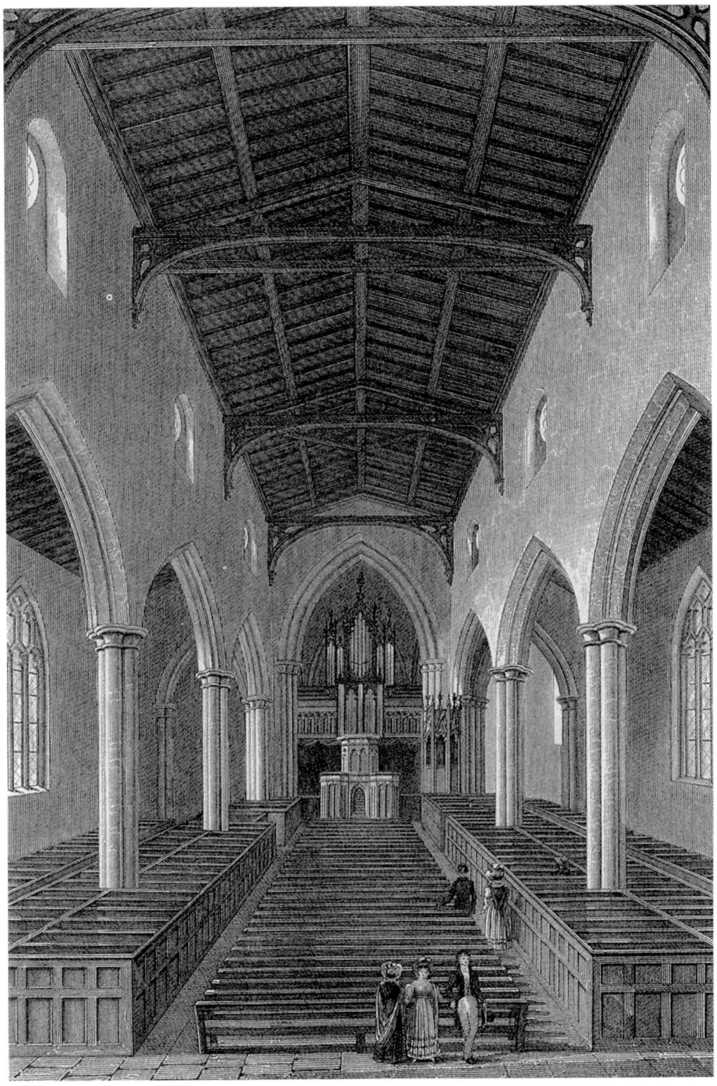

Fig. 3 'Nave of Arundel Church', engraving after Edward Lear, from Rev. M.A. Tierney, *The History and Antiquities of the Castle and Town of Arundel*, 1834, vol. ii, opposite p. 643 (Private Collection).

During this period, Lear, as he later put it, 'leaned more and more to landscape', with the short trip to Ireland in 1835 leading to the much longer and extensive tour of the Lake District in 1836. Part of the reason for this was his deteriorating eyesight, which had worsened owing to years of close ornithological work; as he recorded in his letter to John Gould from Knowsley in October 1836: 'my eyes are so sadly worse, that no bird under an Ostrich shall I soon be able to see to do.'[23] Lear was always much concerned with his health, and his letters frequently contain detailed records of it, leaving the impression that he was often ill. However, despite his infirmity, he was able to undertake arduous journeys which would have been beyond many Victorian tourists. Lear later described 1836 as the year 'when my health failed a good deal', but the record of his activity

23. See Appendix B, and *Selected Letters*, p. 23.

in this year belies this statement and is really quite remarkable; the distances he covered, the poor weather he endured and the number of drawings which he produced are all testimony to his hard work and do not suggest poor health. The 1836 tour is important because it set a pattern which Lear adhered to for the rest of his life; the preparation, the hard conditions, the thoroughness with which he approached the task, the long daily journeys combined with intense sketching, were all repeated in his later topographical tours. The only difference is that Lear's English journey did not result in a published book, as was the case with some of his later continental journeys, and it is our loss that no written record of the tour survives.

If it was Lear's ambition to achieve fame as a great artist, then his life can be viewed as a series of dead-ends ending in ultimate failure. He never became the famous artist he wanted to be, in spite of all his hard work. Some of these dead ends were glorious, in particular his involvement with natural history illustration, but nevertheless the fact is that they went no further. For the period with which we are dealing, his visits to Ireland in 1835 and to the Lake District in 1836 were fundamental to his transformation from a natural history draughtsman to a landscape painter, but were both ultimately unproductive of anything else. His enrolment at Sass's School of Art in early 1835[24] and, much later (far too late), at the Royal Academy Schools in 1849, are both part of the programme of artistic self-improvement that runs through his life, but these never enabled him to draw figures with great proficiency, and to join the ranks of the painters he admired. Although he made a precarious living as an artist, all his life he lived from hand to mouth. As Lord Derby, the 15th Earl, grandson of Lear's original patron, confided to his diary in 1870: 'Lear is always in want of money' (Diary, 14 July 1870). Again, in 1880, he wrote, 'he has been out at elbows all his life, & so he will remain to the last' (Diary, 14 Jan. 1880), a sentiment repeated four years later: 'he works hard, sells well, yet seems always in difficulties' (Diary, 18 March 1884).[25] The irony is that, for all his current reputation as a landscape artist, Lear is significantly better known for his nonsense poetry, an aspect of his life which Lear considered at best only a sideline. In moments of depression and loneliness, and when beset with money worries, Lear sometimes felt that he had missed out, but, seen in its totality, his life is not a failure. His friend Fowler later wrote, 'It may be an odd way of designating to what degree he had risen to fame, but when he died there were many obituary notices of him, as of a prominent man gone from us',[26] adding that he was best known for his nonsense verse. Thanks in part to the enormous quantity of Lear's surviving writings, some of them very self-revelatory, we know a great deal about the ups and downs of his life. Although there is much less evidence for this early period, what survives is all of a piece with the later material. It is this combination of humour and sadness, of fame and failure, that appeals to something in all of us.

24. Noakes 2006, pp. 36–7.
25. Diaries of 15th Earl of Derby, Liverpool Record Office.
26. Smith, p. 103.

LEAR AND LITHOGRAPHY

Michael Twyman

Edward Lear's involvement with lithography spanned most of his working life, and his range in the medium – as natural history illustrator, topographical lithographer, and whimsical illustrator of his own limericks – marks him out from other lithographers. What is more, in the course of his lithographic career he mastered crayon drawing on stone, tinted lithography, and the making of pen-and-ink sketches on specially prepared transfer paper. Who else, at least in Britain, figured so prominently in three very different fields of lithography, let alone worked convincingly on both stone and transfer paper? But for all his versatility – or perhaps because of it – Lear remained outside the mainstream of British lithography; even after his death, though acclaimed in all three fields, his special role as a lithographic all-rounder has not been fully appreciated.

So little is known of Edward Lear's early life and introduction to lithography that it is possible to draw most of the important threads together, even in as short a piece as this.[1] Curiously for one so immersed in recording views at a later stage, landscape lithographs figure hardly at all in his *oeuvre* in the years up to 1837 when he left England for a life abroad. Had he died in 1837 he would be remembered solely as a natural history illustrator, with his *Illustrations of the Family of Psitticadae, or Parrots* (1832) standing as his undoubted masterpiece. By April 1831, an anonymous but well-informed writer of an overview article on lithography in the *Library of the Fine Arts* had drawn attention to 'A splendid work of Parrots, by E. Lear',[2] and in 1847, by which time Lear had already left England and published his first sets of topographical lithographs, it was again his natural history illustrations that attracted attention. In that year W. S. Williams delivered a paper on lithography to the Society of Arts in which he chose to mention 'the parrots and tortoises of Mr Lear' – among other natural history lithographs – as being 'valuable for their fidelity to nature, and attractive from their beauty'.[3] But he made no mention of either his *Views in Rome and its Environs* (1841) or – perhaps understandably – his more recent *Illustrated Excursions in Italy* (1846). Thus the two most important survey articles on British lithography of the 1830s and 1840s helped to characterise him as a specialist in natural history.[4]

1. My principal sources for Lear's early life and work are Noakes 1985, Noakes 2006, and Reade 1949.

2. 'A view of the present state of lithography in England', *Library of the Fine Arts*, vol. i, no. 3 (April 1831), p. 212.

3. Williams 1847–8, p. 235.

4. Surprisingly, Lear's expertise in lithography was acknowledged as early as 1833. In a letter to Arthur Aitkin of the Society of Arts (Royal Society of Arts B6/22 Lear), he reveals that he had been consulted about a lithographic transfer paper, which had been submitted by a Mr Cardano. The paper was referred to the Society's Committee of Polite Arts on 13 March 1833. Why Lear should have been approached by the Society remains a mystery, though it had already subscribed to his *Parrots*. At this stage, well before his *A Book of Nonsense*, Lear

As others have made clear, the evidence we have of Lear's introduction to drawing and lithography is very thin, largely because he destroyed his early diaries.[5] What is known is that his career as an artist took shape in the period 1828 to 1830 when he began to earn his living by taking on a variety of free-lance work, much of it rather trivial.[6] By the end of this period, while still in his teens, he had begun drawing on stone the work that made his name: a set of forty-two hand-coloured lithographs, printed by Charles Hullmandel, for *Illustrations of the Family of Psitticadae, or Parrots* (1832). Original in its portrayal of birds as living creatures and mature in its handling of the lithographic crayon, it was a remarkable introduction to ornithological illustration, especially for someone of Lear's age. It must also have been something of a financial risk, as there was no great tradition for large-format plate books of birds as there had been for topographical ones. Audubon's mammoth work on the *Birds of America* had begun publication in 1827, with aquatint plates produced for him by Robert Havell and others, and in 1829 the young Benjamin Waterhouse Hawkins had started drawing on stone the plates for John Edward Gray's *Illustrations of Indian Zoology*, 2 vols (London: Treuttel & Würz, 1830–34), but Lear's *Parrots* marked a turning point in ornithological illustration.

With a few exceptions, which will be discussed below, Lear's lithographic work lay entirely with natural history illustration until he left England in 1837. His *Parrots* came out in twelve parts between November 1830 and April 1832 in an edition of 175 hand-coloured copies (it was never completed as planned and the final two parts were not issued). Forty-one of its forty-two plates were drawn in crayon lithography, ink-work being reserved for dark touches on claws, beaks, and eyes.[7] Lear produced numerous preparatory drawings for the publication, including copiously annotated studies of live birds,[8] which supports the view that he did not go into the lithographic side of the exercise lightly.

In their format and treatment the plates of Lear's *Parrots* provided the model for the series of bird books published by John Gould in forty volumes over a twenty-year period, starting in 1832.[9] It was also through the *Parrots* that Gould was introduced to Hullmandel, who was to become his regular lithographic printer. Not only did Gould follow Lear's graphic model, he employed him as

had no experience of transfer lithography, and replied 'As however I understand nothing of that part of the art of Lithography – I have taken it to Mr. Hullmandel ...'.

5. *Letters*, p. xix; Noakes 2006, p. [vii]; Reade, p. 10.

6. Noakes 2006, pp. 15–16; Reade, pp. 8–10; Hyman 1980, pp. 13–16.

7. Plate 23 'Platycercus Stanleyii' (Stanley Parrakeet, adult male) has traditionally been described as an ink-drawn lithograph, and this is certainly how it appears on first inspection. However, traces of crayon work on the bird, though not at all on the branch and vegetation, suggest that initial crayon marks may not have survived the proving stage and were later substantially reinforced with ink, giving the final print the appearance of an ink-drawn lithograph. An alternative interpretation is that Lear tried adding crayon work, somewhat unsuccessfully, to an ink drawn stone in order to provide additional nuances of tone. The crayon work is most obvious on the bird's beak and on the plumage beneath its wing.

8. See in particular Hyman 1980, pp. 20, 24, 25, 28–30, for illustrations of Lear's sketches in the Houghton Library, Harvard University.

9. Jackson 1975, pp. 39–58.

an artist / lithographer in several of his publications, beginning with *A Century of Birds from the Himalaya Mountains* (London, 1832). Lear appears to have been referring to this work when he wrote that Gould's wife Elizabeth commenced lithography 'with a little of my instruction'.[10] Lear continued to work for Gould for most of the time he remained in England, receiving little or in some cases no recognition, and was the major contributor to what is generally considered to have been Gould's finest work, *The Birds of Europe* (1832–7). Elizabeth Gould drew most of the plates, leaving Lear to concentrate on the larger and more exotic birds. Lear put in all the backgrounds to her plates and touched up some of her drawings too,[11] receiving no credit for the work but a copy of the publication gratis.[12] Similarly, he received no recognition for the ten plates he contributed to Gould's first work on a single family of birds, *A Monograph of the Ramphastidae, or Family of Toucans* (London: John Gould, 1833–5), some of which were among his finest bird illustrations. In much the same period he put on stone James Sowerby's drawings for Thomas Bell's *A Monograph of the Testudinata* (London: Samuel Highley, [1832–6]), with Hullmandel again serving as his printer. Years later, the unsold stock of this publication was bought by Henry Sotheran, who republished it as *Tortoises, Terrapins, and Turtles* (London, Paris and Frankfurt: Henry Sotheran and Joseph Baer & Co., 1872).

Effectively these publications mark the end of Lear's involvement with natural history illustration, though they provided him with a deep experience in the field, which he drew on later for some of the images of *A Book of Nonsense* (1846). But as far as his shift to topography and landscape is concerned, all that his many bird plates provided by way of experience were their contextual elements: branches, twigs, leaves, and clumps of grass and foliage. Probably the nearest Lear came to landscape in his natural history work was the design he drew for one of the wrappers of the *Parrots*, which includes an arrangement of vegetation surrounding a crumbling inscriptional stone bearing the word 'Parrots' and, in the very distance, traces of an exotic landscape.[13]

The relatively new process of lithography, which had been seen initially in Britain simply as a means of multiplying an artist's sketches, had matured by the time Lear turned to it. Lithographic printers had spent the best part of the 1820s trying to establish its credentials as a versatile and reliable graphic process that would provide an effective alternative to etching and aquatint for artists. Invented in Germany by Alois Senefelder in or around 1798, lithography had been introduced to Britain in 1801 with the name 'polyautography', only to stagnate for a period until peace was established in Europe after the Napoleonic wars. It was from around 1819, when the inventor's treatise on the subject was published by Ackermann in an English translation as *A Complete Course of*

10. Lear to George Coombe, 19 April 1833 (see cat. 5).

11. Ibid.

12. Ibid.

13. Illustrated Hyman 1980, p. 18; Noakes 1985, p. 83. In addition, plate 40 of the *Parrots*, 'Psittacula torquata' (Collared Parrakeet), depicts the bird flying above a very lightly sketched landscape view.

Lithography, and when Charles Hullmandel set up a lithographic establishment in London, that the struggle to establish lithography among artists and publishers really began. London remained the focus for the process in Britain for decades, and by the close of the 1820s there were perhaps as many as thirty lithographic firms working in the capital, though not all of them producing artists' prints.[14] Initially, landscape and topography provided the principal subjects for those who drew on stone. Charles Hullmandel, as artist himself, published his own *Twenty-four Views of Italy* in 1818,[15] and a few years later publication began of *Britannia Delineata* (1822–3),[16] with lithographs drawn in their distinctive styles by some of the first generation of professional lithographic artists in Britain: James Duffield Harding, William Westall, Samuel Prout, and Charles Hullmandel himself. Only twenty-five plates for the first volume on Kent were ever published, but they were important for establishing the suitability of lithography for landscape and topography by virtue of the quality of the work and, in particular, Harding's drawing and Hullmandel's printing. So successful were the best lithographic artists and printers in London by the mid 1820s that several were invited to contribute to some of the early volumes of Baron Taylor's *Voyages Pittoresques et Romantiques dans l'Ancienne France* (Paris, 1820–70).[17] In the same period the Bavarian George Scharf, Sen. and the Belgian Louis Haghe, both of whom had settled in London and were later to establish reputations as topographical artists, demonstrated the suitability of lithography for natural science illustration. It was Haghe who put on stone all the remarkable illustrations for the first part of George Simpson's *The Anatomy of the Bones and Muscles* (London, 1825), all of which were printed by William Day. And in portraiture, a field Lear avoided, Richard Lane was producing even more delicate and refined crayon lithographs.

The process was therefore beginning to be accepted on a broad front by the time Lear turned to it. The main attraction for artists was that it offered them the opportunity to draw with tools and materials not far removed from what they were used to, notably crayons for half-tone effects and ink applied with the pen or brush for line and solid work. This meant that with some initial training and advice they could make their own drawings on stone instead of having them translated by an intermediary. They would often have had to work on stone in reverse, which would have been an impediment, as Lear was to acknowledge,[18] but the combination of techniques available to artists meant that they were able to avoid the formulaic marks associated with etched and engraved work on metal plates. This allowed natural history illustrators to produce convincing textures to distinguish between fur, feather, beak and claw, and landscape artists to draw

14. Twyman 1976, pp. 9–13.

15. Abbey *Travel*, vol. i, no. 167, pp. 145–51; Twyman 1970, pp. 184–8, pls 86–8.

16. Twyman 1970, pp. 192–200, pls 92–6, 98–101, 105, 107–12.

17. Ibid., pp. 243–51, pls 150–7.

18. Noakes 2006, p. 168. While working on his series of lithographs for *Views in the Seven Ionian Islands* (1863) Lear wrote of 'the impossibility of getting any compensation=spiritual from the views I am drawing, since their being all executed reversed causes them to seem unreal, & without any interest.' (Diary, 4 September 1863).

foreground vegetation and create subtle atmospheric effects that would have been quite beyond the range of traditional printmaking methods. The main drawback of lithography in the early 1820s was its unreliability in printing, and several artists and natural scientists referred to their unfortunate experiences at the hands of poor lithographic printers.[19]

The printer who did more than any other to change perceptions of lithography in Britain was Charles Joseph Hullmandel (1789–1850).[20] The son of a notable musician from Strasbourg, he trained as an artist and learned about the new process at first hand while on the way back from a continental sketching tour. On returning to London he made a set of drawings on stone at the printing establishment of Moser & Harris, which he published privately as *Twenty-four Views of Italy* in 1818. Having gained some practical experience of the process in this way he decided to set up as a lithographic printer himself, with a view to printing the work of artists. In his book *The Art of Drawing on Stone* (London: C. Hullmandel and R. Ackermann, 1824; cat. 4), with later editions of 1833 and 1835, he described in detail and with great clarity how artists should make their drawings on stone. Strongly influenced by Godefroy Engelmann's *Manuel du Dessinateur lithographe* (Paris: 1822, 1824), Hullmandel wrote his book to give artists the confidence to turn to the process, and particularly to his own establishment for the printing of their drawings. Hullmandel's success as a printer and self-publicist can be judged by the fact that it was to him that Géricault went while in London in 1821 to have printed his set of twelve lithographs with the title *Various Subjects Drawn from Life and on Stone*. Hullmandel's manual soon became the Bible for budding lithographic artists in Britain, and was even depicted in an allegorical scene on a competitor's trade card alongside the inventor's treatise.[21] Some of those who had drawn attention to the unreliability of lithographic printers regarded Hullmandel as the one exception, and by 1822 he had begun to provide stones with what he referred to as his 'special facing', which he claimed led to a better match between what the artist drew on stone and the impression obtained from it.[22]

19. For example George Cumberland, Sen., *Scenes chiefly Italian by G. Cumberland* (1821), J.S. Paterson, *Sketches of Scenery in Angus and Mearns* (*c*.1824), and E.A. Crouch, *An Illustrated Introduction to Lamarck's Conchology* (London: Longman, Rees, Orme, Brown, and Green, with J. Mawe, 1827). For the first two, see Twyman 1988, pp. 69–70. Crouch wrote in his introduction, p. iv, 'Some apology may be deemed necessary for the delay which has occurred in producing this work so long after its announcement; to those who are acquainted with the vexatious casualties of Lithographic printing, it will be unnecessary; but to those who are not, it may be proper to state, that many of the drawings, from the breaking of the stones, and other accidents, have been redrawn three or four times over; these and the delays occasionally experienced in procuring specimens of some of the rarer Genera must be my excuse.' It is unclear who printed the plates of this book, though W. Day's imprint appears on one of them and also on the lithographed boards.

20. Twyman 1988.

21. Trade card of J. Robertson, lithographic draughtsman & writer, of 9 Hatton Garden (Department of Prints and Maps, Guildhall Library). Robertson worked from this address from the mid 1840s to the mid 1850s.

22. Hullmandel 1824, pp. 15 n., 44; Twyman 1970, pp. 132–5.

Hullmandel's attempt to establish himself as the artist's printer was supported by a series of drawing books, which came out in parts from the early 1820s through to the 1830s. His main role with the series initially was that of printer, though he contributed drawings to it himself, along with Carbonnier, Harding, Prout and others; but after a succession of changes of title it became 'Hullmandel's lithographic drawing book' for a few years in the second half of the 1820s (see cats. 1–2).[23]

It was Hullmandel to whom Lear turned to print the plates of the *Parrots*, and it has been assumed, probably rightly, that it was at Hullmandel's establishment that he was introduced to drawing on stone. There is no firm evidence one way or another on this point, and it may therefore be worth considering other possibilities. As it happens, as many as five leading London lithographic establishments of the late 1820s shared the printing of Waterhouse's plates for Gray's *Illustrations of Indian Zoology* (1830–4), many of which are dated 1829. This folio publication, which includes hand-coloured lithographs of many exotic birds, was a pioneer work of its kind and may well have been known by Lear. The printing of the plates was shared between Engelmann & Co., W. Day (later Day & Haghe), and Graf & Soret. It was not at all uncommon for several firms to undertake the printing of plates for large-scale publications, mainly in order to share the load and help meet deadlines, but Hullmandel's name is conspicuous by its absence from the imprints of the book's plates. All the printers associated with *Illustrations of Indian Zoology* would have been on any publisher's shortlist of candidates for printing lithographed plates of natural history books around 1830. The fact that Lear went to Hullmandel for his *Parrots* may therefore suggest some earlier involvement with his establishment, or simply an awareness of its very considerable reputation.

Most obviously, like anyone anxious to learn about lithography in Britain around this time, Lear is likely to have come across Hullmandel's manual *The Art of Drawing on Stone*. The book had no real competitor at the time, at least not in the English-speaking world, and its success can be judged by the fact that it ran to two further editions. It may well have been Lear's route through to lithography, either as a preparation for putting his drawings of parrots on stone, or beforehand simply to learn something about this increasingly popular art form. It is also possible that Lear's programme of self-education as an artist had already included exposure to the popular lithographic drawing books that Hullmandel printed, all of which carried details of the services he offered on their wrappers. These drawing books – mainly though not exclusively containing exemplars of landscape drawing – also happened to reveal the possibilities of lithography, and particularly crayon drawing on stone. Leaving aside the possibility of a personal introduction through a mutual friend, there were therefore several routes by which Lear may have found his way to the doors of Hullmandel's Great Marlborough Street establishment, just off Regent Street.

There is good reason to believe that Hullmandel would have gone out of his way to encourage the young Lear had he sought his advice. Late on in his life

23. Twyman 1988, pp. 83, 84, 366 n.193.

the artist Daniel Fowler (1810–94), who emigrated to Canada mid-career, wrote movingly of the encouragement he received from Hullmandel when he showed the printer examples of his early work.[24] Fowler, who knew Lear well, regarded Hullmandel as a good, though stern, judge of art, but any encouragement Lear may have received would have been coloured by the fact that Hullmandel would also have looked on him as a potential client. Though Lear was to turn to Thomas McLean to print and publish his *A Book of Nonsense* in 1846 – a work that would hardly have suited Hullmandel's profile as a printer – Hullmandel printed Lear's two sets of Italian views in the 1840s, one of them as Hullmandel & Walton. All the evidence suggests that Lear and Hullmandel were close friends. In the summer of 1835 Lear wrote that Hullmandel had been invited to one of his dinner parties, and was to bring a friend from abroad,[25] and in the early days of January 1837, more revealingly, 'I have been leeching & sitting up with my old friend Hullmandel who is very ill'.[26] Within a few weeks Lear had moved to 36 Great Marlborough Street, just a few houses down the road from Hullmandel, where he took lodgings for a while.[27] He was also to attend Hullmandel's rather humble funeral at Highgate Cemetery on 21 November 1850, referring to him again as 'a very old friend' in a letter in which he complained, characteristically, of having caught a bad cold on the day.[28]

However skilful a draughtsman Lear may have been before he set to work putting his drawings on stone for the *Parrots*, he would have needed some instruction in lithography. The tools may have been broadly familiar to him, but the methods of using them were not. Hullmandel devoted a chapter of some thirty pages to crayon drawing with the title 'Of the mode of applying chalk to the stone'. Chalk was the term commonly used at the time – and still is by many lithographers – but since it does not suggest a greasy substance to most lay people, crayon seems a more appropriate word to use today. Lear would have learned not to hold his lithographic crayons in the bare hand, since this might have led to greasy marks being inadvertently transferred to the stone from his fingers. In his treatise, Hullmandel illustrated a variety of port-crayons, those he preferred being so light that their weight was not an impediment to producing the most delicate lines. By such means, he observed, 'the evenness of the tint depends merely on the weight of the tool, and not on the firmness of the hand … .'[29] Crayons were made in a variety of grades according to their hardness, but however soft they were, they would have been sharpened to such a fine point that they were liable to break very easily. This meant that they had to be handled differently from graphite pencils, and Lear would have been taught to do this in such a way that they did not break. He would also have been encouraged to use

24. Smith 1979, p. 102.

25. Lear to Fanny Coombe, 19 June 1835 (see Appendix A, p. 206).

26. Lear to Fanny Coombe, 3 January 1837 (cat. 91).

27. On 11 February and 3 March Lear wrote to Fanny Coombe from what he described as his lodgings at 36 Great Marlborough Street. He used mourning paper as his youngest sibling 'Kate' [Catherine] had just died. (Cats. 92 and 93.)

28. *Selected Letters*, p. 111 (letter to Lord Derby, 28 November 1850).

29. Hullmandel 1824, pp. 30–1.

a bridge of some sort that extended across the stone to avoid leaning on it and smudging his drawing. Crayon work could be combined with ink applied with a brush or pen where solid blacks or precise dark marks were required, and highlights could be created by scraping away areas of tone with a mezzotint scraper or other sharp tool.[30]

Artists were advised that the stone should not be warmed beyond room temperature, and that they should avoid moistening it with their breath, if need be by holding a piece of paper in front of the nose and mouth.[31] It has to be admitted that Hullmandel was somewhat alarmist in the way in which he described and represented the consequences of not following his advice,[32] but by doing so he established the general point that drawing on stone with crayon was not – at least when done under his guidance – the straightforward operation it was often held to be. For example, he writes that 'If the chalk be moved too fast, particularly in the full tones, the heat produced by the friction softens the chalk, and from that cause gives to the tints a roughness and coarseness which is sure to be transmitted to the impressions in an increased ratio.'[33] These issues were of particular concern to Hullmandel as he was anxious to produce impressions that reflected accurately and reliably the marks made on stone by the artist. And in a passage describing the making of tints, he writes with feeling about the way crayon strokes should be made in order to produce a rich, soft, and velvety look:

> It is done by not working the chalk too quick, but by producing the touch by a rather slow motion, as if painting with a [pencil] brush; I cannot better describe it, than by saying that it is something similar to the motion of the hand of a person attempting with a soft [quill] pen to write slowly and gracefully a capital *J.* or *S.* when in the full part.[34]

How far Lear followed such advice from Hullmandel or anyone else will probably never be established, but the delicacy of his crayon drawing for the *Parrots*, particularly the controlled hatching on the birds themselves, suggests that his innate talents were supported by some technical training along the lines described by Hullmandel.

Since the plates for the *Parrots* were intended from the outset to be coloured by hand, Lear made little use of the techniques – described at length by Hullmandel – of building up tones in a rather mechanical way by overlaying strokes in several directions.[35] When he did attempt to do so in some of the plates he put on stone after drawings by J. D. C. Sowerby for Thomas Bell's *A Monograph of the*

30. Hullmandel 1824, pp. 36–9. This technique was used to good effect for the highlights on the tail feathers of plate 30 of the *Parrots*, 'Palaeornis rosaceus' (Roseate Parrakeet). See fig. 4, opposite.

31. Ibid., p. 30.

32. See, for example, ibid., Plate XI.

33. Ibid., p. 43.

34. Ibid., p. 42.

35. Ibid., pp. 31–5; Twyman 1970, pp. 122–4, pls 43–7.

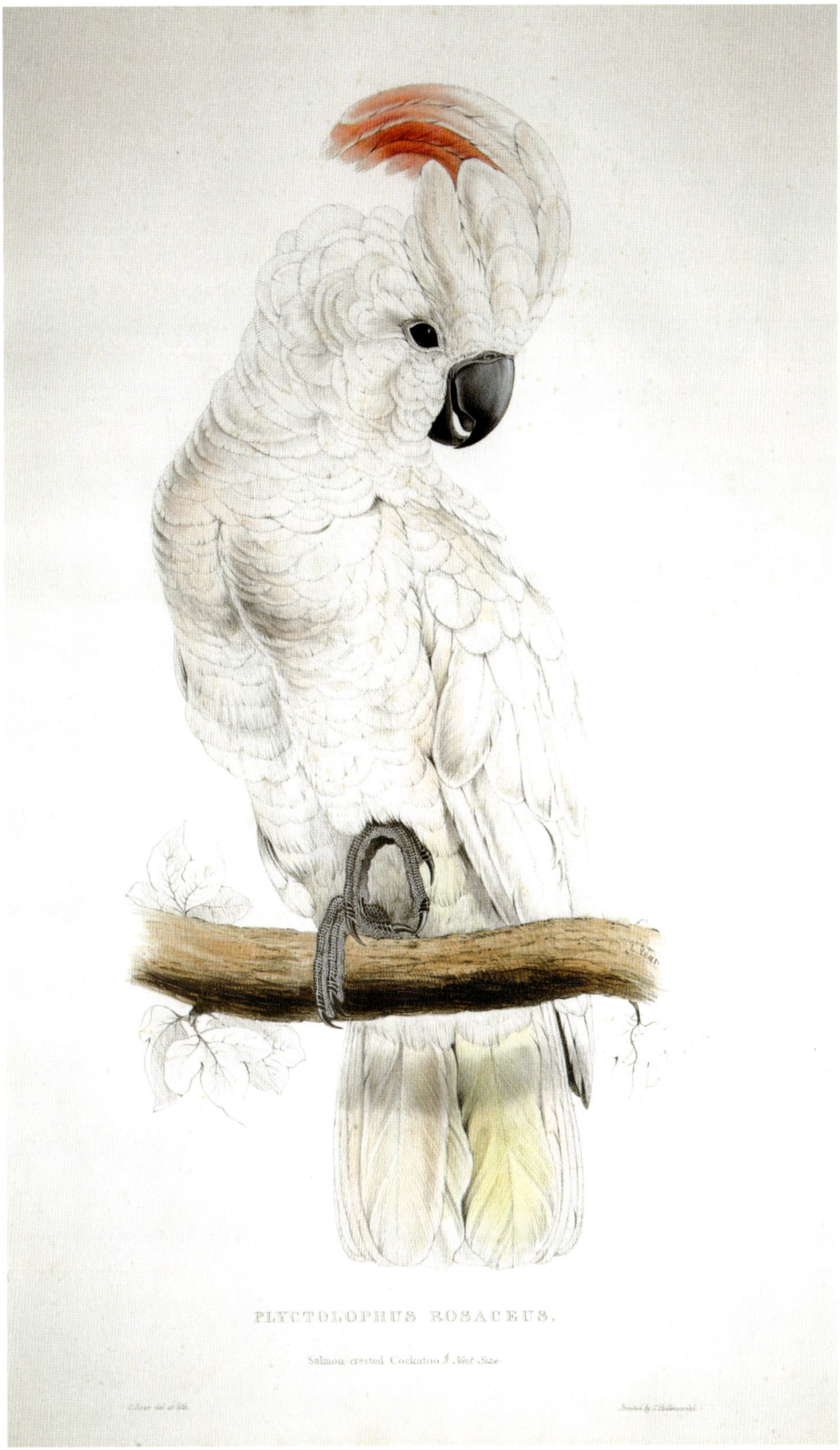

Fig. 4 Edward Lear, 'Palaeornis rosaceus' (Roseate Parrakeet), 1830–2, hand-coloured crayon lithograph, printed by Charles Hullmandel, 54 × 36.4 cm (Private Collection).

Testudinata (London: Samuel Highley, [1832–6]), which was published in 1872 as *Tortoises, Terrapins, and Turtles*, he showed himself singularly unsuccessful (most obviously in some uncoloured plates). On the other hand, numerous plates for the *Parrots* suggest that Lear took on board some of Hullmandel's recommendations: the plumage of his birds takes the form of carefully rendered parallel lines (a feature of Hullmandel's own work as a lithographic artist), and his foliage shows the use of softer crayons that have been drawn seductively across the stone to produce swelling lines, sometimes loosely cross-hatched. Only the rather casual and somewhat indiscriminate hatching on some of the branches is likely to have offended Hullmandel, who drew two different versions of the same natural science illustration for one of the plates of his manual in order to demonstrate what he considered good and bad approaches to crayon drawing.[36] One of these was carefully hatched in order to print well, the other was drawn freely without consideration of such things, with the risk – according to Hullmandel – that the blackness would not lead to a commensurate build up of grease on the stone.

Hullmandel was not the only person from whom Lear may have learned how to draw on stone in the early 1830s. Numerous lithographic artists would have been in and out of the Great Marlborough Street establishment at the time, including George Scharf, Sen. (1788–1860), who continued to work as a natural history illustrator into the 1830s, and the major landscape lithographer of the day, James Duffield Harding (1797–1863). Moreover, the flower painter Valentine Bartholomew (1799–1879), one of Hullmandel's managers, lived on site until 1827.[37] Given Lear's need to draw vegetation as supporting features for his *Parrots* and for Gould's bird publications too, it might be assumed that he picked up something from Bartholomew, if only from seeing his lithographic work.

There remains the question as to whether Lear would have worked on the *Parrots* and his lithographed plates for other publications at Hullmandel's establishment or at home. Lear specialists seem to be uncertain on this point, and there is no clear evidence one way or the other. Lear would surely have been a frequent visitor to Hullmandel's large and rambling establishment, which was at the peak of its success in the 1830s. We have surmised that he was introduced to lithography there, and it may be that a set of eight hand-coloured heads of parrots, mounted onto a single sheet, are among his earliest experiments in lithography.[38] Lear did not reverse his drawings of parrots when he put them on stone, but the three heads from this set that relate to the *Parrots* are mirror images of those in the published plates, which suggests that they were drawn back to front on the stone.[39]

36. Plate VI. The drawings were based on, and are in reverse of, an engraving by James Basire in William Buckland, *Reliquiae Diluvianae* (London: John Murray, 1823), which includes plates that Hullmandel had printed. The actual bone, an ulna of a hyena, is now in the University Museum, Oxford (Q.2100/2).

37. Twyman 1988, p. 58.

38. Victoria & Albert Museum, Department of Prints and Drawings, 29557-96/P026.

39. The remaining five heads do not appear to relate to the publication directly. Though referred to by Lear scholars, notably Reade, p. 22, no-one appears to have offered an explanation

Hullmandel's normal practice – which followed that of the earliest lithographic printers in England – was to hire out his stones to artists. In *The Art of Drawing on Stone* he referred to 'stones obtained from my establishment... being sent out',[40] and in a letter to the Liverpool antiquarian Matthew Gregson he stated unequivocally that he never sold his stones.[41] By hiring out his stones he was able to retain control over them and make sure that he did the printing of the artist's work. Hullmandel's terms for hiring out stones were set out on his invoices as 'from 4d to 18d per Month each, according to their size...'.[42] After paying rental for so many months the hirer usually had the right to retain possession of the stones, which underlines the fact that the purpose of the arrangement was to encourage artists and publishers to retain their printer. Lear's arrangement with Hullmandel must surely have followed similar lines, since he wrote in October 1831: 'I have pretty great difficulty in paying my monthly charges, for to pay colourer & printer monthly I am obstinately prepossessed...'.[43]

All this suggests that Lear worked at home when putting on stone the drawings for his *Parrots*, and also possibly those for some of the other publications he contributed to at the time. In a letter written at the beginning of January 1837, when daylight hours would have been just past their shortest, he wrote of working on a quantity of lithographs every evening in candlelight, leaving the day time for his watercolours.[44] Common sense suggests that he would have hired a few stones at a time to avoid both cluttering his rooms and accruing monthly charges unnecessarily. This would account for the fact that the description he gave of his rooms refers to them as overflowing with prints of parrots,[45] rather than what would have been much more of an encumbrance, stacks or even cases of stones. We can assume that Lear's trips to Hullmandel's establishment would have been fairly regular, not so much to make alterations to proofs, though this was possible even with crayon lithographs by the time Lear began working on stone,[46] but to pass proofs and return stones to have their titles and imprints added by one of Hullmandel's specialist letterers.[47]

for these prints of parrot heads, each of which has been cut out following the limits of the image, as though for a scrapbook. The three images that relate directly to the publication (to pls 5, 16, 30) are perhaps rather less assured in their crayon hatching than the final plates. It is possible therefore that Lear began with the idea of putting his drawings on stone in reverse of his original drawings (so that they appeared the same way round when printed), but abandoned the idea until he was forced to do so for his topographical subjects.

40. Hullmandel 1824, p. 44.

41. Hullmandel to Gregson, Liverpool Record Office, 920 GRE 2/5, 4 Dec [1820]; cited Twyman 1988, p. 62.

42. For example, Twyman 1988, fig. 2.18.

43. Noakes 2006, p. 19; *Selected Letters*, p. 14 (letter to Charles Empson, 1 October 1831).

44. Lear to Fanny Coombe, 3 January 1837 (cat. 91). This seems to have been a common practice, and Daniel Fowler refers to Harding as working on his lithographs at night time so as to devote daylight to work involving colour.

45. Noakes 2006, p. 18.

46. Hullmandel 1827; Twyman 1970, pp. 132–8, pls 58–60; Twyman 1988, fig. 2.27.

47. Twyman 1988, pp. 67, 365 n.132.

Needless to say, we cannot know what Lear's drawings for the *Parrots* would have looked like on the stones, but the prints taken from them suggest that there must have been some loss of marks in the course of production. This appears to have been particularly so in the lightly-drawn background foliage; it is not evident in the birds themselves, where Lear's hatching is generally firm and assured, and usually well disguised by hand-colouring. Not all impressions taken from the same stones are identical. For example, a comparison of a proof before letters of plate 42, 'Psittacula Swinderniana' (Swindern's Parrakeet),[48] shows much more drawing on the main branch and the leaves stemming from it than appears in the plate as published in the Victoria & Albert Museum copy of the publication. The precise reasons for such losses are not now likely to be fully understood, but since the proof shows many lines that have subsequently disappeared, the likelihood is that the stone was too strongly etched at some stage after proofing, leaving the drawing on stone looking very weak. The copy in the Linnean Society Library does not show this loss of marks, which means that it must have come about in the course of printing the edition. The more general weakness of lines in the foliage of the plates of the *Parrots*[49] is more likely to have been the result of over-etching at the initial proving stage, though some responsibility for the lightest of these marks could also lie with Lear, who may not have observed all Hullmandel's strictures. Failings of the kind discussed here were what had brought lithography into disrepute a few years earlier; however, they were not to be expected at Hullmandel's establishment in the early 1830s, and in this particular case were not – as far as I am aware – remarked upon by Lear.[50]

The plates for the *Parrots*, and most of those for the *Testudinata* were hand-coloured in imitation of the original drawings on which they were based. Colour-printing of pictorial lithographs was a few years away,[51] and even when it was highly developed artistically and technically half a century later, major natural history books continued to be hand-coloured long after the practice had been abandoned in other fields. It can be assumed that Lear coloured a single impression of his natural history lithographs as an exemplar for others to follow, and the prospectus for the original edition of *Testudinata* reveals that a Mr Bayfield was responsible for the hand-colouring of its plates and for those of the *Parrots* too.[52]

48. Victoria & Albert Museum, Department of Prints and Drawings, 29557.23/P026.

49. Particularly in pls 8, 15, 16, 24, 25, 33, 40, and most often in the outlines of leaves.

50. Though a few years later Harding was to note in his diaries that some of his work had suffered at the hands of Hullmandel's printers. He reported the unsuccessful proving of a drawing on 8 February 1840 and in the following month (on 14 and 18 March) that the proving of two drawings of his was only 'tolerably successful'. More seriously, in January 1847, he was involved in a dispute with the proprietors of *Scotland Delineated* over payment for 'all the Drawings Mr Hullmandel had spoiled', which lingered on until the end of May, when the matter was settled. Courtauld Institute of Art, James Duffield Harding Archive (CI/JDH).

51. Twyman 2007, pp. 29–93.

52. Introduction to the 1872 edition of *Tortoises, Terrapins, and Turtles Drawn from Life by James de Carle Sowerby F.L.S. and Edward Lear* (London, Paris and Frankfurt: Henry Sotheran and Joseph Baer & Co., 1872). Citing the original prospectus of around 1832, it states that 'The

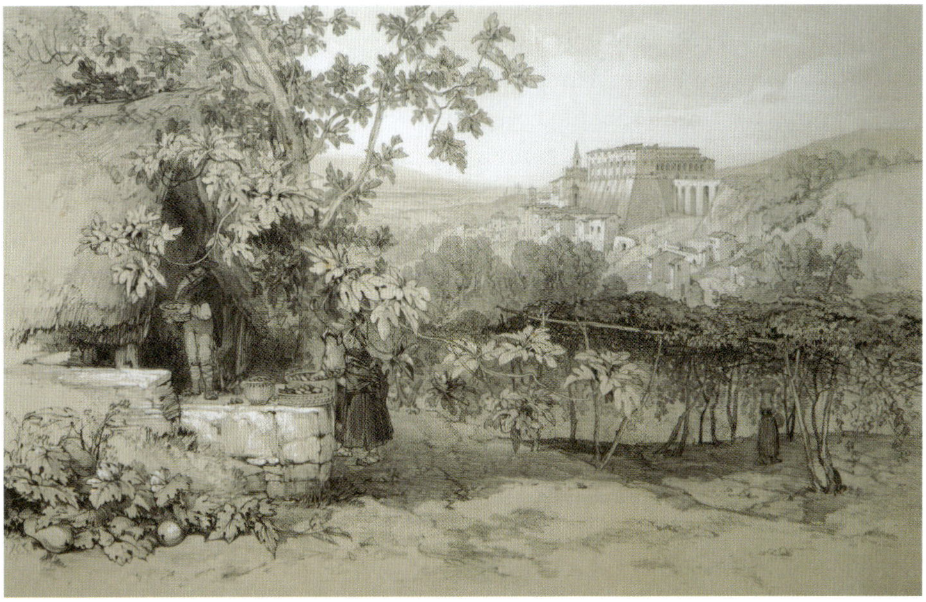

Fig. 5 Edward Lear, 'Genazzano', from *Views in Rome and its Environs*, 1841, tinted lithograph, printed by Charles Hullmandel, 23.1 × 36.4 cm (Private Collection).

Arrangements for the production of the plates for the *Views in Rome and its Environs*, which Lear put on stone at least in part while staying with Lord Derby at Knowsley Hall in August 1841,[53] are likely to have been somewhat different from those made for his earlier lithographs. Hullmandel printed these plates too, and we have to assume that the stones were transported to and from Knowsley in crates of the kind described and illustrated in *The Art of Drawing on Stone* for those 'residing in the country, or distant towns'.[54] There were lithographic houses in nearby Liverpool by this time, but Hullmandel would only have been prepared to print from his own, specially treated stones. If all the twenty-five drawings for the publication had been put on stone at Knowsley, Lear (and Hullmandel too) must have worked with considerable speed, as the book came out in the Autumn of the same year with plates in tinted lithography, each of which would have required two stones (see fig. 5). A couple of proofs of Italian landscapes by Lear in the Victoria & Albert Museum,[55] both printed in black on buff stock and touched up in white gouache, suggest that Lear's method of working in tinted lithography involved three stages: making a drawing on stone and having it proofed in black on tinted stock; adding white to the proof as a guide to the production of a tint stone; and drawing the tint stone to produce the required effect. Lear's short stay at Knowsley Hall in this period may not

Plates will be lithographed by Mr. Lear, coloured (so as to form the most perfect *facsimiles* of the drawings) by Mr. Bayfield. The joint talent of these excellent artists, exhibited in the illustrations of the Psittacidae of the former gentleman, renders it unnecessary to say that the ability of the painter will be ably seconded by that of the lithographer and colourist.'

53. Noakes 2006, p. 48.

54. Hullmandel 1824, p. 91, plate VII, figs. 8, 9.

55. Department of Prints and Drawings, Victoria & Albert Museum, 'Unidentified landscape', E.737-1939/ES 102 H; 'Castel Fusano', E.1039-1887/ES 1024.

have been long enough to cater for the considerable to-ing and fro-ing between the Hall and Hullmandel's establishment. It is possible, therefore, that the relatively simple tint stones for this publication were drawn by one of Hullmandel's lithographers at Great Marlborough Street, and that Lear simply worked on a proof impression along the lines of the two surviving prints discussed above.[56]

The two published sets of Italian views of the 1840s marked a clear shift in Lear's lithographic career, and more generally as an artist, towards topography and landscape. Since the present publication focuses on his output up to and including 1837, this aspect of his work will not be pursued into the 1850s and 1860s, though it seems sensible to consider early stages in this change of direction. Natural history illustration was his main means of earning a living before he was enabled by Lord Derby and Robert Hornby to travel to Rome in 1837.[57] But we have to ask two questions about the later development of Lear's lithographic career. To what extent did the lithographic work he undertook before leaving England prepare him for his later topographical publications? And, given the number of landscape drawings he made of the Lake District, why he did not turn them into a set of lithographs, either soon afterwards or at a later stage?

Neither question is easily answered, but a few miscellaneous crayon lithographs, which Lear must have made before going on his travels abroad, provide evidence of his concern to master landscape lithography. Other Lear lithographs of this kind may survive, but the ones that have been traced by so far are: 'Tor Mohun Church. Devon' (cat. 10), which was lithographed by Lear from a sketch by Lady Georgiana North and bears Hullmandel's imprint; a view of Knowsley Hall from the lake (fig. 10, p. 75); two crayon studies of trees (one dated 1834) (cats. 7 and 9); and a landscape in tinted lithography, 'Wastwater & the Screes, from Wastdale', showing a path receding into the distance and a figure to the right leaning against a wall (cat. 47).

The first of these lithographs may be the earliest of the five and seems to relate to Lear's work as a drawing master; it is likely to have been drawn before

56. The first of these proofs relates to 'Cervara', a plate in *Views in Rome and its Environs* (1841), though the lithograph was redrawn for the publication. It is not clear why this was so, but the rocks in the right foreground of the proof are poorly drawn and also show many alterations of a kind that would have led to difficulties when printing an edition. Lear produced a revised drawing on stone along similar lines, with minor but obvious compositional differences. The white gouache highlights on the proof print, which are assumed to have been drawn by Lear, were largely ignored in the tint plate that was added to Lear's revised image. In the published print importance must have been attached to establishing a difference between the tones of the sky and the actual landscape, particularly the hilltop town, and to reinforce this interpretation many of Lear's highlights within the landscape were suppressed. This seems to support the hypothesis that the tint stones were put on stone by one of Hullmandel's staff artists. Additional evidence for this interpretation stems from Lear's Preface to *Illustrated Excursions in Italy* (1846), in which he wrote 'I have executed the whole of the Lithographic drawings from my own sketches, and have endeavoured to preserve a close fidelity to the Originals.' (p. [vii]). The second of these touched up proofs relates to 'Castel Fusano', plate 25 of *Illustrated Excursions*.

57. See cat. 93 and Noakes 2006, p. 38.

he had a continuing source of income from the work he did for Gould. Nothing much can be deduced from its immature lithographic style, since it was put on stone by Lear after a sketch by Lady Georgiana North, who may have been responsible for the rather naïve treatment of the perspective of the buildings and the peculiar junction between the tower in the foreground and a group of trees in the middle distance. Curiously, the more distant trees overlap the tower – which suggests rather uninformed copying – and by no standards can the print be considered a work of lithographic maturity.

The other four lithographs all reflect in varying degrees the impact James Duffield Harding must have made on the young Lear. Harding provided Hullmandel with the long-term services of a skilled lithographic artist. And though he worked on stone independently in his own studios, mostly at night, he was prepared to put himself at Hullmandel's disposal and explore the potential of some of the latter's technical innovations. The connection between the two men began around 1820 when Harding made his first lithograph. It continued through to Hullmandel's death in 1850, and over the years Lear was able to benefit considerably from the fruits of the cooperation of the two men.

The trees Lear drew in four of these miscellaneous lithographs owe a lot to Harding, whose sketches in the various parts of 'Hullmandel's lithographic drawing book' would have been available for him to study around the time he was setting out on his path as an artist (see cat. 2). This series of drawing books had no text, but Harding, whom Ruskin came to regard, after Turner, as 'unquestionably the greatest master of foliage in Europe',[58] went on to describe his approach to drawing foliage in *Elementary Art: or, the Use of the Lead Pencil* (Charles Tilt, 1834, 2nd edition 1838):

> … much that contributes to effect roundness in the individual folds of a Tree proceeds from the appearance of flexibility in the leaves, gained by making the first strokes incline a little upwards, and gradually, as they proceed downwards, making them perpendicular; at which point only would the true shape of the leaf be seen; – the others exhibiting this in a less degree, because they are seen more in perspective, and overlap each other in whole or in part. Though no leaf is here individually and entirely drawn, or attempted to be drawn, so much is done as to suggest the rest, and the eye and the mind are better satisfied.[59]

Bearing in mind Lear's longstanding quest for some form of training in drawing, it was almost inevitable that his approach to landscape lithography should have been influenced by Harding, the recognised master in the field. Lear could hardly have avoided seeing his lithographs and it also seems highly likely that he was familiar with his drawing books and his ideas on and instructions for drawing trees.

58. Ruskin 1903–12, vol. iii, p. 578.

59. J. D. Harding, *Elementary Art; or, the Use of the Lead Pencil Advocated and Explained*, 2nd edn (London: Charles Tilt, 1838), p. 43. References to the plate numbers of the original have been omitted. This is an improved version of an almost identical passage that appeared in the 1st edn of 1834 (p. 42). (See cat. 6.)

In these miscellaneous crayon lithographs Lear appears to have been struggling to come to terms with what Harding advocated. The treatment of the trees in 'Tor Mohun Church. Devon' suggests an early stage in Lear's path to landscape drawing, and the tree to the left in the view of Knowsley Hall a more advanced, but perhaps rather self-conscious application of Harding's principles. The two individual tree studies, both of which stand firmly within the nineteenth century tradition for such images,[60] show a growing assimilation of Harding's approach to drawing trees; the massing of clusters of foliage is more convincing, and the overall effect more natural than in what are assumed to be his earlier works. The lithograph of a pine tree (cat. 9) is based on a surviving graphite drawing (cat. 8), and is in reverse of the original; it shows modifications to the token landscape setting, but both the graphite drawing and the lithograph smack of the kind of composition Harding used in his drawing-book sketches. The trunk of the tree, in both the drawing and the lithograph made after it, show that Lear had begun to learn from Harding how to convey both a sense of form and something of the specific characteristics of a tree.

The 'Wastwater and Screes' lithograph, a landscape in what became known as the tinted style, takes Lear away from the drawing-book study to a landscape sketch. It is almost certainly the latest of the five prints. Here his trees are set within a natural and uncontrived setting, and the clouds give some sense of the prevailing weather. His handling of the crayon on the black stone is more fluid than it was in the other miscellaneous lithographs discussed here, and the trees in the left foreground show a confident use of the scraper to produce a variety of effects. The loose handling of the foreground, with its broken fence and stone wall, goes beyond the formulaic treatment of his tree studies and builds on the experience he must have gained from drawing countless clumps of grass and foliage for Gould. This seems to have been the major contribution that Lear's natural history illustration made to his topographical lithography, and it is evident later in the rather exaggerated treatment of vegetation in some of the foregrounds of his Italian views.

The print's pale and rather ill-fitting tint stone has pin-hole registration marks at the top right and bottom left corners of the tint, which were the means by which its drawn areas were made to fit with the black image. Highlights on the lake and on parts of the foreground (for example, the man's hat, the top of the wall and uprights of the fence) must have been removed by scraping away the tint completely with some sharp instrument. But more adventurously Lear created varied tones in the sky, which is a clear indication that he was aware of experiments undertaken by Hullmandel and Harding in the mid 1830s (which are discussed below). Lear is likely to have produced the varied tones in the sky of this print in four stages. In stage one, a proof from the black, crayon-drawn stone would have been transferred to a fresh stone. This would then have been covered

60. Examples include François Villiers-Huet, *Rudiments and Characters of Trees* (London: R. Ackermann, 1806), and H.W. Burgess, *Eidodendron: Views of the General Character and Appearance of Trees Foreign and Indigenous as Connected with Picturesque Scenery* (London: J. Dickinson and Colnaghi, 1827).

all over with a coating of transparent wax, varnish or other greasy substance (which in this state would have printed as a solid). Lear would therefore have had a guide for the work he had to do on the tint stone, which included removing the solid coating entirely with a sharp instrument for the highlights, and partially removing it with a wire brush or a coarse cloth to produce the mid tones of the clouds. Finally, Lear would have re-defined the clouds by reinstating the full tone of the tints in the sky with lithographic ink.

This landscape sketch provides a connection with the main group of drawings in the exhibition, and also points to the future. But why, as far as we know, is it the only such Lear lithograph? The Lake District was already fertile ground for publishers of prints,[61] and it might be supposed that there would have been a market for a set of lithographed views of the kind shown in this exhibition. The process of lithography was ideally suited to conveying the majesty and mystery of Lake District scenery, and all one can conclude, somewhat weakly, is that the lure of Italy and the life of a wanderer in the South, coupled with a degree of financial independence, pushed any idea Lear may have had of producing further lithographs of this kind to one side.

By 1837, when Lear set out on his serious travels abroad, the prevailing style of lithography had begun to change. The two developments were entirely coincidental, but both were to have a major bearing on Lear's lithographic work. Changes in lithography came about through improvements to methods of working on tint stones made by Hullmandel in conjunction with his friend and working partner Harding. Tinted lithography (which made use of a second working, usually straw or buff in colour, to support a black lithograph) was common in the very early days of the lithographic process, particularly in Germany.[62] It grew from the experiences of early lithographers, who found that the drawings they had made on stone (which has a distinct tone) looked rather bald when printed on white paper. Some early lithographs were printed on tinted stock to compensate for this loss of background tone; others were provided with a further printing in a tint for the same reason. The second of these approaches had the greater potential as it allowed for some parts of the tint stone to be removed to produce highlights, as in drawings touched up with white gouache. It was this method that became popular in the early decades of the nineteenth century. Hullmandel was very familiar with it, in both theory and practice, and included an account and an example of it in *The Art of Drawing on Stone*.[63] But at this stage, only pure lights could be removed from the tint stone, which limited the range of possible applications and effectively ruled out its use for subtle effects in skies.

In the 1830s Hullmandel applied his mind to making improvements in tinted lithography, which are recorded in an album he compiled to document many of

61. Abbey *Scenery*, nos. 183–95, pp. 112–22; Peter Bicknell and Robert Woof, *The Discovery of the Lake District 1750–1810; a Context for Wordsworth* ([Grasmere]: Trustees of Dove Cottage, 1982), and *The Lake District Discovered, 1810–1850: the Artists, the Tourists and Wordsworth*, (Grasmere: Trustees of Dove Cottage, 1983).

62. Twyman 1965.

63. Hullmandel 1824, 'Of printing with two plates', pp. 81–2, pls XIII, XIV.

his lithographic innovations.[64] They were part of a package of improvements for artists that Hullmandel introduced to make lithography more 'painterly', culminating in his patented process of 'lithotint' (1841), a method of applying lithographic washes of varying strength to stone. Hullmandel's improvements to tinted lithography focused on methods of producing a variety of tones within the tint stone by combining positive marks drawn with the stump and negative ones that resulted from partially rubbing away dark tones with a wire brush or coarse cloth. These experiments were undertaken in collaboration with Harding and prepared the way for this artist's future publications. One experiment is precisely described as 'Trial for producing variety of tint in a tint stone which enabled Mr Harding to produce his "Sketches at Home & abroad & established and introduced what has since been called, the tinted style in 1835'.[65] *Sketches at Home and Abroad* (London: Charles Tilt, 1836) came out the following year in a form of tinted lithography that was not nearly as daring as some of the experiments in Hullmandel's album.[66] Nevertheless, it had an immediate influence and led to the publication of countless sets of topographical and landscape lithographs by other artists showing variation of tints within the tint stone.[67] Harding was able to promote tinted lithography still further by the inclusion of several examples of it in the second edition of his *Elementary Art; or the Use of the Lead Pencil* (London: Charles Tilt, 1838). Tinted lithography offered several advantages over monochrome work. First, and most obviously, it mapped onto the longstanding fashion for the Claude glass, which was still being used as a means of endowing English views with the golden glow of the Italian *campagna*. Secondly, it provided a lithographic parallel to the growing practice – which Lear adopted – of drawing on tinted paper. Thirdly, it meant that prints could be published that worked successfully in both plain and hand-coloured states, particularly in their skies, since the tint was usually light enough to have little effect on hand-colouring, whereas even very light crayon hatching on a black impression was likely to have a deadening effect on it.

Tinted lithography was the method Lear came to adopt for his sets of overseas views, beginning with *Views in Rome and its Environs* (1841) and *Illustrated Excursions in Italy* (1846). If further support is needed for Harding's influence on Lear it is to be found in the latter's acceptance of the tinted style for these publications. Bearing in mind the experiments in Hullmandel's album, and the likelihood that Harding would have wanted to claim priority in the use of the new form of tinted lithography, 'Wastwater & the Screes from Wastdale' can be dated late 1836 or early 1837, a date which is supported by the fact that Lear is known to have been in the Wastdale area in mid September 1836 (see cats. 42–6). Not only did Lear model his tinted lithography on that of Harding, including the

64. Hullmandel, 'A Collection of proof impressions and experiments made by C. Hullmandel in his attempt to improve the art of lithography' (*c.*1818–40) (St Bride Library, London, 15582). See Twyman 1988, pp. 72–8.

65. Ibid', f. 24; reproduced Twyman 1988, figs 2.30, 2.31.

66. Abbey *Travel*, vol. i, no. 29; Twyman 1970, pp. 203–6, pls 115–16.

67. Twyman 1970, pp. 206–25.

use of the technique of putting foreground highlights slightly in relief in imitation of impasto gouache,[68] but his self-confident handling of the crayon and bravado treatment of some foregrounds echo the former's tendency to allow style to override observation.

In a little over ten years, Lear's involvement with lithography had taken him from natural history illustrator to topographical artist. Initially, it seems, he picked up what he needed to know about drawing on stone from Hullmandel and his circle in order to reproduce his remarkable water-colour studies of parrots. From 1834, and most probably before, he was struggling to master landscape and particularly the drawing of trees, with Harding as his major mentor. From a comparative novice in the field Lear became an accomplished exponent of topographical lithography in the 1840s, adopting the new tinted style that Hullmandel and Harding had developed just a couple of years before he headed for Italy in July 1837.

Acknowledgements: the Librarian of the Linnean Society Library; the staff of the Department of Prints and Drawings, Victoria & Albert Museum; Angela Roche (who allowed me to see the British Museum's group of Lear lithographs while they were waiting for a conservation report); and Charles Nugent for sharing his knowledge of Lear with me.

68. This technique was referred to by Harding in his *Elementary Art* (1838, p. 78): 'The white, which is sold in a liquid state, should be very much diluted with water for the skies and middle distances; but on the foreground objects it should be so thick as to be in relief from the paper, more especially on the very small touches of light.' The use of thick gouache in foregrounds was simulated very effectively in tinted lithography by scraping away the tint stone for the lights, or etching it deeply, so as to produce an embossed effect in the printing. *Sketches at Home and Abroad*, was a pioneering work in the use of this technique, which was taken further in other publications, most obviously in J.C. Bourne's *The History and Description of the Great Western Railway* (1846) (see Twyman 1965, p. 51 and pl. 6).

CATALOGUE

Note: all items are by Edward Lear
unless otherwise stated.

[1]

LEAR, LANDSCAPE AND LITHOGRAPHY

In common with many middle-class households, the ability to draw was held to be an accomplishment in the Lear family, and the young Edward was taught by his elder sisters Ann and Sarah. All his life he felt the want of professional teaching and, although he was to make his living as an artist, he was certainly a slow starter and some of his early efforts are barely above the level of polite drawing-room accomplishment. In 1822, Sarah Lear married and moved to Arundel in Sussex, where Lear seems to have been a frequent visitor and which provided the material for his earliest landscape drawing.

In 1827, the Lear family broke up on his father Jeremiah's retirement; the young Edward set up house with his eldest sister Ann in Grays Inn Road in London, and began to make his living as an artist. The few drawings that survive from this period show uneven levels of accomplishment. His still-life drawing can be very good, as seen in his watercolour entitled 'Eleanor's Geranium', dated June 1828 (Private Collection; Noakes 1991, p. 32), but when he has to invent, as in his drawing of a panther from Miss Fraser's album, dateable to about 1830 (Private Collection; Noakes 1991, p. 34), his rendering of natural forms is repetitive and formulaic.

Lear's earliest surviving landscape drawing is of Peppering House in Sussex and is dated 1829 (fig. 1, p. 3). This was the home of the Drewitt family, with whom Lear became very intimate. Fanny Drewitt was about Lear's age; by the time of Lear's earliest surviving letter to her in September 1830, she was being courted by George Coombe. The date of their marriage is unknown but, as there were two children by April 1833, one of whom is described as 'new', they must have been married in 1831. Lear's letters to them, always addressed separately as George and Mrs George, are an invaluable source for this very early period in Lear's life.

The drawing of Peppering House is in pencil only, and there is no evidence that Lear was using watercolour to record landscape at this period; the progression from the 1829 view of Peppering House to the 1834 view of Parham House (cat. 11) does not involve the use of colour. At some point in the late 1820s Lear began to turn his attention to lithography. Originally considered as a mechanical process for multiplying images, lithography had gained in popularity during the 1820s. One of its most important practitioners and apologists was Charles Hullmandel (1789–1850), and it was probably from his exhaustively detailed manual of lithography, *The Art of Drawing on Stone*, published in 1824 (cat. 4), that Lear learnt the process. Certainly, Hullmandel was a good friend by the 1830s and printed most of Lear's lithographs.

Those for which Lear is best known are the forty-two lithographs of parrots which were published as *Illustrations of the Family of Psittacidae, or Parrots*, in 1832, having been published in parts from November 1830. The Parrot prints have little or no landscape backgrounds, but nevertheless Lear was beginning to turn his attention to landscape draughtsmanship. His model in this field was the watercolourist and lithographic artist James Duffield Harding (1797–1863), who worked closely with Hullmandel on a series of drawing books for amateurs from the mid 1820s; Harding's drawing style, particularly his depiction of trees, provided a model for Lear for at least the next decade. Lear's contribution to the field of natural history illustration, both on his own account and in his (mostly unacknowledged) work for John Gould, is now rightly acclaimed. At the time, however, he was living from hand to mouth and doing bread and butter work for Gould, whose wife he claimed in 1833 to have taught lithography; landscape provided a break from this routine.

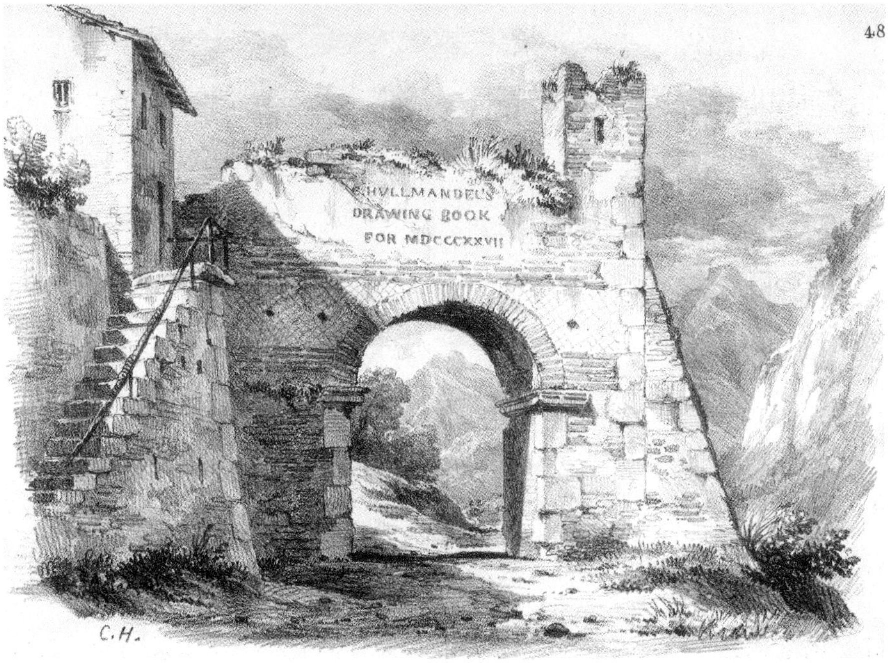

Cat. 1

CHARLES HULLMANDEL (1789–1850)

1 *A Building and an Archway in a Mountainous Landscape*
Title page for *C. Hullmandel's Drawing Book for MDCCCXXVII*
Signed with initials on the stone, numbered 48
Lithograph, 17.1 × 23.8 cm
Private Collection

As the wrapper for one of the part issues makes clear, *Hullmandel's Drawing Book* was published monthly with four lithographs in each issue. This now detached print was the last of the year, and has been cut down to remove the publication details from the lower margin.

CHARLES HULLMANDEL (1789–1850), after JAMES DUFFIELD HARDING (1797–1863)

2 *Trees in a Landscape with a Bridge Beyond*
Plate 6 in *C. Hullmandel's Drawing Book for MDCCCXXVII*
Signed with initials on the stone, numbered 6
Lithograph, with the imprint reading 'Pub^{d}. by J. Dickinson 114, New Bond Street, 1827.', 26.2 × 17.9 cm
Private Collection
Illustrated on p. 36

This is the bound copy of *Hullmandel's Drawing Book for 1827*, open at one of the lithographs of a James Duffield Harding drawing. The book contains forty-eight prints: twenty after Harding, twelve after Samuel Prout, eight after C. Carbonnier, and eight after Hullmandel himself. These prints, which had no explanatory text, were intended as prototypes for amateurs to copy. As a fledgling artist, Lear would certainly have seen drawing books such as this, and it was Harding's style, in particular in the rendering of trees and foliage, which was the strongest influence on him.

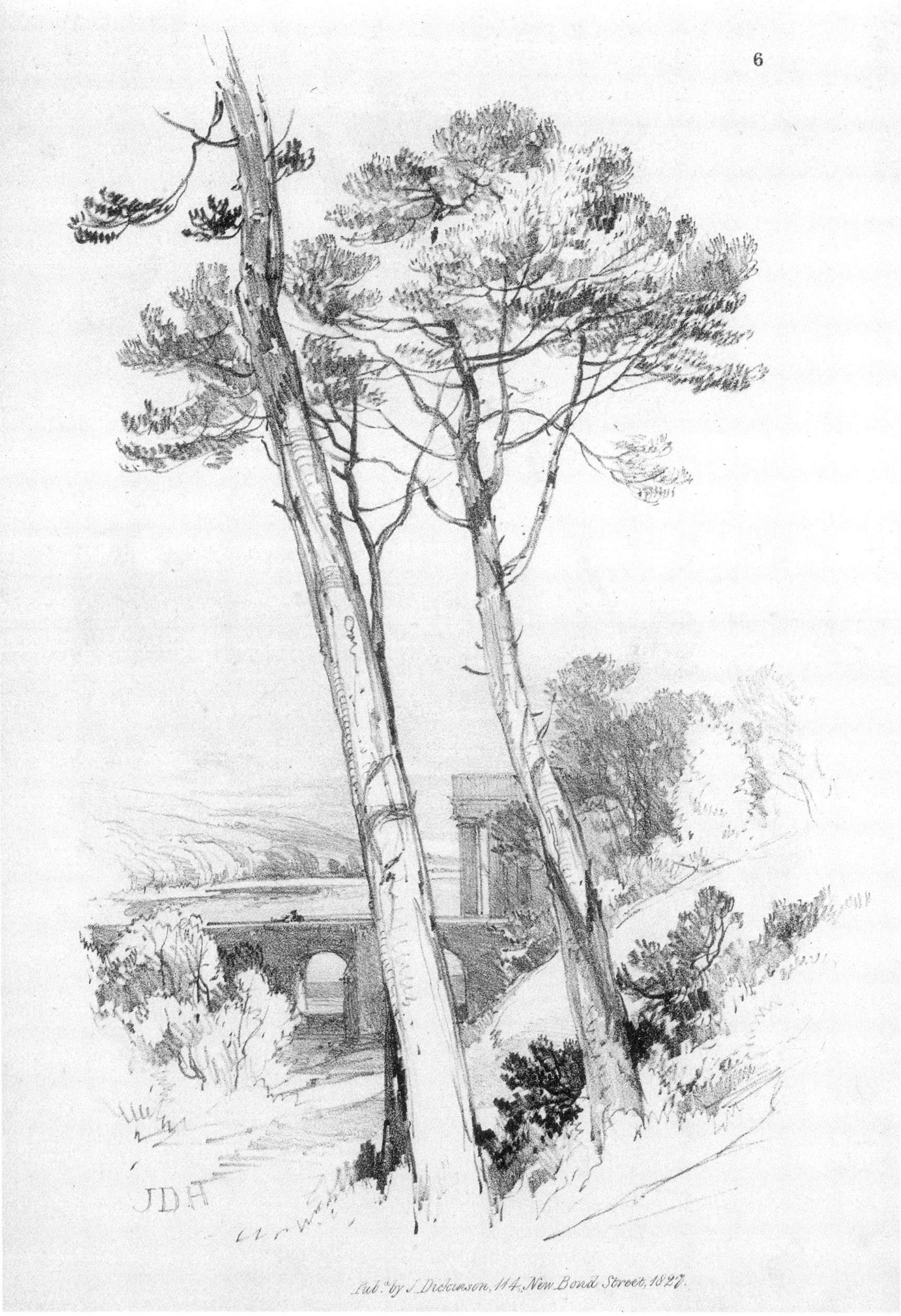

Cat. 2

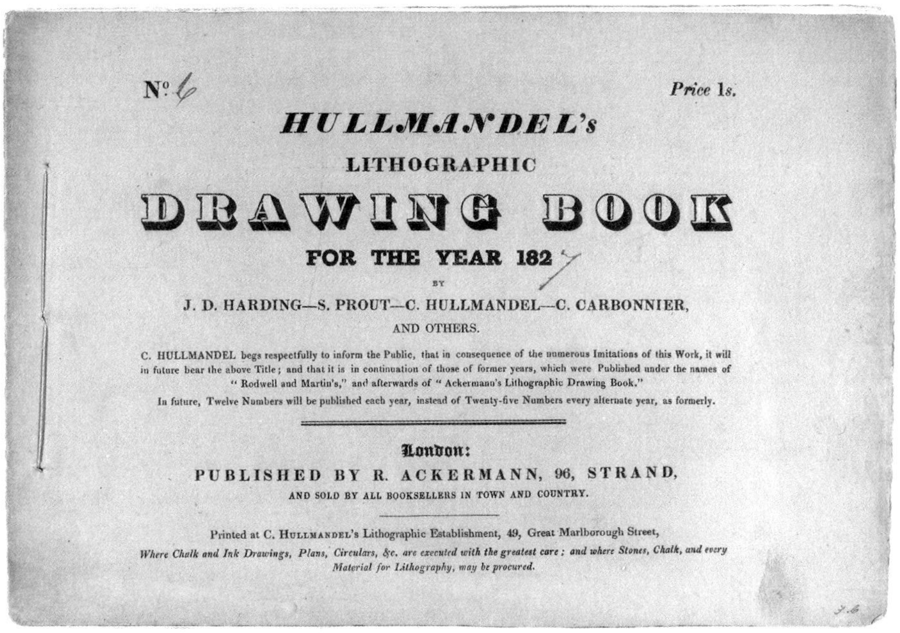

Cat. 3

3 Wrapper for No. 6 of *C. Hullmandel's Drawing Book for MDCCCXXVII*

Containing four prints after Harding
With handwritten numbers added to the printed text
19 × 28.2 cm

Private Collection

This wrapper is the sixth (i.e. the June) issue of *Hullmandel's Drawing Book* for 1827 and contains Plates 21–4 of the book, four lithographs after Harding; the digits for the Number and for the year have been added in longhand. The cooperative nature of the drawing book is clear from the wrapper, with Hullmandel and Ackermann both being named. Hullmandel was a businessman as well as an artist and printer, and was clearly using the *Drawing Book* series to publicise his activities as a printer of other artists' work.

CHARLES HULLMANDEL (1789–1850)

4 'Of the Mode of Holding the Chalk'

Plate I from *The Art of Drawing on Stone Giving a Full Explanation of the Various Styles, of the Different Methods to Be Employed to Ensure Success, of the Modes of Correcting, as Well as of the Several Causes of Failure*
London: C. Hullmandel and R. Ackermann, 1824
Lithograph, 17.5 × 25 cm

Private Collection

Illustrated on p. 38

This, Hullmandel's manual of lithography, was published in 1824, and consisted of ninety-two pages with a title page (see fig. 2, p. 4) and nineteen lithographic plates grouped at the end. The book is broken down into 135 numbered paragraphs, in which Hullmandel systematically goes through the lithographic process in great detail. The sections have titles such as: 'Of the Mode of Supporting the Hand when

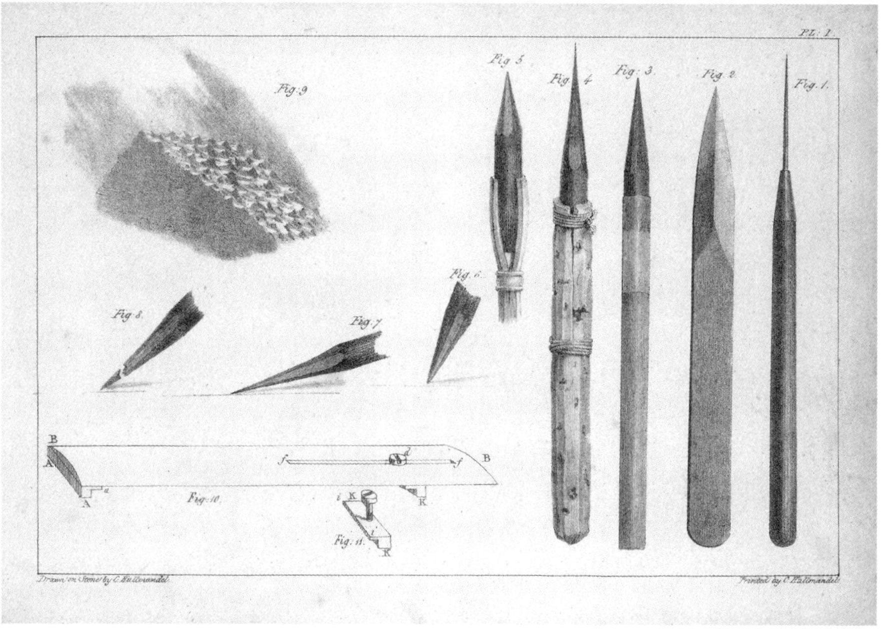

Cat. 4

Drawing on Stone', 'Of the Tools Necessary for Drawing on Stone', 'Of the Mode of Applying Chalk to Stone' and 'Of Some Causes of Failure'.

Some of Plate I is described on pp. 24–5 of the book in a section entitled 'Of the Mode of Holding the Chalk'. The passage reads:

> As lithographic chalk is more brittle than lead pencil, it requires some precautions in the mode of holding and cutting it, according to the intensity of the tint intended to be produced.
>
> 41. When delicate tints are wanted, the pencil must be cut long and slender, as in fig. 4, plate 1; when middle tints, as in fig. 3, and when dark ones are to be produced, still more obtuse, as in fig. 5.
>
> 42. If, in drawing dark tints, the chalk is held sloping, as in fig. 8, it is sure to break; indeed, I know few pencils that would not: the darker the tint or the line, the more upright the chalk must be held, see fig. 6. When clouds and other light tints are to be produced, it matters little how sloping it is held, as in fig. 7.

Although it is not known how Lear learnt the practice of lithography and he himself never commented on it, the inference is that he learnt from Hullmandel, whose good friend he certainly was and who printed most of his lithographs. This book would therefore have been one with which Lear was intimately familiar.

5 *Letter to George Coombe, from 61 Albany Street, Regent's Park, London*

19 April 1833
Autograph manuscript with postal stamps and seal
The Frederick Warne Archive
See pp. 202–4 for full text

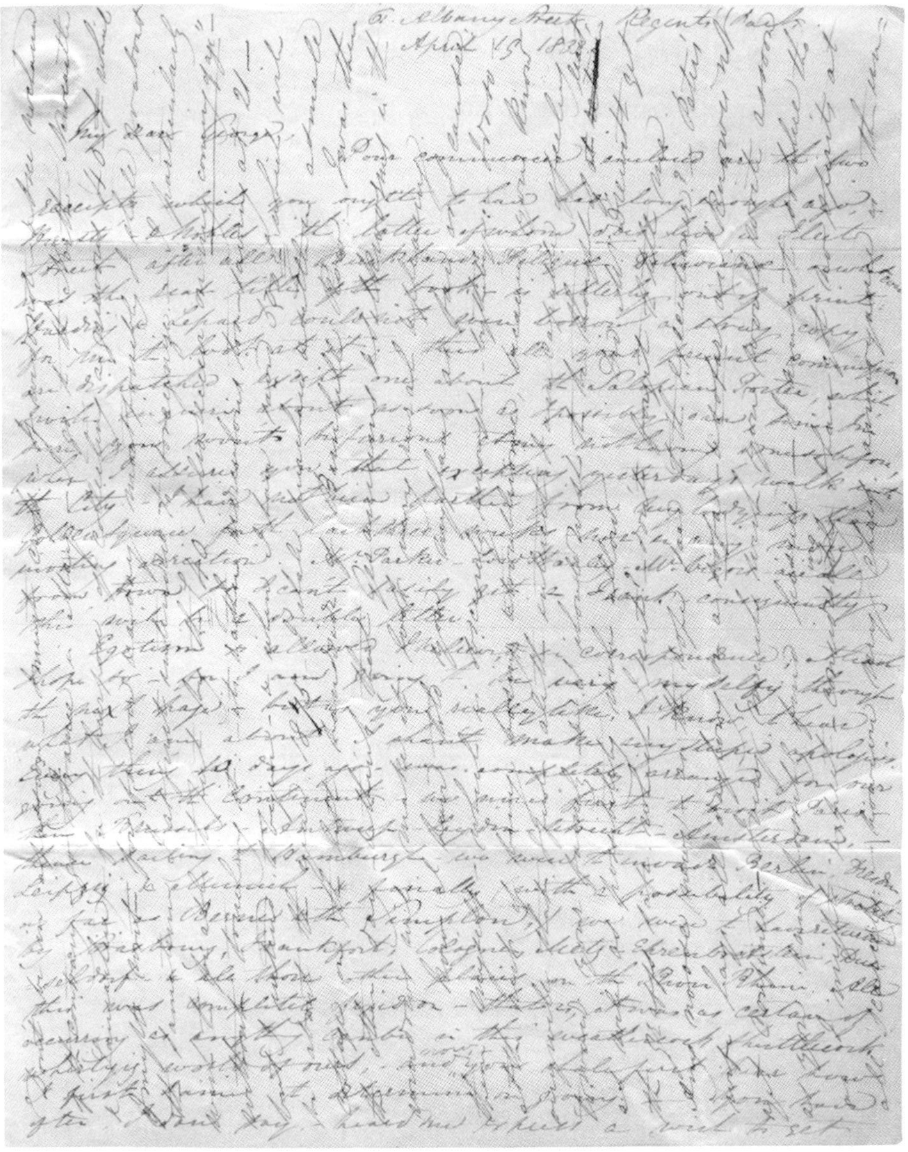

Cat. 5

An invaluable source for Lear's early life is the group of rediscovered letters written to George Coombe and his wife Fanny (née Drewitt), which were offered at Christie's on 29 June 1995 and are now in the Frederick Warne Archive. The Drewitt family were childhood friends of the Lear family, who lived at Peppering near Arundel in Sussex. Lear's connection with the area derives from his sister Sarah who married Charles Street in 1822 and went to live near Arundel. This letter is written from 61 Albany Street, Regents Park, which were Lear's London lodgings from April 1832 until the end of January 1834.

At this date, postage cost eight pence for a single sheet, and, since Lear was unable to find someone to frank it for him, he was forced to overwrite the text at right angles so that page four is written over page one (see illustration above) and page five over page two, with consequent problems of legibility. As Lear says at the end of the first paragraph: 'Mr Parker—Lord Stanley—Mr Vigors—are all from town so I can't easily get a Frank—consequently this will be a double letter.' The way in which the single sheet was folded in half, the half sheet then folded in on itself in quarters, and this finally folded in the opposite direction in thirds before being sealed, is clearly visible. A fascinating glimpse of relations among the Lear siblings is provided by the postscript, added after the letter had been folded in half, but before subsequent foldings: 'There is no occasion, if you please, to tell Mrs Street any of my proceedings: you know none of my sisters are confidantes of mine.'

Most of this long and chatty letter is concerned with Lear's plans to go the Continent with John Gould in connection with his work on *The Birds of Europe*. At the time of writing, the trip had not taken place owing to the illness of Mrs Gould, as described in the letter; later that summer, in July, Gould did visit the Continent, and it is highly likely that Lear accompanied him, although no letters survive recording the journey. Lear and Gould were intimately connected at this time; Lear wrote in this letter, 'I do all the backgrounds to the European birds besides various touchings up'. The letter gives a full account of Lear's relations with the Gould family, his plans 'as far as I see them myself' and goes into some detail over his financial position following the publication of *Psittacidae*, referred to as 'my Parrots'; it provides a detailed and tantalising snapshot of the life of the young ornithological artist, then aged only twenty, who refers jokily to his imminent coming of age at the beginning of page four.

JAMES DUFFIELD HARDING (1797–1863)

6 'Beech Trees from Buckhurst Park'

Plate XXIV, from *Elementary Art; or, The Use of the Lead Pencil, Advocated and Explained*
London: Charles Tilt, 1834
Signed with initials on the stone
Lithograph, with the imprint reading 'London Published by Charles Tilt 86 Fleet Street', 21.5 × 30.4 cm
The London Library

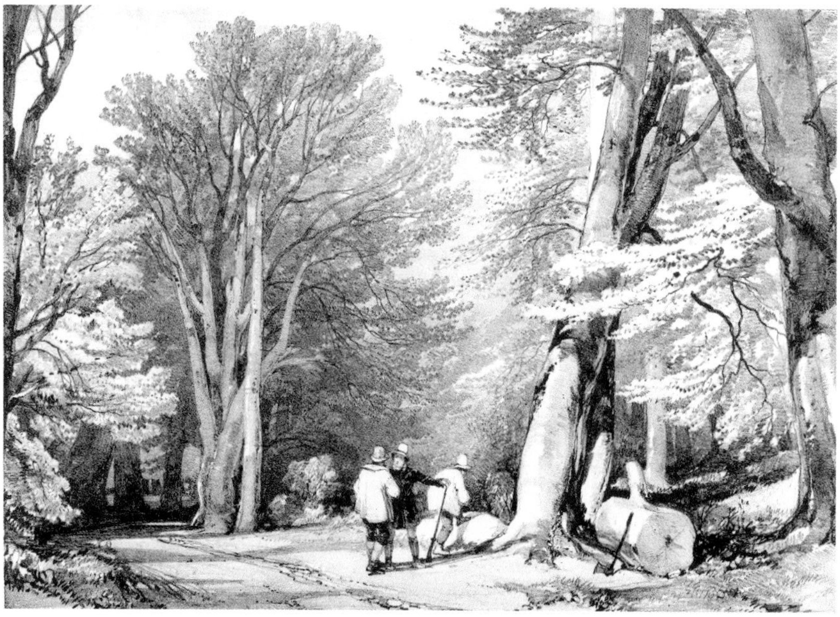

Cat. 6

Harding was primarily a watercolour painter and was elected a member of the Society of Painters in Watercolours in 1821; he exhibited there regularly until his death, apart from a period from 1846, when he attempted to become a member of the Royal Academy by sending oils for exhibition there. Despite his failure to join the Academy, Harding's reputation stood a great deal higher in the nineteenth century than it does today, and he was a very well-known and popular drawing master and teacher. Ruskin, who was his pupil in the early to mid 1840s and whose style was for a time strongly influenced by him, wrote in Volume I of *Modern Painters* that Harding was, after Turner, 'the greatest master of foliage in Europe' (Ruskin 1903–12, vol. iii, 578).

As well as contributing to topographical publications, Harding wrote several drawing manuals, of which this one *Elementary Art, or The Use of the Lead Pencil*, first published in 1834, must have been seen by Lear. In the Preface, Harding makes his aims clear, 'The object of the Author in undertaking the present Work, has been, to place before those who desire to study the Arts of Design, and especially those who practise, for the first time, the use of the Lead Pencil, such simple rules for their guidance, as will enable them to see how Nature may be represented by Art.' As well as containing drawing exercises, and compositions after H.P. Briggs and Edwin Landseer, the book contains nine lithographs after Harding; these all show Harding's great skill at drawing trees, which was a strong influence on Lear.

7 *An Ash Tree*

Signed with initials
Lithograph, 43.2 × 32.6 cm, sheet size
Provenance: presented by E. Rawdon Smith in 1954
The British Museum (1954-11-3-392)
Illustrated on p. 42

8 *A Figure beside a Scots Pine Tree with a Cottage and a Barn beyond*

Signed and dated 1834
Pencil, on grey paper, 36.4 × 24.8 cm
Provenance: presented by E. Rawdon Smith in 1954
The British Museum (1954-11-3-402)
Illustrated on p. 42

This is a study for cat. 9, with the background altered in the finished print.

9 *A Figure beside a Scots Pine Tree with a Cottage beyond*

Signed with initials and dated 1834
Lithograph, 42.2 × 32.1 cm, sheet size
Provenance: presented by E. Rawdon Smith in 1954
The British Museum (1954-11-3-391)
Illustrated on p. 42

This, and cat. 7, both somewhat stained, are Lear's earliest surviving dateable landscape lithographs; one of them still has its preparatory drawing (cat. 8). There is no evidence (and Lear never makes any revelations) as to who taught him lithography, but the evidence is very strong that it was Charles Hullmandel. Certainly, they were

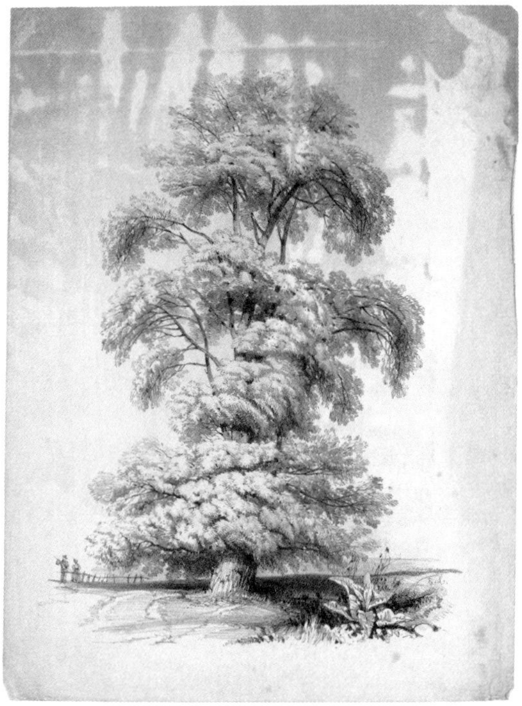

Cat. 7

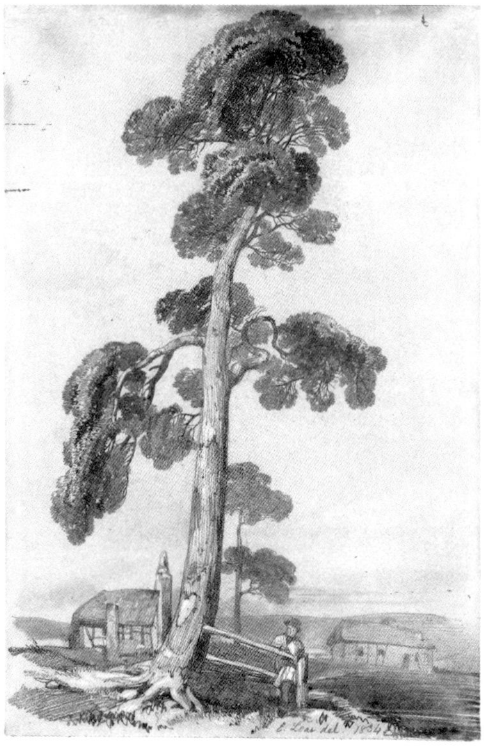

Cat. 8

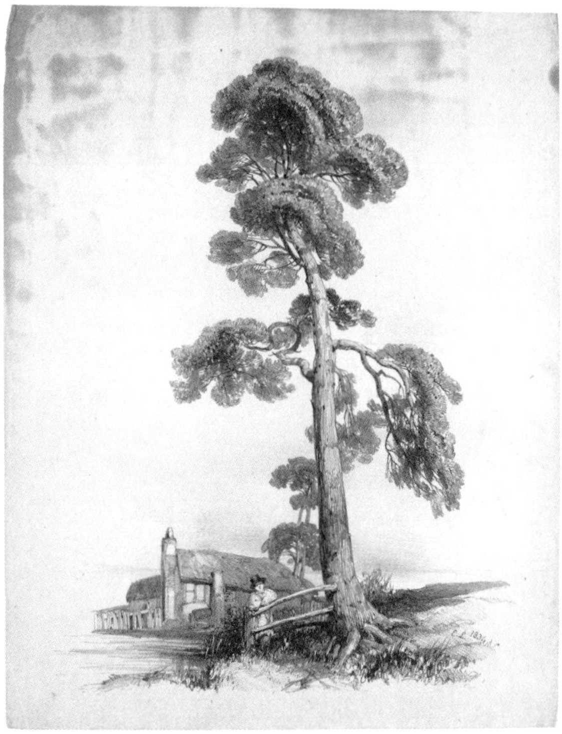

Cat. 9

very friendly around this time, and, although he does not say so, Daniel Fowler probably met Lear at Hullmandel's lithographic premises at Great Marlborough Street. Fowler was a pupil of James Duffield Harding, who worked closely with Hullmandel, and Fowler and Lear later travelled to Europe together in 1837. The execution of these lithographs is somewhat crude, as one would expect from someone learning the practice. They were probably not issued in large numbers, but the fact that they show two different types of tree indicates that they might have formed part of a set illustrating a number of different species.

10 *Tormohun Church, Devon*

Lithograph, on India paper, with the imprint reading 'Lithog. by E Lear from a Sketch by Lady Georgina North, printed by C. Hullmandel', 14.3 × 19.1 cm (image size)
Provenance: presented by Dr. Gray in 1854
British Museum (1854-2-11-100)

This slightly crude lithograph is not dated but is surely a very early attempt at the medium, and probably only ever existed in a few impressions. An indication of the circumstances in which such prints were produced is provided by the fact that Hullmandel's letterer has misspelt the lady artist's name, leaving out an 'a'. She was in fact Lady Georgiana North (1798–1835), the younger daughter of the 3rd Earl of Guilford, and may have been a pupil of Lear's in London. Another possible connection is that she was related by marriage to the Stanleys of Alderley, since her aunt

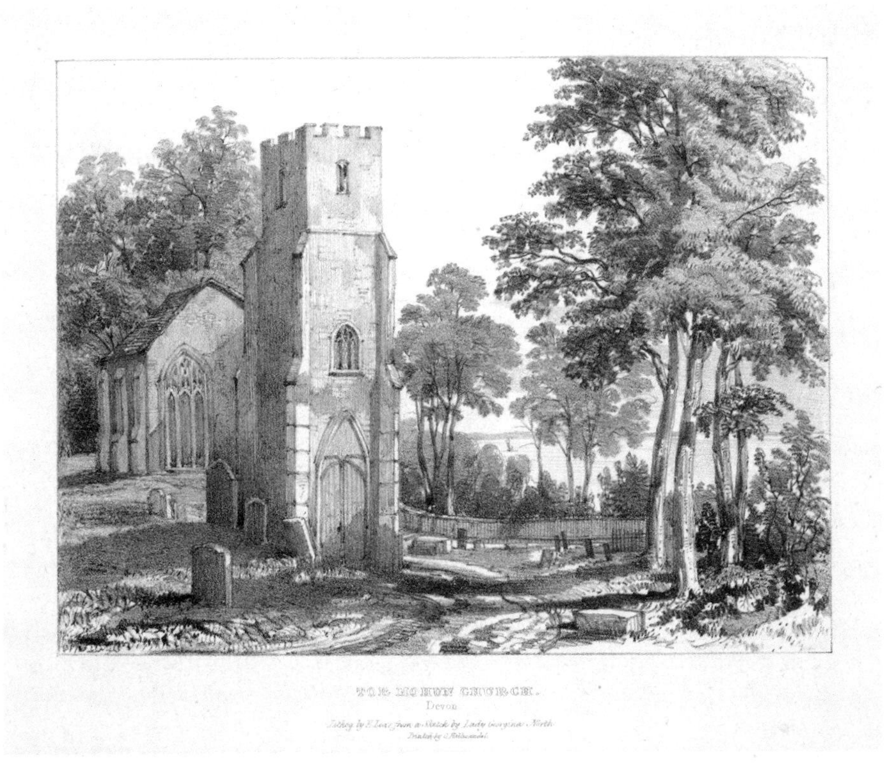

Cat. 10

Lady Anne North was the third wife of the 1st Earl of Sheffield, whose eldest daughter Lady Maria Holroyd was the wife of Sir John Stanley of Alderley (created Baron Stanley of Alderley in 1839). Lear was very close to the Stanleys of Alderley, and travelled in Ireland with some members of the family in August 1835. The medieval church of Tormohun was the original church for what was to become the modern resort of Torquay.

11 *Parham House from the South*

Signed, inscribed and dated 'E.Lear. del: / Parham. 1834.'
Pencil heightened with white, on buff paper, 26.7 × 36.8 cm
Provenance: presented to the current owner in 1947
Private Collection

Lear second eldest sister Sarah (1793–1874) married Charles Street, a banker in Arundel, in 1822, and Lear often visited them during his childhood. The Tudor manor house of Parham is not far from Arundel; at this date, it was the property of the Zouche family. On the death of the 13th Baron Zouche in 1828, Parham and the Zouche title passed to his elder daughter Harriet Anne (1787–1870), who was married to Robert Curzon, a younger son of the 1st Viscount Curzon; their sons, Robert (b. 1810), who became 14th Baron Zouche, and Edward Cecil (b. 1812), were Lear's near contemporaries, although it is not known whether he knew them. It is known that Lear was staying at Peppering House near Arundel, the home of the Drewitt family, in September and October 1834; there are dated drawings done in Peppering and its vicinity, and two drawings of trees in the park at Parham, inscribed 'Parham' and dated 30 September and 13 October 1834 at the Yale Center for British Art (B1997.7.8 and 13). This is the only known Lear drawing of the house. Around 1830, Lady Zouche had instituted a thorough renovation of Parham, in which one of the main alterations was the moving of the main entrance from the south to the north of the house, where it remains today. This drawing provides an important record of the appearance and fenestration of the south front of the house after the Zouche alterations and before the extensive renovations of the twentieth century, which took place after the house was sold to the Pearson family in 1922.

12 *Undated letter to Fanny Coombe, from 28 Southampton Row, London*

19 or 20 June 1835
Autograph manuscript
The Frederick Warne Archive
Illustrated on p. 46; see p. 205 for full text

This undated note to Fanny Coombe seems to be the final part of another letter or parcel; it is obviously very close in date to the letter of 19 June 1835 to George Coombe which describes the misfortunes of Lear's planned bachelor party (see Appendix A). It was written from London shortly before Lear left for Knowsley for the summer (he left on the evening of 20 June), and the 'long epistle' to George Coombe promised in the first part is therefore cat. 14, written from Knowsley on 24 June.

The letter describes Lord Derby's solicitude towards the aspiring artist, who was nearly forty years his junior and of much more humble status:

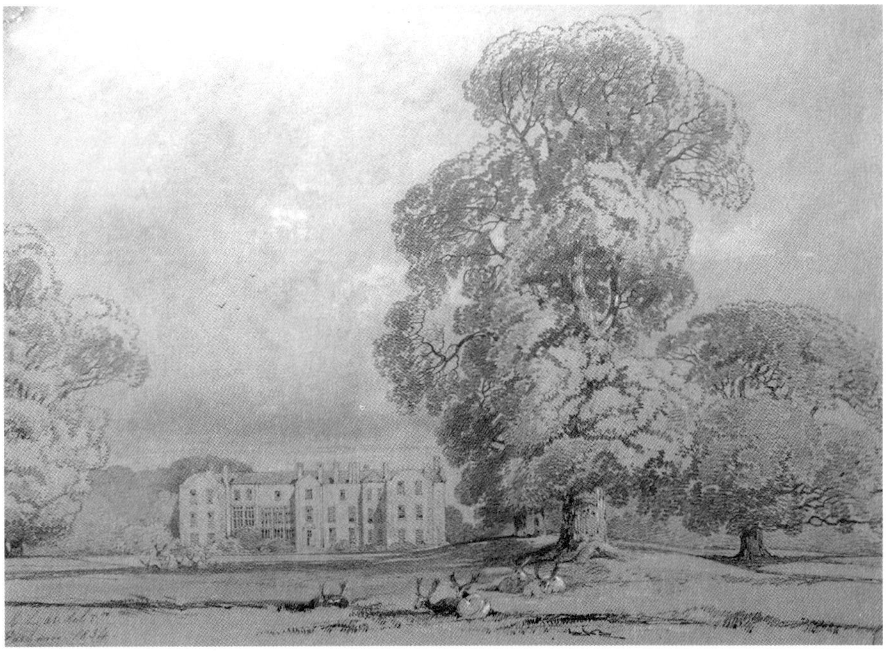

Cat. 11

> Lord D … has behaved with great kindness: two or 3 things while he was in town were particularly marked:—such as at the Gardens & Zoological meetings—shaking hands with me before all the great bodies—& in calling & sitting for a long half hour at 28 Southampton Row [Lear's London lodgings from the middle of February 1834 until late January 1837]. These attentions—little in themselves—have a great effect when coming from people of rank—to us small fry of artists—& it is very praiseworthy of noblemen to make use of such means to bring young beasts forward one step in life.

Lear also tells an amusing anecdote about his patron's deafness: '"My Lord—" said I—"I hope your head is better"—for he had had a bad headache the day before. "Oh!"—replied he—"I have found a remedy for that. I have taken all the little birds out & put in one Cockatoo & three large red Macaws."' Lear makes a brief mention at the end of the letter of his artist friend Daniel Fowler, who had just returned with a portfolio of sketches made on a year's tour of Europe ('early yesterday morning in rushed Daniel Fowler red hot from Rome.' – letter, 19 June 1835); Lear had met Fowler (1810–1894) who was a pupil of James Duffield Harding, at Hullmandel's studio (see p. 5). Lear describes Fowler's drawings of Germany, the Alps and Italy in this letter as 'without *exception* the *finest sketches* I ever saw from any artist's portfolio: some are beyond wonderful.' The sketches and Fowler's friendship were an important influence on Lear at this time.

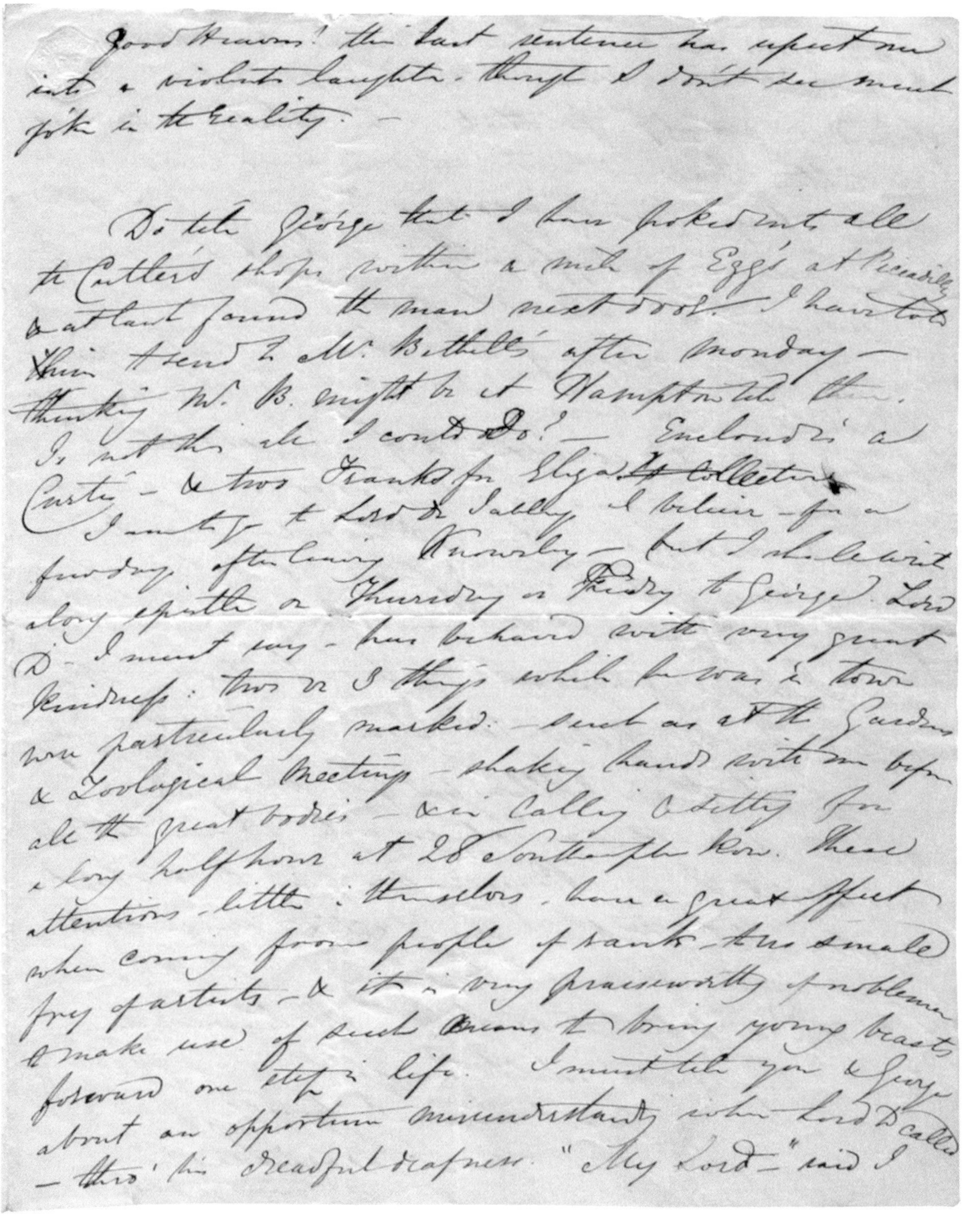
Good Heavens! the last sentence has upset me into a violent laughter - though I don't see much joke in the reality. -

Do tell George that I have poked into all the Cutler's shops within a mile of Egg's at Piccadilly & at last found the man next door. I have told him to send to Mr. Bethell's after Monday - thinking Mr. B. might be at Hampton till then. Is not this all I could do? - Enclosed is a Cast - & two Franks for Eliza's collection.
I am to go to Lord de Tabley I believe - for a few days after leaving Knowsley - but I shall write a long epistle on Thursday or Friday to George. Lord D. - I must say - has behaved with very great kindness: two or 3 things while he was in town were particularly marked: - such as at the Gardens & Zoological Meeting - shaking hands with me before all the great bodies - & in calling & sitting for a long half hour at 28 Southampton Row. These attentions - little in themselves - have a great effect when coming from people of rank - to us small fry of artists - & it is very praiseworthy of noblemen to make use of such means to bring young beasts forward one step in life. I must tell you & George about an opportune misunderstanding when Lord D called - thro' his dreadful deafness. "My Lord -" said I

Cat. 12

[2]

LEAR AND KNOWSLEY

Lear's first publication was *Illustrations of the Family of Psittacidae, or Parrots*, which was issued in twelve folio parts between November 1830 and the early months of 1832, and as a book of forty-two hand-coloured lithographs in April 1832. His work on this book brought him to the attention of Lord Stanley, who on the death of his father in October 1834 became the 13th Earl of Derby; Lord Stanley was President of the Zoological Society in June 1830, when Lear applied for permission to make drawings of the parrots belonging to the Society. From at least 1831, Lear was working for Lord Stanley, drawing the animals and birds in the private menagerie at Knowsley Hall, the large country estate of the Stanley family in Lancashire. It is not known when Lear first visited Knowsley; his first surviving letter from there dates from June 1835 and describes the housekeeper as 'a new one since I was here', implying that there had been a previous visit. There were presumably other earlier ones; indeed Lear wrote in 1851, '22 years ago I first went to Knowsley', suggesting that he went there as early as 1829 (*Letters*, 18). It should be borne in mind, however, that Lear is not always accurate in his memories of dates.

For the visits of 1835 and 1836, where the evidence of letters and dated drawings is more full but still very incomplete, it is clear that Lear used Knowsley as a base for several months at a time. In 1835, Lear arrived at Knowsley on 21 June and there is a drawing of the house dated 5 September (cat. 28). In between those dates, he paid visits to other grand houses in Lancashire and Cheshire, as well as making trips to Anglesey and Ireland; after visiting Lathom on 17 and 18 September 1835 (cats. 30 and 31), he arrived back in London on 14 October. In 1836, we do not know when Lear arrived at Knowsley but the letter of 24 August (cat. 37) describing 'passing ... a consecutive 6 weeks ... this year at Knowsley', which he left 'about 10 August', suggests that he arrived there at the end of June as in the previous year. After his tour of Lancashire and the Lake District, he returned to the house on 30 October; the date of his return to London is not known. Lear was back at Knowsley again for Christmas 1836, and returned on 19 May 1837, staying until the end of the month. By 1837 he was almost treating Knowsley as a second home, and wrote on 3 January, 'I was much pressed to remain ... & ... have now received an invitation to come when I please without being asked.' Considering the amount of time that Lear spent at Knowsley, it is remarkable how few drawings of the house survive. There are three quite sketchy pencil drawings of the house and two of the park and grounds at the Yale Center for British Art (B1997. 7.15–17 and 18–19, figs. 6 and 7, p. 48), and apart from these all the drawings that survive, three in number, are in this exhibition. They represent only a fraction of the drawings that must once have existed; at least one of them was made into a lithograph (fig. 10, p. 75). The Lathom drawings provide evidence that it was Lear's practice to produce drawings of the houses he visited; in his letter of 20 July 1835 (cat. 15), he mentions visits to Tabley House, Dunham Massey, Oulton Park and Beeston Castle, suggesting the subjects of drawings which are now lost.

The Knowsley Hall which Lear visited had grown from a medieval hunting lodge into a very large house, built over several periods. Basically L-shaped, the south wing contains under later additions the medieval core of the house, while the east wing was built in the early Georgian period under the direction of the 10th Earl; this large house had been extended yet further in the early nineteenth century in the medieval style. Lear's letters, only a few of which now survive, describe the house, its staff and its guests with all the enthusiasm of a truly impressed visitor. But Lear was not just a visitor; by the time that he left Knowsley at the end of May 1837, he had come to feel like one of the family. He wrote in his final letter of 8 July 1837 (cat. 104) before his departure for Europe: 'let me go back to Knowsley—to leave which cost me a great deal of pain … I have been very happy at different times in many places as you know very well: but having had a longer duration of comfort in Lancashire I shall always look back to it as the best home I have ever met with.'

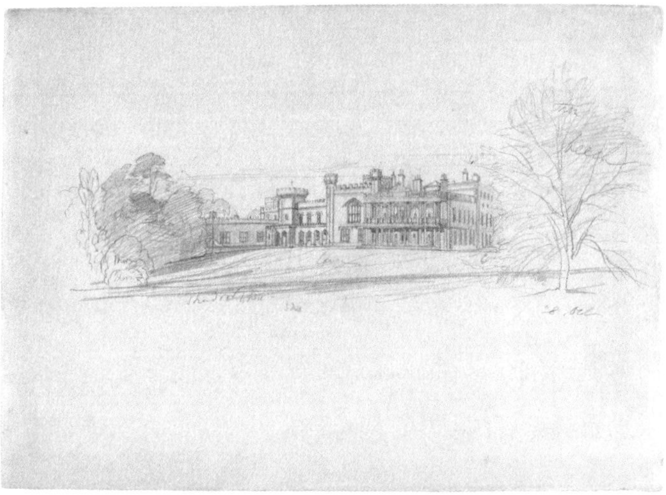

Fig. 6 Knowsley Hall: the South and East Fronts, dated 28 October, and inscribed with notes, pencil, 27 × 38.3 cm (Yale Center for British Art, B1997.7.15).

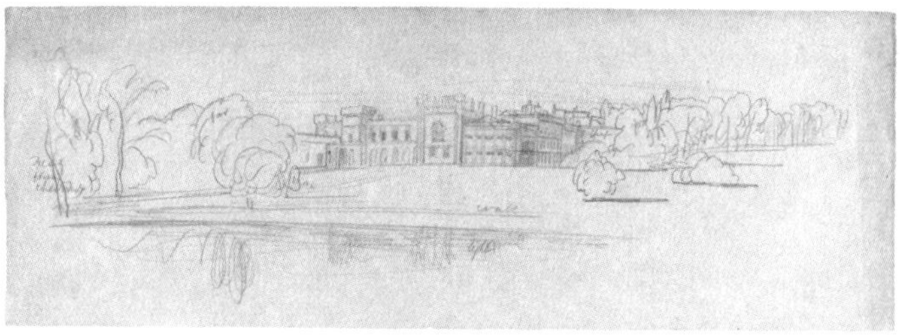

Fig. 7 Knowsley Hall: A Distant View of the South and East Fronts, inscribed with notes, pencil, 13.5 × 38.1 cm (Yale Center for British Art, B1997.7.16).

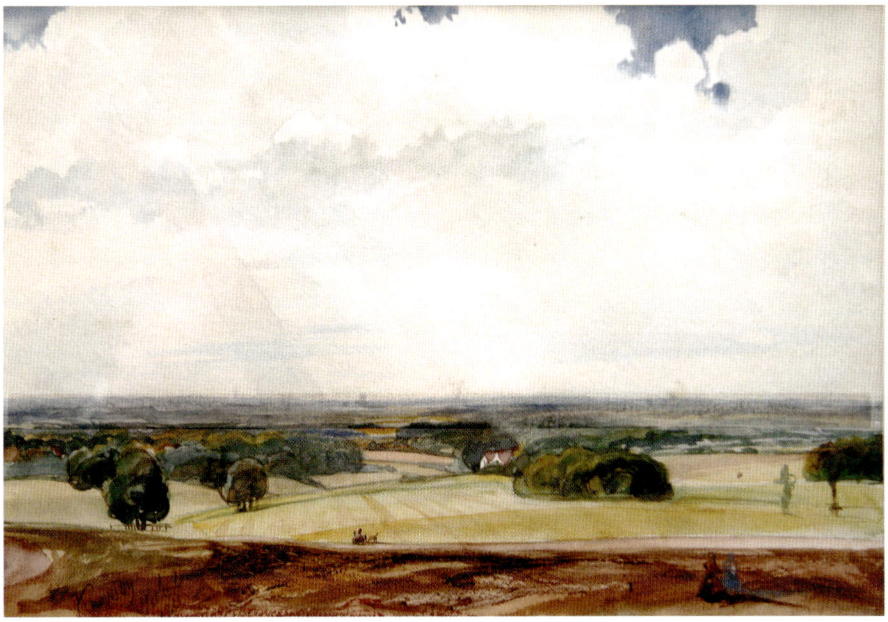

Cat. 13

13 *View over the Park at Knowsley*

Inscribed and dated 'Knowsley / July 4 / 1835'
Watercolour with touches of white heightening, 17 × 25 cm
Provenance: Anon. Sale; Christie's, 18 Mar. 1986, lot 150 (£2,800); Anon. Sale, Sotheby's, 14 Nov. 1991, lot 155 (unsold); Anon. Sale, Sotheby's, 1 Apr. 1993, lot 133, purchased by current owners (£850)
Private Collection

This view of the Park at Knowsley has the distinction of being the earliest known watercolour landscape by Lear. Although he used watercolour for his natural history illustrations, it was not a medium which he used for landscape at this period, preferring to employ a soft pencil on coloured paper to give the effect of a lithograph. Having probably learnt the lithographic process from Charles Hullmandel, and being well versed in the landscape lithographs of James Duffield Harding, Lear much preferred a monochrome finish to his landscape drawings, which remained the norm for several years to come.

Soon after arriving at Knowsley, Lear wrote to George Coombe on 24 June 1835: 'I keep my promise of writing early to you—though possibly there would be a better chance of amusing you if I waited longer before I did so. It is about seven o'clock—the rain is coming down in torrents, and the vast pancake of landscape from here to Liverpool is all in a beastly gray mist.' (cat. 14). The view described is similar to that in this watercolour, although by 4 July the weather had obviously improved.

14 *Letter to George Coombe, from Knowsley Hall, Lancashire*

24 June 1835
Autograph manuscript
The Frederick Warne Archive
Illustrated on p. 50; see pp. 207–9 for full text

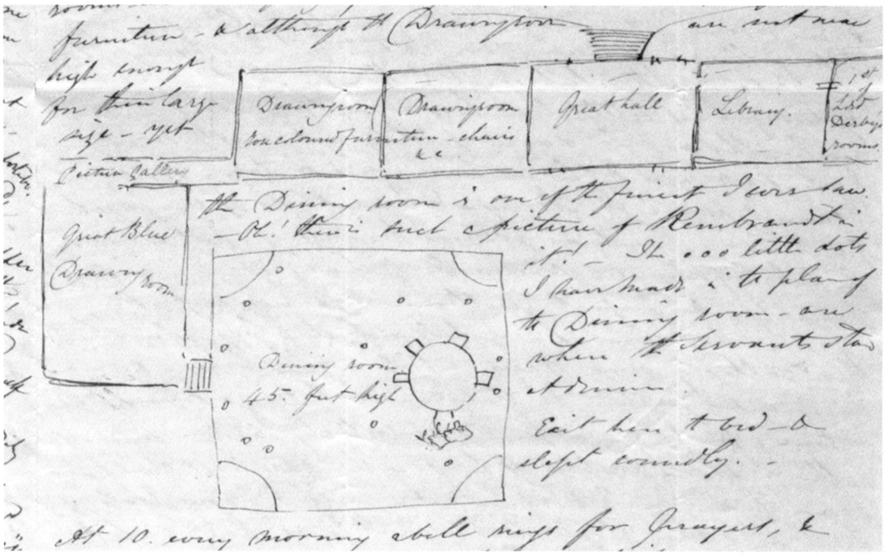

Cat. 14

Written at Knowsley Hall in the very early morning ('It is about seven o'clock … nearly 4 mortal hours to breakfast'), this letter describes Lear's coach journey there from London, which he left on the evening of Saturday 20 June. Lear travelled on the outside of the coach, where the seats were cheaper:

> My companions … fell asleep—& I sung aloud to the delight of Coachy who was rather drunk.—Made a good supper in Bedfordshire—& at 8 next morning reached Birmingham—perfectly frozen, to make a beastly breakfast of far gone eggs—& high beef. All Sunday was a lovely day … The delays … caused us to get to Prescot about 8—so as no one was waiting for my luggage—I ordered it to be brought immediately to the Hall, & I walked over myself.

Lear's position at Knowsley was an awkward one; he was a gentleman and therefore the social equal of his host, but he was visiting the house as a servant of Lord Derby to make drawings of the animals in the menagerie. The situation was resolved, but it required Lord Derby to make the move; Lear

> was told that supper would be presently in the housekeepers room;—thither, (adapting myself to circumstances) I went & soon made a good meal. Of course —as I saw how matters were going to be—I took *all* the pains in the world to make myself pleasant—& all things were going on swimmingly—when, lo! —a messenger from Lord D. begged me to come immediately to him. To my surprise his Lordship was in the Passage, where he gave me a regular *shake* of the hand, & apologized for my having been put where I was. 'I intended of course,' quoth he—'that you should have been *one of us*—& not dine with the servants.'—Pray—he continued—finish your supper & then come & join us in the drawing room. Ergo I finished my supper—& then to the eminent opening of eyes of the good people assembled—my modesty was obliged to desire that one of them would forthwith worrie [*sic*] me to the presence chamber.

Lear was very grateful to his host for admitting him upstairs; later in the letter he writes: 'Really his extreme kindness is quite extraordinary—he takes opportunities continually of shewing it—& is without partiality—a perfect Gentleman in every respect', but he was nevertheless overawed by his grand surroundings and companions. At the end of the letter, he makes his feelings clear to his old friend:

> The connexion—the change of air—& the tone of society one sees are the bright side of the matter. The darks I don't bother you with. Now I beg & implore you & Fanny to concoct me a long letter next week. Consider I have no creature of my own grade of society to speak to—& without my saying more—believe that I *shall be heartily* glad of some symptoms of old acquaintance in the shape of a letter.

The central part of the letter contains a description of the guests at the house, all members of the Hornby family (see Appendix D), and of the principal rooms ('although the Drawing rooms are not near high enough for their large size—yet the Dining room is one of the finest I ever saw'). Within the letter is a sketch map of the principal rooms and their locations (see the illustration of a detail from the letter), which provides a record of the house before the remodellings of the late nineteenth and the twentieth centuries. Lear describes the dining room—the only room in the house with its location unaltered today—as '45 feet high' and adds 'Oh! There is such a picture of Rembrandt in it!'; this is the famous Rembrandt painting 'Belshazzar's Feast', purchased by the 10th Earl of Derby *c.*1736 and sold from the Knowsley collection to the National Gallery, London, in 1964 (NG6350).

15 *Letter to George Coombe, from Knowsley Hall, Lancashire*

20 July 1835
Autograph manuscript with postal stamps and seal
The Frederick Warne Archive
Illustrated on p. 52; see pp. 209–10 for full text

By the time Lear wrote this letter he had been in the north for a month, and its contents describe the general pattern of his days. His correspondents in Sussex would have loved hearing about the aristocratic company he was keeping, and Lear panders to their voyeurism, although professing to be tired of the life.

> I am sick of splendour—vomiting with excess of pomp—longing for a little porter out of a pewter pot—& some bread & cheese eaten with my fingers ... I have been passing a most delightful week at Tabley Hall—Lord de Tabley's—Everybody ought to see Lady de Tabley before they die—she is a most glorious creature:—& not less delightful than beautiful—in fact, I never felt more at home in my life—so kind & unaffected were the whole family & guests. One day we—(the Parkers, de Tableys—& I,) went to Lord Stamfords', a fine old place [i.e. Dunham Massey]—& lionized all about it,—another was spent in a similar excursion to Sir Philip Egerton's [i.e. Oulton Park],—whose Lady is *preterpluperfection*, (she used to be called 'the pride of Cheshire',) & whose house is little inferior. Another of my white days was a gipsey party to Beeston Castle—sublime old ruins—from whose towers 300 feet high one might break ones neck really with satisfaction—the lovely rides you may very well conclude I enjoyed—but above all I put the glorious Raspberry beds, at Tabley Hall!—How I did stuff & cramm—they called me 'raspberry Lear'.—Every evening at this lovely house—we had lots of music: Lady de T. & I duett wonderfully—& I only marvel at my not being hired as nurse to the baby—who was always quietted by my playing the Accordion.

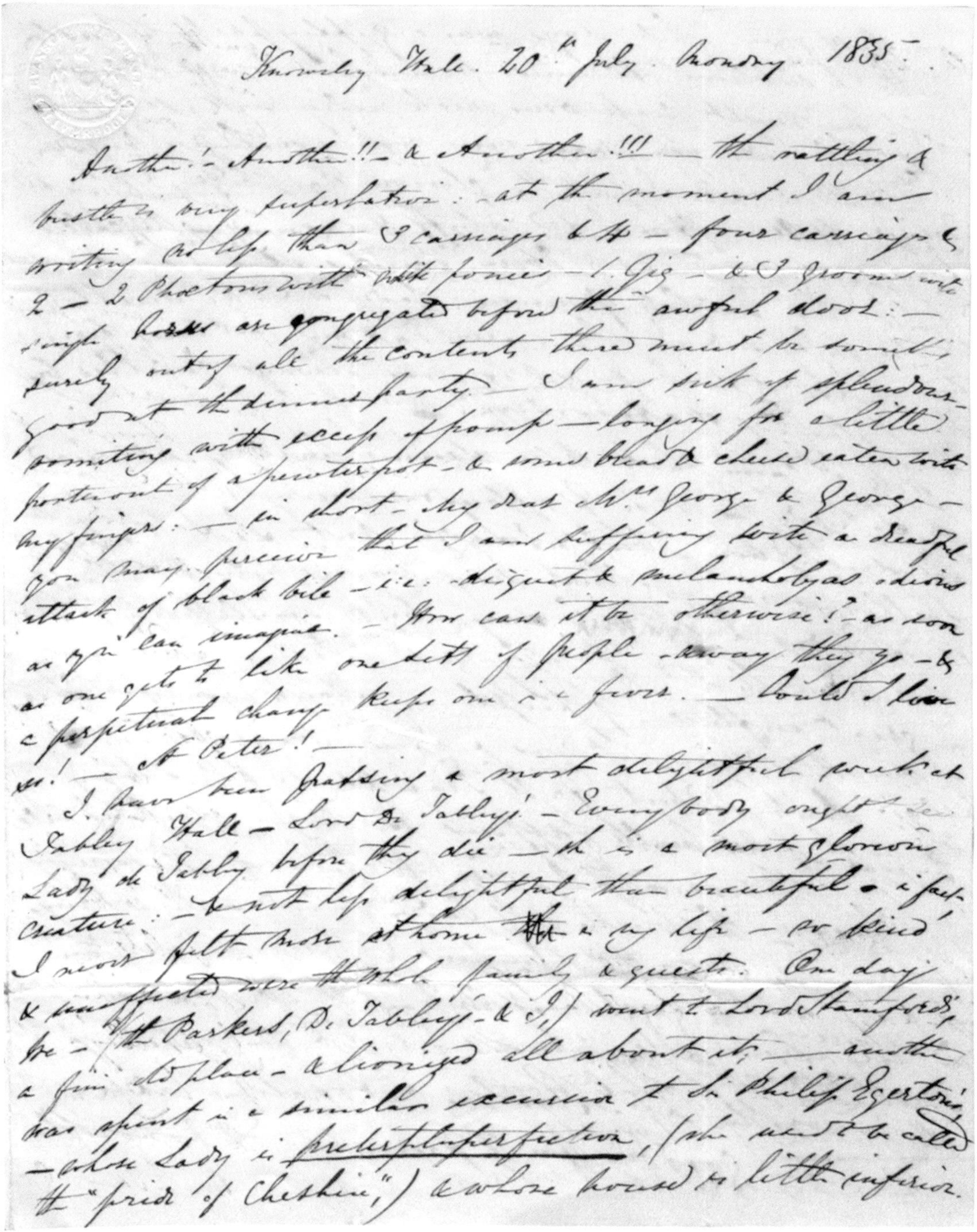
Knowsley Hall. 20th July. Monday 1835.

Another!—Another!!—& Another!!!—the rattling & bustle is very superlative:—at the moment I am writing no less than 8 carriages & 4—four carriages & 2—2 Phaetons with white ponies—1 Gig—& 3 grooms with single horses are congregated before the awful door:—surely out of all the contents there must be something good at the dinner party.—I am sick of splendour—vomiting with excess of pomp—longing for a little porter out of a pewter pot—& some bread & cheese eaten with my fingers:—in short—my dear Mrs George & George—you may perceive that I am suffering with a dreadful attack of black bile—i.e. disgust & melancholy as odious as you can imagine.—How can it be otherwise?—as soon as one gets to like one sett of people away they go—& a perpetual change keeps one in a fever.—Would I love so!—St Peter!—

I have been passing a most delightful week at Tabley Hall—Lord De Tabley's—Everybody ought to see Lady de Tabley before they die—she is a most glorious creature:—& not less delightful than beautiful.—I never felt more at home in my life—so kind & unaffected were the whole family & guests. One day (we—the Parkers, De Tableys—& I,) went to Lord Stamford's, a fine old place—& lionized all about it;—another was spent in a similar excursion to Sir Philip Egerton's—whose Lady is preterpluperfection, (she used to be called the "pride of Cheshire,") & whose house is little inferior.

Cat. 15

The casual name-dropping, outlining visits to three of Cheshire's greatest stately homes, hints at drawings which remain to be discovered. Surprisingly, Lear did not visit Tatton Park, which is only a couple of miles from Tabley and which he certainly would have passed on his way to Dunham Massey. No visit to Cheshire was complete without a visit to Beeston Castle, perched high on its rocky crag eight miles south-west of Tabley overlooking the Cheshire plain; David Cox was similarly fascinated by the site a few years later, but sadly no drawings survive giving Lear's impressions of it. Lear returned from Tabley to Knowsley for a large dinner party on Saturday 18 July. Numerous other guests arrived the following Monday, and Lear prepares with foreboding for yet another dinner on the Tuesday evening: '[Monday's] dinner *nearly* killed me—& today's *will* I think *quite*.' The ending of the letter is typical; while he professes to hate the high life, he describes it with relish for his impressionable friends: 'Goodbye—I am too wretched to add anything but that I am now going to stick my head in a bush of fern ever so far off where there is nobody to bother me. Yours ever [truly?], Edward Lear. Pray tell little Fanny & Marion never to envy a fine life. There were 8 Edwards at dinner the other day. between 20 & 30 servants to wait at dinner.—'

16 *Letter to George Coombe, from Knowsley Hall, Lancashire*

24 July 1835
Autograph manuscript
The Frederick Warne Archive
Illustrated on pp. 56–7; see pp. 210–12 for full text

It was Lear's practice to start a letter and then return to it later, so this long and very interesting one commences, 'Though I only just sent off a letter yesterday I commence another—as I shan't finish it all at once'. The letter was begun on Friday 24 July and completed on the evening of Saturday 25 July, and thus describes the eventful happenings of those two days rather like an on-the-spot reporter, so that it reads almost like a running commentary.

The letter begins with a description of the brilliant weather: 'What lovely weather for a whole week! ... it is the first *warmth* I have felt these 5 weeks'. This is conducive to outdoor games:

> Spite of the heat—cricket is all the fashion, or rather rage at Knowsley just now: morning, noon, & night—bats & balls have no sinecure. After breakfast,—the green,—for there is an immense lawn before the house, is covered with the most odd gamesters—Sir J. Shelley—Miss S.—Lady Ellinor H. [i.e. Lord Derby's daughter] & all the children male & female play away till I should think their brains nearly fry: it is very amusing to see ... After luncheon—out the males rush again, & then there is a match general—grooms—riders—footmen —& aristocrats all in a bundle:—not that I saw percieve the unfortunate grooms do anything but become fags—(isn't that the word?—)—catching & throwing the ball. I fear the game is carried on on rather an exclusive principle—since Sir John—the Stanleys—Hopwoods. & Penrhyns are always at the wickets when I look out of window.—It is now half after 2 at midday—& the sun quite broiling over the misty distance.

Lear was at Knowsley to draw the animals: 'All to day I have been drawing an insane partridge who will sit still on no account whatever—little beast,—& now I am so hot as to be utterly incapable of any activity [erased word] in the world'. But the usual activities of the household were to be violently interrupted: 'Hark!—what a screaming—they are crying Fire—I declare—Fire! fire! fire!—Engines!—Water. God bless us—the noise increases & all the cricketters are rushing toward the out buildings across the lawn: I smell smoke—a chimney on fire I dare say—must go & see'. There follows an hour-by-hour account of the fire, which appears to be the only record of this event:

> 4. O'clock. I date from Knowsley now—but before you get my letter I sadly fear Knowsley Hall will have ceased to be. The house has taken fire behind the kitchen ... The engines are playing—but can do little execution—the fire is so central—they are unroofing the house—Water—water is the universal cry—the dignities are done away with—we are all in shirts & trowsers & perspiration ... The fire has entirely destroyed the painted Chamber—& Mr Stanley's room is already reached—featherbeds are rolling down the stairs—curtains—clothes—books—furniture are being tossed from windows—the heat is dreadful ... Awful state of violence—they are tearing away the carpets—but the pictures are destroyed in the painted chamber—Down comes Belshazzar [the Rembrandt painting]—for in another half hour the fire must reach the great dining room:—ladders—shrieks—men—women—engines—water—soot—falling tiles—wet blankets flames—smoke—its excessively horrible. The alarm bell still rings & the peasantry flock in from all quarters—but to very little purpose.
>
> 5., O'clock. The fire has been quite subdued on the inside by the plan of breaking away some windows thro' which the water has played effectively. I am quite knocked up with working in the hot [room?] & have been violently sick—& [then?] fainted. The scene now is all before the house—& worthy any painters looking at ... 6 o'clock. All is safe.—they still pump—but there is no further danger. Had all this occurred in the night—everything must have been lost.—Lord D. is dreadfully shaken by it ... The drawing room & dining room are such a scene as has never been seen before in Knowsley:—Yet in this most clockwork of establishments even now everything is beginning to go on as usual.
>
> Saturday. 25.th July. 1835. ... This morning the workmen are all busy at the late place of fire—but that is all to keep yesterday's disturbance in memory.

The fire is described in the manner of a breathless observer, and at this point the letter is only punctuated with dashes; it concludes with a description of the coming and going of more guests, and ends: 'Must go & draw a Kangaroo.'

17 *Letter to Fanny Coombe, from Beaumaris, Anglesey*

6 August 1835
Autograph manuscript
The Frederick Warne Archive
Illustrated on pp. 58–9; see pp. 212–13 for full text

A visit to Wales, by this date obligatory for any artist who wished to study landscape scenery, had been in Lear's mind for some time. In the letter written to George Coombe on 24 June soon after arriving at Knowsley (see cat. 14), he wrote: 'I have some idea I shall not stay long—for I hear them talking of some Races—which will bring down an immense party. In that case I shall go immediately to town—& give up Wales entirely—as my money will be short instead of long'. The letter here, written from a hotel in Beaumaris, Anglesey, is, however, the only record of Lear's visiting Wales.

Composed in haste before breakfast, the letter describes how members of the house party at Knowsley persuade Lord Derby to make a visit to Puffin Island, which lies just off the coast of Anglesey in Conwy Bay a few miles north-east of Beaumaris:

> Well one day Capt Stanly Mr Penrhyn asked Lord D. if he was going to Puffin Island—a Rocky isle near Anglesea—whither he goes yearly generally at the Puffin time—those birds breeding there by millions. Lord D said it was nearly too late—but for the last 10 days the subject was never allowed to rest—till his Lordship was finally coaxed into fixing the jaunt for the 4th Tuesday—I who could not see any pleasure in shooting parties refused when Ld. D. offered my being one of them—but hearing that Beaumaris was to be to stay for a day or two—I altered & went. Up we all got on Tuesday & breakfasted at 8:—at 9 we 5 Ld. D. Col. H Capt S. Mr. Penrhyn & myself rolled away in the four horse carriage—2 keepers—& a valet & footman following with luggage in a chariot & a gig. Of course the Lord Lieutenant's cavalcade made a deviation at Liverpool. & a crowd came to the quay. Very merry & jolly we were: bounce we went into a little boat & were soon on board the Lewellyn Steamer. ... As for the scenery as you approach Wales—it is beyond expression! The inn we went to is opposite Penmanmawr—& delightful it is. Before dinner we went all over Sir R Bulkeley's park ... Wednesday [5 August]– a mizzly dizzly day—& I almost unable to move for a headache—off we went tho' at 11 in a sailing boat to Puffin Land—the birds were gone: adjourned to rabbit shooting—sketched ashtrees & made love to Welsh washerwomen while it rained. lunched. came home at 6—all wet through ... This morning is again lovely up & roaming about & just time in life to write this.

As the roads along the North Wales coast were so poor, Lord Derby's party travelled by boat to Anglesey from Liverpool, and returned by the same means. Lear's letter ends: 'we return at 10 o'clock to filthy Liverpool', with the postscript added showing that at least one of the party was suffering from overindulgence: 'Lord D. has just asked for a "raw egg"'. On arriving in Liverpool, Lear went immediately to Ireland, which, rather like the visit to Wales, seems to have been a spur-of-the-moment decision, so is not mentioned in this letter.

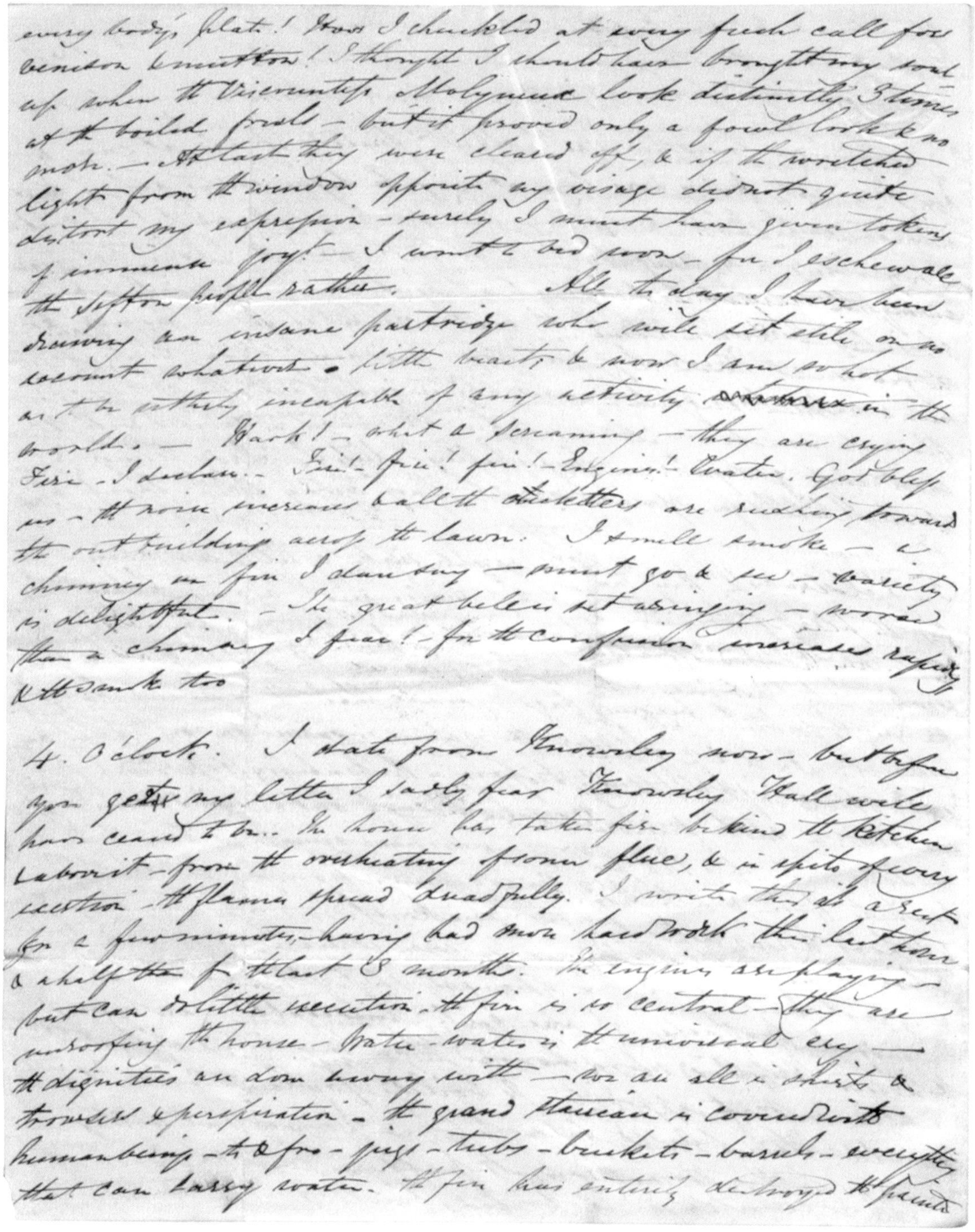
every body's plate! How I chuckled at every fresh call for venison & mutton! I thought I should have brought my soul up when the Viscountess Molyneux look distinctly 3 times at the boiled fowls — but it proved only a fowl look & no more. — At last they were cleared off, & if the wretched light from the window opposite my visage did not quite distort my expression — surely I must have given tokens of immense joy. — I went to bed soon — for I eschewed the Sefton people rather. All the day I have been drawing an insane partridge who will sit still on no account whatever — little beast, & now I am so hot as to be utterly incapable of any activity whatever in the world. — Hark! — what a screaming — they are crying Fire — I declare. — Fire! — fire! fire! — Engines! — Water. God bless us — the noise increases & all the [illegible] are rushing toward the out buildings across the lawn. I smell smoke — a chimney on fire I daresay — must go & see — variety is delightful. — The great bells set a-ringing — worse than a chimney I fear! — for the confusion increases rapidly & the smoke too

4. O'clock. I date from Knowsley now — but before you get my letter I sadly fear Knowsley Hall will have ceased to be. — The house has taken fire behind the kitchen laboratory — from the overheating of some flue, & in spite of every exertion the flames spread dreadfully. I write this as a rest for a few minutes, having had more hard work this last hour & a half than for the last 3 months. The engines are playing — but can do little execution — the fire is so central — they are unroofing the house — water — water is the universal cry — the dignities are done away with — we are all in shirts & trowsers & perspiration — the grand staircase is covered with human beings — to & fro — jugs — tubs — buckets — barrels — everything that can carry water. The fire has entirely destroyed the present

Cat. 16

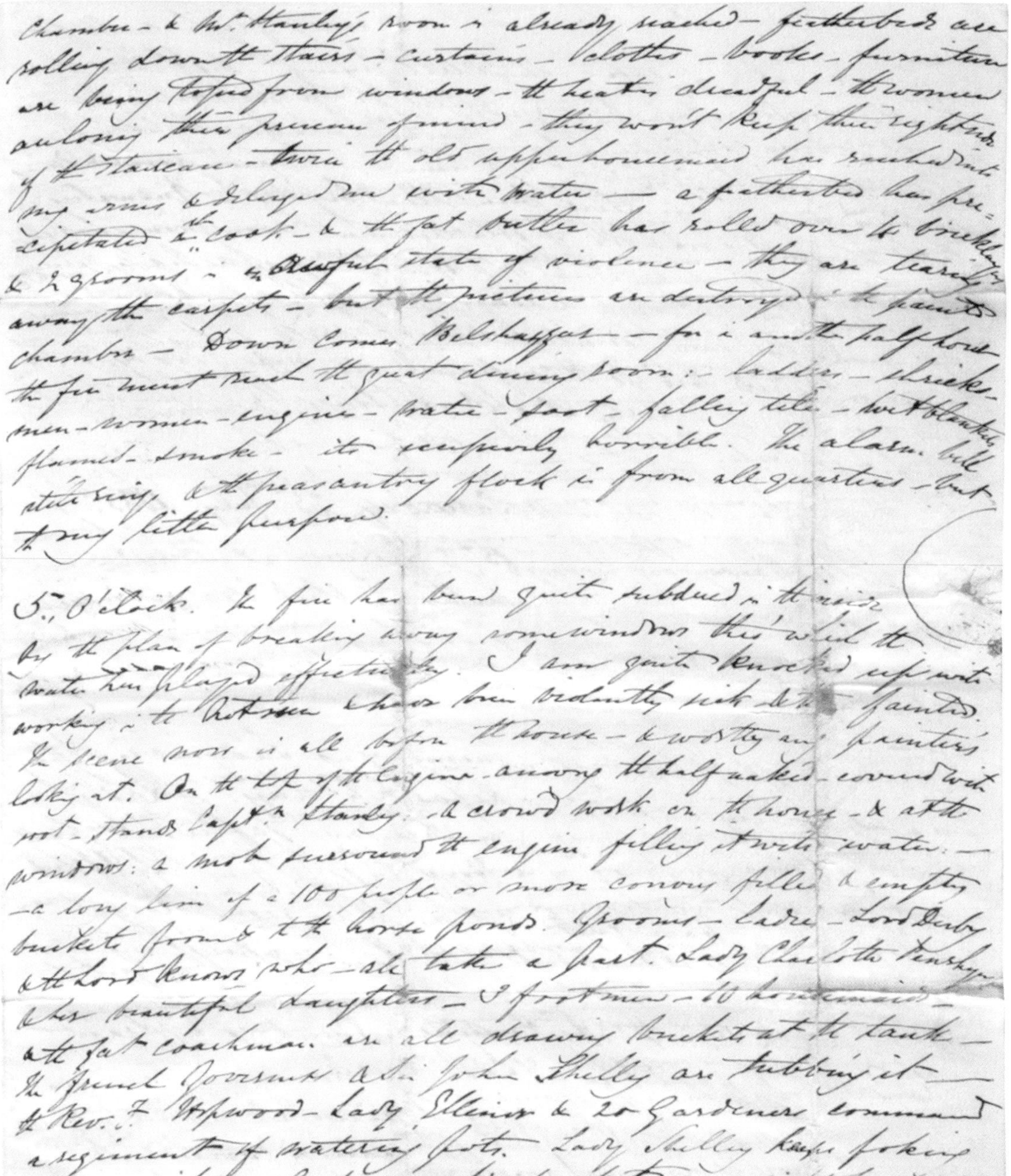
Chamber – & Mr. Stanley's room is already reached – featherbeds are rolling down the stairs – curtains – & clothes – books – furniture are being tossed from windows – the heat is dreadful – the women are losing their presence of mind – they won't keep their right side of the staircase – twice the old upper housemaid has rushed into my arms & deluged me with water — a featherbed has precipitated the cook – & the fat butler has rolled over the kitchen & 2 grooms in a dreadful state of violence – they are tearing away the carpets – but the pictures are destroyed in the painted chamber – Down comes Belshazzar – for in another half hour the fire must reach the great dining room: – ladders – shrieks – men – women – engines – water – soot – falling tiles – wet blankets – flames – smoke – it is seriously horrible. The alarm bell still rings, & the peasantry flock in from all quarters – but to very little purpose.

5. O'clock. The fire has been quite subdued in the rooms by the plan of breaking away some windows thro' which the water has played effectually. I am quite knocked up with working in the hot room & have been violently sick & then fainted. The scene now is all before the house – & worthy any painter's looking at. On the top of the engine among the half naked – covered with soot – stands Captn Stanley. A crowd work on the horses – & at the windows: a mob surround the engine filling it with water: — a long line of a 100 people or more convey filled & empty buckets from & to the horse ponds. Grooms – ladies – Lord Derby & the Lord knows who – all take a part. Lady Charlotte Penrhyn & her beautiful daughters – 3 footmen – the housemaids – & the fat coachman are all drawing buckets at the tank – The French Governess & Sir John Shelley are tubbing it — the Revd F Hopwood – Lady Eleanor & 20 gardeners command a regiment of watering pots. Lady Shelley keeps poking about with a leaky washing bucket. Some right honorable children who can do nothing else are sounding the alarm bell. All the country is coming – but the fire gives under long

Cat. 16

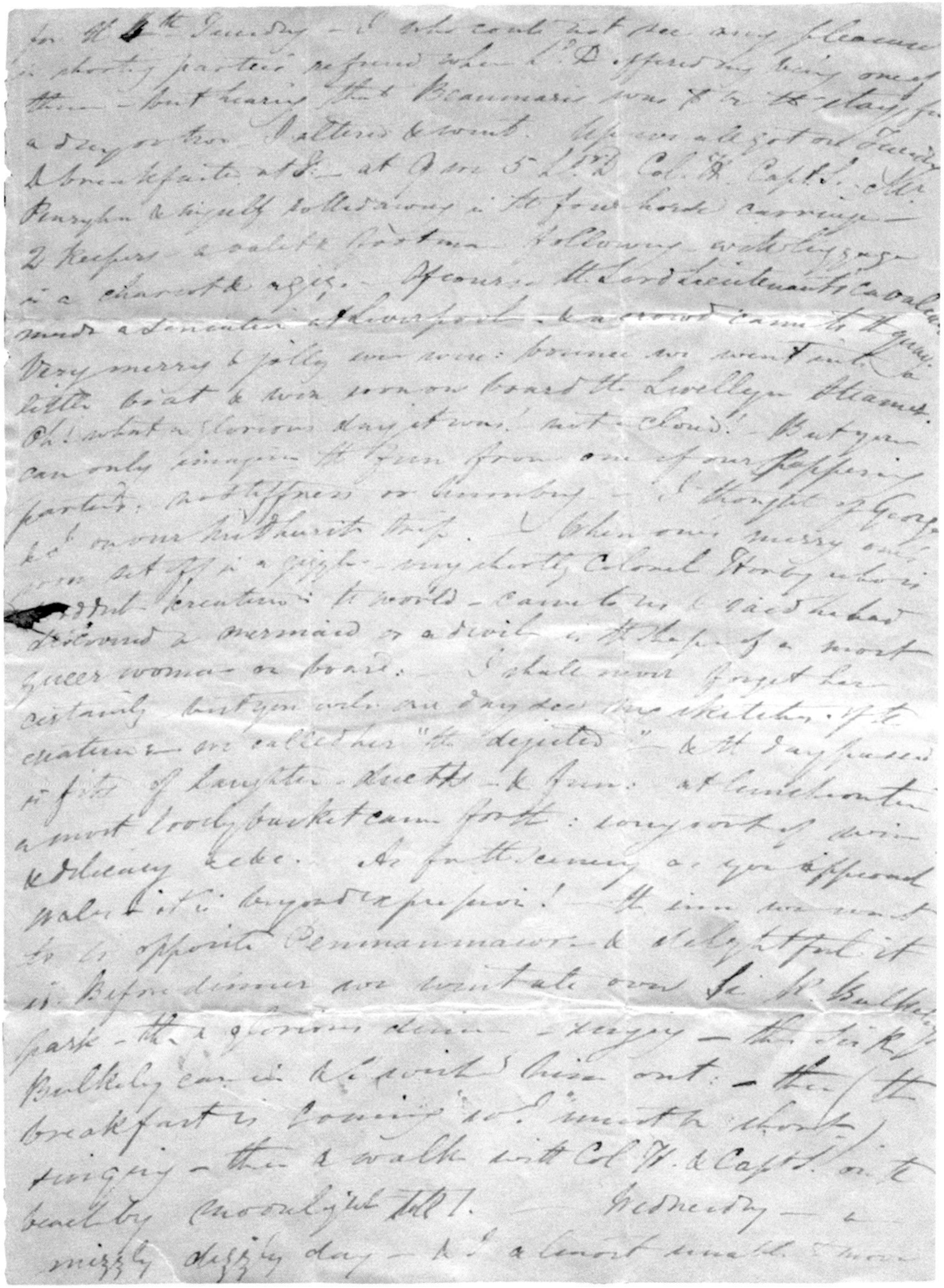
for the 4th Sunday — I who could not see any pleasure
in shooting parties refused when Ld D. offered my being one of
them — but hearing that Beaumaris was to be the stay for
a day or two I altered my mind. Up we all got on Sunday
& breakfasted at 4 — at [illegible] 5 Ld D. Col. H. Capt. [illegible] — Mr
Penrhyn & myself rolled away in the four horse carriage —
2 keepers — a valet & footman following with luggage
in a chariot & [illegible] — Of course the Lord Lieutenant's cavalcade
made a sensation at Liverpool — & a crowd came to the quay.
Very merry & jolly we were: [illegible] we went into a
little boat & were soon on board the Llewellyn Steamer.
Oh! what a glorious day it was! not a cloud! — But you
can only imagine the fun from one of our happiest
parties: no stiffness or humbug — I thought of George
&c. on our [illegible] trip. — When our merry one
[illegible] set off in a giggle — very shortly Colonel Hornby who is
[illegible] creature in the world — came to us & said he had
discovered a mermaid or a devil in the shape of a most
queer woman on board. I shall never forget her
certainly but you will one day see the sketches of the
creature — we called her "the dejected" — & the day passed
in fits of laughter sketches & fun: at luncheon time
a most lovely basket came forth: every sort of wine
& delicacy &c &c. As for the scenery as you approached
Wales it is beyond expression! The inn we went
to is opposite Penmaenmawr — & delightful it
is. Before dinner we went all over Sir R. Bulkeley's
park — then a glorious dinner — singing — then Sir R.
Bulkeley came in & we [illegible] out: — then (the
breakfast is coming so I must be short)
singing — then a walk with Col H. & Capt. [illegible] on the
beach by moonlight till 1. — Wednesday — a
mizzly drizzly day — & I almost [illegible] more

Cat. 17

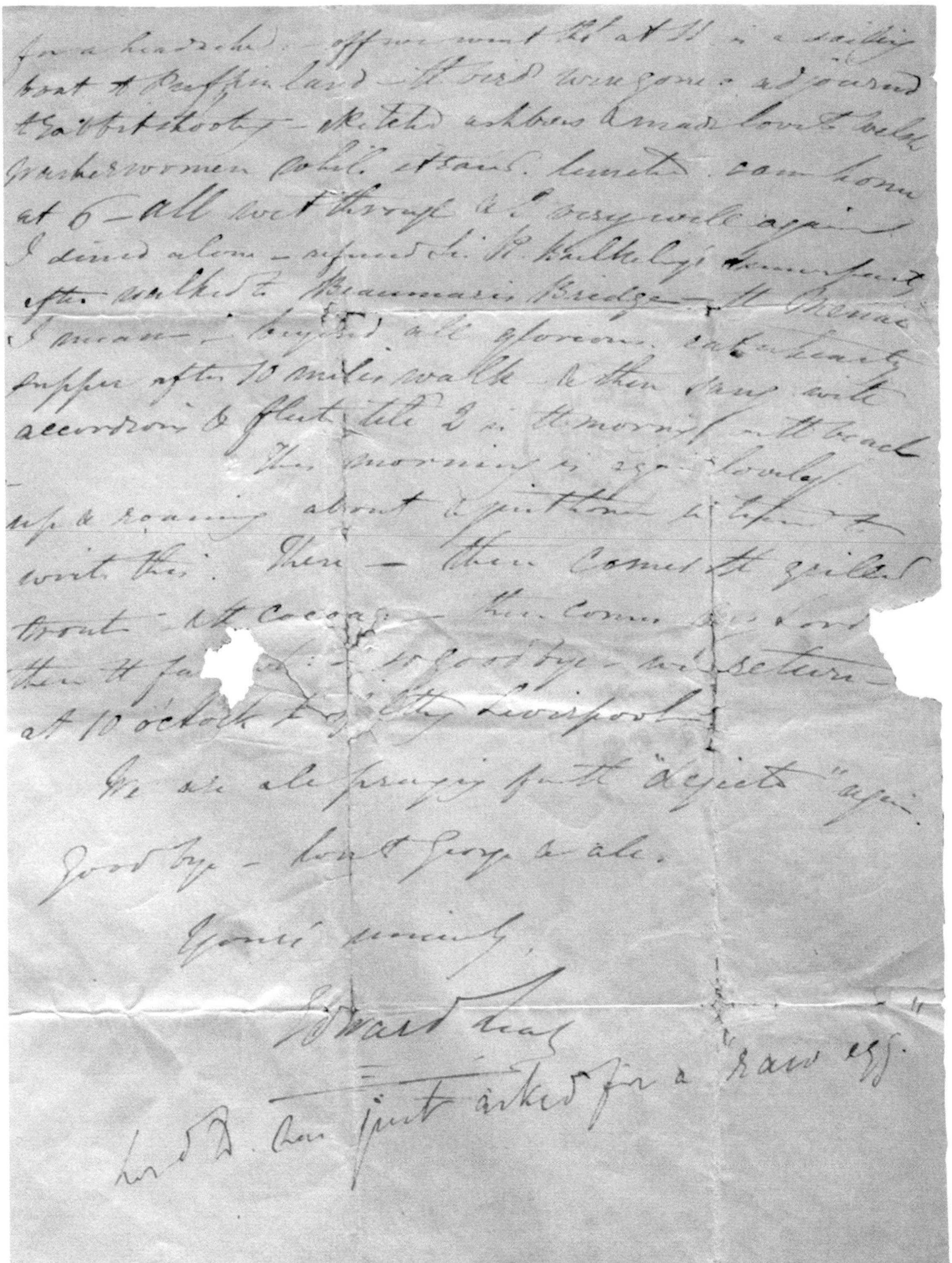

for a headache — off we went tho' at 11 in a sailing
boat to Puffin land — the birds were gone — adjourned
to rabbit shooting — sketched as there & made love to welch
washerwomen whilst [illegible] lunched — came home
at 6 — all wet through but very well again —
I dined alone — refused Sir R. Bulkeley's dinner party
after walked to Beaumaris Bridge — the Menai
I mean — laughed all afternoon — eat a hearty
supper after 10 miles walk — & then sang with
accordion & flute till 2 in the morning on the beach
This morning is [illegible] lovely —
up & roaming about & quite time to [illegible]
write this. Then — then comes the grilled
trout — the cocoa — then comes [illegible]
then the farewell — the goodbyes — we return
at 10 o'clock to filthy Liverpool —
We are all praying for the "[illegible]" again.
Good bye — love to George & all.
Yours sincerely,
Edward Lear
Lord B. has just asked for a "raw egg."

Cat. 17

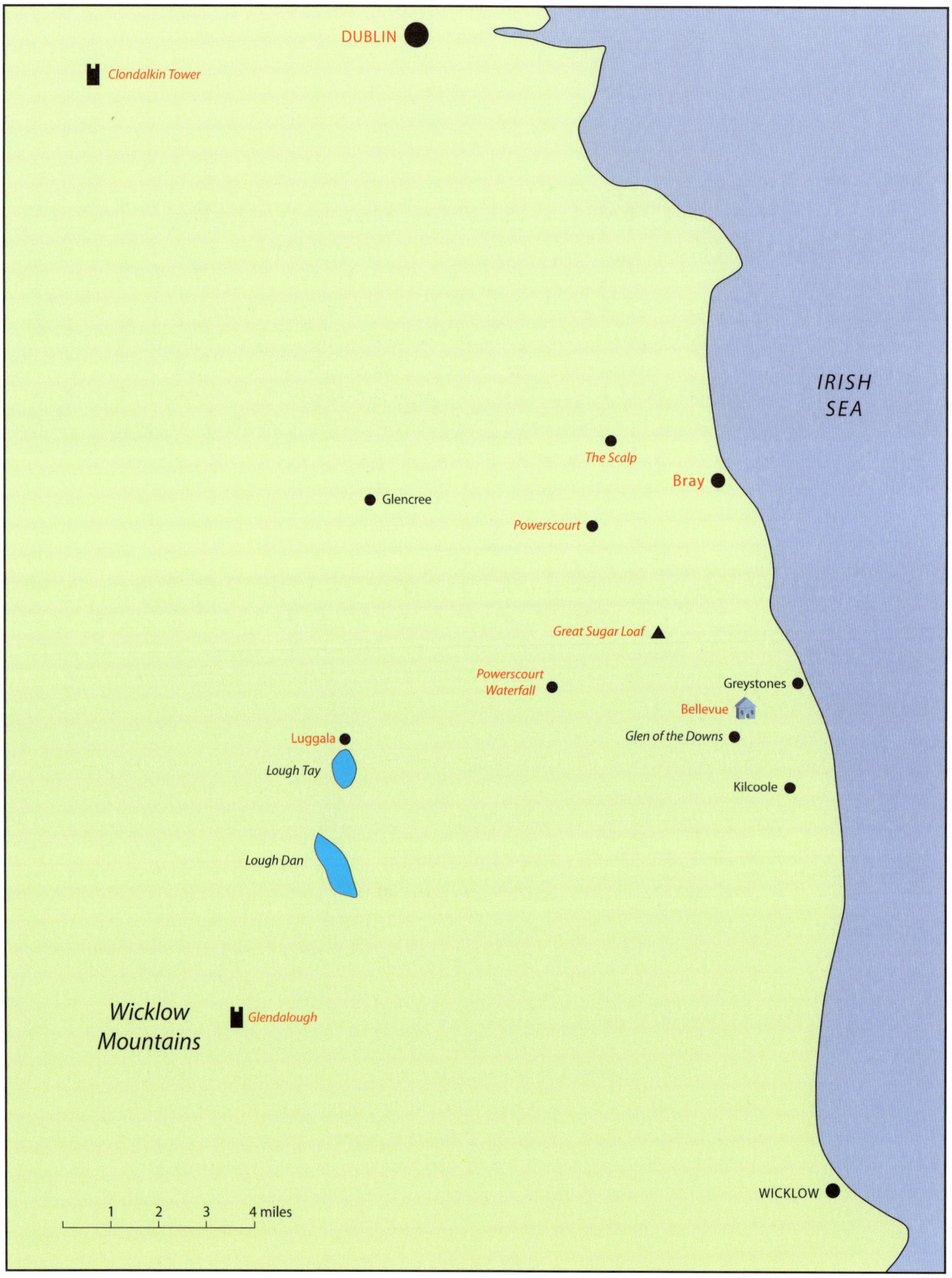

LEAR AND IRELAND

Lear's exact route through Wicklow in April 1835 is impossible to establish. Only the places which it is known that he visited or drew are marked in red.

[3]
IRELAND: AUGUST 1835

The evidence for Lear's first visit to Ireland is very scant (he visited for the second time in 1857). We do not know for certain when he arrived in Dublin, nor exactly when he left. All that is known is that he was in Anglesey on 6 August, apparently about to return to Liverpool by boat (see the letter written that day, cat. 17), and that he was back at Knowsley by 1 September (cat. 27). It is now known that Lear had four companions in Dublin, although it is unclear whether they travelled over from England together. The first of them was the Rev. Edward Stanley (1779–1849), the younger brother of Sir John Stanley of Alderley, who was created Lord Stanley of Alderley in 1839. He was a liberal churchman who had been Rector of Alderley since 1805, and was appointed (to Lear's excitement – see the letter of April 1837, cat. 94) Bishop of Norwich in 1837. The second companion was the Rev. Edward Stanley's son, Arthur Penrhyn Stanley (1815–1881). He had been at Rugby, and was in 1835 at Oxford, where he was elected a Fellow of University College in 1838. He became a leading liberal theologian and was appointed Dean of Westminster in 1864; the disappearance of his papers and of his correspondence with Lear, who was a close friend, is a great loss to scholarship. Also present was Arthur's younger brother Edward (1819–1849). The fourth traveller was Edward Leycester Penrhyn (*c.*1790–1861), who was the Reverend Edward Stanley's brother-in-law (and therefore Arthur Penrhyn Stanley's uncle) as well as Lord Derby's son-in-law (he had married Lady Charlotte Stanley in 1823). Edward Penrhyn had been on the boat trip to Puffin Island with Lear, and it was probably him who suggested linking up with the other Stanleys travelling to Ireland.

The main reason for the journey was the annual meeting of the British Association for the Advancement of Science (BAAS), which took place in Dublin from 10 to 15 August 1835. The BAAS was founded in 1831 by a group of scientists who were disillusioned by the elitist and conservative attitude of the Royal Society, and is still in existence today. It is a learned society with the object of promoting science, directing general attention to scientific matters, and facilitating interaction between those working in various scientific fields. Its aims are 'to give a stronger impulse and a more systematic direction to scientific enquiry, – to promote the intercourse of those who cultivate Science in different parts of the British Empire, with one another, and with foreign philosophers, – to obtain a more general attention to the objects of Science, and a removal of any disadvantages of a public kind, which impede its progress' (*Proceedings*, p. 5). The disparate elements within the BAAS were mercilessly lampooned by Charles Dickens in *The Mudfog Papers* (1837–8), where the society was satirised as the Mudfog Association for the Advancement of Everything. The Rev. Edward Stanley was an amateur zoologist and published *A Familiar History of Birds* in two volumes in 1835;

he had joined the BAAS in November 1831, and at the Cambridge meeting of the society in 1834 described himself as a 'Naturalist'. The BAAS was divided into seven Sections distinguished by the letters A to G; Section D, that of Zoology and Botany, was the one obviously of interest to Stanley and Lear. Dickens divides his Mudfog Association into five Sections; Section A is Zoology and Botany, which contains some 'remarks on the disappearance of dancing-bears from the streets of London, with observations on the exhibition of monkeys as connected with barrel-organs', and the Supplementary Section, E, is devoted to Umbugology and Ditchwaterisics.

The Dublin Meeting of 1835 was the fifth of the BAAS and the first to take place outside mainland Britain. The Irish were keen to impress and attract the most prestigious visitors, and a great deal of care and organisation therefore went into the planning of the Meeting and the events that went with it. To supplement the daily boats from Liverpool and Holyhead, Sir John Tobin, a Liverpool merchant, offered free passage from Liverpool to Kingstown (Dun Laoghaire) on board his best steam vessel, *Sir William Penn*; this sailed on Friday 7 August, returned to Liverpool on the Saturday and sailed again on Sunday 9 August (Morrell & Thackray, p. 182–3). It is not known whether Lear was on this boat, or whether he went to Holyhead from Beaumaris, and sailed from there. On arrival in Dublin, lavish hospitality was laid on for the visitors. The events, learned and social, were recorded in detail by the Dublin printer Philip Dixon Hardy, who published a volume entitled *Proceedings of the Fifth Meeting of the British Association for the Advancement of Science, held in Dublin, during the Week from the 10th to the 15th of August, Inclusive. With an Alphabetical List of Members enrolled in Dublin.*This volume was published quickly, and anticipated the official 1835 Report, published in London by John Murray, by more than six months. Lear's name, giving the Dublin address, 20, Dame Street, is recorded in the 'List of Members Enrolled' (fig. 8), as are those of the three Stanleys and Edward Penrhyn, who each gave their English addresses. The Zoology and Botany Section of the BAAS (Section D) held its meetings in the Board-Room of the Royal Dublin Society in Kildare Street; this building (fig. 9) was the former Dublin home of the Dukes of Leinster, who sold it to the Dublin Society in 1814. It remained the home of the Dublin Society until 1924, and is now the home of the Oireachtas, the parliament of the Republic of Ireland.

The Meeting combined lavish entertainment and hospitality with scientific lectures and papers. The paper submitted to Section D on Monday 10 August was 'on the Formation of a Natural Arrangement of Plants' (*Proceedings*, p. 19); this was followed by dinner at Morrison's Hotel. On Tuesday 11 August, a Colonel Sykes read a paper 'on the Geographical Range of Birds and Animals, in which he pointed out the very close analogy, and in some cases probable identity of the Indian and European species' (ibid., p. 41). Lear was almost certainly at this meeting, and at the '*dejeuner*' that day given at the Gardens of the Zoological Society, which was described as a 'magnificent entertainment', where 'there were laid covers for five hundred' (ibid., pp. 47–8).

), M.R.I.A.
R.S.L. Brompton, London
ler, 16, Gardiner's-place
M.B. 10, Hardwicke-place
ourgh
unty of Wexford
, 45, Harcourt-street
, LL.D. Bristol
tol
ristol
Armagh
arrickfergus
Glasgow
on
. Ordnance Survey Office

Law, Hamilton, 39, Sackville-street
Lloyd, G., M.D. Leamington
Lendrick, James, 4, Hatch-street
Lynch, Francis I. Stevens's Hospital
Lawless, John, 4, Russel-street
Lanyon, Charles, Naas
Lear, Edward, 20, Dame-street
Long, Thomas, 19, Mary-street
Littledale, Harold
Leslie, Charles, 40, Bride-street
Lucas, William, Tommey's Hotel
Lingwood, Robert, Cambridge
Leatham, J. A. Wakefield
Lambert, Alexander, Ballinrobe
Lindsay, George, Dublin Castle

Fig. 8 Detail of the list of names of members enrolled in the British Association for the Advancement of Science in 1835, showing Lear's name and Dublin address.

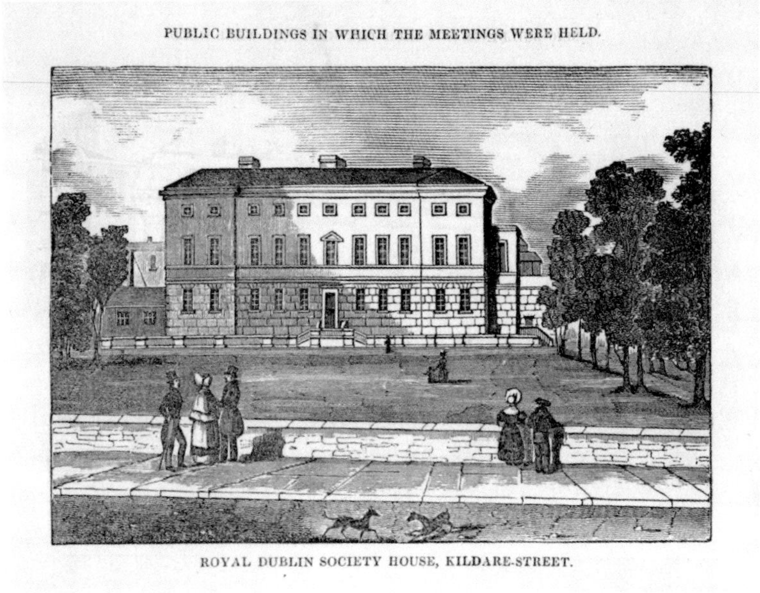

Fig. 9 'Royal Dublin Society House, Kildare-Street' (Leinster House), one of the 'Public Buildings in which the meetings were held', wood engraving reproduced in *Proceedings*.

On Wednesday 12 August, the paper that was read was on 'the structure of the horizontal branches of the of the natural family of Coniferae' (ibid., p. 60), with the '*dejeuner*' that day described as being 'on a scale of princely magnificence' (ibid., p. 65). On Thursday 13 August, after papers on the discovery of a live toad in a piece of sandstone, and another on plants and ferns indigenous to Ireland, the party divided into two. A smaller group, including the poet Thomas Moore, the French philosopher Alexis de Tocqueville and the mathematician Charles Babbage, dined with the Lord Lieutenant, the Earl of Mulgrave, at the Vice-Regal Lodge in the Phoenix Park. A larger number, described as 'upwards of 300', of whom Lear was probably one, were taken by special train to Kingstown (Dun Laoghaire), where they dined at Marsh's Hotel in Salt Hill. According to the Dublin *Proceedings*, 'the profusion and excellence of the viands were such as to afford the utmost satisfaction ... The Rev. Mr Stanley having proposed the health of Captain Portlock [the President of the Zoological Society], and that gentleman having briefly returned thanks, the members retired at half past seven o'clock ... So many individuals arrived at Salt Hill, that it was found necessary to have the two great rooms, and three smaller ones in the establishment appropriated for the accommodation of the guests ... the company ... returned to town in a train specially reserved for them' (ibid., pp. 94–5). The last two days of the Meeting proceeded in a similar vein, with a feast provided by the Royal Dublin Society in marquees in the Botanical Gardens on the Friday for more than 1,300 people, and a farewell banquet on Saturday 15 August given by the Provost and Fellows of Trinity College for more than 300 members of the Association (Morrell & Thackray, pp. 182–5). Not surprisingly, the combination of meals and lectures was satirised by Dickens: 'I cannot close my account of these gigantic researches and sublime and noble triumphs without repeating a *bon mot* of Professor Woodensconce's ... that learned gentleman entered the hall yesterday ... and ... said ... "This is what we meet for; this is what inspires us; this is what keeps up together, and beckons us onward; this is the *spread* of science, and a glorious spread it is."' The Dublin *Proceedings* concluded: 'Thus terminated a week of Meetings as interesting and important, as any ever held in the metropolis of Ireland' (p. 128).

When the Meeting was over, Lear was free to explore Dublin and its environs; only Arthur Stanley, Edward Penrhyn and Lear are mentioned as making the tour into the Wicklow Mountains, which means that Arthur's father and younger brother were left in Dublin. The only documentary evidence to survive, which is itself mostly second-hand, is from *The Life and Correspondence of Arthur Penrhyn Stanley, D.D. Late Dean of Westminster*, published in two volumes by Rowland E. Prothero in 1893. This book quotes from and paraphrases letters and journals which are no longer extant; the 1835 trip is briefly mentioned in Volume I:

> Part of Stanley's first Long Vacation (1835) was spent in a visit to Dublin, where he joined his father at a meeting of the British Association. Though unable, as he confesses, 'to enter into the scientific business from my ignorance of the subject,' he was keenly interested in seeing the eminent men who were assembled at the meeting, and in hearing the debates on social questions. His stay in Dublin was diversified by a visit to Glendalough and the Seven Churches, in company with his uncle Penrhyn and Mr. Lear (Afterwards well known as the gifted artist of that name.)
>
> 'Luggelaugh had been very beautiful, but Glendalough was perfect. You come down between woody hills on a narrow valley, with two lakes

> glimmering in the sunset, closed at the end by the cliffs of Lugduff, and with finely-shaped hills and woody rocks jutting into it. At the entrance of the valley is the Round Tower, and three [?] of the Seven Churches, small and in ruins, but the most interesting ruins I ever saw … The guide was, however, sufficient to drive away all sentiment. He began by shouting Moore's poem on Glendalough at the top of his voice, and then went on with a profusion of legends. … He nearly broke my legs by trying to make them meet round a stone cross, which is necessary to secure a beautiful wife and a good fortune.'
>
> He adds a string of similar stories, ending with a description of his
>
> 'ascending shoeless with Mr. Lear along a narrow ledge—a mauvais pas on a small scale—and helped round the corner by an old woman surnamed Kathleen, who popped us into the hole (St Kevin's bed) just like a bathing-woman, saying all the time, 'Don't be fretful, my dear.' We drove on to sleep at Belleview, Mrs. Latouche's place, but … did not reach it till 9.30.' (Stanley, vol. i, pp. 146–7)

As far as can be guessed from the few drawings that survive, Lear seems to have followed the main tourist routes through Wicklow. The nearly contemporary *Ireland: Its Scenery, Character, &c.*, by Mr and Mrs S.C. Hall, published in 1841–3, observed:

> We must not, however, mislead the tourist into the notion that a great expenditure of time is necessary to examine the county of Wicklow. The whole of its leading attractions may be visited within three days – long summer days; but a week will amply suffice to introduce him to every one of its beauties and peculiarities … the tour need not exceed sixty miles – easily accomplished in three or four days.'(ii, 197).

The account of County Wicklow in Hall's *Ireland* (vol. ii, pp. 193–256), which has the travellers entering the district through The Scalp on the Enniskerry Road and, after visiting Powerscourt, the Glen of the Dargle, Luggala and Glendalough, returning via Bray, probably follows the route that Lear took a few years earlier. A more contemporary account, by Leitch Ritchie in *Ireland – Picturesque and Romantic*, has the traveller entering the district via Bray, then proceeding to Enniskerry, the Glen of the Dargle, Powerscourt, Luggala, Glendalough, Arklow and south into Wexford (pp. 51–122).

18 *Clondalkin Tower, Co. Dublin*

Pencil, on blue-grey paper, 13.2 × 8.8 cm (irreg.)
Provenance: acquired by Agnew's from Mary F. Shaw; purchased from Agnew's in January 1989 (with 6 others) (£1,650); sold privately to the current owner in 1989
Private Collection, Ireland

Clondalkin Tower is the only tower in Ireland with an expanded base, and the sole tower now standing in the Dublin area to be complete with cap during the nineteenth century. This view is taken from the north. Clondalkin, located about seven miles west of Dublin, is not on the way to Wicklow, and would therefore have been a separate excursion from the city.

19 *Clondalkin Tower, Co. Dublin*

Pencil, on blue-grey paper, 13.1 × 8.8 cm
Provenance: acquired by Agnew's from Mary F. Shaw; purchased from Agnew's in January 1989 (with 6 others) (£1,650)
Private Collection

This view of the tower is taken from the south; the doorway, which is not visible, faces east towards the now vanished church.

20 *The Great and Little Sugarloafs, from The Scalp, Co. Wicklow*

Inscribed on the mount
Pencil heightened with white, on grey paper, 10.3 × 16.5 cm
Provenance: Robert A. Hornby (d. 1857); Anon. Sale; Sotheby's, 18 March 1982, lot 9 (2 in lot) (£320); acquired by the present owner
Private Collection, Ireland

The viewpoint for this distant view of the distinctive Great and Little Sugarloafs is possibly Prince William's Seat. The Enniskerry Road through The Scalp is visible behind the trees in the left foregound. 'By the Enniskerry Road ... the county is entered at "the Scalp," a chasm in the mountain which separates it from the county of Dublin. The mountain appears to have been divided by some sudden shock of nature ... Through these overhanging cliffs the road runs; enormous granite blocks, of many tons in weight, having been "rolled back" out of the path of the traveller' (Hall, vol. ii, pp. 197–8). Leitch Ritchie wrote: 'The Sugarloaf hills seem to haunt the steps of the traveller. They are seen from every point of view' (Ritchie, p. 54).

21 *The Great and Little Sugarloafs, Co. Wicklow*

Pencil, on grey paper, 8.2 × 13 cm
Provenance: acquired by Agnew's from Mary F. Shaw; purchased from Agnew's in January 1989 (with 6 others) (£1,650)
Private Collection
Illustrated on p. 68

This is probably drawn from Lord Powerscourt's Deerpark, the site of the famous waterfall painted by countless artist visitors and, in view of his fondness for painting waterfalls the following summer, surely drawn by Lear in 1835, although no such drawing has survived. This view is taken looking due east.

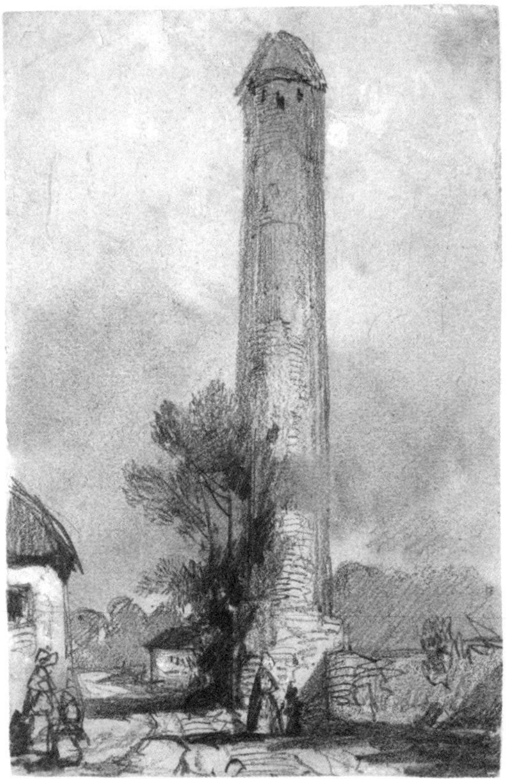

Cat. 18

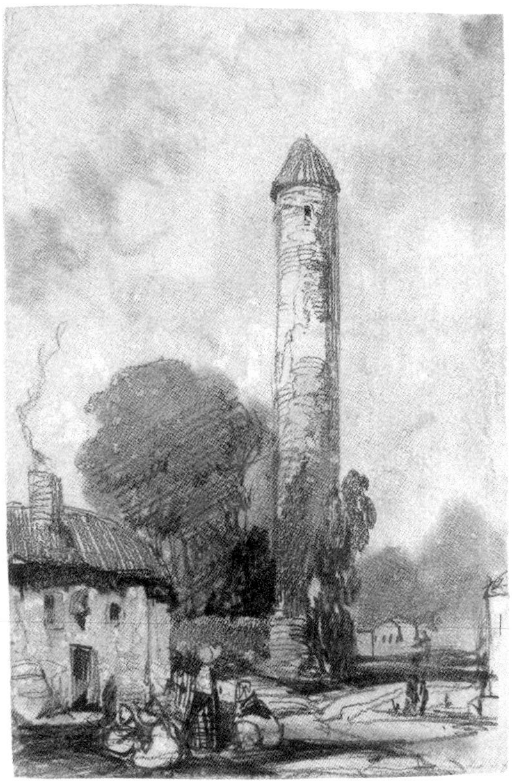

Cat. 19

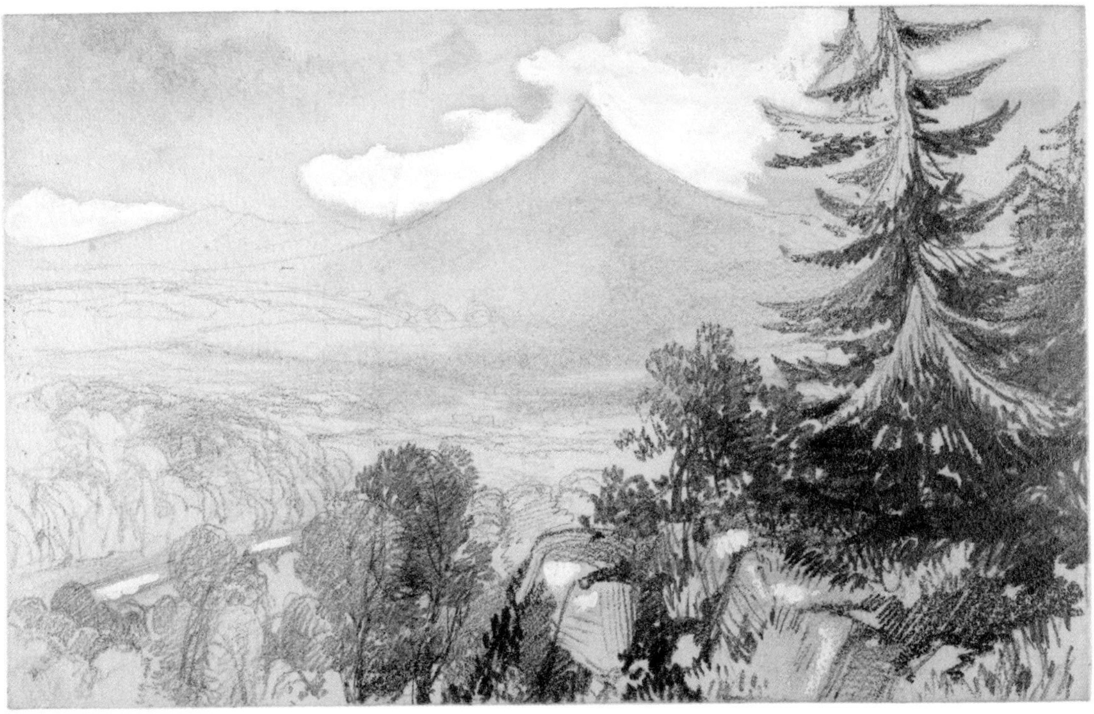

Cat. 20

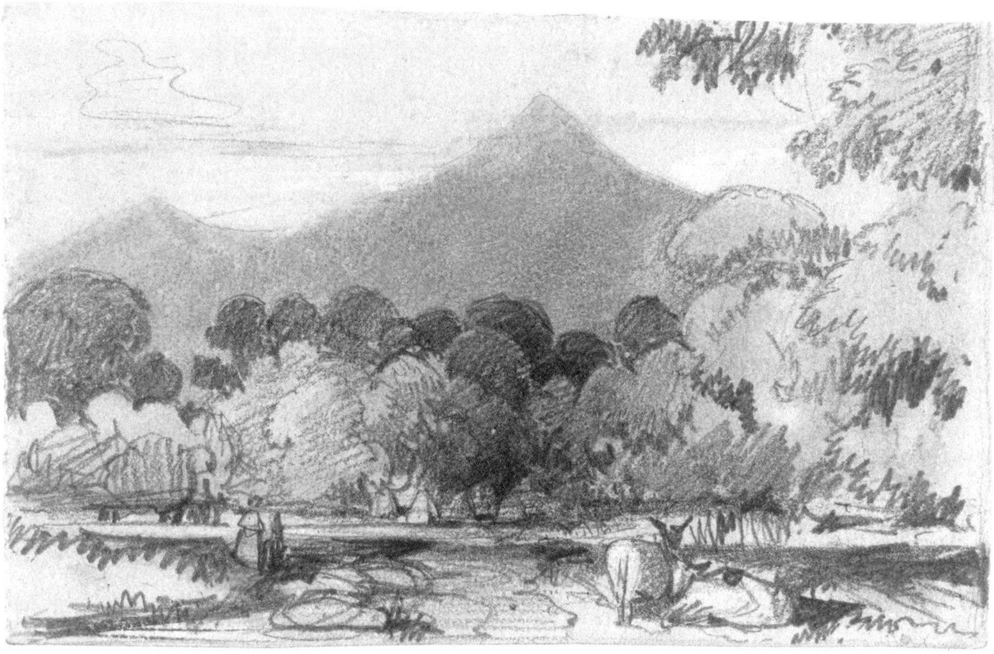

Cat. 21

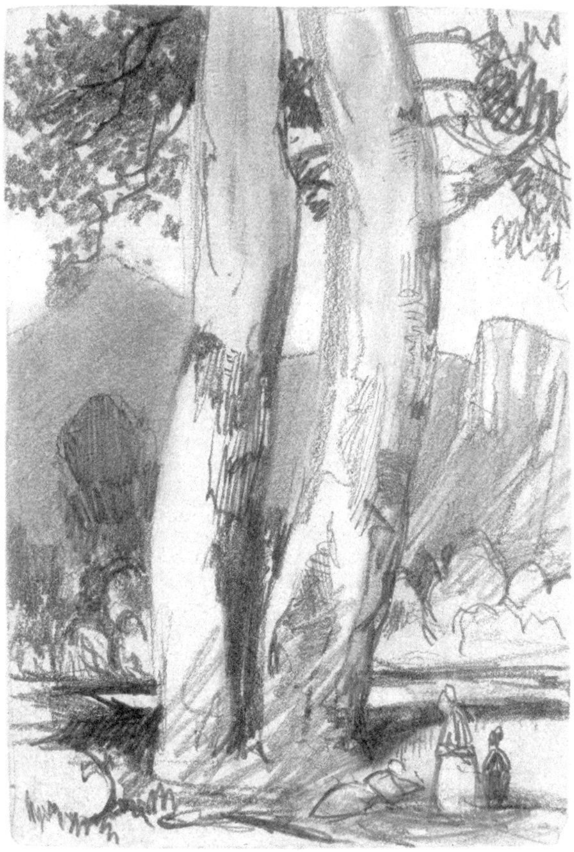

Cat. 22

22 *Figures beside Trees with an Escarpment beyond, probably in the Powerscourt Demesne, Co. Wicklow*

Pencil, on grey paper, 12.6 × 8.8 cm
Provenance: acquired by Agnew's from Mary F. Shaw; purchased from Agnew's in January 1989 (with 6 others) (£1,650)
Private Collection

The cliffs in the background are probably those that flank the famous waterfall. Hall describes the scene: 'The demesne of Powerscourt contains 1400 acres; the natural advantages of the locality have been heightened and improved by taste … the whole is so completely inclosed by mountains, apparently "inaccessible to mortal feet," as to realise the picture of the "happy valley." The "waterfall" … is, perhaps, the most magnificent fall in the county of Wicklow.' (Hall, vol. ii, p. 202).

23 *Loch Tay looking North, Co. Wicklow*

Pencil, on blue-grey paper, 9.7 × 12.8 cm (irreg.)
Provenance: acquired by Agnew's from Mary F. Shaw; purchased from Agnew's in January 1989 (with 6 others) (£1,650); sold privately to the current owner in 1989
Private Collection, Ireland

This shows a view looking north over part of Loch Tay, with the rocky scarp of Luggala on the left. The open land on the right is the location of Luggala Lodge, then the property of the La Touche family, where it was possible to stay the night. 'At one end of the lake is the pretty cottage-mansion of Mr. Latouche' (Hall, vol. ii, p. 209); an earlier guide book records that 'a part of the building is allocated for respectable strangers where, in the spirit of Irish hospitality, beds and attendants are provided' (John Carr, *The Stranger in Ireland*, 1806). It is likely that Lear and his companions availed themselves of this hospitality.

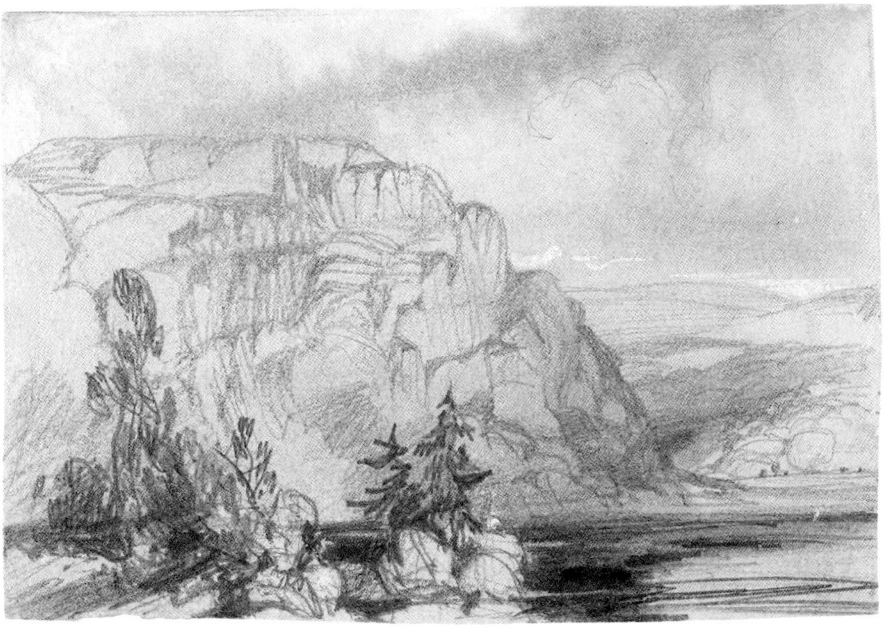

Cat. 23

24 *The Round Tower at Glendalough, Co. Wicklow*

Pencil, on blue-grey paper, 12.5 × 8.7 cm (irreg.)
Provenance: acquired by Agnew's from Mary F. Shaw; purchased from Agnew's in January 1989 (with 6 others) (£1,650); sold privately to the current owner in 1989
Private Collection, Ireland

Situated in a valley deep in the Wicklow Mountains, the Monastery at Glendalough originally dates from the time of St Kevin in the sixth century. Although it ceased to function as a monastery around the fourteenth century, it has continued as a place of pilgrimage up to the present day, its proximity to Dublin making it one of the premier tourist sites in Ireland. In Lear's day, as recorded in Stanley and also (at considerable length) in Hall, the monastery site abounded in importunate and enthusiastic unofficial guides. The cap on the Round Tower was not restored until 1876.

No visit to Glendalough can be short, and it is likely that Lear and his companions spent the best part of a day there. Although only this one drawing survives of a building downstream from the Lower Lake, the account in Stanley makes it clear that they also visited St Kevin's Bed on the Upper Lake, so they must have covered the area thoroughly, and other drawings of the site must once have existed. Certainly, Glendalough made enough of an impression for Lear to produce an illustrated eight-page poem on the subject of St Kevin and the Gentle Kathleen, where the lines are adapted from those of Thomas Moore (published by D. Gallup, New Haven, 1973).

25 *The Banqueting-room in the Demesne of Bellevue, with a Distant View of Wicklow Head*

Inscribed on the mount, pencil heightened with white, on grey paper, 10.6 × 16.5 cm
Provenance: Robert A. Hornby (d. 1857); Anon. Sale; Sotheby's, 18 March 1982, lot 9 (2 in lot) (£320); acquired by the present owner
Private Collection, Ireland

As is recorded in Stanley, after visiting Glendalough Lear and his companions stayed at Bellevue, the country house of the Dublin banking family, the La Touches, near Delgany and about four miles south of Bray. The house and its various garden buildings are described in Samuel Lewis's *Topographical Dictionary of Ireland* (2 vols, London: 1837): 'The scenery is richly diversified, and the neighbourhood is embellished with numerous seats, of which Bellview is the chief. It is situated in the Glen of the Downs, which is a deep ravine formed by a disruption of the mountain ... with precipitous sides, richly clothed with wood ... The stately mansion ... [was built in 1754 and] has been subsequently enlarged by the addition of wings. Behind it is a conservatory 264 feet in length, furnished with many rare exotics ... The demesne, containing above 600 acres, commands a variety of magnificent prospects. There are several walks leading to the Octagon House, Banqueting-room, and Turkish Tent; and within it is a park of 55 acres well stocked with deer.' (vol. i, p. 450). When Lear visited the house it was in its heyday, and the remarkable glass conservatory or glazed passage, which snaked across the lawn for several hundred yards and joined the house to a succession of large greenhouses, still stood. In 1835, Bellevue was the property of Mrs. Elizabeth La Touche, the elderly widow of Peter La Touche, who had died in 1828. After several years standing derelict, the house was demolished in the 1950s, but some of the garden buildings, now ruinous, still stand, including this one. A contemporary guide book records this building: 'Below the octagon house

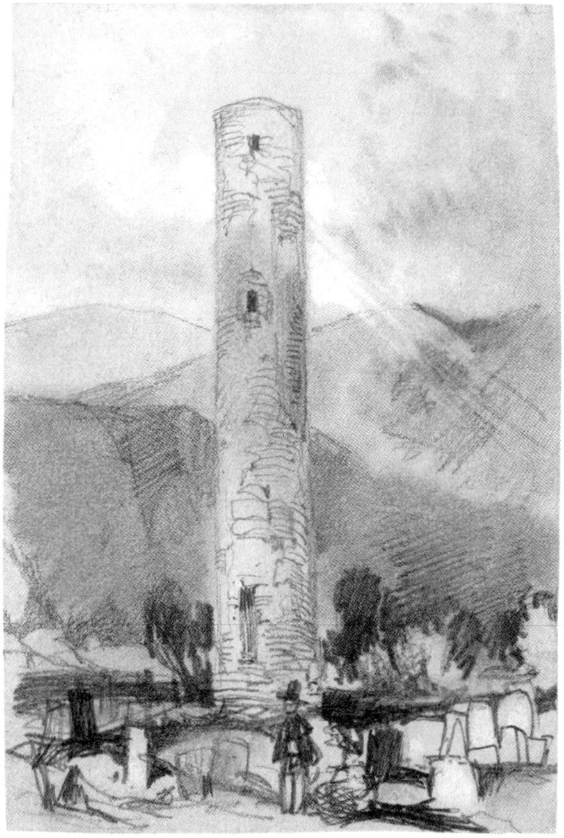

Cat. 24

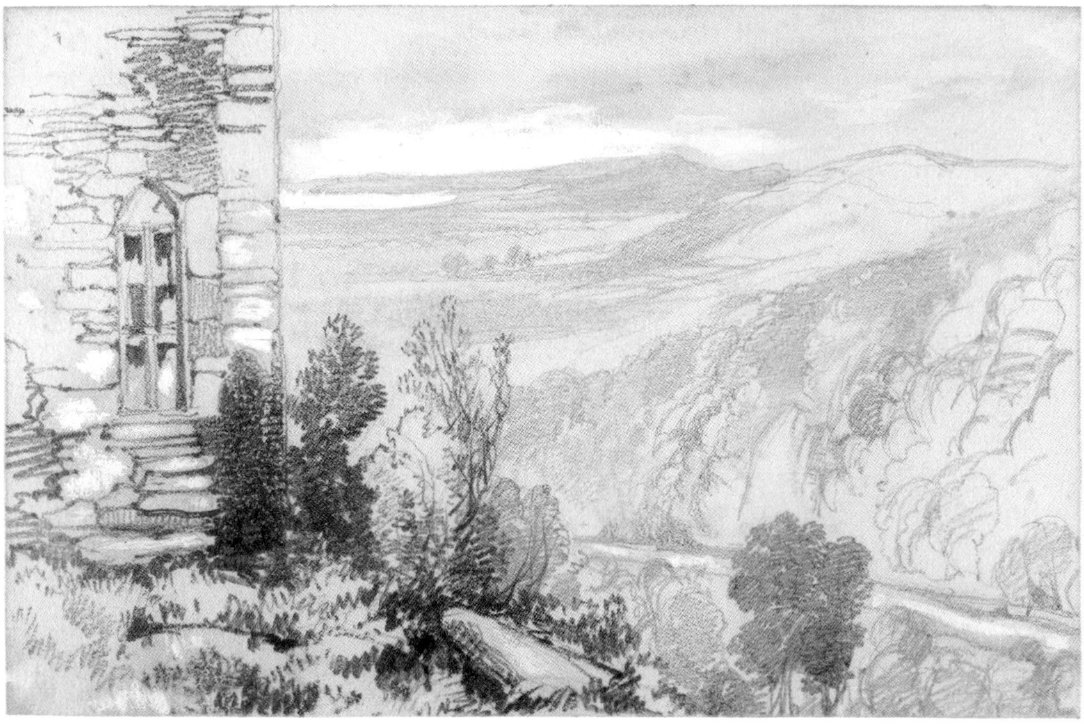

Cat. 25

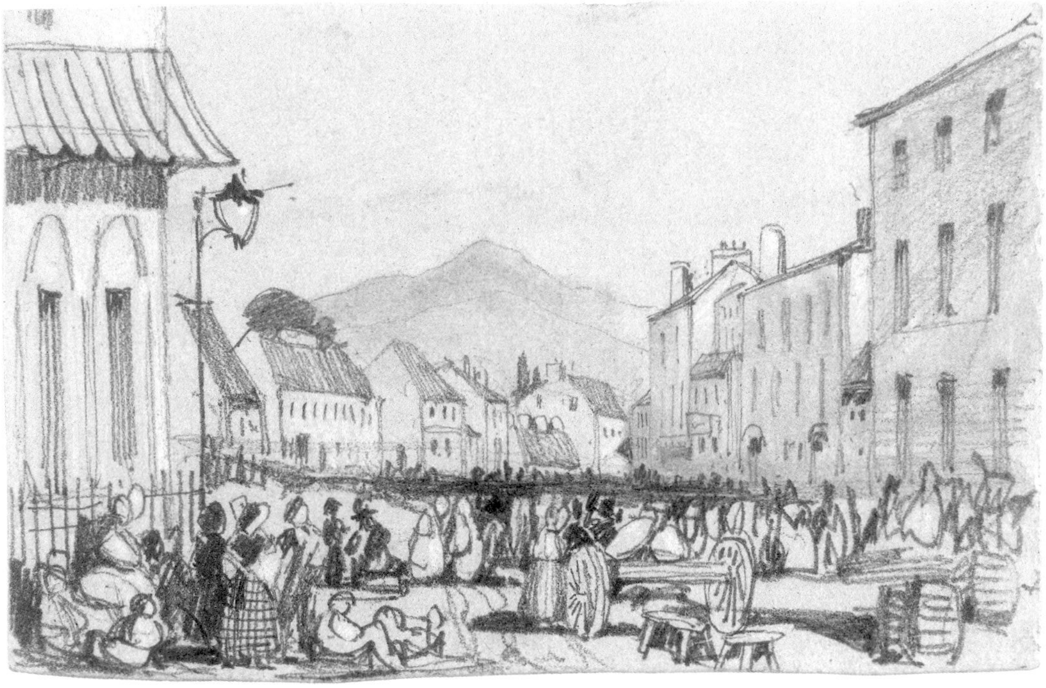

Cat. 26

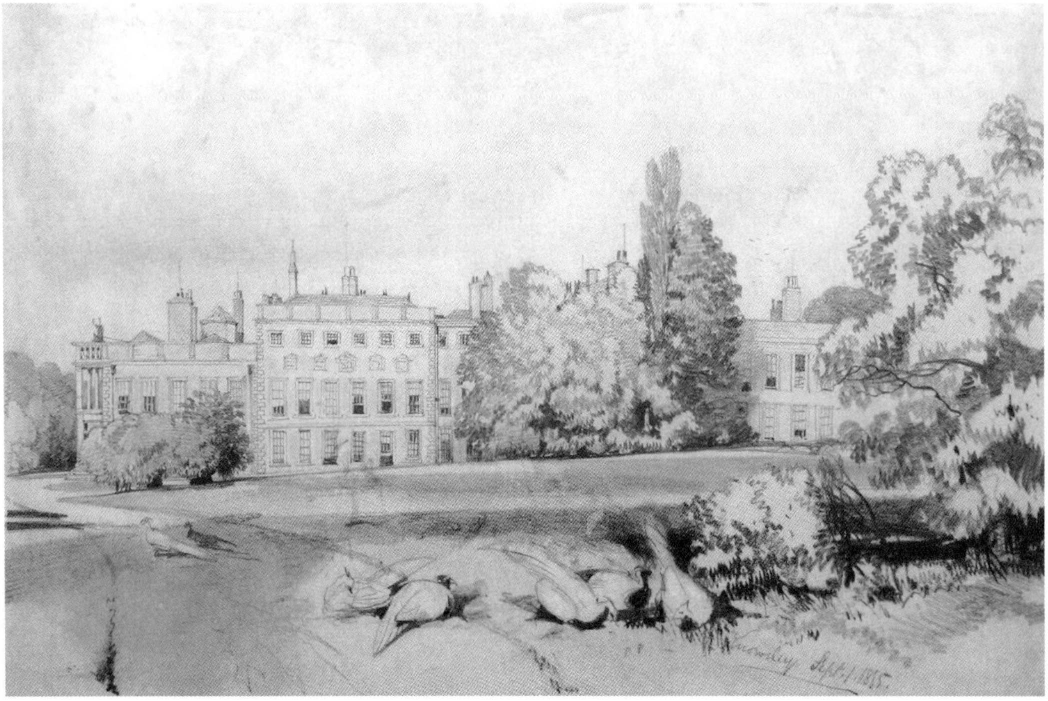

Cat. 27

is a very curious building of rustic masonry, or rock-work, called the Banqueting-room; it is built in the Gothic style, and in imitation, probably, of an apartment excavated from a solid rock' (*Guide to the County of Wicklow*, new ed., 1835, p. 45).

26 *Bray, with the Little Sugarloaf in the Distance, Co. Wicklow*

Pencil, on blue-grey paper, 8.2 × 13 cm

Private Collection

This is an important record of the main street in Bray looking south towards the Little Sugarloaf. The view, which records the appearance of the town before the arrival of the railway in 1854, is taken from outside the Market House on Market Day. Markets were then held on Tuesdays and Saturdays. As Lear must have gone to Bray after Glendalough and Bellevue, which is near Delgany, he was therefore visiting the town on the way back to Dublin, and this must therefore have been drawn on either Saturday 22 or Tuesday 25 August, since by Saturday 29 August he was surely on his way back to England. Described by Ritchie as 'the favourite summer resort of the "genteel people" of Dublin' (p. 54), Bray in 1835 was already a popular bathing place, and Quin's Hotel, just out of sight on the left of Lear's view, was one of the best hotels in Ireland. The Quin family also ran a coach service, and theirs was the logical place to change horses on passing through the town, which is probably what Lear did on his way from Bellevue to Dublin. This is the last drawing of Ireland by Lear to survive.

27 *Knowsley Hall from the East*

Inscribed and dated 'Knowsley Sept. 1. 1835.'
Pencil and stump with touches of white heightening, on grey paper, 21.6 × 36.2 cm
Provenance: the 13th Earl of Derby, and by descent

Lent by The Earl of Derby

Lear's view of Knowsley, drawn soon after his return from Ireland, shows the east side of the house, the construction of which began in the 1720s and continued until 1737. The central portion of this wing (hidden behind the trees) was completely rebuilt in the early twentieth century.

28 *Knowsley Hall from the North-west*

Inscribed and dated 'Knowsley. / Sept. 5.1835.'
Pencil, on grey paper, 25.4 × 34.9 cm
Provenance: the 13th Earl of Derby, and by descent

Lent by The Earl of Derby

Illustrated on p. 74

From this point, the L-shaped nature of the house is very clear. The principal entrance front to the left can be clearly seen. At right angles to it is the earlier wing; the two round turrets flanking a doorway date from the late fifteenth century, but have been recased in the medieval style along with the rest of the wing.

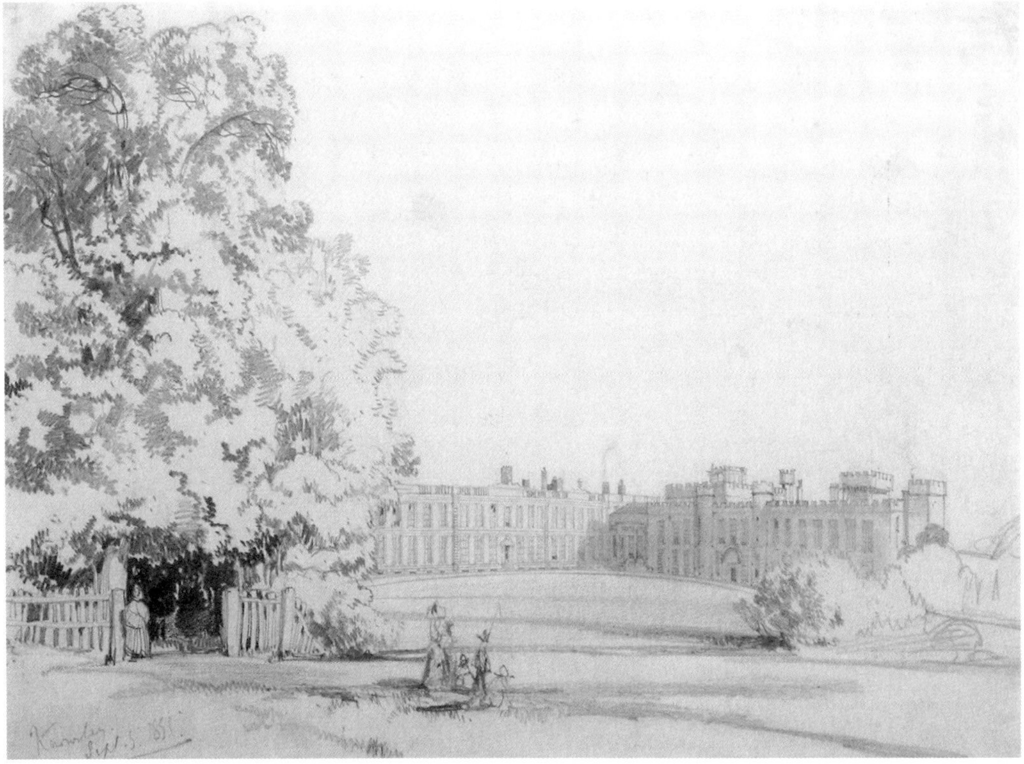

Cat. 28

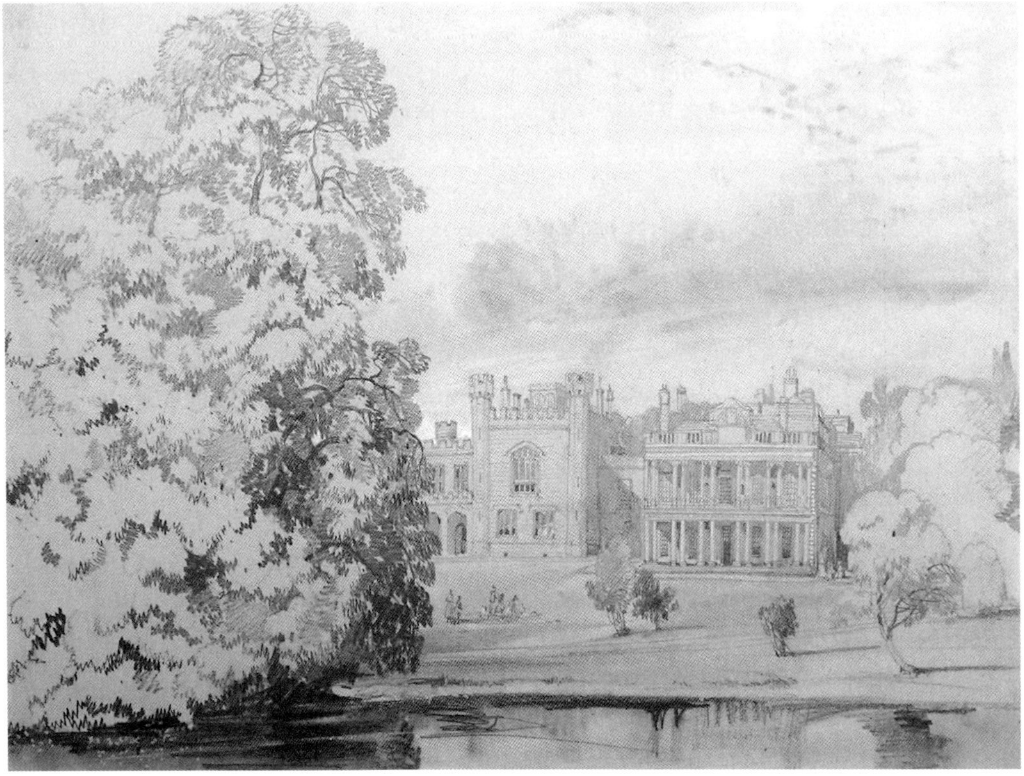

Cat. 29

29 *Knowsley Hall from the South*

Pencil, 25.5 × 33.1 cm
Provenance: the 13th Earl of Derby, and by descent
Lent by The Earl of Derby

On the right of this view is the handsome five-bay portico of two storeys, with paired columns on the ground and first floors, which represents the climax of the early Georgian rebuilding of the house. To its left is the State Dining Room, which had been built to the designs of John Foster between 1810 and 1821. This drawing is related to a lithograph, which is Lear's earliest known topographical print (fig. 10, present location unknown). The viewpoint is virtually the same, but it shows more of the house to the west of the State Dining Room.

30 *Lathom House, Lancashire, from the North*

Inscribed and dated 'Lathom. / Sept.18.1835.'
Pencil and black chalk, on blue-grey paper, 17.5 × 25.8 cm
Provenance: presented by Sir Hugh Walpole in 1938
The King's School, Canterbury
Illustrated on p. 76

This recently discovered drawing provides a record of one of the great lost Palladian houses of Lancashire. Not only was Lathom House, near Ormskirk, on the site of the former principal seat of the Stanley family in Lancashire, it was also at this date the property of Baron Skelmersdale, a close relative by marriage of Lord Derby. In 1825 Emma Caroline Bootle-Wilbraham (her father was created Baron Skelmersdale in 1828) had married Lord Derby's heir, Edward Stanley, who later succeeded his father as the 14th Earl in 1851. The Skelmersdales and the Derby families were thus intimately connected, and it is not surprising that Lear knew them also; in a letter written to Fanny Drewitt from Knowsley on 19 May 1837 (cat. 95), Lear records lunching with the Skelmersdales at their house in Grosvenor Square and '[taking] leave of the Lathom people', so clearly he was on good terms with them.

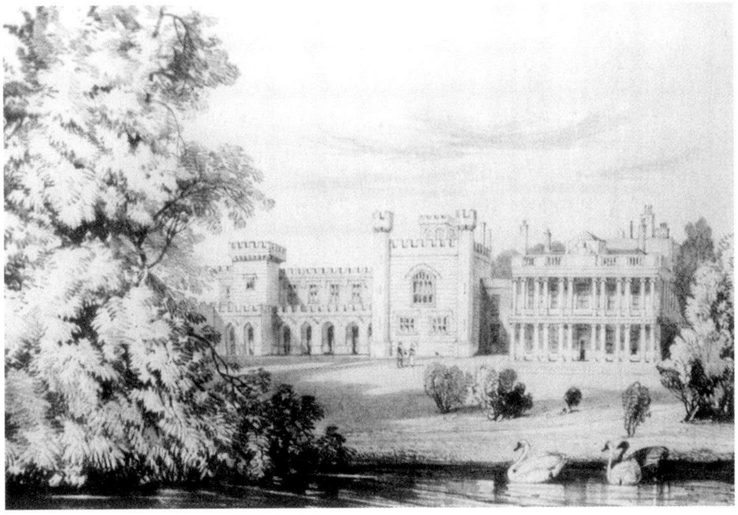

Fig. 10 Knowsley Hall from the South, lithograph, 22 × 29.7 cm (location unknown).

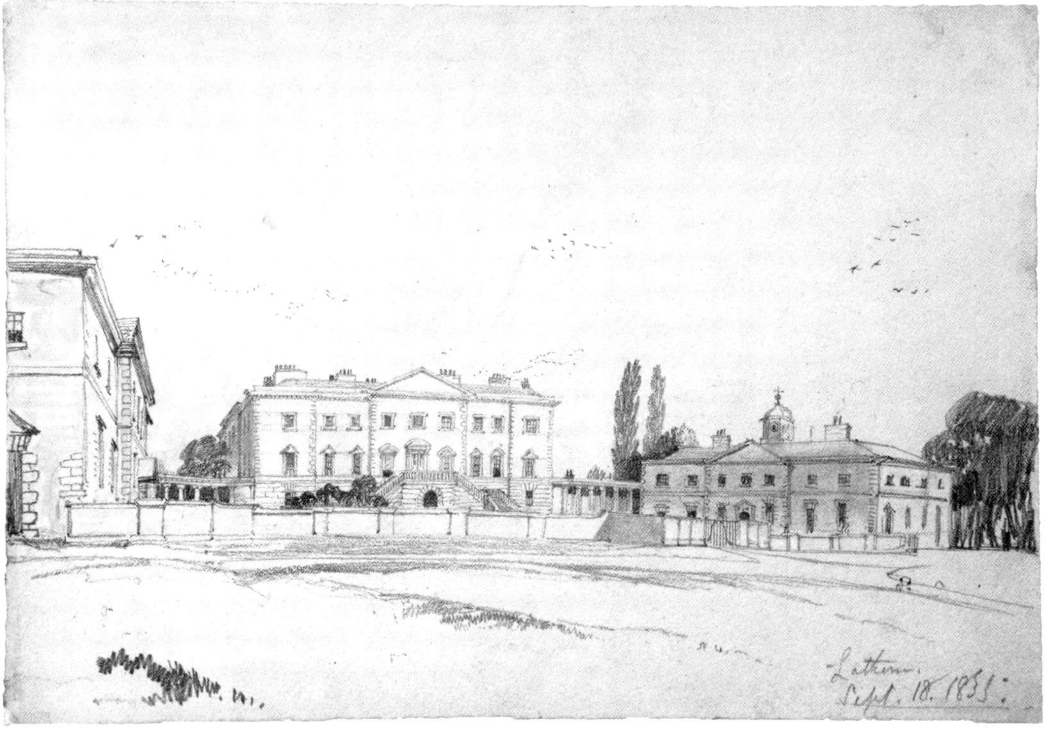

Cat. 30

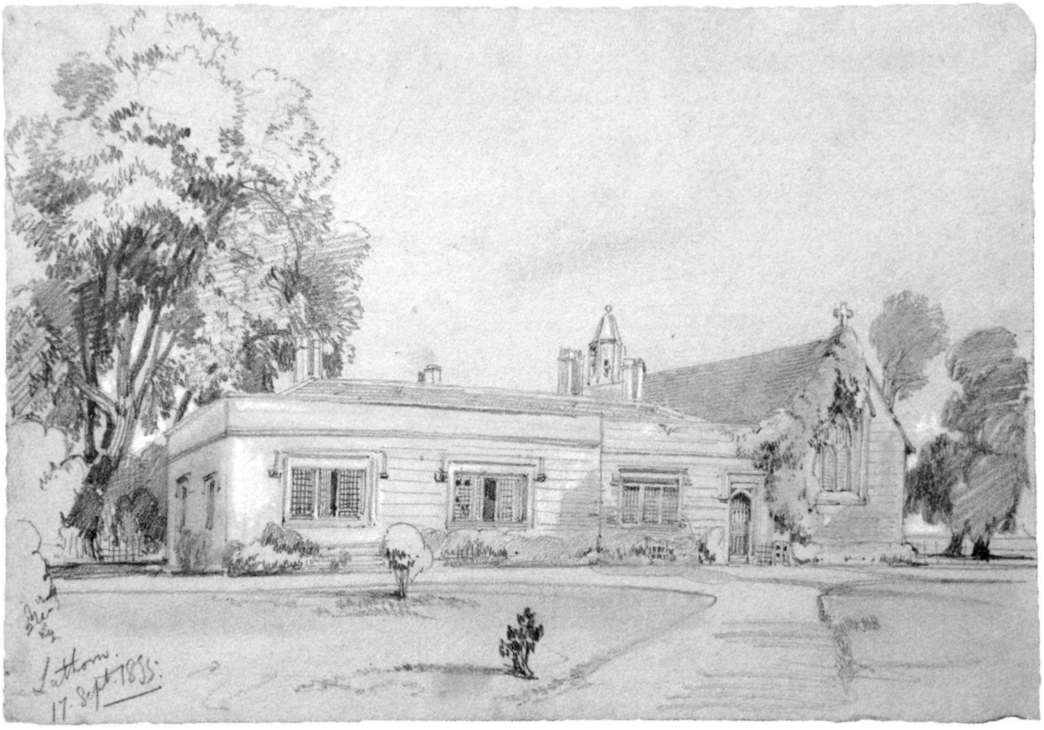

Cat. 31

Lathom House had originally been the main residence of the Stanley family, and was the scene of a prolonged and bloody siege during the Civil War in 1644, when it was heroically held against the Parliamentarians by the Countess of Derby. Having been destroyed and passed out of the family, it was rebuilt as a grand Palladian mansion by the Venetian architect Giacomo Leoni for Sir Thomas Bootle and completed *c.*1740. Lear's drawing shows the north front of the house with the projecting service wings connected by colonnades; the house is shown before the addition of an attic storey to the centre, which was added in 1862. Sadly, owing to the profligacy of the 3rd and last Earl of Lathom (1895–1930) – the Barony of Skelmersdale was raised to an Earldom in 1880 – the main house was demolished in 1925; the service wings stood until 1960, but only the western one (on the right in Lear's drawing) now remains, recently converted into flats.

31 *The Chapel and School, Lathom, Lancashire, from the South*

Inscribed and dated 'Lathom. / 17 Sept. 1835.'
Pencil and black chalk with touches of white bodycolour, on blue-grey paper, 17.3 × 26 cm
Provenance: presented by Sir Hugh Walpole in 1938
The King's School, Canterbury

Standing about a third of a mile to the west and north of Lathom House, the Chantry Chapel at Lathom was founded by the 1st Earl of Derby in 1500 and consecrated in 1509. With its attached almshouses, it remained in use after the Reformation and has thus outlived both the medieval and Palladian Houses nearby. Originally, the Chapel had a priest's house attached, but this was demolished in the eighteenth century and replaced by a School, visible to the left in Lear's drawing and now converted into a house. After more recent restorations, the Perpendicular doorway is the only remaining genuine external feature from the original building; it is clearly visible in Lear's drawing in the south wall between the Chapel and the School.

[4]
THE 1836 TOUR

Lear's plan of campaign for his tour of north Lancashire, Westmorland and Cumberland in the late summer of 1836 was considerably more ambitious than his spur-of-the-moment sketching tour of counties Dublin and Wicklow the previous year. Although in the same medium and also on coloured paper, the drawings produced are larger and more numerous. In his letter to George Coombe, written from Whittington Hall near Kirkby Lonsdale on 6 September (cat. 40), he wrote: 'Tomorrow I go on my last visit,—Col: Bolton's of Storrs [i.e. Storrs Hall on Windermere]...& from *there*—I intend taking walks from different Inns all over the Lakes: that's if the weather is tolerant'. He was armed with letters of introduction from Lord Derby and others; although it is likely that he made use of these to stay at Ponsonby Hall at Calder Bridge and at Wasdale Hall at the south-western end of Wastwater, it is probable that he stuck to his stated intention and stayed in inns.

It was certainly Lear's practice later in his career to prepare for a sketching tour with extensive research in guide books before setting out, and there is no reason to think that this was not the case with his first major tour. By the 1830s, there was a plethora of tourist literature on the Lake District. A number of guide books had been recently published or republished. The ones that Lear must have consulted were:

Edward Baines, *A Companion to the Lakes of Cumberland, Westmoreland, and Lancashire; in a descriptive account of a family tour, and excursions on horseback and on foot. With a new copious and correct Itinerary*, published in 1834; this was the third edition, the first having come out in 1829.

Leigh's Guide to the Lakes and Mountains of Cumberland, Westmoreland, and Lancashire. Illustrated with a map of the country, and maps of Windermere, Derwent Water, Borrowdale, Ullswater, Grasmere, Rydal Water, and Langdale, 1835, third edition (the first was in 1830).

Allison's Northern Tourist's Guide to the Lakes, of Cumberland, Westmorland, and Lancashire; wherein the mountains, lakes, and scenery are correctly described; and the stages and favourite excursions distinctly pointed out, 1835, fifth edition (of *Shaw's Guide*, first published in 1812). Both this and *Leigh's Guide* were designed to be put in the pocket.

George Tattersall, *The Lakes of England*, 1836 (the vignette engraving on the title page of this is dated 15 April 1836 and shows a dismounted tourist leading a horse down a slope).

Lear probably also looked at the 1835 fifth edition (with considerable additions) of Wordsworth's *Guide through the District of the Lakes in the North of England*, first published in its original form in 1810. This was the last edition on which the poet worked, but it is of limited use as a practical guide to visitors.

Lear's plans for the tour were reasonably fluid. Although he wrote in his letter of 24 August (cat. 37) that he expected to return to Knowsley in September, he did not in fact do so until the end of October. The reason for this extension of time was surely the weather, as it is quite clear from the numerical sequence of drawings that several days at a time were unproductive of drawings; Lear worked in the open air, and could not work in the rain. Occasionally, he seems to have been surprised by the rain while drawing, as is shown by the rain marks on some of them , but he certainly never started one in the rain; he could thus be idle for several days in succession because of the weather. Lear was accustomed to starting work very early in the morning (the drawing of St Mary's Church, Nether Alderley, cat. 96, is inscribed '4. AM.') and when the weather was good could produce as many as six drawings a day in addition to covering the miles.

Because it was Lear's normal practice to get franks for his letters off the people he was staying with in order to save himself the cost of postage, he was unable to do this while staying in inns, which is probably why no letters survive between that of 6 September (cat. 40) and that of 31 October, written the day after his return to Knowsley (Houghton Library). Unless other letters surface, the only evidence for the journey that Lear made is the drawings themselves. The drawings that survive from the tour proper, that is after leaving Storrs Hall and until returning to Knowsley, are all in soft pencil and stump (some with white heightening and some with watercolour added) on blue-grey paper and mostly measure approximately 7 by 10¼ inches (17.5 by 26 cm); this size corresponds to an eighth of an imperial sheet (approximately 22 by 30 inches). Most of the drawings are dated precisely to the day. At a later date (that day, or at least within a few days, while the journey was fresh in his mind) Lear went through them and gave them numbers in pen and brown ink, so that they are in the order in which he made them; this was a practice that he continued throughout his life with his working drawings. Sadly, at some future date, many of the drawings have been slightly cropped, which has meant that either the whole or part of the date and/or the number has been removed. It is sometimes impossible therefore to give an absolutely precise date for some of the drawings, although the geographical location and the survival of dates on other drawings of the same area enable the researcher to make an educated guess.

The Lake District Sketches

Although he had been away from Knowsley for nearly a month and had produced in that time many sketches, Lear began a new numerical sequence when he began his tour of the Lakes proper on 9 September 1836. No. 1 is the classic view across Windermere from Lowwood and dates from that day (fig. 21, p. 107); no. 124 is another view of Windermere, this time taken from near Bowness and drawn on 20 October (cat. 85). Lear wrote to John Gould from Knowsley on 30 October: 'I left Knowsley, (only half my work done,) on the 12 August for a sketching tour, & really it is impossible to tell you *how, & how enormously* I have enjoyed the whole Autumn. The counties of Cumberland & Westmd [*sic*] are superb indeed, & tho' the weather has been miserable, yet I have contrived to walk pretty well over the whole ground, & to sketch a good deal beside. I hope too, I have improved somewhat—(hard if I haven't after slaving as I have done) but you will judge when I get back.' He was not exaggerating and had been working hard; although on rainy days he could not work or travel, on clear ones he was able to produce as many as six drawings. This means that it is possible to estimate that there were once between 130 and 140 Lake District sketches recording the tour between 9 September and the end of October. Of this number, about half are traceable, or have appeared on the market in the last fifty years.

Productive as this tour was, it was remarkably unproductive of anything else. Although Lear mentions working on commissions in a letter of January 1837, writing of 'some pencil drawings (18 or 20) ordered for sundry Lancashire folks' and '8 large Lithographs, 20 Landscapes—3 Watercol: drawings—besides other trifling things', it is probable that not all of these were Lake District related. Considering the number of sketches produced, it is remarkable how few finished works resulted. The reason for this may lie in Lear's personal circumstances, which changed so drastically for him in February 1837 (the news is reported in a letter of 3 March, cat. 93) so that worries about money and his hand-to-mouth existence ceased for a time. The prospect of moving to Rome and studying there for two years pushed the recently completed Lake District tour into the background, and it seems that the sketches were never returned to.

Although Lear did return to the Lake District, probably in 1850 and certainly in 1858, it was only for a visit to Wansfell Holme, the rented Hornby house on Windermere, and he never again undertook a long and arduous sketching tour like that of 1836 in an English climate. The Lake District sketches therefore were no longer useful to Lear, since he was unlikely to receive English commissions, and it seems that he gave them away during his lifetime. It is not known when he did this. In 1870, he could still recall the visit to Cumberland, since he wrote in *Journal of a Landscape Painter in Corsica*: 'nor was there there, as here, an undergrowth of silvery birch, suddenly recalling Coolhurst or Cumberland' (entry for 12 May 1870, *Journal of a Landscape Painter in Corsica*, 1870, p. 141). In October 1876, Lear looked back on his journeys and wrote in his diary: 'Worked all day long looking over sketches—more than three cabinets full, so that today & yesterday I seem to have lived over again every year of my life from 1824—Sussex—Lancashire, the Rhine—Rome—Naples—Campagna, Abruzzi—Sicily, Calabria—Sicily again—Apulia—Corfu—Greece, Constanty[z]a, Albania, Greece & Thessaly—Egypt—Ionian Isles, Athos, Palestine, Malta, Cornice, Venice, the Lakes, Dalamtia, Crete, Corsica, India.' Barring Sinai, this is a complete record of all the places Lear visited, omitting second or third visits to places he had already been. When he puts Lancashire in the list, he means Knowsley, but it is surely significant that Cumberland and Westmorland are not mentioned, suggesting that by this date he no longer had the sketches. By the 1880s, when he came to put together the set of 200 Tennyson illustrations, it seems that the Lake District sketches were no longer in his possession, since there are only six English subjects among them, the furthest north being in Staffordshire.

It is significant that all of the surviving Lake District sketches have a Nevill family provenance. On hearing of William Nevill's death in January 1874, Lear described him as 'my dear and oldest friend'; William Nevill was a childhood friend of Lear and had several children, of which one, Allan, was Lear's godson (*Selected Letters*, p. 289 n.24). William, Allan and another son, Ralph, were all apparently given Lake District sketches by Lear; in the case of Allan, he was apparently bequeathed them. According to a letter in the British Museum files, the six Lake District drawings that were purchased by the museum in 1942 were given to Ralph Nevill (the vendor's father) by Lear, and, according to the 1958 Arts Council exhibition catalogue, all the drawings (forty-two in all), which then belonged to the book seller H.V. Day and subsequently were sold to Colnaghi before being dispersed in 1960, came from the same source. It is possible that all the drawings, with the exception of those bequeathed to Allan, were in fact given to William, before descending to Ralph (as with the Devil's Bridge drawing, cat. 39), and that the vendor's memory in the 1942 British Museum letter was at fault. The vendor's letter refers to her collection as numbering 'about twenty', however, whereas there must have been at least forty-eight, if what she said about their provenance was true.

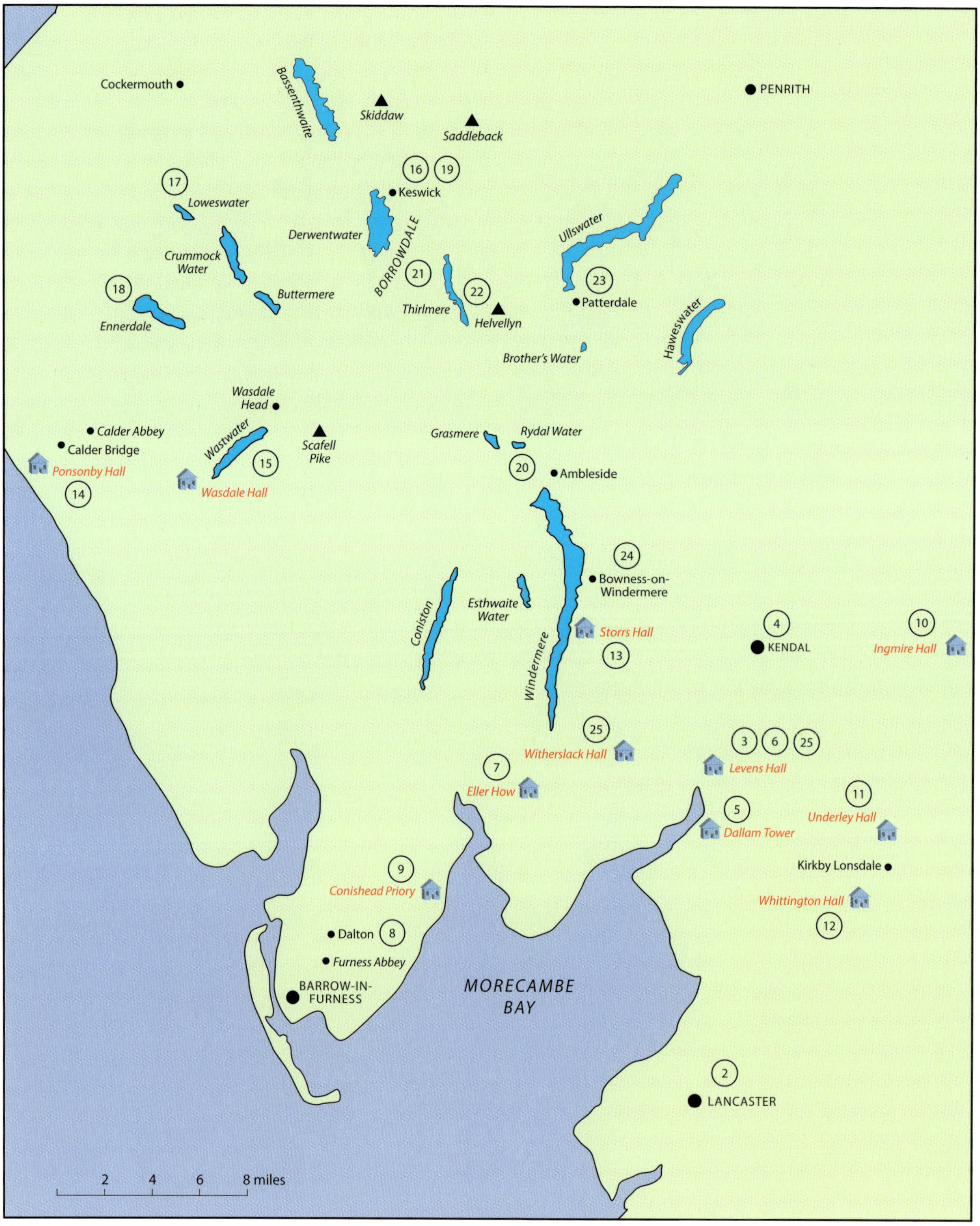

LEAR'S 1836 TOUR

The circled numbers on the map refer to the stages on the itinerary opposite. The houses where Lear is known or thought to have stayed are marked in red.

1. Left KNOWSLEY 10 or 12 August

2. LANCASTER – ?10/12–16 August. Stayed with Hornbys.

3. LEVENS – 17–?20 August

4. KENDAL – 20 and 21 August (Sunday). Saturday Market Day; very wet.

5. DALLAM TOWER – 22 and 23 August (?).

6. LEVENS HALL – 24–26 August (Lear says a week). Letter to Fanny Coombe (24 Aug.; cat. 37).

7. ELLER HOW – 26–29 August. Lear probably left Monday morning (the 29th). Visits to Cartmel and Holker.

8. DALTON (i.e. Furness) – Views of Furness Abbey – 29 and 30 August. Stayed in an inn. Wet.

9. CONISHEAD PRIORY – 31 August –3 September (?). Climbed Birkrigg.

10. INGMIRE HALL (near Sedbergh) – 4 Sept. (Sunday). Maybe earlier (?).

11. UNDERLEY HALL (near Kirkby Lonsdale) – ?4 and 5 Sept.

12. WHITTINGTON HALL (near Kirkby Lonsdale) – Letter to George Coombe (6 Sept.; cat. 40).

13. STORRS HALL (via Kendal) – 7–9 Sept. New numbering sequence of drawings begins. Langdale Pikes from Lowwood (no. 1).

14. 10 Sept. Skiddaw and Saddleback from Dunmail Raise (2). Travelled by coach (?) to Calder Bridge. Stayed at PONSONBY HALL with the Stanleys (?).

    12 Sept. Calder Abbey (no number).

15. 14–18 Sept. In and around Wasdale and Wastwater. Probably stayed at WASDALE HALL and at a farm at WASDALE HEAD (no inn at that date).

    19 Sept. Over Styhead Pass. Styhead Tarn (31) and Scawfell Pike and Lingmell (32).

16. 20–26 Sept. Based in KESWICK (?). Views of Derwentwater and Bassenthwaite.

17. 27 Sept. Travelled over to Buttermere via Newlands Valley. Views of Buttermere and Crummock Water (51–4). Stayed night SCALE HILL, LOWESWATER (?).

    28 Sept. Loweswater (56). Crummock Water (59). Stayed night SCALE HILL (?).

18. 29 Sept. Walked (?) over to Ennerdale via Floutern Tarn. Views of Ennerdale Water and Valley (61–3). Stayed night ANGLER'S INN, ENNERDALE (?).

19. 30 Sept. Buttermere (71). Back to KESWICK (?).

    1-3 Oct. No drawings. Must have been very wet.

20. 4 Oct. Vale of Keswick (73). Headed south on horse (?) via St John's in the Vale past Thirlmere to GRASMERE or AMBLESIDE (?) (74–7).

    5 Oct. Skelwith Force (78). Grasmere from Red Bank (80).

    5-7 Oct. Explored Grasmere, Rydal and Ambleside. Rydal Water (93).

21. 8 Oct. Travelled up Langdale over Stake Pass and down into BORROWDALE (97–101), on horse (?).

    9 and 10 Oct. Exploring Borrowdale (106 and 107).

22. 11 Oct. Walked/rode via Watendlath and Armboth Fell to Wythburn (southern end of Thirlmere). Stayed night NAG'S HEAD, WYTHBURN (?).

23. 12 Oct. Walked/rode via Dunmail Raise and Grizedale Tarn (?) to PATTERDALE.

    12–15 Oct. Exploring Ullswater and environs.

    15 Oct. Helvellyn from the west (122).

24. 15–20 Oct. Over Kirkstone Pass to BOWNESS. Bad weather (?).

    20 Oct. Bowness and Windermere (124).

25. 20-30 Oct. Travelled back to KNOWSLEY. Visited Town Head and Fell Foot, Windermere. Visited WITHERSLACK HALL and LEVENS HALL on way.

    30 Oct. Arrived at Knowsley in the evening.

    31 Oct. Letter to John Gould (Appendix B).

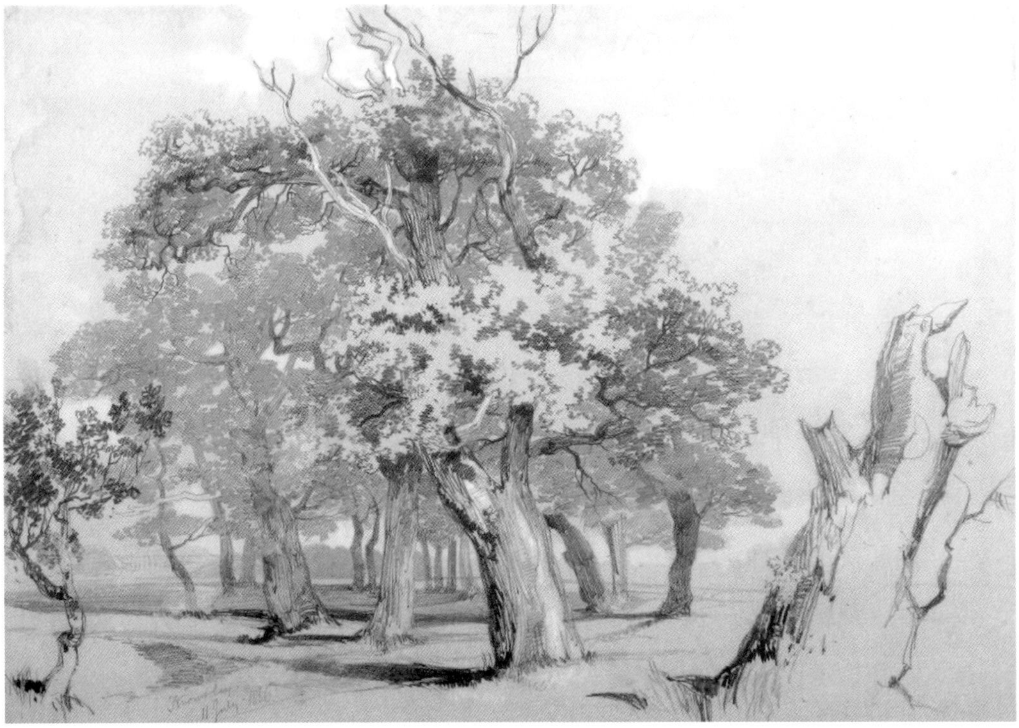

Cat. 32

32 *Trees in the Park at Knowsley*

Inscribed and dated 'Knowsley. / 11 July. 1836'
Pencil with touches of white heightening, on grey paper, 34.9 × 51.4 cm
Provenance: the 13th Earl of Derby, and by descent
Lent by The Earl of Derby

This is the only drawing which survives from Lear's stay at Knowsley before he set off on his tour of Lancashire and the Lake District around 10 August 1836. The park at Knowsley is one of the largest in Britain, its wildness and untamed nature standing in marked contrast today with the nearby urban sprawl of Liverpool and the proximity of the motorway. In Lear's day it was also impressive, and this study of oak trees with a distant view of the house to the left is strongly indebted to the work of James Duffield Harding, who had established his reputation as a drawing master and teacher with the publication of *Elementary Art or, the Use of the Chalk and Lead Pencil, Advocated and Explained*, first published in 1834 (see cat. 6).

On 24 June 1835 Lear wrote to George Coombe: 'The trees—oh! the trees!—"what once be thought wise Giants—now seemed dwarfs."—Positively there is not a tree in the whole park fit to draw—though there is promising timber enough:—after Parham & Arundel I see nothing but Gooseberry bushes' (see cat. 14). But this should be taken with a pinch of salt and seen as Lear pandering to his recipient's prejudices. There were many fine trees in the park at Knowsley, and Lear's memory of them remained fresh as late as 1839 (see cat. 107).

10 August – 29 August
from Knowsley to Furness Abbey

In his letter of 24 August written from Levens Hall to Fanny Coombe (cat. 37), Lear wrote: 'I left Knowsley on a sketching tour—but as Lord Derby [and other relatives] all thrust ... letters into my hand to different friends,—my life is one of extreme gaiety—& vastly little improvement ... from that time till now—I have been happiness personified—for a more exquisite country than Westmoreland I never dreamed of'. His first port of call was the town house in Castle Park, Lancaster, the home of Edmund George Hornby, Lord Derby's nephew. Lear wrote: 'Those lovely days about 10 August—I spent at Lancaster—with the Edmund Hornbys—a delightful family. Mrs Hornby—the mountains of Westmoreland—the Castle—& the Lunatic Asylum—are all balanced in my mind—you might see them all at once—& each was perfection in its way.' Edmund Hornby (1799–1865) was Constable of Lancaster Castle, which was then, as now, a prison; there is a drawing by Lear dated 1836 of the entrance to the castle (Private Collection), the viewpoint of which is very close to the house Lear was staying in. No other drawings from this visit have yet come to light; there is a drawing of trees beside a stream, which is dated August 1836 (fig. 11), but this presumably shows a view in the Lancashire countryside.

Lear probably spent nearly a week in Lancaster, and moved on to Levens Hall, of which there are dated drawings from 17 to 19 August; he then visited Kendal, where he spent at least one night. According to the evidence of a drawing and the Levens letter, Lear was in Kendal on 20 August, which was a Saturday and Market Day, and 21 August. The drawing, dated 20 August, is inscribed jokingly 'Umbrellifera' (fig. 12, p. 86) and shows a group of (mostly) women with their umbrellas up, presumably

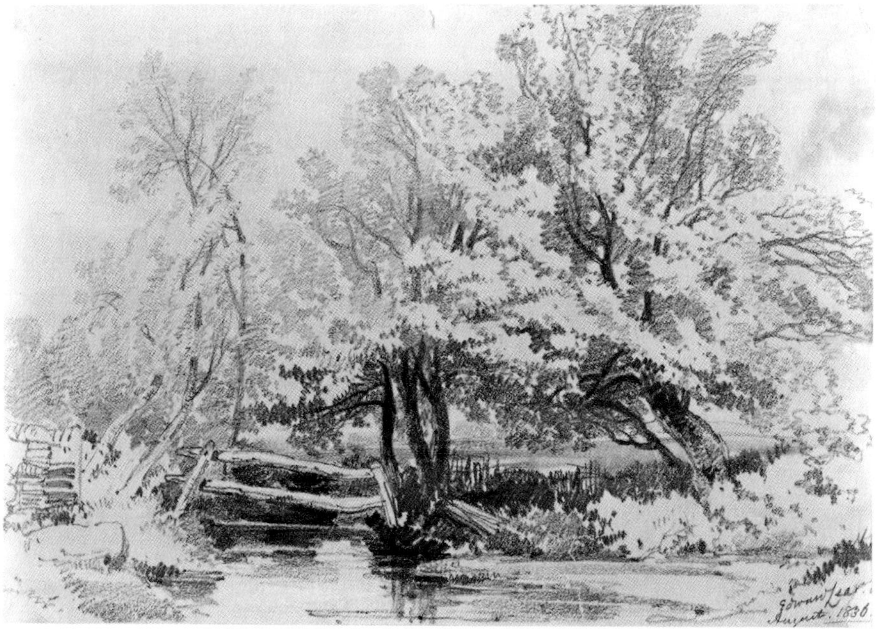

Fig. 11 Trees beside a Stream, signed and dated August 1836, pencil, 16.5 × 23.8 cm (Huntington Art Collections, 66.37).

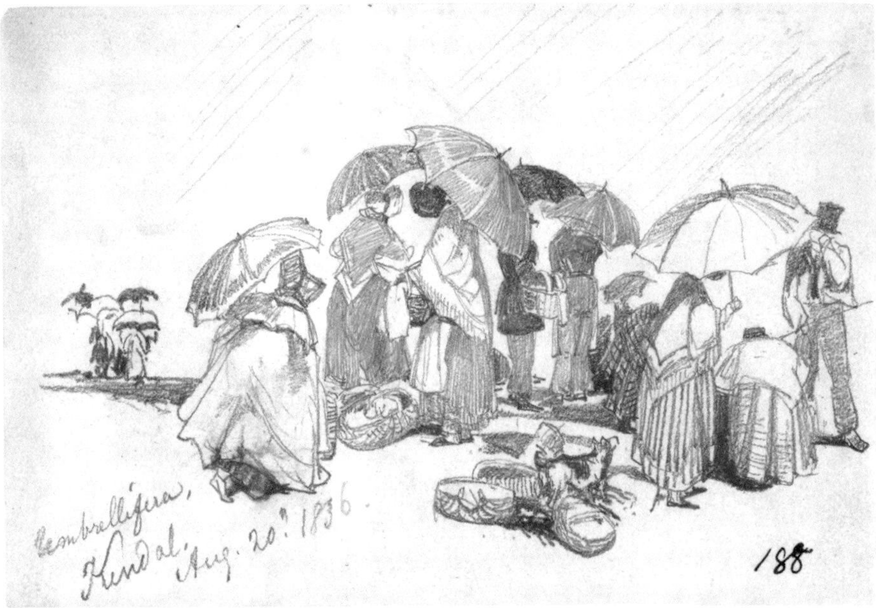

Fig. 12 A Group of Figures attending Kendal Market, inscribed and dated 'Umbrellifera, / Kendal. / Aug. 20. 1836.', numbered 188, pencil, on blue-grey paper, 12.4 × 17 cm (Department of Printing and Graphic Arts, The Houghton Library, Harvard University).

attending the Market; the Levens letter corroborates the fact that it was a rainy day: 'I went to Kendal—Nature's slopbasin—where it always rains ... & din'd there on Sunday [i.e. 21 August]'. The letter goes on to mention a visit to Dallam Tower (fig. 13), called, unfortunately for posterity, 'beyond a letter's description'; Lear was probably there on 22 and 23 August, and returned to Levens, three miles away to the north, on 24 August. The only drawings of Levens that survive date from Lear's first visit to the house (cats. 33–6); he probably spent the time on his second visit exploring the surrounding area.

The only drawing that survives from this second visit is now at Yale (fig. 14). Formerly described as 'A Ruined Tower House', it has recently been identified as a view of Hazelslack Tower, a small pele tower near Arnside two miles south-west of Milnthorpe. The inscription and the date have been cut, but it was presumably drawn some time between 22 and 26 August. Other drawings from these days remain to be discovered; as it is known that Lear drew Hazelslack Tower, it is hard to believe that he did not also draw Arnside Tower, the considerably larger pele tower two miles south-west, or Beetham Hall a mile to the east.

Thanks to the Levens letter and a second letter, written from Whittington Hall, near Kirkby Lonsdale, on 6 September (cat. 40), Lear's itinerary for this part of the tour can be pieced together with some accuracy, although the exact dates of his stay at each port of call remain unknown, and can only be guessed at. In the Levens letter, he wrote: 'On Friday [i.e. 26 August] I go to Mr Webster's'; this is Eller How, Lindale, near Grange, the home of the Kendal architect George Webster (fig. 15, p. 88). Lear was probably there from 26 to 28 August; the Whittington letter describes the visit, hinting at drawings yet to be discovered, 'Followed this—a visit to Eller how ... This—tho' very handsome—was not a palace ... Some exquisite scrambles

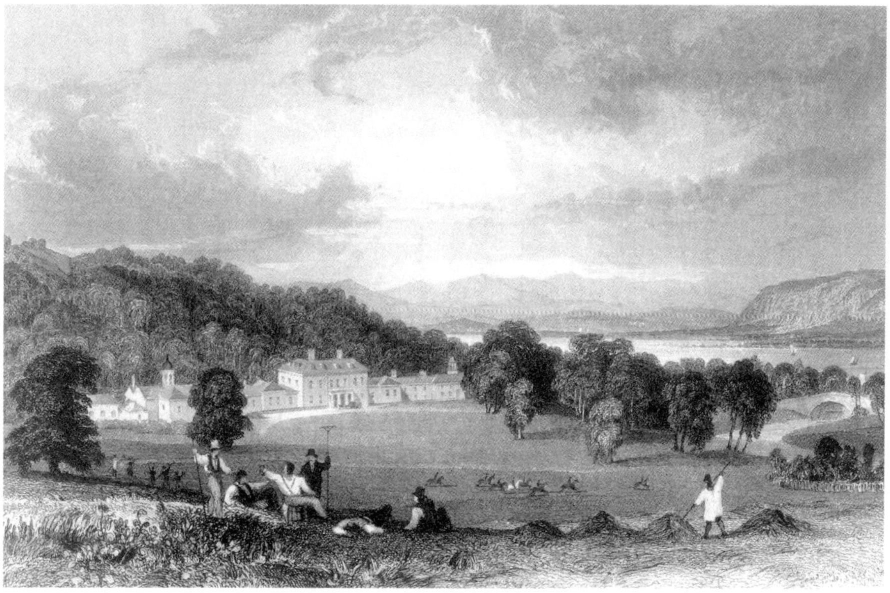

Fig. 13 'Dallam Tower, near Milnthorp', engraving after Thomas Allom, 1834, from *Westmorland, Cumberland, Durham, and Northumberland, Illustrated. From Original Drawings by Thomas Allom, George Pickering, &c. with Descriptions by T. Rose*, 1832–5 (The Wordsworth Trust).

The early eighteenth century house had been remodelled and much extended by George Webster for Colonel George Wilson (1782–1853) in 1826. The Colonel, originally Colonel Smyth, had acquired the house in 1824 through his wife, Sarah (d. 1831), and had assumed the surname Wilson in 1825.

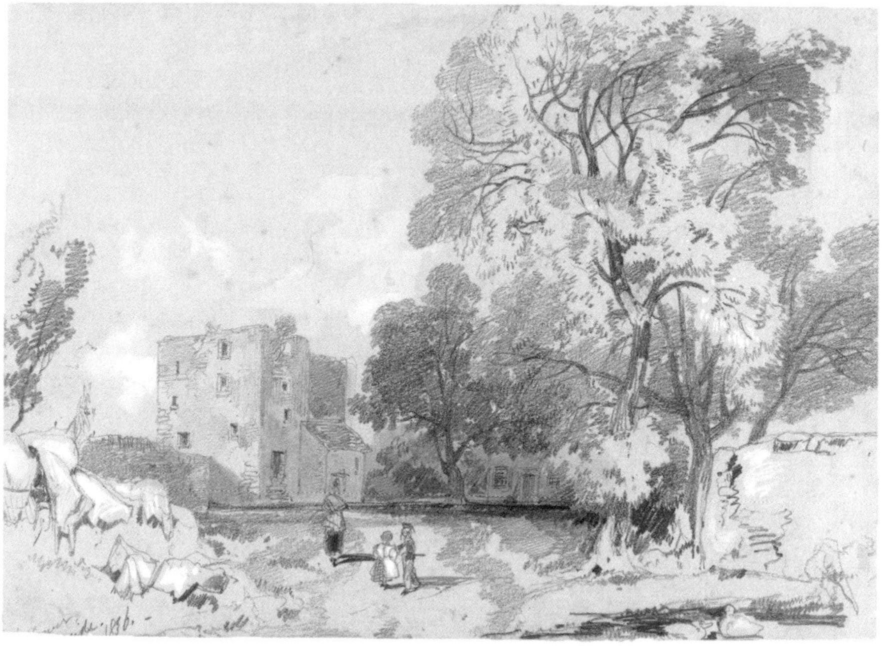

Fig. 14 Hazelslack Tower, near Arnside, inscribed and dated '–Tower / [Arn]side. / [date cut] 1836.', pencil heightened with white, on blue-grey paper, 23 × 32.8 cm (Yale Center for British Art, B1997.7.34).

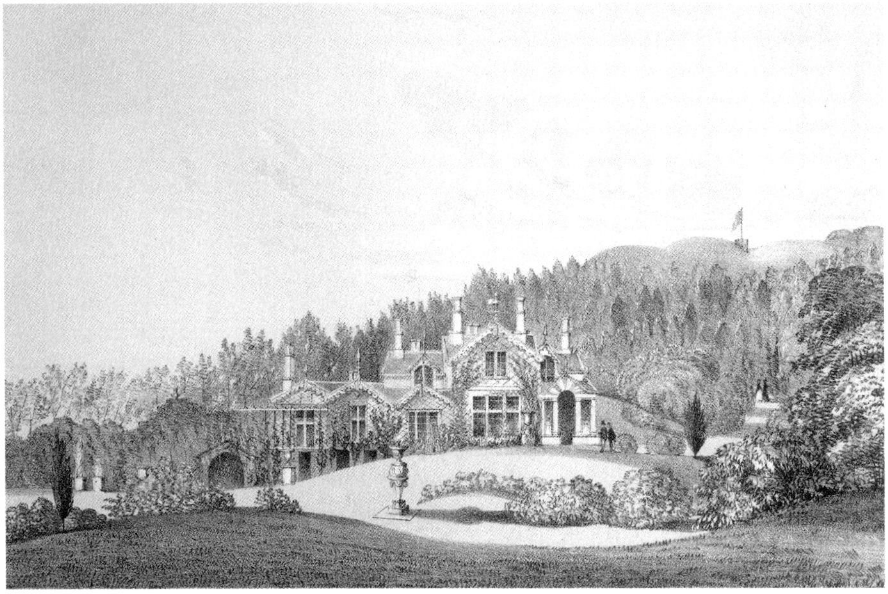

Fig. 15 Eller How; lithograph from E. Twycross, *Mansions of England and Wales: County Palatine of Lancaster*, 1847, Vol. II, plate 31. Eller How was built as a country retreat by Francis Webster *c.*1818; he died there in 1827, and the house was extended by his son George (1797–1864), Lear's host in 1836. (Barrow Library.)

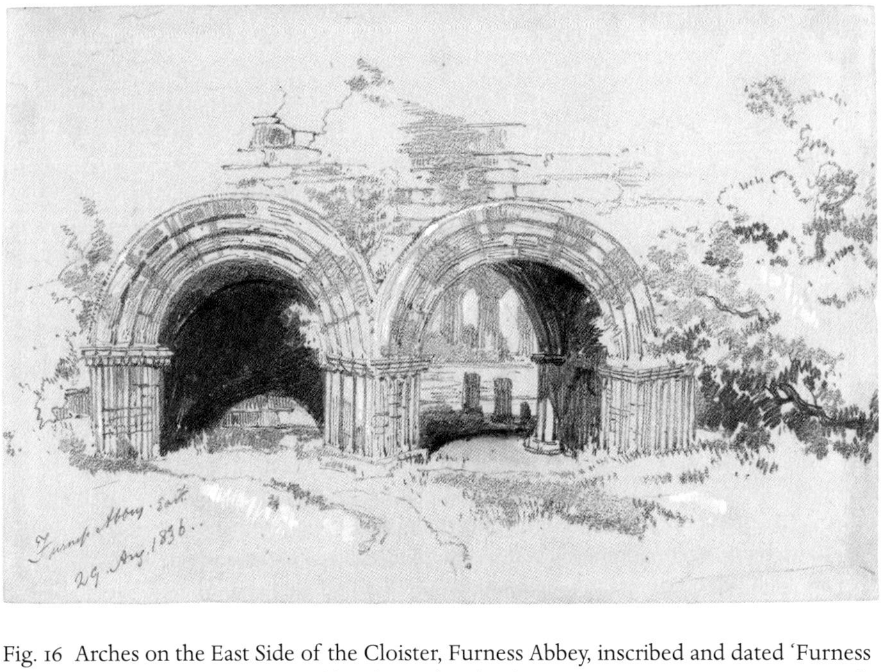

Fig. 16 Arches on the East Side of the Cloister, Furness Abbey, inscribed and dated 'Furness Abbey. East / 29 Aug. 1836.', pencil heightened with white, on grey paper, 20 × 30.5 cm (Yale Center for British Art, B1997.7.23).

I got nevertheless over the hills—& really the Bay of Morecambe is more lovely than anything I ever saw!—I omit parties to see Cartmel Abbey—Lord Burlington's &c &c'. 'Lord Burlington's' is Holker Hall, Cark-in-Cartmel, which Lear's host, George Webster, was to remodel for the Earl in 1838–41.

Eller How was, as Lear implies, not large; it was also full of children, whom Lear describes as 'not nice' (George Webster had four children born between 1829 and 1834, rather too young for the artist to enjoy their company). Lear was probably glad to move on and, avoiding travelling on Sunday, probably left Lindale on the morning of Monday, 29 August; the Whittington letter continues: 'I then went to Dalton—a most outoftheway town in the Peninsula of Furness—hoping to get some sketching at the noble ruins of Furness Abbey … it poured deluges from 5 in the morning till 8 at night—& I played the philosopher for two days in an old Inn where the people scarcely spoke English'. A drawing of the southernmost two of the five arches on the east side of the cloister at Furness Abbey, dated 29 August (fig. 16) confirms the letter, and is the only drawing now locateable recording Lear's visit to the Abbey. A second drawing of the Abbey (now untraced) was sold at Christie's, 20 April 1971, lot 127; the date of 30 August on it confirms Lear's statement that he spent two days there trying to sketch .

In the English Heritage guide to Furness Abbey, first published in 1965, the arches are described as 'a magnificent series of five round-headed arches which constitute one of the glories of the abbey'; it is fortunate that the rain held off long enough for Lear to draw them.

33 *Levens Hall: View from the South-east, with the Gardens and the Howard Tower*

Dated [Augus]t 17 1836
Pencil heightened with white, on blue-grey paper, 23.9 × 35.4 cm
Provenance: presented by the artist to Ralph Nevill, F.S.A. (d. 1917); by descent to his daughter, Mrs B C Bamber; purchased from Mrs B C Bamber in 1942 (£10 for six drawings)

The British Museum (1942-12-11-1)

Illustrated on p. 91

Levens Hall is by far the largest Elizabethan house in Cumbria and, at the time of Lear's visit, was the home of the heiress Mary Howard (d. 1877) and her husband Colonel the Hon. Fulke Greville Howard (d. 1846). It was work for Mrs Greville-Howard which had kept Lear in London in June. In a letter written on 2 June to Lord Derby, Lear wrote: 'I ought to be able to mention the times of my coming to Knowsley, but I am doing some Lithographic drawings for Mrs. Greville=Howard, & as she is out of town, & I have promised to do one more on her return, (which will be, I imagine, in about 10 days,) I am not yet my own master' (*Selected Letters*, p. 21); the subject of these drawings is not known. The medieval tower-house had been much extended, altered and enlarged, most recently, at the time of Lear's visit, by the addition of a tower, known as the Howard Tower, at the south-east corner of the house, which was projected as early as 1807 but not completed until 1820. Lear waxed lyrical about Levens Hall; in the letter written from there (cat. 37) he described it as 'perhaps the finest existing specimen of an antique house' and continued:

> From Henry the 8th's time downward not a thing has been altered about it:—except the Gardens—which are James the 2ds.—& perfectly wonderful in their way: Consider no shrub—no plant ever allowed to grow without cultivation! avenues—[oriels?]—squares—walks of yew trees—centuries old—30 or 40 feet

high—cut into cows—bottles—hats—& every possible shape—unaltered by an inch since 1680!! Imagine turf between walls of high beech trees—all magically shorn quite even—& looking like fable & nonsense!! Then the house itself—every wall & room covered with oak—carved [massively?] a foot deep—the chimnies 8 feet wide,—no grates—only peat burning—the windows recessed—with little cut panes—arms painted on all,—the ceilings fretted—the floors solid oak—chairs tables—buffets—all carved oak,—the chairs highbacked—the sofas of damask or tapestry with pointlace hangings of Cardinal Wolsey's date,—the hall hung profusely with armour—the very staircase scattered with jackboots—gauntlets—& spears of 1400—the bedrooms courious little oaky nooks—gloomy with little windows & crimson tapestry—& approached up turrets by stone stairs—!!—only imagine this! For the reality is far beyond what I can describe. On the whole it is the most perfect piece of antiquity extant,—& if you add to this,—that the people are admirable—& the park & country round exquisite—you won't wonder I am pleased.

Lear also had an excellent social time at Levens, as the letter from Whittington Hall (cat. 40) written nearly two weeks later records: 'I believe I told … how dancing, music, & dining made the time very short:—also how I enjoyed myself at Colonel Howard's—that curious old hall—where ghosts are as common as mice,—& you sit among armour & starched ruffs till you find even your own limbs growing stiff & mouldy'.

34 *Levens Hall: the Interior of the Small Drawing-Room with the Chimneypiece*

Inscribed and dated 'Levens / Aug.18.1836', numbered 7
Pencil heightened with white, 25 × 35.9 cm
Provenance: presented by the artist to Ralph Nevill, F.S.A. (d. 1917); by descent to his daughter, Mrs B C Bamber; purchased from Mrs B C Bamber in 1942 (£10 for six drawings)

The British Museum (1942-12-11-2)

The most recently published guide book, Tattersall's *Lakes of England* (1836), wrote: 'Levens Hall … is more remarkable for its singularity than for intrinsic beauty either of situation or architecture … Like all other old houses, it is inconvenient and dark, with one very wide staircase, and a great many narrow, innumerable passages, and enormous fireplaces; but the oaken carvings with which it abounds are most elaborate and elegant … The Chimney-front in the North Dining-room, (likewise of oak) represents the Five Senses, the Four Seasons, and the Four Elements, supported by Sampson and Hercules' (pp. 17–18).

35 *Study of an Interior at Levens Hall and Studies of Figures at Kendal*

Inscribed and dated lower left 'Levens. / Aug.18. / 1836.', inscribed and dated centre right 'Kendal. / 20t. Aug.', and numbered 187
Pencil, 15.5 × 23 cm
Provenance: presented by Sir Hugh Walpole in 1938

The King's School, Canterbury

Illustrated on p. 92

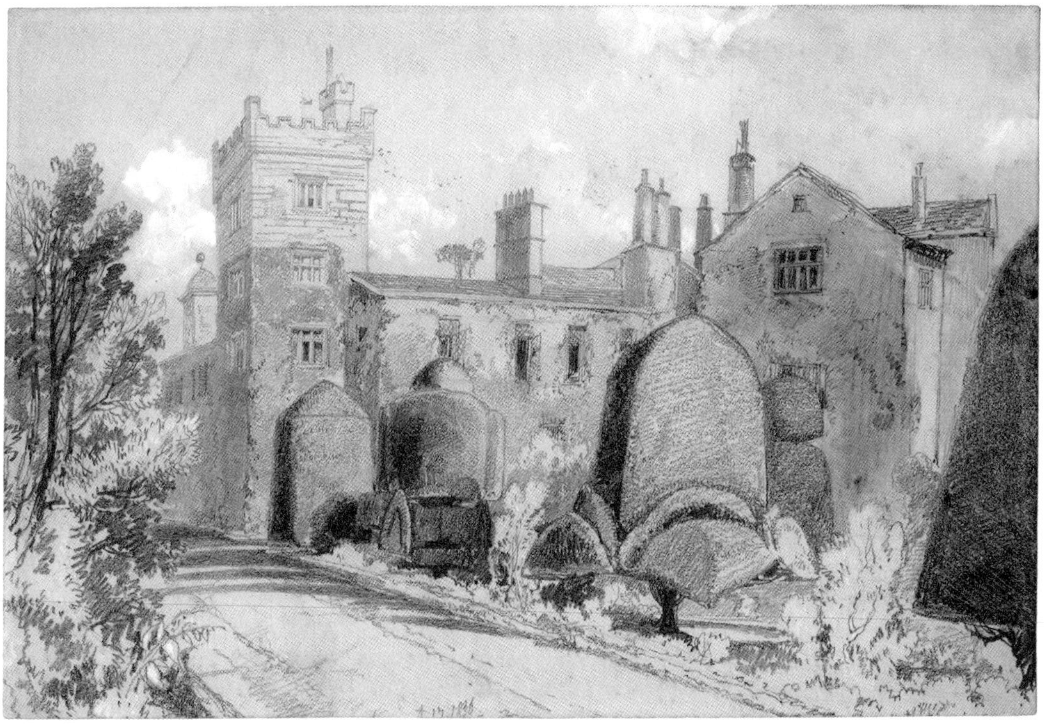

Cat. 33

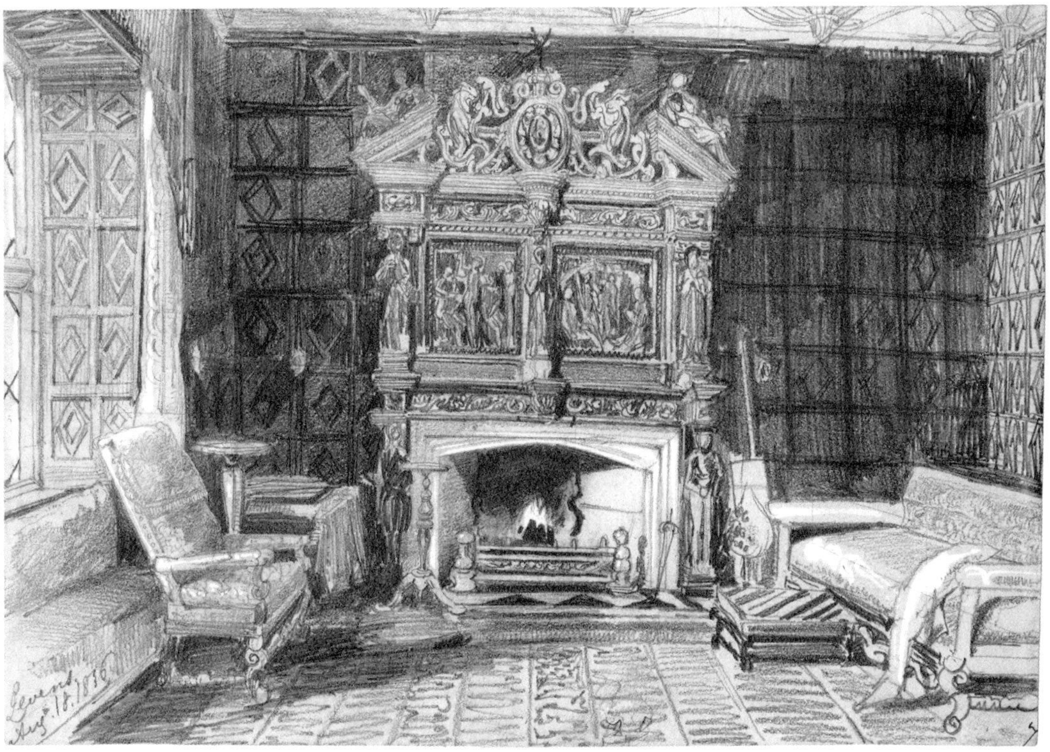

Cat. 34

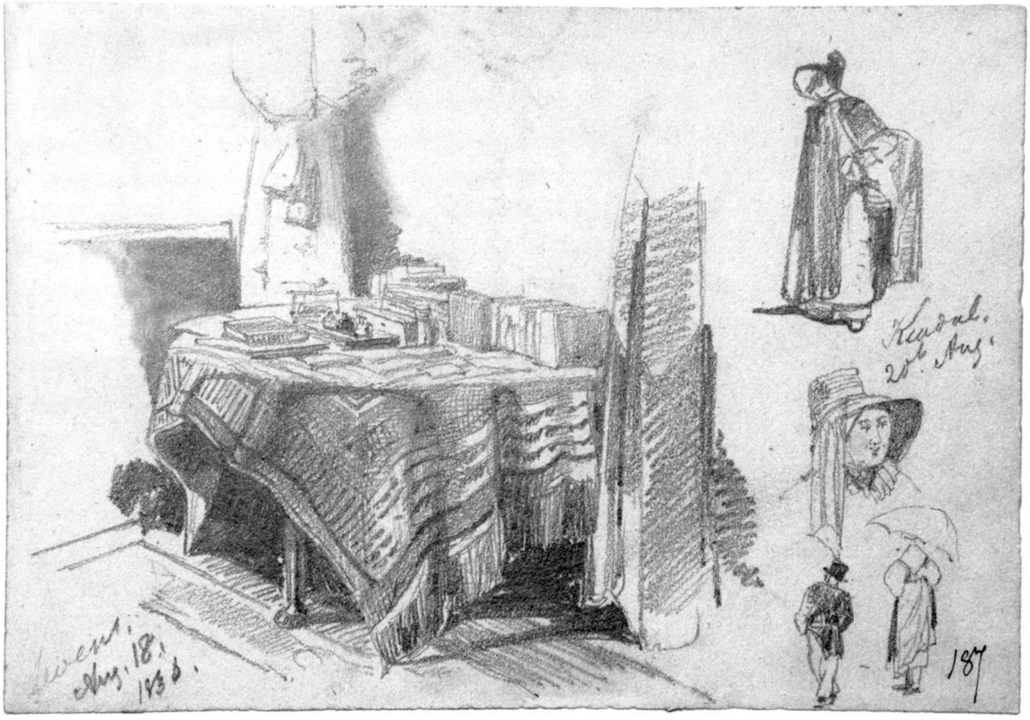

Cat. 35

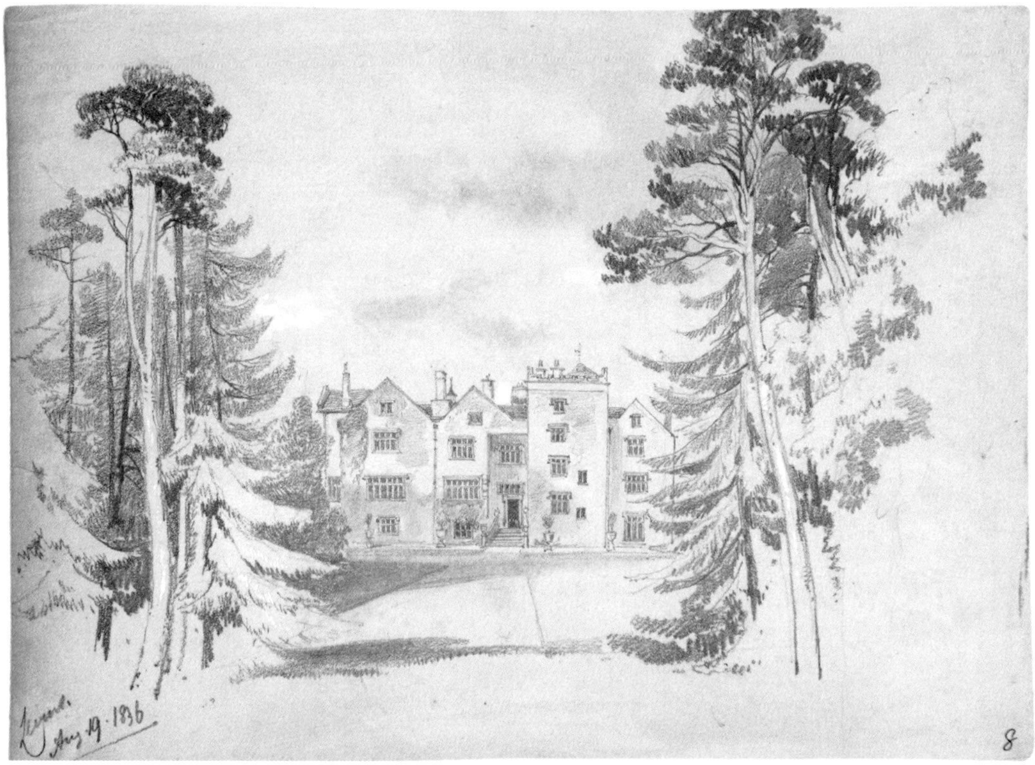

Cat. 36

The drawing at the Houghton Library, 'Umbrellifera, Kendal' (fig. 12, p. 86), is numbered 188, but the view of Levens (cat. 36) is numbered 8, indicating that, at this stage of the tour, Lear was operating two different numbering sequences. On 9 September he began a new sequence (see fig. 21, p. 107 and cat. 41).

36 *Levens Hall: the North Front*

Inscribed and dated lower left 'Levens. / Aug.19. 1836', and numbered 8
Pencil with touches of white heightening, on blue-grey paper, 25.5 × 36 cm
Provenance: presented by Sir Hugh Walpole in 1938

The King's School, Canterbury

37 *Letter to Fanny Coombe, from Levens Hall, Milnthorpe, Westmorland*

24 August 1836
Autograph letter

The Frederick Warne Archive

Illustrated on pp. 94–6; see pp. 215–16 for full text

This very important letter, written from Levens Hall, establishes part of the chronology of Lear's sketching tour; the information contained in it can be confirmed and supplemented by known drawings. The letter describes his leaving Knowsley ('I never remember passing so happy a consecutive 6 weeks as I did this year at Knowsley… knowing that I could not meet with better fun—or better friends elsewhere—I did not set out with all the alacrity with which a tourist ought to begin his journey.'), his visit to the Hornbys in Lancaster, and his arrival at Levens.

Levens is described as 'perhaps the finest existing specimen of an antique house' and 'the most perfect piece of antiquity extant'; its features and characteristics are expounded with all the enthusiasm of a modern tourist brochure. This was in fact Lear's second stay at the house, as he writes towards the end of the letter: 'from Levens I went to Kendal … & din'd there on Sunday [21 August]—Thence I came to Milnthorpe & Dallam Tower … & today [Wednesday 24 August – the letter is written at midnight] I have returned here for some festivities tomorrow.' He continues with his future plans: 'On Friday [26 August] I go to Mr Webster's [Eller How, at Lindale, near Grange-over-Sands; Mr Webster is George Webster, the Kendal architect], & then to Underley—Whittington & Kirby Lonsdale:—after this (for I have not yet seen the Lakes) … to Messrs. Bradylls [Conishead Priory, near Ulverston]—Townleys [Town Head, near Newby Bridge]—Starkies [Fell Foot, near Newby Bridge]—& Col: Boltons on Windermere [Storrs Hall]—so I shall stand a chance of seeing some society.'

Lear starts the letter 'I am already half asleep', and ends it 'I am worn out', giving a sketch of his daily routine: 'I get up at 5—walk all day—& [dine?] at 7, I am generally done for by 12'. As is shown by the other letter that survives from the tour, written from Whittington Hall, near Kirkby Lonsdale, on 6 September (cat. 40), Lear did not exactly stick to the itinerary given here; he actually visited Conishead Priory *before* heading back to Underley and Whittington Hall. Armed with the letters of introduction he describes at the beginning this letter, his ports of call did not change, only the order in which he visited them.

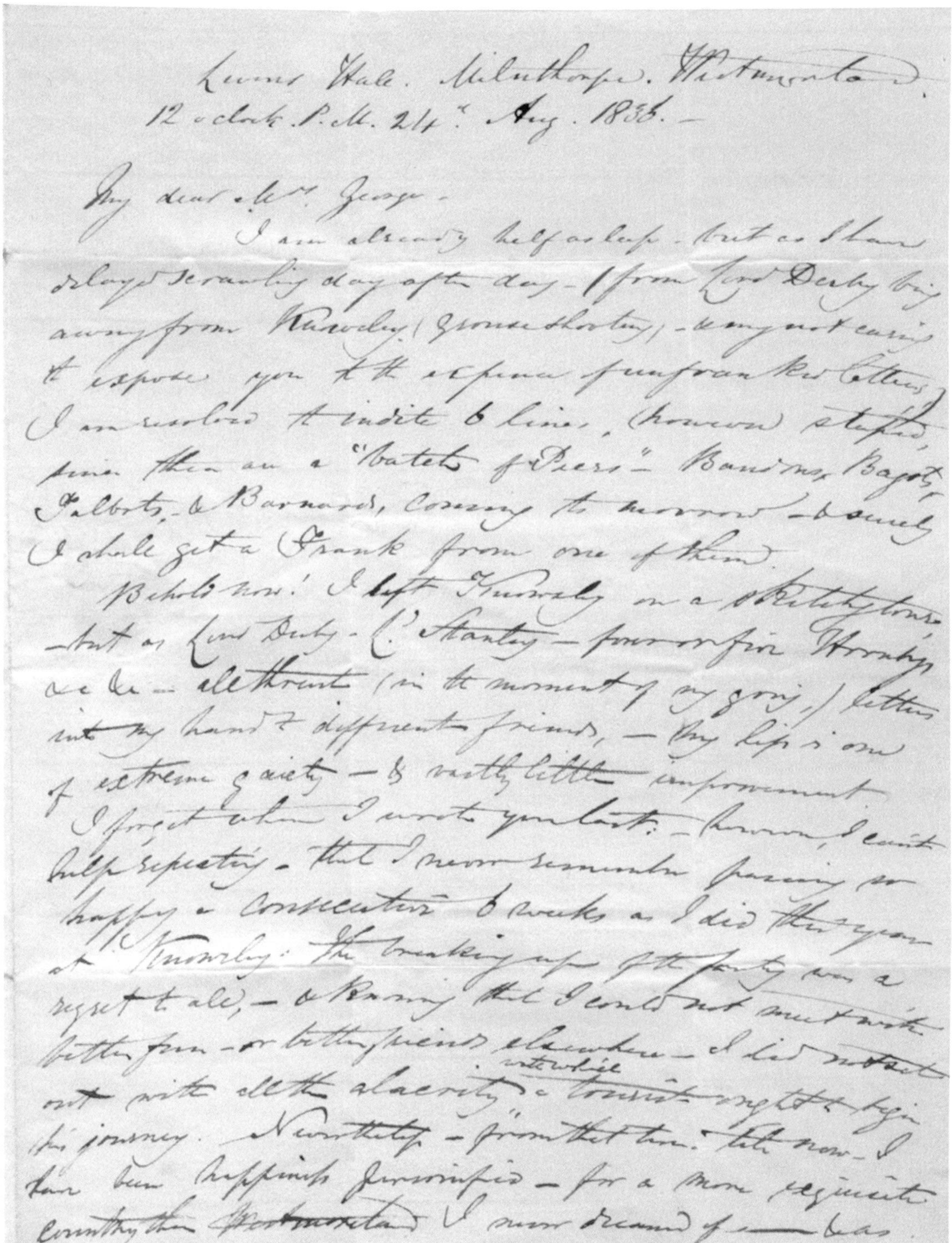

Levens Hall. Milnthorpe. Westmorland.
12 o'clock P.M. 24th Aug. 1836.–

My dear Mr George.–

I am already half asleep – but as I have delayed scrawling day after day – (from Lord Derby being away from Knowsley (grouse shooting) – & my not caring to expose you to the expence of unfranked letters) I am resolved to indite 6 lines, however stupid, since there are a "batch of Peers" – Bandons, Bagots, Talbots, & Barnards, coming to morrow – & surely I shall get a Frank from one of them.

Behold now! I left Knowsley on a sketching tour – but as Lord Derby – (& Stanley – four or five Hornbys &c &c – all thrust (in the moment of my going,) letters into my hand to different friends, – my life is one of extreme gaiety – & vastly little improvement.

I forget when I wrote you last: – however, I can't help repeating – that I never remember passing so happy & consecutive 6 weeks as I did this year at Knowsley: the breaking up of the party was a regret to all, – & knowing that I could not meet with better fun – or better friends elsewhere – I did not set out with all the alacrity (otherwise) a tourist ought to begin his journey. Nevertheless – from that time till now – I have been happiness personified – for a more exquisite country than Westmorland I never dreamed of – tho' as.

Cat. 37

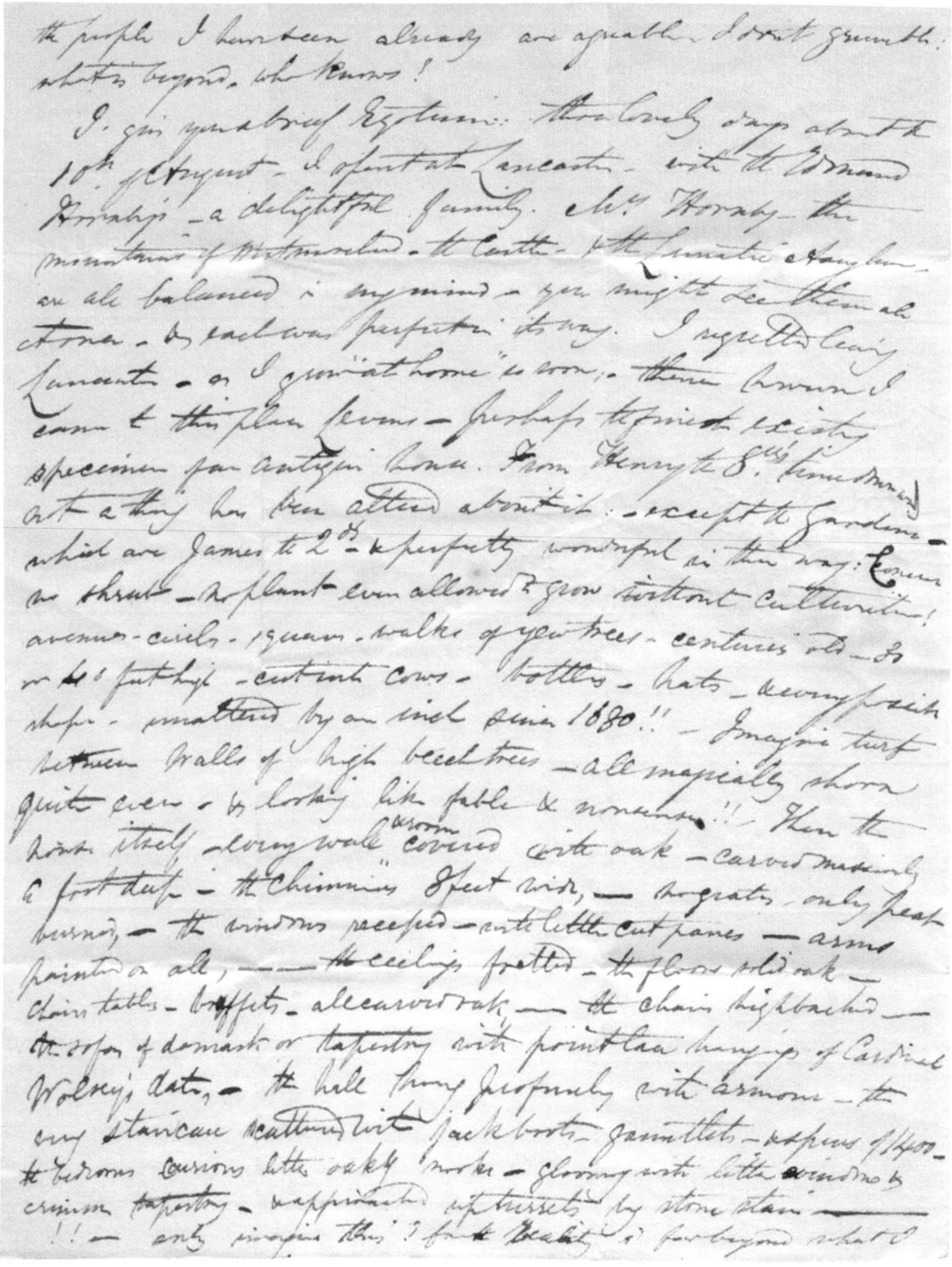
the people I have seen already are agreeable. I don't grumble: what's beyond, who knows!

I give you a brief Synopsis: three lovely days about the 10th of August, I spent at Lancaster with the Edmund Hornbys — a delightful family. Mrs Hornby — the mountains of Westmoreland — the Castle — & the Lunatic Asylum — are all balanced in my mind — you might see them all at once — & each was perfect in its way. I regretted leaving Lancaster — as I grow at home so soon; — thence however I came to this place Levens — perhaps the finest existing specimen of an antique house. From Henry the 8th's time downward not a thing has been altered about it — except the Gardens which are James the 2d — & perfectly wonderful in their way: Scarce one shrub — no plant even allowed to grow without cultivation! avenues — circles — squares — walks of yew trees — centuries old — 30 or 40 feet high — cut into cows — bottles — hats — every possible shape — unaltered by an inch since 1680!! — Imagine turf between walls of high beech trees — all magically shorn quite even — & looking like fable & nonsense!! Then the house itself — every wall & room covered with oak — carved massively 6 foot deep — the chimneys 8 feet wide, — no grates — only peat burning — the windows recessed — with little cut panes — arms painted on all, — the ceilings fretted — the floors solid oak — chairs tables — buffets — all carved oak, — the chairs high backed — the sofas of damask or tapestry with point lace hangings of Cardinal Wolsey's date, — the hall hung profusely with armour — the very staircase scattered with jack boots — gauntlets — & pieces of 1400 — the bedrooms curious little oaky nooks — gloomy with little windows & crimson tapestry — & approached up turrets by stone stairs — !!! — only imagine this! I find Reality is far beyond what I

Cat. 37

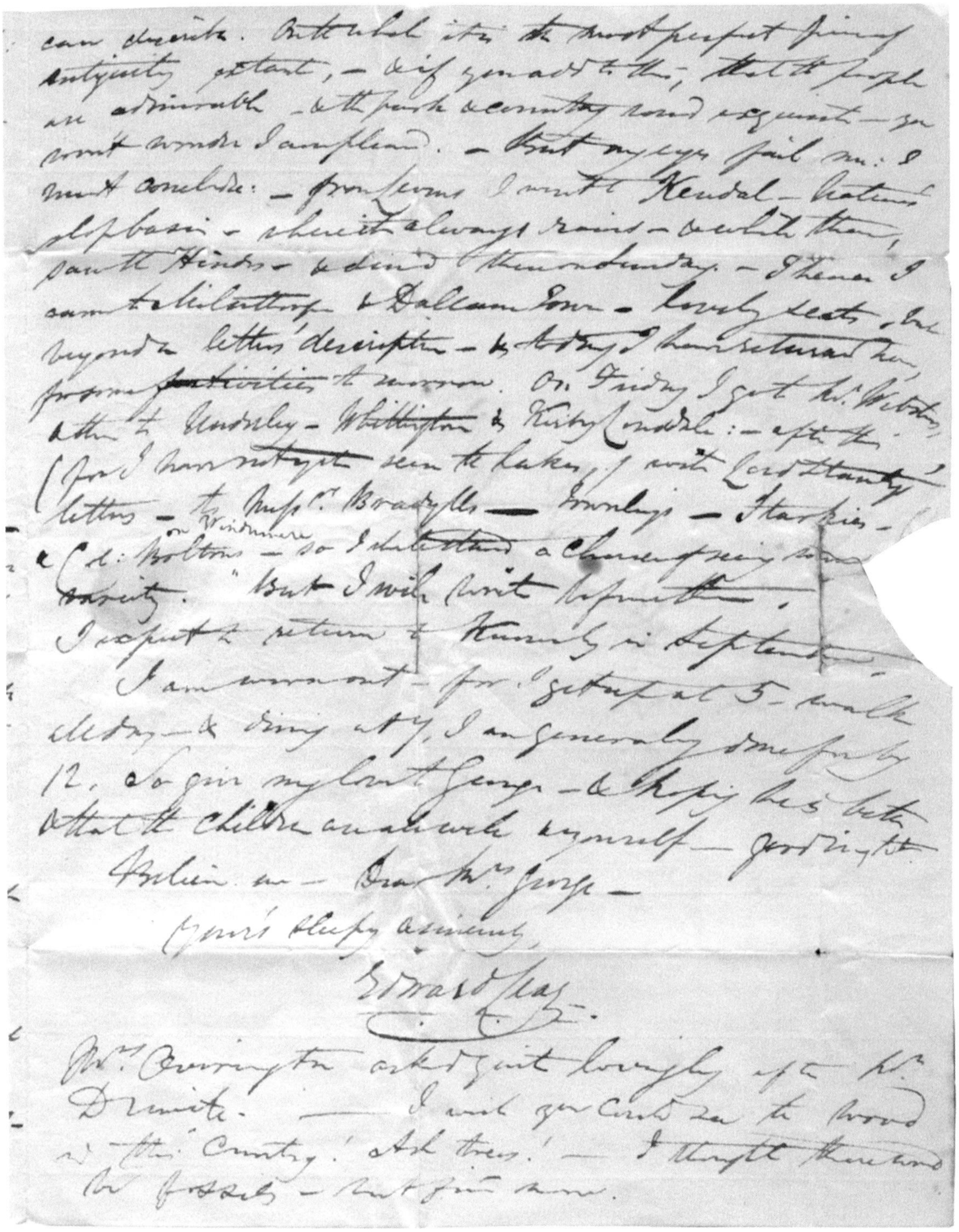

can describe. On the whole it is the most perfect piece of antiquity extant, — & if you add to this, that the people are admirable — & the park & country round exquisite — you won't wonder I am pleased. — But my eyes fail me: I must conclude: — tomorrow I went to Kendal — hateful slop basin — where it always rains — & while there, saw the Hindes — & dined there on Sunday. — Thence I came to Milnthorpe & Dallam Tower — lovely seats, but beyond a letter's description — & today I have returned here from ~~festivities~~ tomorrow. On Friday I got Mr. Webster's letter to Underley — ~~Whittington~~ & Kirby Lonsdale: — after this (for I have ~~not yet~~ seen the lakes,) I wait Lord Stanley's letters — to Mrs. Cr. Braddylls — Towneley's — Starkie's — Col: Boltons on Windermere — so I shall have a chance of seeing some variety. But I will write before then.
I expect to return to Knowsley in September.

I am worn out — for I get up at 5 — walk all day — & dine at 7. I am generally done up by 12. So give my love to George — & I hope he's better & that the Children are all well & yourself — good night.

Believe me — Dear Mrs. George —

Your's sleepy & sincerely

Edward Lear.

Mrs. Orrington asked quite lovingly after Mr. Drewitt. — I wish you could see the wood in this country! Ash trees! — I thought there would be fossils — but find none.

Cat. 37

End of August – 8 September
from Conishead to Windermere

It may have been Lear's intention to go on a sketching tour, but the young artist was fond of company and his letters often describe musical parties; as he wrote on 24 August, 'my life is one of extreme gaiety—& vastly little improvement' (cat. 37), and again on 6 September, 'dancing, music, & dining made the time very short' (cat. 40). After spending a damp couple of days staying at an inn in Dalton-in-Furness, Lear was very glad to pay a visit to Colonel Thomas Braddyll at Conishead Priory just to the south of Ulverston; as he later wrote: 'So then I set off with a note from Lord Derby—to the finest house in these parts— Mr Bradyll's—whose family are Saxon, & so old, that Adam is supposed to have been brought up in it. Conceive any place so lovely!—Enormous sycamores & ash bury it—great rocks shelter it from cold—& all the slopes down to the sea—where the Bay appears on each side & on one hand Helvellyn—the other far in the distance Pile Castle & the Isle of Man!—the landscape shown was my least pleasure: for the 3 Miss Bradylls are 20 degrees beyond perfection—& what with all sorts of singing & music with them, their father, & Brother, & Admiral Sotheran,—a band of 2 accordions-flute-harp-guitar & piano—we minded not the rain a tittle' (cat. 40).

At the time of Lear's visit, Conishead Priory (fig. 17) had been partly rebuilt in the Gothic style by Philip Wyatt; he was employed in 1821 but dismissed for lack of progress in 1828. The house was eventually completed by George Webster between 1839 and 1844; it is now the Manjushri Buddhist Centre.

Lear's letter of 6 September (cat. 40) implies that he spent more than just a night at Conishead, but, with only one recorded dated drawing, it is impossible to know for sure; a drawing inscribed 'Charley, a King Charles Spaniel of Conishead Priory' and dated 1 September 1836, was sold at Sotheby's, 2 May 1962, lot 24 (current location unknown). Aside from drawing one of the Braddyll family dogs, Lear certainly had time to explore the surrounding countryside, but only one drawing is now

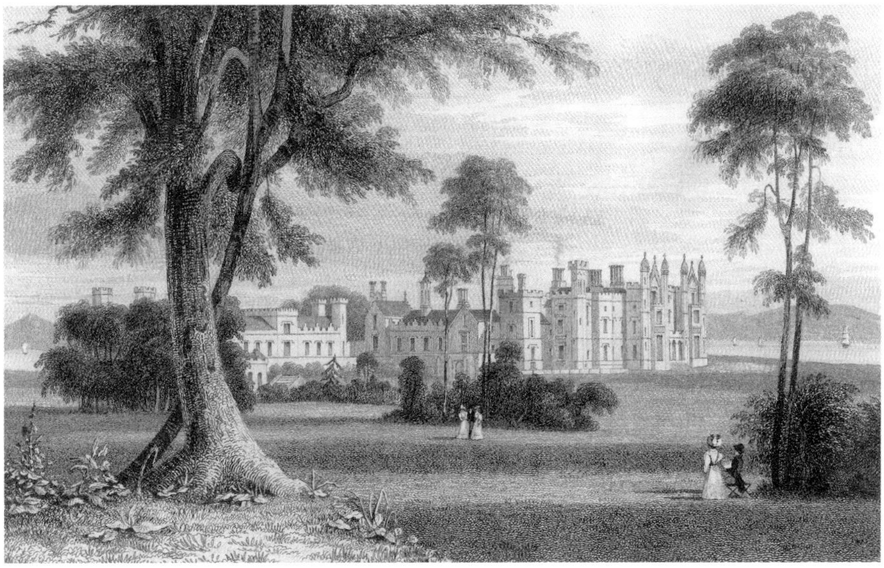

Fig. 17 'Conishead-Priory, near Ulverston', engraving after J. Harwood, 1830, from *Lancashire Illustrated, from Original Drawings, by S. Austin, J. Harwood, and G. & C. Pyne, with Descriptions*, 1831 (Private Collection).

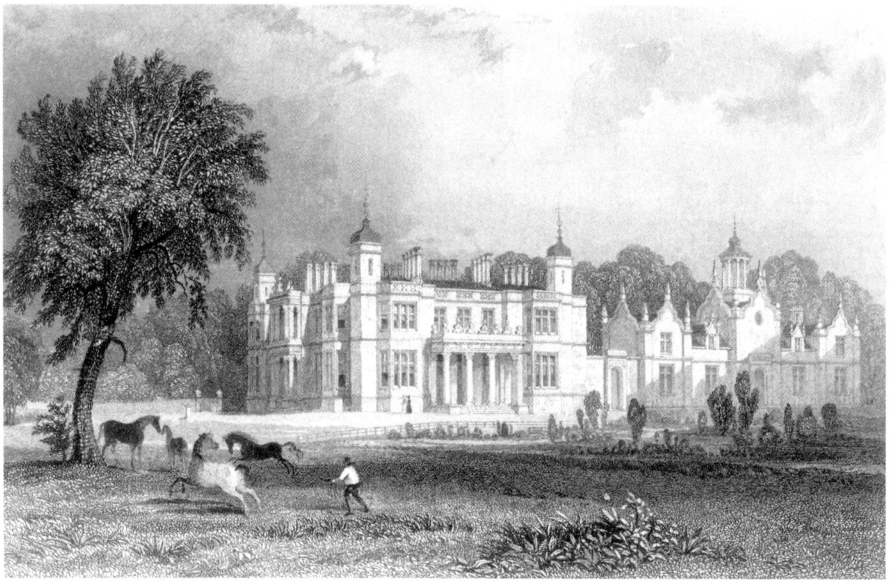

Fig. 18 'Underlay Hall, Westmorland', engraving after Thomas Allom, 1834, from *Westmorland, Cumberland, Durham, and Northumberland, Illustrated. From Original Drawings by Thomas Allom, George Pickering, &c. with Descriptions by T. Rose*, 1832–5 (The Wordsworth Trust).

locateable which records this aspect of the visit (cat. 38). According to the letter, in the first few days of September, Lear travelled from Conishead to Ingmire Hall near Sedbergh, home of the Upton family, and then south to Underley Hall near Kirkby Lonsdale. Underley Hall (fig. 18) had been recently built by George Webster in 1825–8 for Alexander Nowell, who had made a fortune in India; Lord Derby's letters of introduction gave the young artist the opportunity to mix with new money as well as old, and he wrote on the 6th, 'Of Underley, I may add, that Mr Nowell its proprietor is a rich possessor of East Indn. property, and the valuable splendour there beats credibility!—& such living! curries! pilaus! champagnes!—Dear me!' Lear was probably at Underley on 4 or 5 September before moving on to Whittington Hall, but only one drawing (cat. 39) survives from this period to confirm the content of the letter, which hints at the likely subject matter of drawings which are no longer extant. His intention after leaving Underley was to pass through Kendal and stay at Storrs Hall on Windermere before beginning his tour of the lakes. Lear had been having a fine time partying in the houses of Lancashire and Westmorland, and wrote on 6 September: 'At this place & here & elsewhere—nothing can be more friendly or hospitable, & I assure you that I leave each batch of new friends with regret' (cat. 40).

38 *View to the North from Birkrigg, Furness, Lancashire*

Signed '[E]. Lear.del.', dated 1837, and inscribed on the reverse
Pencil, black chalk and stump, on blue-grey paper, 8.9 × 17.2 cm
Provenance: the Braddyll family, Conishead Priory (?); Robert A. Hornby (d. 1857); Anon. Sale; Sotheby's, 18 Mar. 1982, lot 13 (3 in lot) (£1,200); Anon. Sale; Sotheby's, 20 Nov. 1986, lot 11 (with 1 other) (£750); Spink, English Watercolour Drawings, Annual Exhibition, 1987, no. 25 (£1,600); John Dayton (d.2003); Anon. Sale; Sotheby's, 30 July 2005, lot 282 (£1,200), acquired by the present owner
The Wordsworth Trust (2006.47.2)

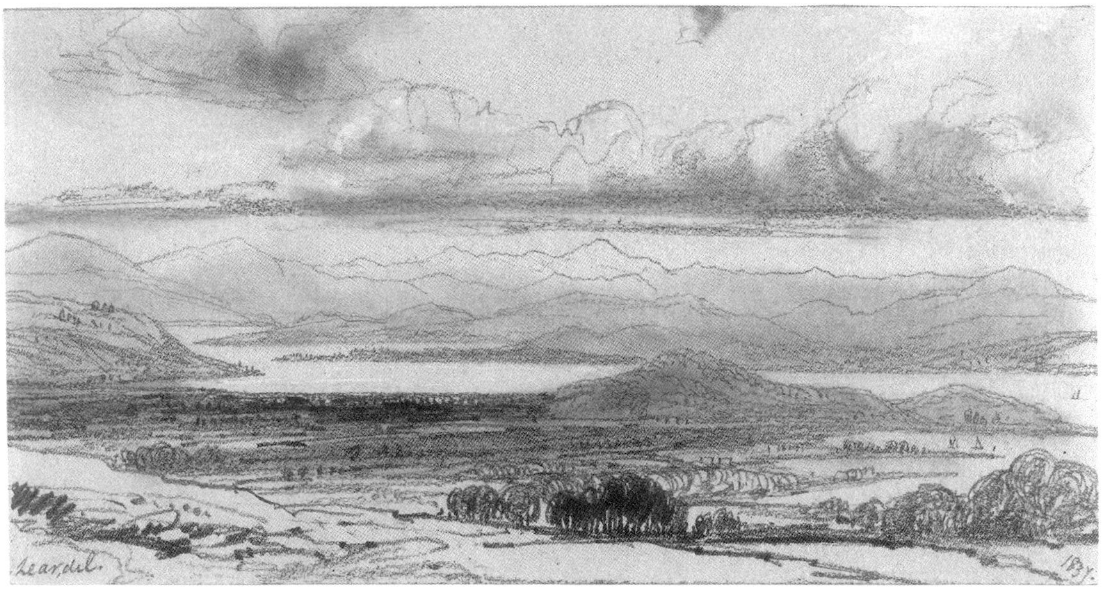

Cat. 38

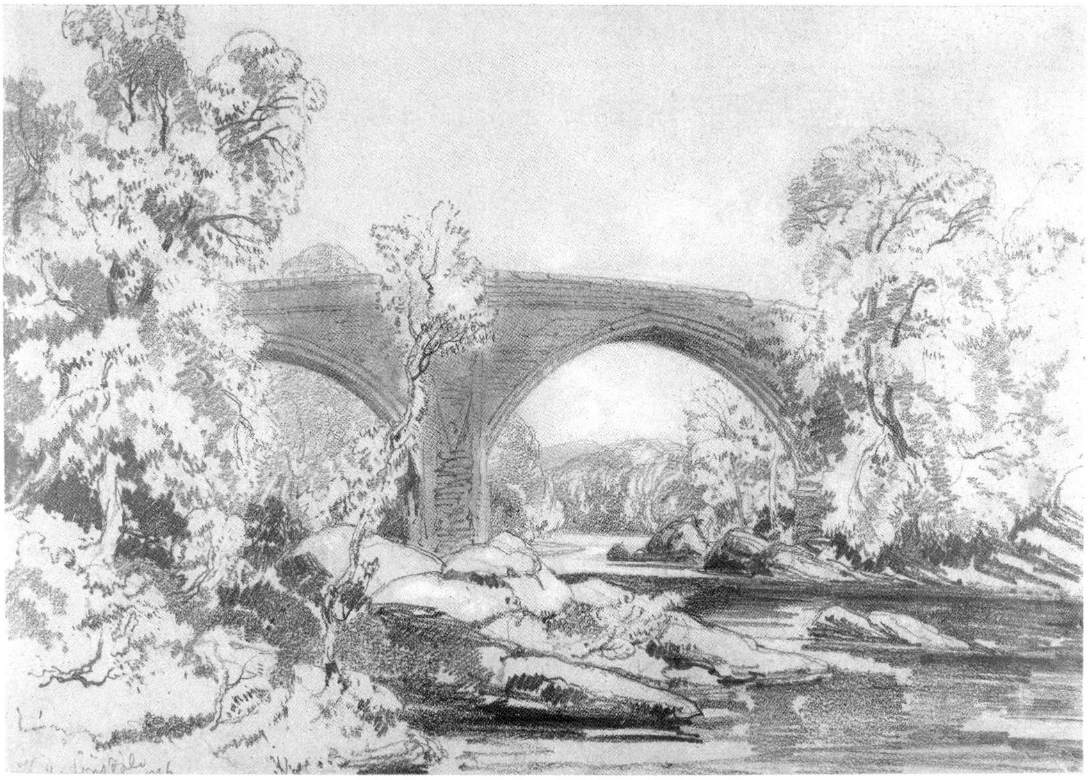

Cat. 39

This is one of the few drawings to survive which derive from Lear's stay at Conishead; it is dated 1837 but is based on a sketch made in early September 1836. Originally one of three drawings showing the view in different directions from Birkrigg, the limestone outcrop to the south of Ulverston, this may have been a commission from the Braddyll family, Lear's hosts at Conishead, and is therefore one of the 'pencil drawings (18 or 20) ordered for sundry Lancashire folks', mentioned in his letter of 3 January 1837. Joseph Onwhyn's *Pocket Guide to the Lakes* (London: 1841) described the view: 'Birkrigg Fell is of no great elevation; it adjoins the common, or is in fact part of it; and it is worthwhile for the tourist to leave the main road in order to gain the summit ... The prospect, in the direction of Ulverston, is ... of infinite beauty; it is the best bird's eye view of Ulverston town that can be had; and the mountains beyond, streaking the whole edge of the horizon with their wavy summits, have a remarkably fine effect' (p. 139).

39 *The Devil's Bridge, Kirkby Lonsdale, Westmorland*

Inscribed and dated '[Kirkby] Lonsdale / [183]6'
Pencil heightened with white, on buff paper, 24 × 34.8 cm
Provenance: William Nevill (d. 1874), a friend and contemporary of the artist; by descent to Ralph Nevill, F.S.A. (d. 1917); Anon. Sale: Sotheby's, 24 Sept. 1987, lot 71 (£620 to Spink); Spink, Annual Exhibition, 1988, no. 41 (£2,500); purchased by the current owner from James Thompson, Kirkby Lonsdale, in 1992 or 1993

Private Collection

Illustrated on p. 99

Until the appearance of the letter written to George Coombe from Whittington Hall on 6 September (cat. 40), Lear's exact movements on his tour could only be inferred from dated drawings. Although the date on this drawing has been cut off, the evidence of the letter means that it has to have been drawn in early September. The Whittington letter records visits to Ingmire Hall, a mile to the west of Sedbergh, and Underley Hall, a mile to the north of Kirkby Lonsdale, before his arrival at Whittington, two miles to the south of the town down the Lune valley. It is most likely that this view of the Devil's Bridge, which is taken from the west bank of the Lune looking upstream through the bridge, was drawn on the short journey between Underley and Whittington, which Lear probably made on 5 September.

Edward Baines published his *Companion to the Lakes of Cumberland, Westmoreland, and Lancashire* in 1829. It was a popular book, and a second edition 'with a new, copious, and correct Itinerary' was published in 1830; Lear probably used the third edition of 1834. This edition described the Devil's Bridge as follows: 'The bridge is of immemorial antiquity; it is a long, lofty, firm and handsome structure, but ... narrow ... At least no two carriages of a larger size can pass each other ... Like many other very clever works executed in difficult circumstances, this bridge has been ascribed to the devil' (pp. 46–7).

40 *Letter to George Coombe, from Whittington Hall, Kirkby Lonsdale*

6 September 1836
Autograph letter

The Frederick Warne Archive

Illustrated on pp. 103–6; see pp. 217–18 for full text

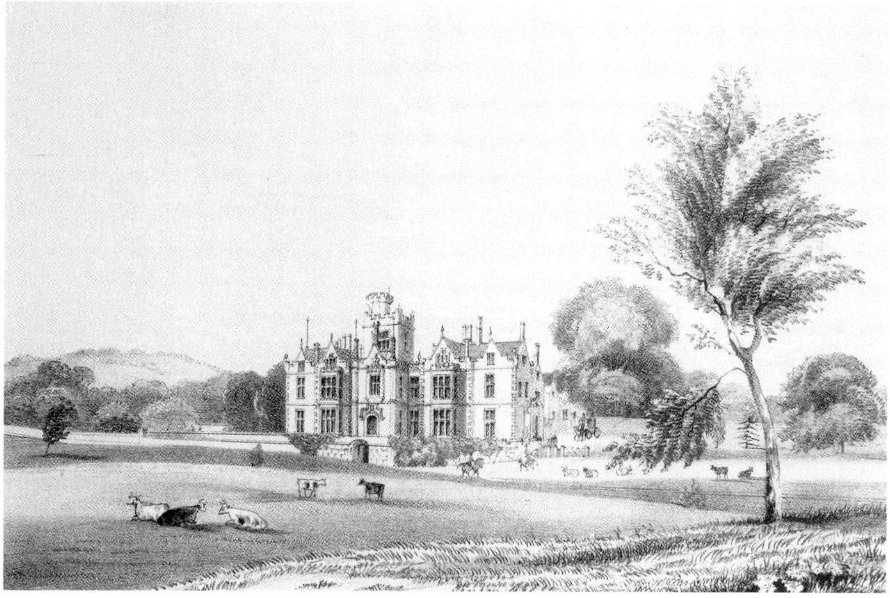

Fig. 19 Whittington Hall, lithograph from E. Twycross, *Mansions of England and Wales: County Palatine of Lancaster*, 1847, Vol. II, plate 9 (Barrow Library).

This is the longer of the two letters that survive from Lear's 1836 tour, and was written from Whittington Hall (fig. 19), a few miles to the south of Kirkby Lonsdale. At the time of Lear's visit Whittington had been newly rebuilt to the designs of his recent host George Webster; it was constructed between 1831 and 1836, replacing the home of the Sunderland family (the Lake District amateur artist Thomas Sunderland had been born there in 1744). Lear's host at Whittington was Thomas Greene (1794–1872), MP for Lancaster, who had purchased the estate piecemeal during the 1820s.

The letter is full of information about Lear's recent movements and his future plans:

> I have now been a month in the Lake Country—& have seen nothing of a Lake at all! … almost all this time I have only made studies of rain … In Consequence of this wet season, I have been paying a succession of visits—pleasures & palaces, one after another—& just enough of fair sunshine, to get a ramble now & then in this most lovely of all counties. Wales is in my opinion—far below Westmoreland,—the foliage—the forms of the hills, here are all superior.—I believe I told Mrs George how I staid at Lancaster on leaving Knowsley—how I saw the prison & the Lunatic Asylum—& other sundries: how dancing, music, & dining made the time very short:—also how I enjoyed myself at Colonel Howard's [Levens Hall] … also how I went to the Wet City of Kendal, where it always rains … spent another week at Col: Howards after this … Followed this—a visit to Ellerhow—where there were Mr Webster's good natured family … Some exquisite scrambles I got nevertheless over the hills—& really the Bay of Morecambe is more lovely than anything I ever saw!—I omit parties to see Cartmel Abbey—Lord Burlingtons &c &c. I then went to Dalton—a most outoftheway [*sic*] town in the Peninsula of Furness—hoping to get some sketching at the noble ruins of Furness Abbey … I played the philosopher for

two days in an old Inn where the people scarcely spoke English—till I was tired. So then I set off with a note from Lord Derby—to the finest house in these parts— Mr Bradyll's [Conishead Priory, fig. 17, p. 97] … that splendid priory,—how sorry I was to leave it !—But I did, &—(still in the rain,) I came to Ingmire Hall—Underley Hall—& now Whittington hall: of all which I may say—they are exquisite mansions full of pleasant society in a lovely country … I go today to sloppy Kendal! … Tomorrow I go to my last visit,—Col: Bolton's of Stoors, I believe the finest seat in the Lakes.

Storrs Hall (fig. 20), the last grand house which it is known that Lear visited before heading into the central lakes, was the home of Colonel John Bolton (1756–1837), a Liverpool shipping magnate, who had made a fortune from the slave trade. Bolton had bought the estate in 1806 and had had the house designed in 1808–10 by Joseph Michael Gandy (1771–1843); he was quite elderly at the time of Lear's visit and died early the following year. It was at Storrs that Lear must have met the Staniforths, whom he mentions staying with in his letter to John Gould written after returning to Knowsley (see Appendix B), since the Rev. Thomas Staniforth (1807–1887) was John Bolton's heir, his mother Mary Littledale being sister to Bolton's wife Elizabeth; possibly, given John Bolton's age, the Staniforths were acting as hosts at Storrs. Constable had stayed in the earlier house on the site thirty years earlier; Lear was probably there from 7 to 9 September. He must have known that he was not getting enough work done, and that the time had come to stop partying and get on with the sketching tour; his letter of 6 September continues: 'I have *refused*—(don't stare,) to go to Lord Lonsdale's—(Lowther Castle,) as this sort of life is all very fine—but very improper. I expect to meet a very gay party—Lowthers & Littledales at Storrs—& from *there*—I intend taking walks from different Inns all over the Lakes: that's if the weather is tolerant—if not—I shall toddle back to Knowsly.' It was from this point that the real work of the sketching tour began.

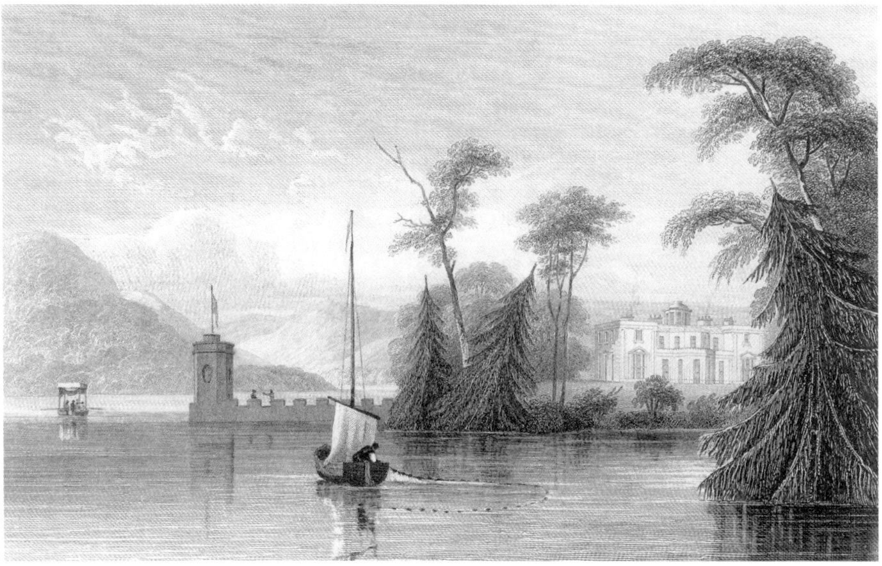

Fig. 20 'Storrs, Windermere Lake', engraving after J. Harwood, 1830, from *Lancashire Illustrated, from Original Drawings, by S. Austin, J. Harwood, and G. & C. Pyne, with Descriptions*, 1831 (Private Collection).

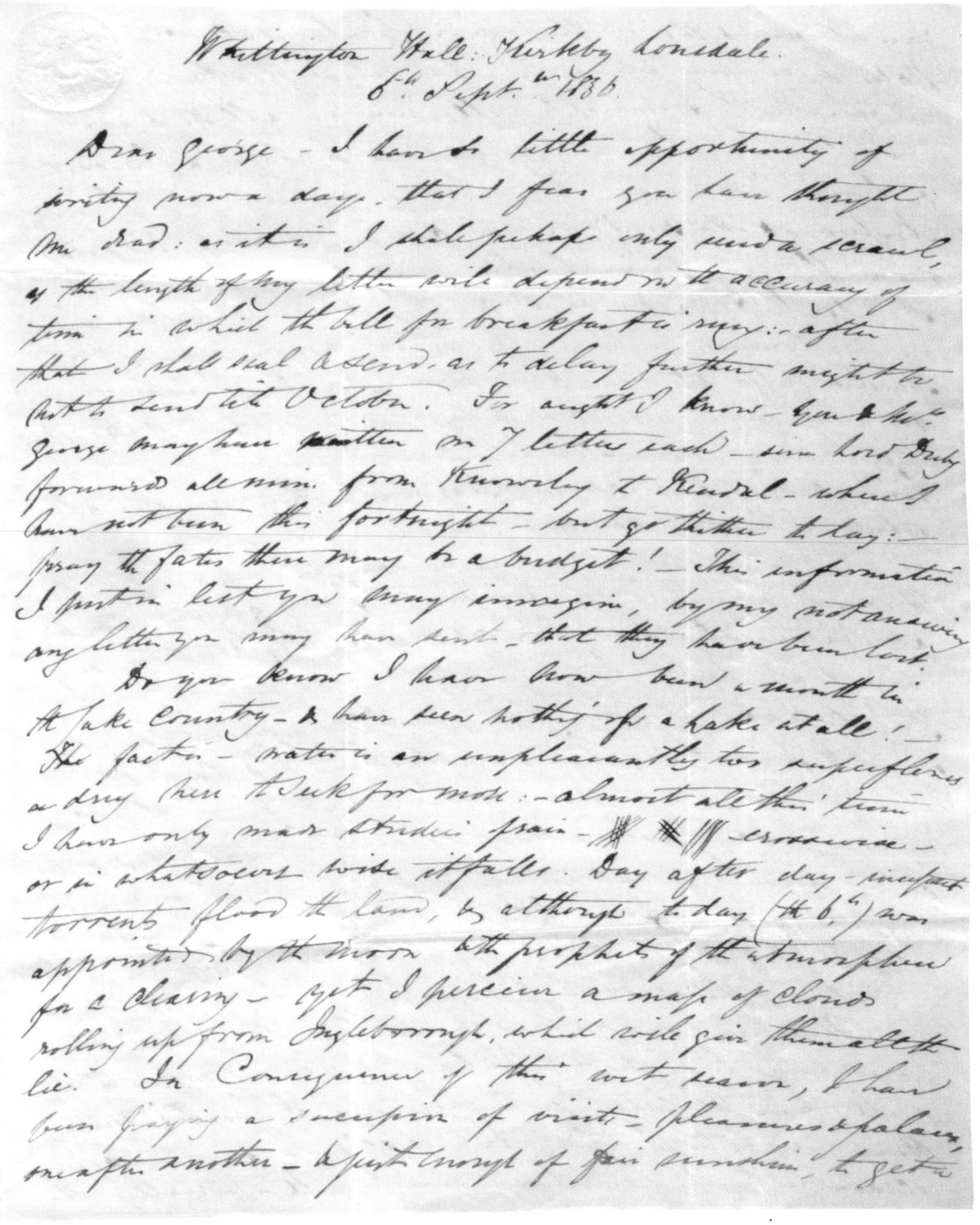
Whittington Hall: Kirkby Lonsdale.
6th Sept. 1836.

Dear George – I have so little opportunity of writing now a days, that I fear you have thought me dead: as it is I shall perhaps only send a scrawl, as the length of my letter will depend on the accuracy of time in which the bell for breakfast is rung: – after that I shall seal & send, as to delay further might be not to send till October. For aught I know – Ayre & Mr George may have written me 7 letters each – since Lord Derby forwarded all mine from Knowsley to Kendal – where I have not been this fortnight – but go thither today: – pray the fates there may be a budget! – This information I put in lest you may imagine, by my not answering any letter you may have sent – that they have been lost.

Do you know I have now been a month in the Lake Country – & have seen nothing of a Lake at all! – The fact is – water is so unpleasantly too superfluous a drug here to seek for more: – almost all this time I have only made studies of rain – //// \\\\ //// – crosswise – or in whatsoever wise it falls. Day after day – incessant torrents flood the land, & although today (the 6th) was appointed by the moon & the prophets of the atmosphere for a clearing – yet I perceive a mass of clouds rolling up from Ingleborough, which will give them all the lie. In consequence of this wet season, I have been paying a succession of visits – pleasures & palaces, one after another – in spite though of fair sunshine, to get a

Cat. 40

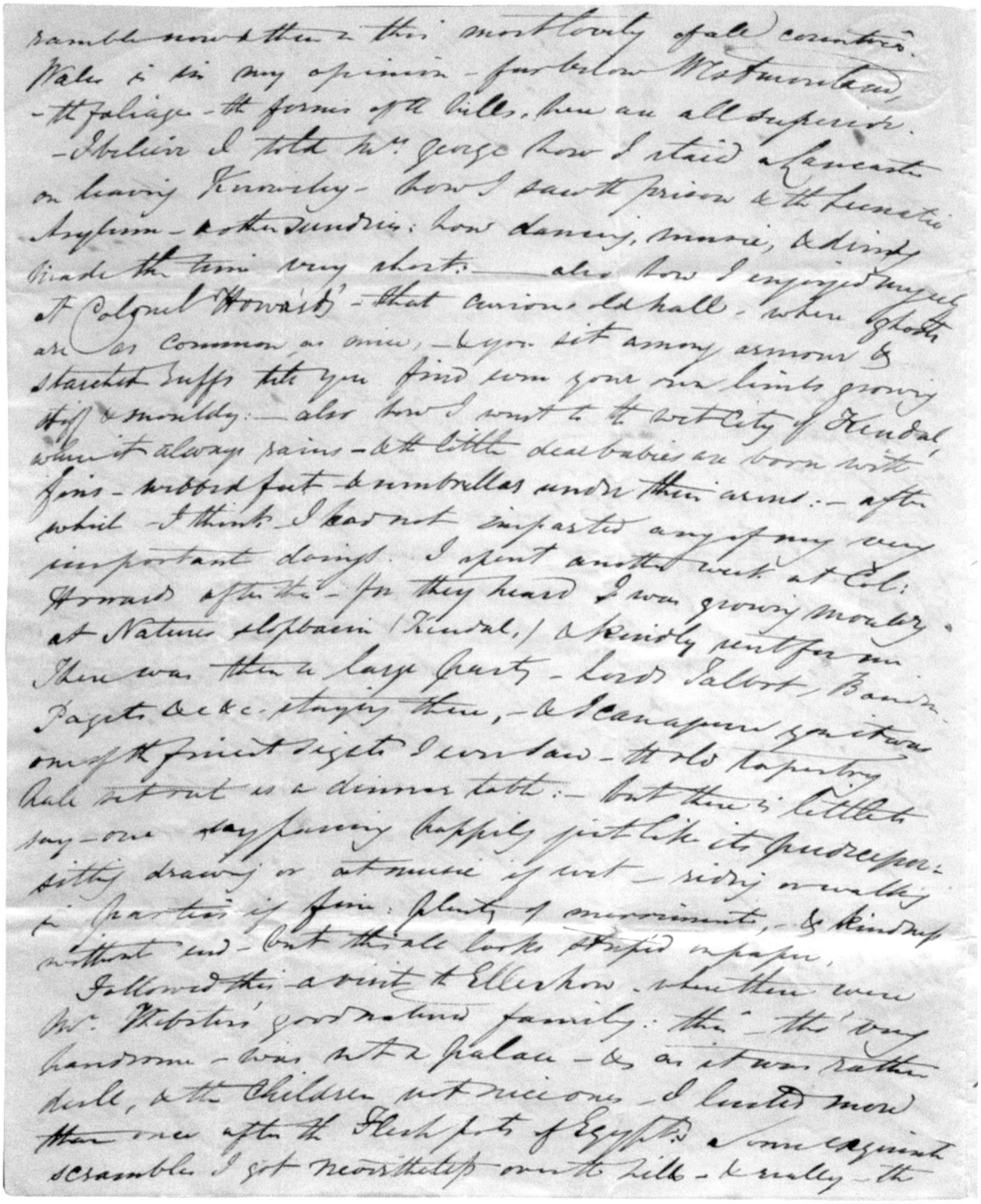

ramble now & then in this most lovely of all countries.
Wales is in my opinion – far below Westmoreland
– the foliage – the forms of the hills, here are all superior.
– I believe I told Mr George how I staid at Lancaster
on leaving Knowsley – how I saw the prison & the Lunatic
Asylum – & other sundries: how dancing, music, & drinking
made the time very short: — also how I enjoyed myself
at Colonel Howard's – that curious old hall – where Ghosts
are as common as mice, – & you sit among armour &
starched ruffs till you find even your own limbs growing
stiff & mouldy: — also how I went to the wet City of Kendal
where it always rains – & the little dear babies are born with
fins – webbed feet – & umbrellas under their arms: – after
which – I think I had not imparted any of my very
important doings. I spent another week at Col:
Howard's after this – for they heard I was growing mouldy
at Nature's slopbasin (Kendal,) & kindly sent for me.
There was then a large party – Lord Talbot, Bonds,
Pagets &c &c. staying there, – & I can assure you it was
one of the finest sights I ever saw – the old tapestry
hall set out as a dinner table: – but there is little to
say – one day passing happily just like its predecessor:
sitting drawing or at music if wet – riding or walking
in parties if fine: plenty of merriment, – & kindness
without end – but this all looks stupid on paper.
Followed this a visit to Ellershaw – where there were
Mr. Webster's good natured family: this – tho' very
handsome – was not a palace – & as it was rather
dull, & the children not nice ones – I lusted more
than once after the Flesh pots of Egypt. Some exquisite
scramble I got nevertheless over the hills – & really – the

Cat. 40

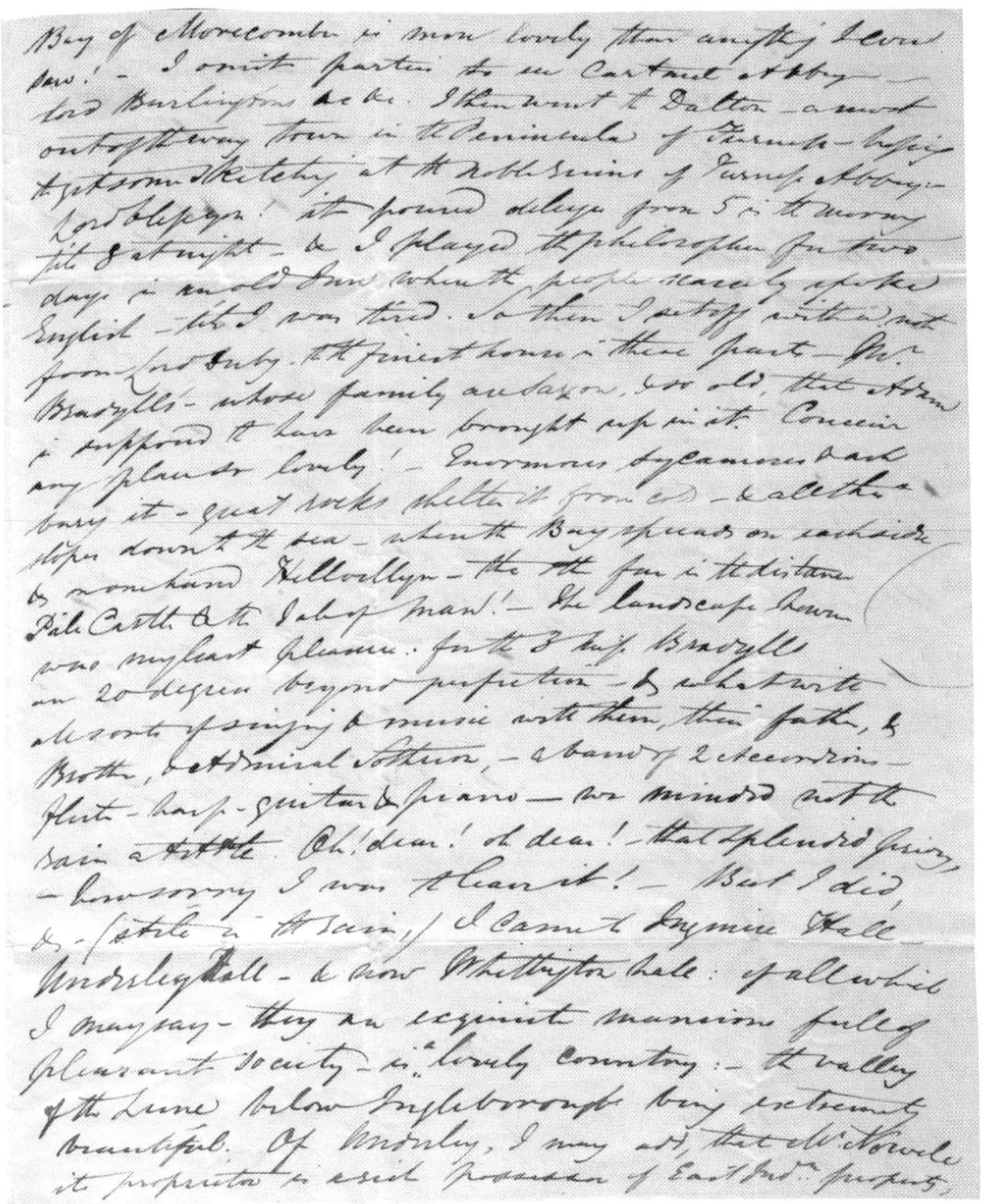
Bay of Morecombe is more lovely than anything I ever
saw! — I omitted parties to see Cartmel Abbey —
Lord Burlington's &c &c. I then went to Dalton — a most
out of the way town in the Peninsula of Furness — hoping
to get some sketching at the noble ruins of Furness Abbey —
Lord bless you! it poured deluge from 5 in the morning
till 8 at night — & I played the philosopher for two
days in an old Inn where the people scarcely spoke
English — till I was tired. So then I set off with a note
from Lord Derby, to the finest house in these parts — Mr
Braddyll's — whose family are Saxon, & so old, that Adam
is supposed to have been brought up in it. Conceive
any place so lovely! — Enormous sycamores & ash
bury it — great rocks shelter it from cold — & all the
slopes down to the sea — where the Bay spreads on each side
& mountains Helvellyn — &c the sea in the distance
Peel Castle & the Isle of Man! — The landscape however
was my least pleasure: for the 3 Miss Braddylls
are 20 degrees beyond perfection — & what with
all sorts of singing & music with them, their father, &
Brother, & Admiral Sotheron, — a band of 2 accordions —
flute — harp — guitar & piano — we minded not the
rain a little. Oh! dear! oh dear! — that splendid giving
— how sorry I was to leave it! — But I did,
& — (stole in the rain) I came to Ingmire Hall —
Underley Hall — & now Whittington Hall: of all which
I may say — they are exquisite mansions full of
pleasant society — in a lovely country: — the valley
of the Lune below Ingleborough being extremely
beautiful. Of Underley, I may add, that Mr Nowell
its proprietor is in rich possession of East Indn property,

Cat. 40

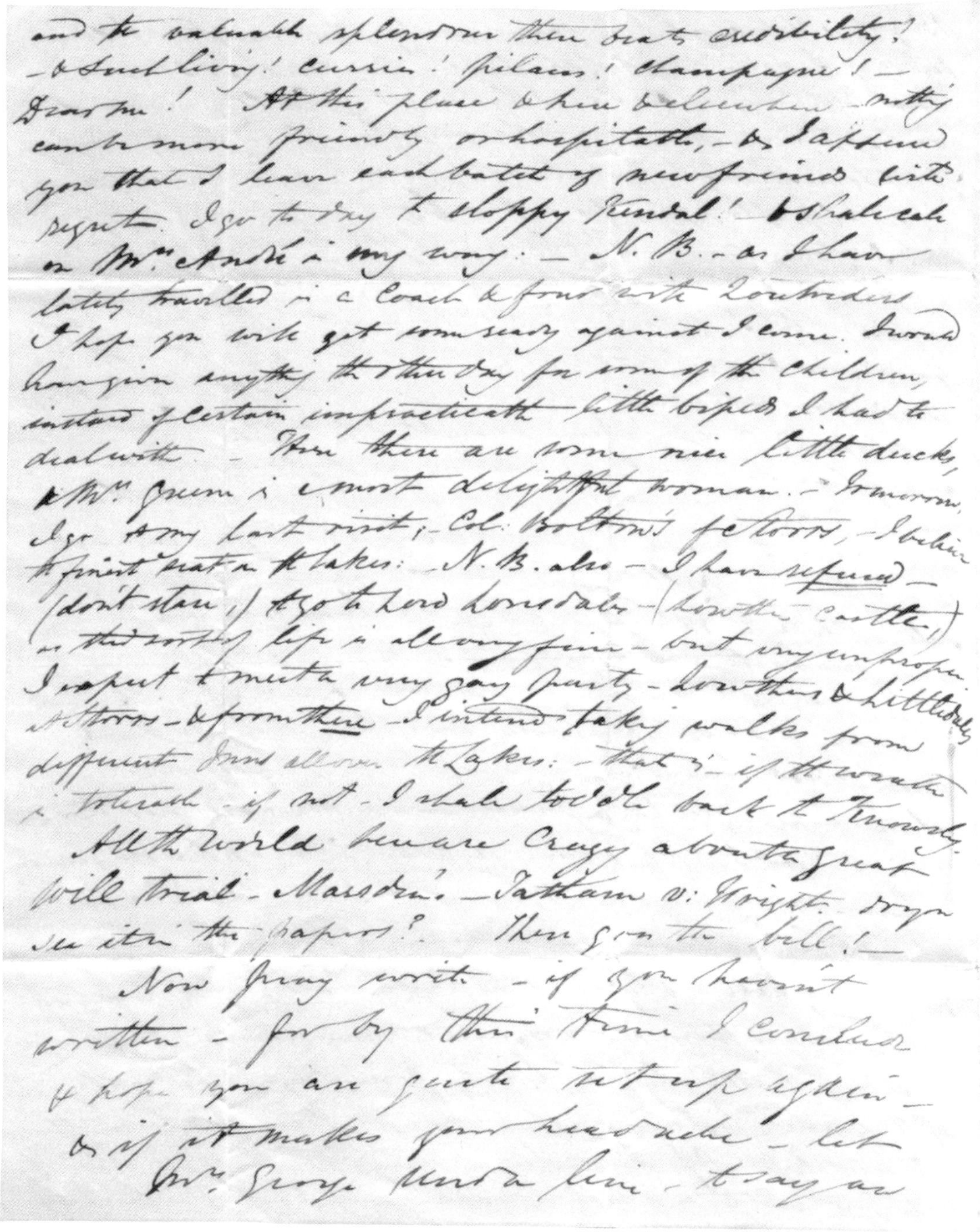
and the valuable splendour there beats credibility!
– & such living! curries! pilaus! champagne! –
Dear me! At this place & here & elsewhere – nothing
can be more friendly or hospitable, – & I assure
you that I leave each batch of new friends with
regret. I go to day to sloppy Kendal! – & shall call
on Mrs André in my way: – N. B. – as I have
lately travelled in a Coach & four with Lowthers
I hope you will get some ready against I come. I would
have given anything the other day for some of the Children,
instead of certain impracticable little bipeds I had to
deal with – Here there are some nice little ducks,
& Mrs Green is a most delightful woman. – Tomorrow
I go to my last visit, – Col. Bolton's of Storrs, – I believe
the finest seat in the lakes: – N. B. also – I have refused –
(don't stare,) to go to Lord Lonsdale's – (Lowther Castle,)
as that sort of life is all very fine – but very improper
I expect to meet a very gay party – Lowthers & Littledales
at Storrs – & from there – I intend taking walks from
different Inns all over the Lakes: – that is – if the weather
is tolerable – if not – I shall toddle back to Knowsley.
All the world here are crazy about a great
will trial – Marsden! – Tatham v: Wright. do you
see it in the papers? There goes the bell! –
Now pray write – if you haven't
written – for by this time I conclude
& hope you are quite set up again –
or if it makes your head ache – let
Mrs George send a line – to say ar

Cat. 40

9–12 September
from Windermere to Calder Bridge

It was generally Lear's practice to number his drawings, and, on leaving Storrs Hall, he began a new numerical sequence, presumably in order to mark the beginning of his tour of the Lakes proper. The first drawing in the series, dated 9 September and numbered 1, is the classic view of the Langdale Pikes from Lowwood (fig. 21).

There was an inn at this site, later to be replaced by the Lowwood Hotel built in 1850, and Lear may have spent the night there; Wordsworth wrote in his *Guide through the District of the Lakes* (1835): 'Low-wood Inn, a mile from the head of Windermere, is a most pleasant halting-place; no inn in the whole district is so agreeably situated for water views and excursions' (p. 6). In Lear's drawing, the clouds are lowering over the lake with the promise of rain; the presence of several figures on the shore who appear to be carrying umbrellas indicate that this is a likely prospect. The Lowwood drawing, made in the afternoon or early evening, as is shown by the shadows, is the only one from the first day of the tour; afterwards Lear either spent the night at Lowwood or travelled a few miles north to Ambleside to find accommodation.

The weather was obviously better on the second day, but only one drawing survives from it (cat. 41). As previously noted, Lear was armed on setting out from Knowsley with letters of introduction. It is not known for certain where he stayed on any of the nights of the tour after he left Storrs Hall. The next known dated drawing after the view taken from the top of Dunmail Raise on 10 September is the view of Calder Abbey dated 12 September but unnumbered (fig. 22, p. 108).

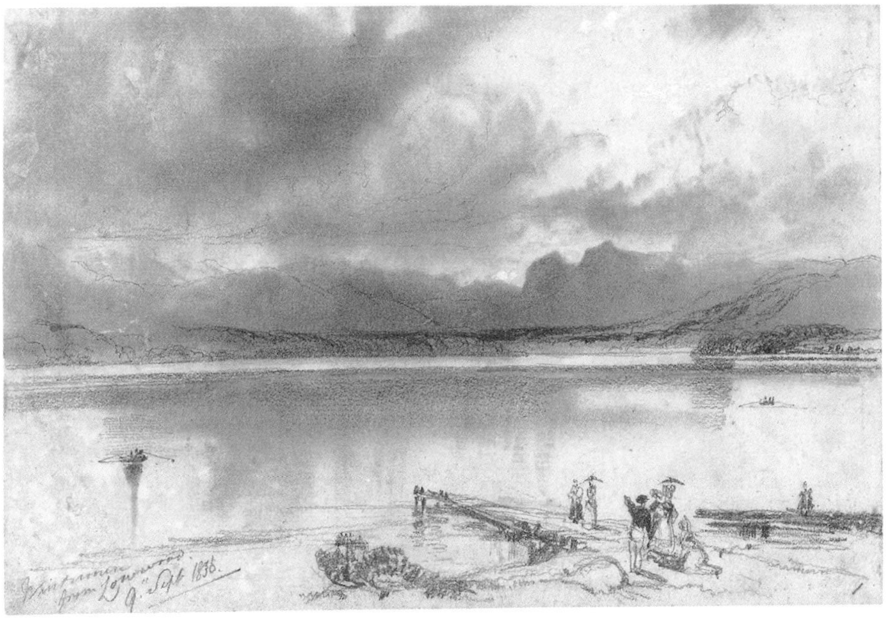

Fig. 21 The Langdale Pikes from Lowwood, inscribed and dated 'Windermere / from Lowwood. / 9. Sept. 1836', numbered 1, pencil and stump, on blue-grey paper, 17.1 × 26 cm (Private Collection, ex-Christie's, 20 November 2003, lot 53).

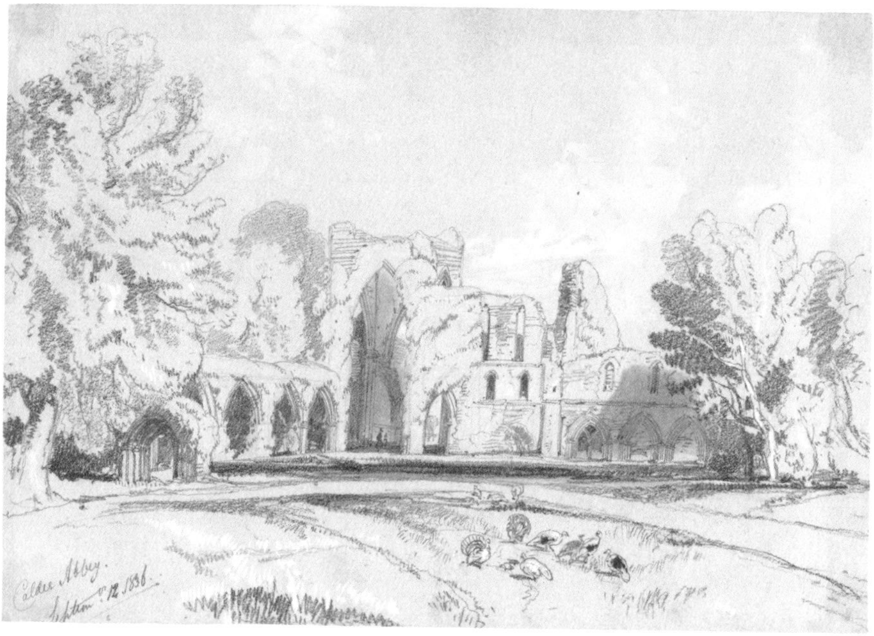

Fig. 22 Calder Abbey, inscribed and dated 'Calder Abbey. / Septembr. 12. 1836', pencil and stump, heightened with white, on blue-grey paper, 23.2 × 33.3 cm (Yale Center for British Art, B1997.7.24).

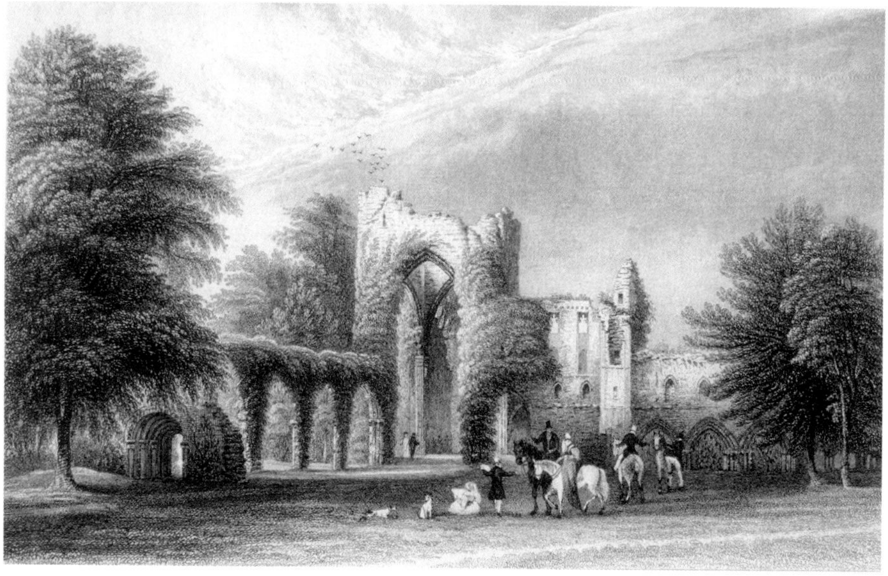

Fig. 23 'Calder Abbey, Cumberland', engraving after George Pickering, 1835, from *Westmorland, Cumberland, Durham, and Northumberland, Illustrated. From Original Drawings by Thomas Allom, George Pickering, &c. with Descriptions by T. Rose*, 1832–5 (The Wordsworth Trust).

The viewpoint for Lear's view of Calder Abbey (fig. 22) is virtually identical with this contemporary engraving. The later house built on part of the abbey site stands to the south of the ruins, and is out of view.

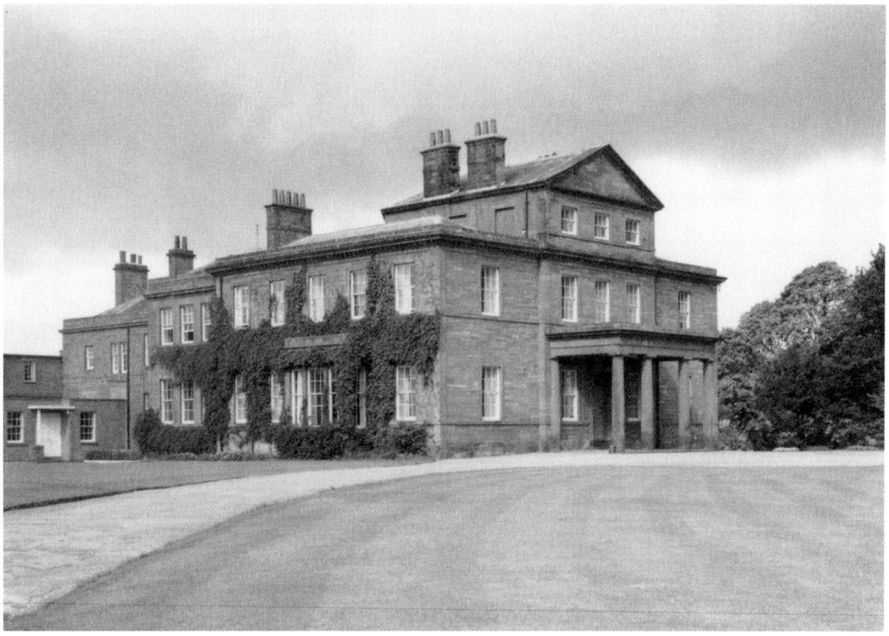

Fig. 24 Pelham House (formerly Ponsonby Hall), Calder Bridge, Cumbria. Lear probably stayed at this house, which was the property of a branch of the Stanley family (A. Taylor).

Calder Abbey (fig. 23) had been for many years the property of the Senhouse family, and had been inherited by Mary Senhouse (1793–1884) in 1805; she married Captain Thomas Irwin (1789–1877) in 1823, and Lear therefore knew the house as the property of the Irwins. In 1836 Captain Irwin was the High Sherriff of Cumberland. Although it is possible that Lear had a letter of introduction to the Irwins at Calder Abbey, it is much more likely that he visited Ponsonby Hall in Calder Bridge, which was the property of another branch of the Stanley family.

Ponsonby Hall (fig. 24) had been built using designs by James Paine, *c.*1775, for George Edward Stanley and was in 1835 the property of his son Edward Stanley (1790–1863), a kinsman of Lord Derby, to whom Lear would surely have had a letter of introduction; at the time of Lear's visit, Stanley was the MP for West Cumberland. Now known as Pelham House, it is the property of BNFL and currently houses the offices of the Nuclear Decommissioning Agency; the gateposts bearing the Stanley arms still stand at the entrance on the A591 in Calder Bridge.

41 *View of Thirlmere from Dunmail Raise*

Inscribed 'Skiddaw & Saddleback / from Dunmail Raise' and dated Sept. 10. 1836, numbered 2

Pencil and watercolour, 17.7 × 26.1 cm

Provenance: presented by the artist to the Nevill family; by descent in the Nevill family until sold to H.V. Day (bookseller) of Dorchester, Dorset, before 1958; purchased from H.V. Day by Colnaghi, 29 Dec. 1959 (£18); sold to Dr F. Springell, 28 Mar. 1960 (£29 15s); acquired by the current owner from Dr Springell in 1960

Private Collection

Illustrated on p. 110

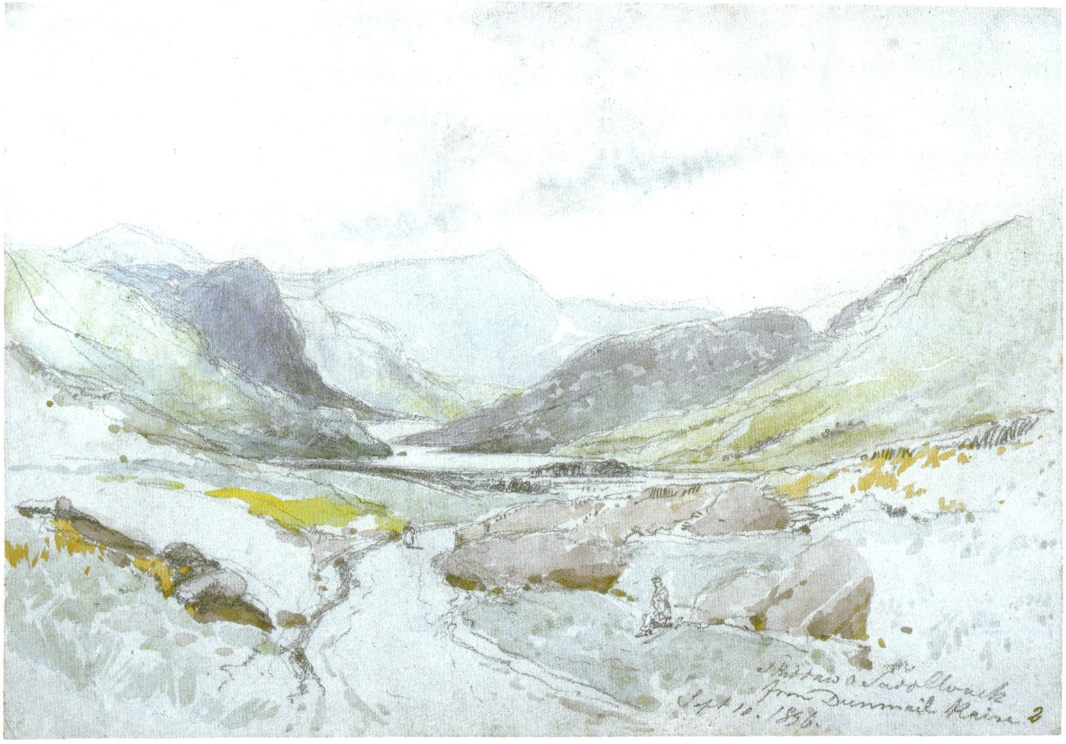

Cat. 41

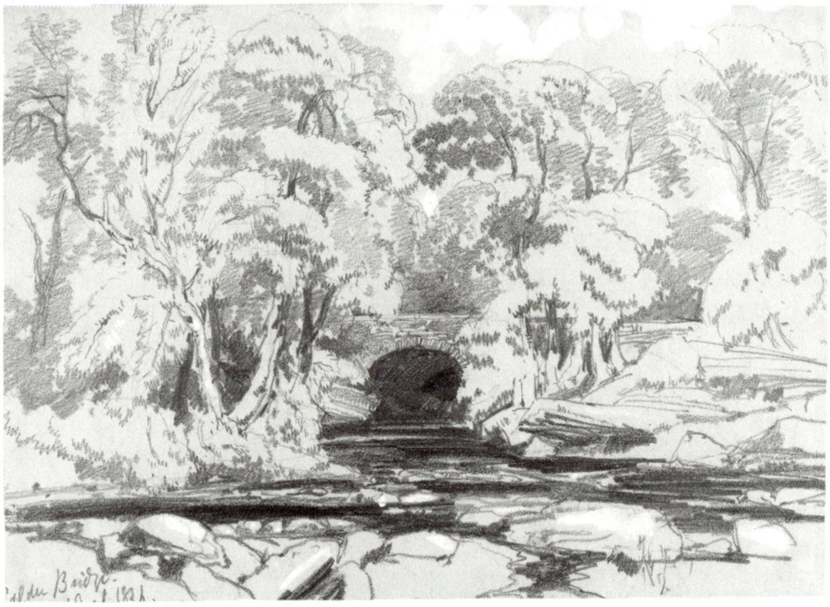

Fig. 25 On the Calder at Calder Bridge, inscribed and dated 'Calder Bridge / [date cut] 1836.', pencil and stump, heightened with white, on grey paper, 24.2 × 34.4 cm (Yale Center for British Art, B1997.7.33).

This is the the only drawing that survives from the second day of the tour, drawn from Dunmail Raise, the old border between Westmorland and Cumberland, and looking down over Thirlmere. Although inscribed 'Skiddaw & Saddleback', only part of the former is visible, to the left and behind Raven Crag, which shows up black in the far distance; the mountain in the central distance is Lonscale Fell; Saddleback (or, to use its ancient, now revived name, Blencathra) is not visible. This is one of only a handful of drawings done on the Lakes tour which have had watercolour washes added.

On his journey to Calder Bridge, Lear would have passed by Thirlmere, gone through Keswick and on to Cockermouth on the newly built coach road along the southern shore of Bassenthwaite; later in the month he revisited some of these places in order to draw them, but no sketches appear to have been made at this time. After Cockermouth, the road took him out to the coast at Whitehaven and on to Calder Bridge via Egremont. The reason for the lack of drawings (there is only one to be fitted into the numerical sequence) is unknown; possibly the weather was inclement, or perhaps Lear was in a coach and could not stop. The only other drawing to survive is inscribed 'Calder Bridge', although sadly both the date and the number have been cut (fig. 25). The view shows the bridge over the Calder just after the entrance gate to Ponsonby Hall on the drive that leads from the main road to the house; the view is taken from downstream and was probably drawn soon after arrival at Ponsonby Hall.

13–19 September
Wastwater and Wasdale Head

Due to the fact that no letters survive, it is only possible to piece together Lear's itinerary at this point from known dated drawings. Sadly, in several cases the drawings have had their inscriptions, dates or numbers partially or completely cut, so it is not possible to follow the artist's footsteps with absolute accuracy. However, the fact that the composite drawing of nine thumbnail sketches (cat. 45) contains two of Wasdale Hall suggests that Lear may have stayed there (fig. 26); it is not known where, or indeed whether, Lear stayed at Wasdale Head (fig. 27) at the other end of the lake. It is possible that he stayed at Wasdale Hall all this time, or that he found accommodation in a farmhouse at Wasdale Head, since all the guide books make it clear that there was no inn in the hamlet at that date. Wherever he stayed, it is known that Lear attempted some adventurous climbs among the Scawfell group of mountains, before he headed over Styhead Pass into Borrowdale on 19 September.

Wordsworth noted of Wasdale: 'Wastdale is well worth the notice of the Traveller who is not afraid of fatigue: no part of the country is more distinguished for sublimity' (p. xvii). Lear seems to have explored the area thoroughly; during his stay in the Wasdale area, he walked all round the shores of Wastwater. The drawings that survive represent only a fraction of those he must have made, and nineteen are missing from the numerical sequence. The drawing 'View from the Shore of Wastwater',

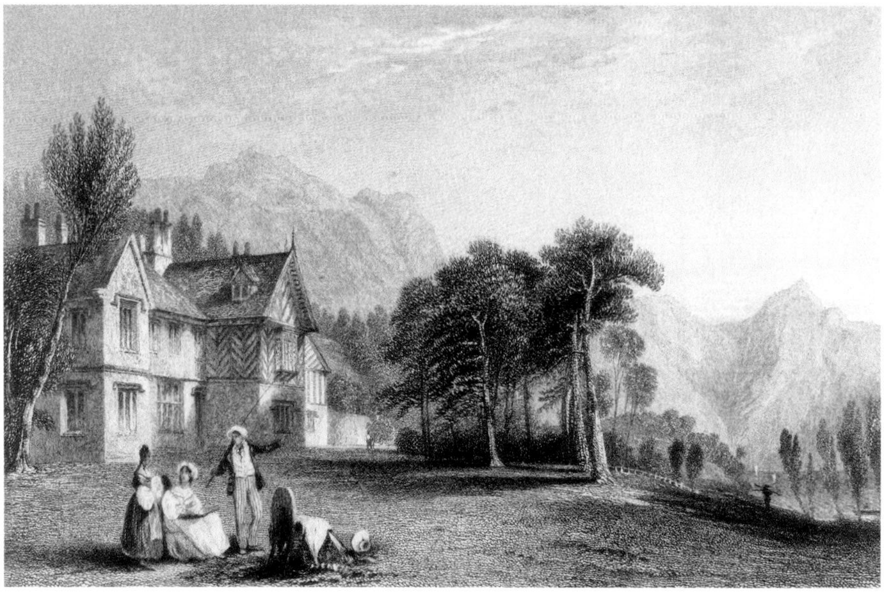

Fig. 26 'Wasdale Hall, Cumberland', engraving after Thomas Allom, 1835, from *Westmorland, Cumberland, Durham, and Northumberland, Illustrated. From Original Drawings by Thomas Allom, George Pickering, &c. with Descriptions by T. Rose*, 1832–5 (The Wordsworth Trust).

At the time of Lear's visit, Wasdale Hall had been recently built (a stone set in the wall of one of the attic rooms is dated 1829), and the land around it laid out and planted, by the Huddersfield banker Stansfeld Rawson (1778–1856); it is now the Youth Hostel.

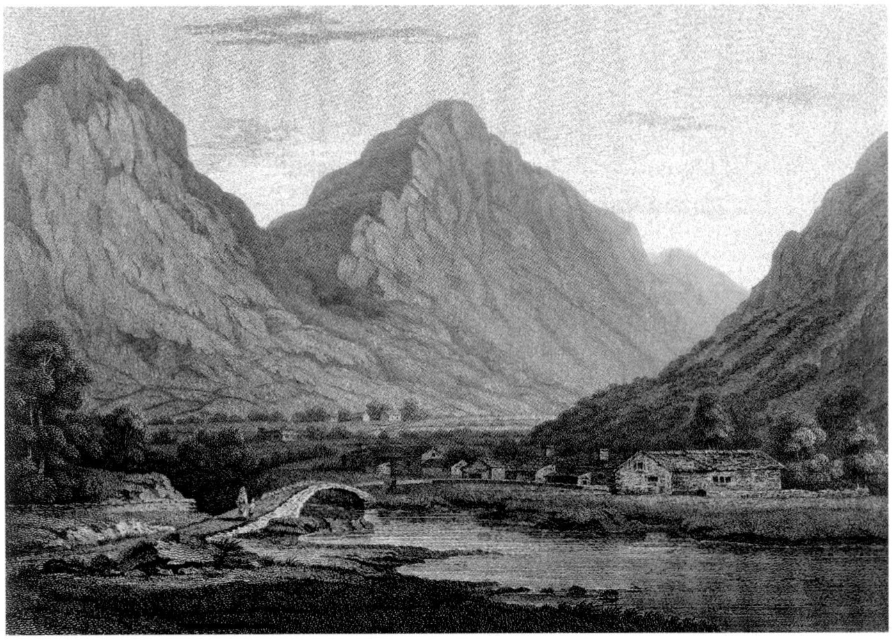

Fig. 27 'Wastdale Village', engraving after Joseph Farington (1815), published in *The Lakes of Lancashire, Westmorland, and Cumberland; Delineated in Forty-three Engravings, from Drawings by Joseph Farington, R.A.*, 1816 (The Wordsworth Trust).

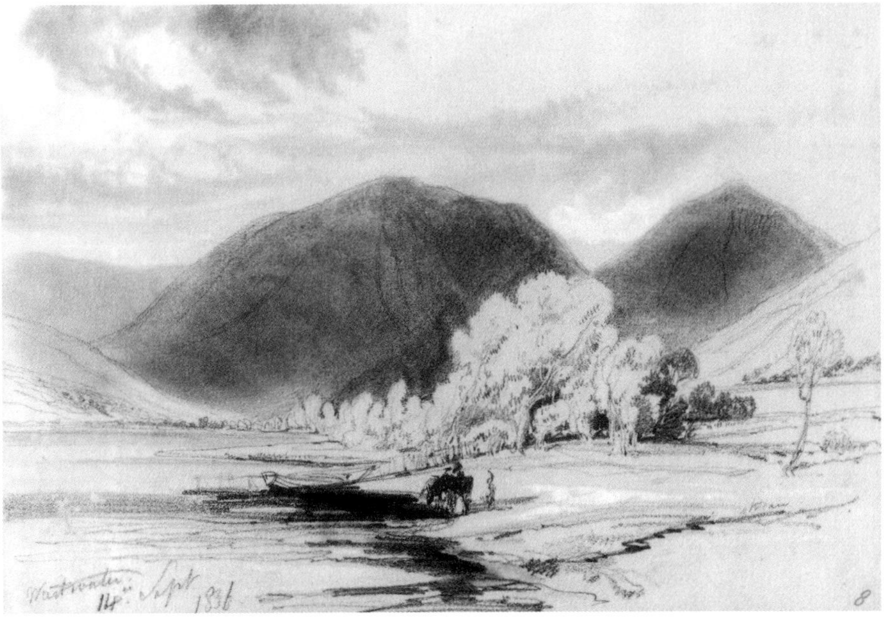

Fig. 28 Kirkfell and Great Gable, inscribed and dated 'Wastwater. / 14. Sept. 1836.', numbered 8, pencil and stump heightened with white on grey paper, 17.5 × 26 cm (Private Collection, ex-Sotheby's, 11 Apr. 1991, lot 57).

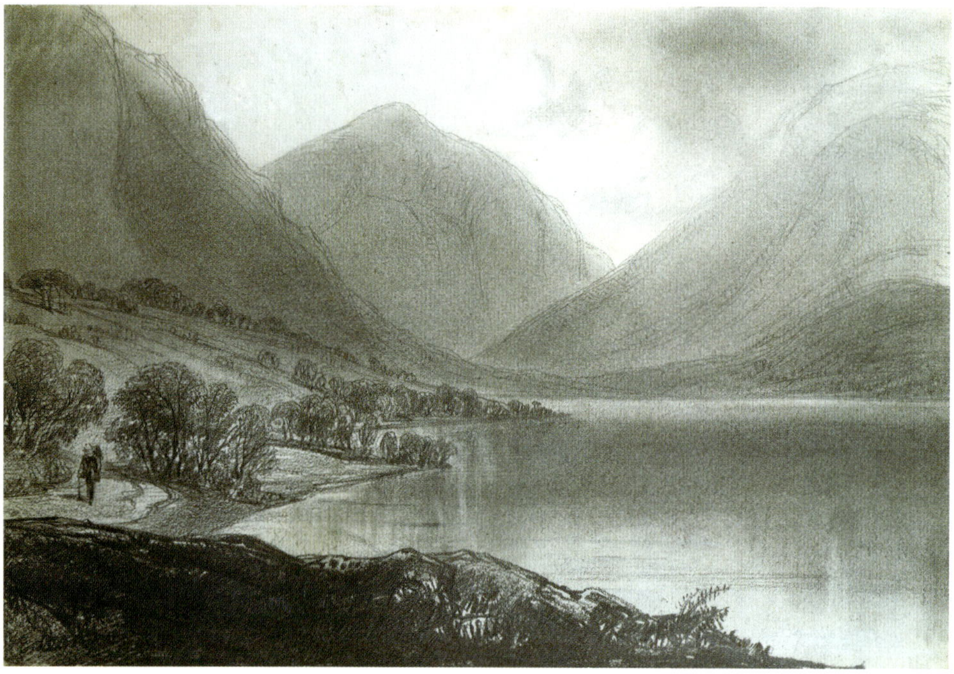

Fig. 29 Wastwater and Great Gable, signed, pencil heightened with white, on grey paper, 17.9 × 26.2 cm (Victoria & Albert Museum, E.750-1939).

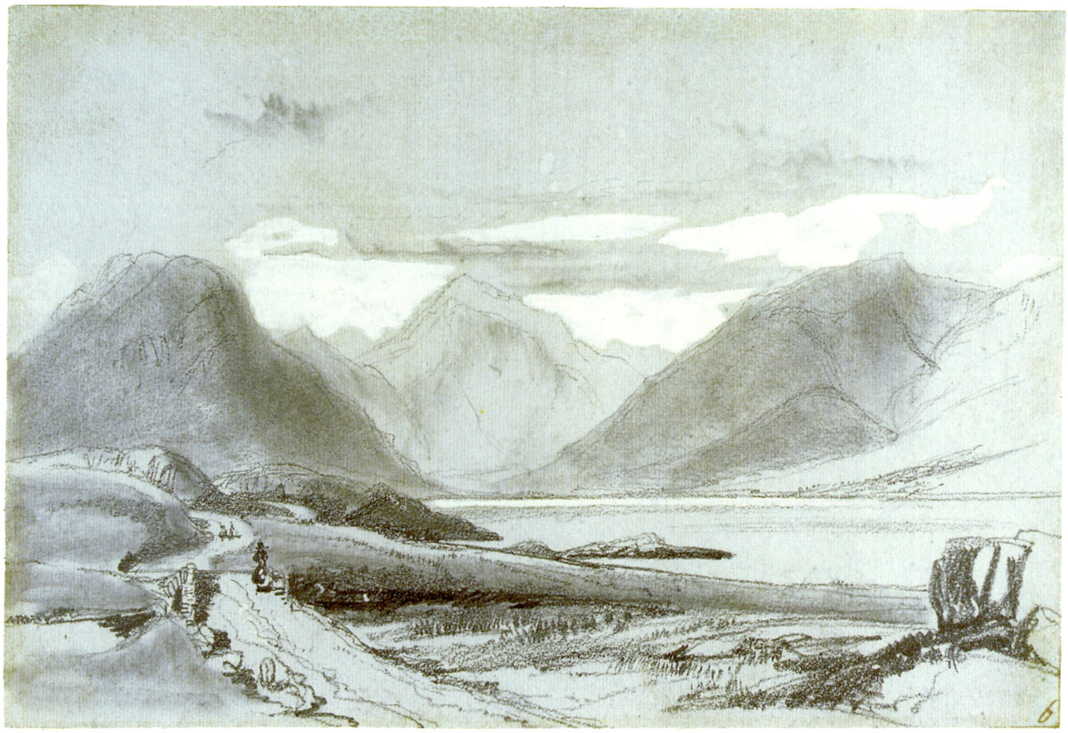

Cat. 42

numbered 6 (cat. 42) corresponds with one of the thumbnail sketches in the composite drawing (cat. 45). A drawing of Kirkfell taken from the shore of the lake near the top of its north-eastern side is inscribed and dated 'Wastwater / 14. Sept. 1836' and numbered 8 (fig. 28, p. 113).

There is a finished pencil drawing in the Bovisand album at the Victoria & Albert Museum, catalogued as 'Landscape with a lake among mountains', which shows the classic view up Wastwater with Great Gable in the distance (fig. 29); there must have been a sketch for this drawing in the numerical sequence. Other drawings which must once have existed, since they survive as thumbnail sketches in the composite drawing (cat. 45), are Wastwater looking up the Lake towards Wasdale Head, Wastwater looking towards the south (see cat. 47), and Wasdale Hall from across the Lake.

42 *Distant View of Wasdale Head with Yewbarrow, Great Gable and Lingmell*

Numbered 6
Pencil and stump heightened with white, on grey paper, 16.9 × 25.5 cm
Provenance: bequeathed by the artist to his godson, Allan Nevill; by descent in his family until sold at Christie's, 20 November 2003, part of lot 77, where acquired by current owner

The Wordsworth Trust (2004.119.5)

Although this sketch is not dated, working on the assumption that Lear was producing five drawings a day when the weather was good, and knowing that number 8 is dated 14 September, we can probably date it to that day also. The sketch corresponds with one of the thumbnail drawings in the sheet of composite sketches (cat. 45).

43 *Pikes Crag from Hollow Stones*

Inscribed 'Lingmell & Scawfell Crags' and 'Muckledore', dated Sept. 15. 1836 and numbered 11
Pencil and stump heightened with white, on grey paper, 17 × 24.4 cm
Provenance: Mrs E.B. Bakhurst; Sotheby's, 6 Nov. 1969, lot 70 (£80 to John Baskett)

Private Collection, on loan to Winchester College

Illustrated on p. 116

The survival of this sketch, which corresponds with the top left thumbnail drawing in the sheet on composite sketches (cat. 45), indicates that Lear was prepared to venture a considerable distance from the footpaths and to do some serious scrambling, since this is not far from the summit of the highest mountain in England. His later claim to know the peaks well – 'I know every corner of Westmorland; Scawfell Pikes is my cousin, and Skiddaw is my mother-in-law' – may therefore not be without foundation, although both peaks mentioned are in Cumberland. The sheet is inscribed 'Lingmell', but that mountain is out of view to the left. The buttress in front of him which Lear describes as 'Scawfell Crags' is in fact Pikes Crag, and 'Muckledoor', Lear's mishearing of Mickledore, the rocky col between Scafell and Scafell Pike, is out of view round to the right.

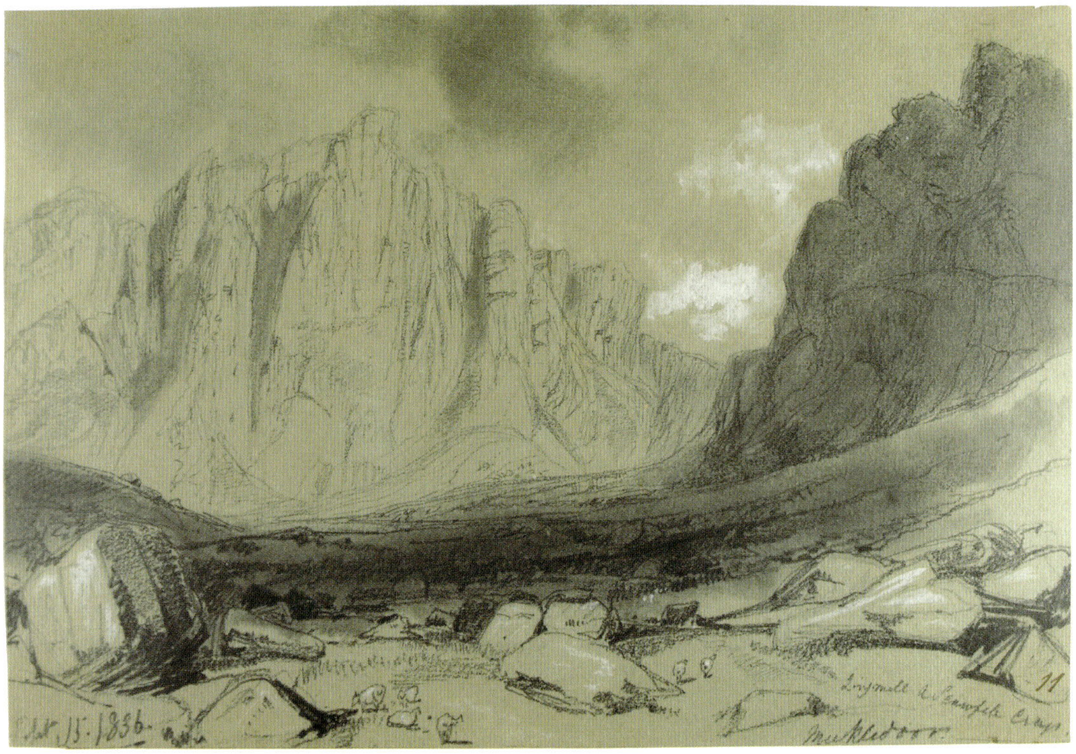

Cat. 43

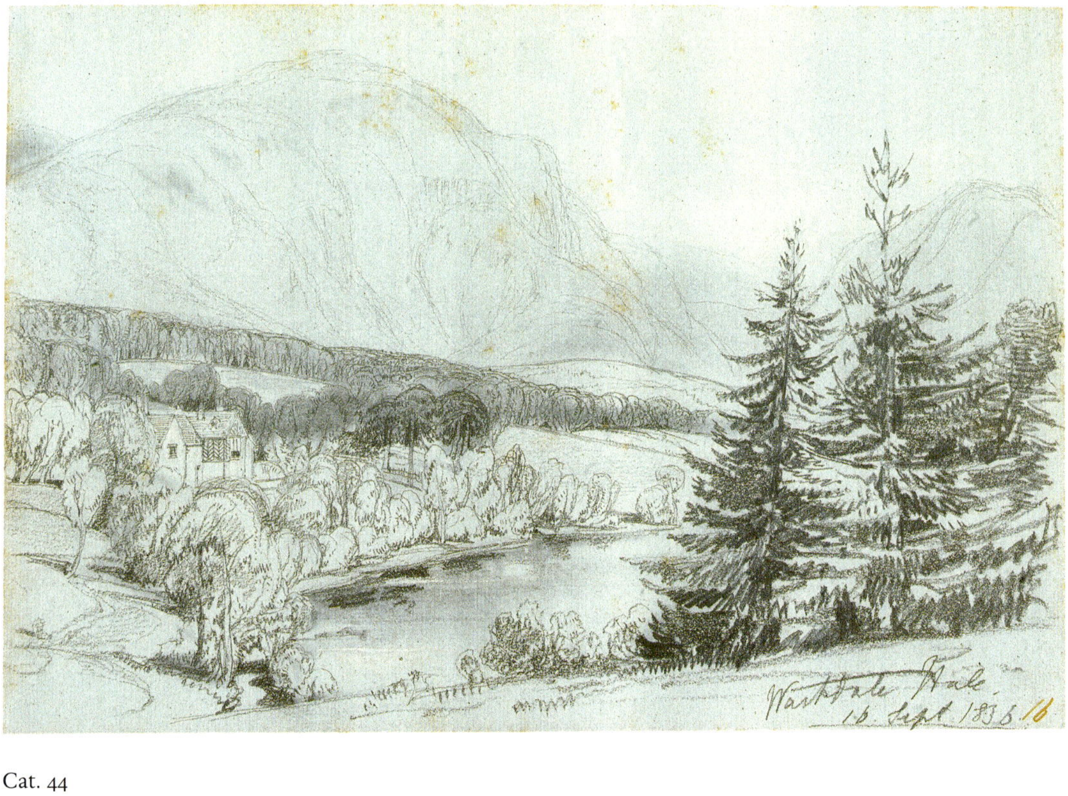

Cat. 44

44 *Wasdale Hall*

Inscribed and dated 'Wastdale Hall. / 16. Sept. 1836', numbered 16
Pencil and stump, on grey paper, 17.1 × 26 cm
Provenance: presented by the artist to the Nevill family; by descent in the Nevill family until sold to H.V. Day (bookseller) of Dorchester, Dorset, before 1958; purchased from H.V. Day by Colnaghi, 29 Dec. 1959 (£13); sold to Dr F. Springell, 28 Mar. 1960 (£21 5s); acquired by the current owner from Dr Springell in 1960
Private Collection

This sketch corresponds with the composition of one of the thumbnail drawings in cat. 45. Another sketch of the house, seen from across the southern end of Wastwater, with Buckbarrow behind, is recorded by the composite sheet. The drawing next in the numerical sequence, drawn on the same day and numbered 17, is inscribed 'Yewbarrow. Wastwater' ; it was drawn from the western shore of the lake looking towards Wasdale Head (fig. 30).

45 *Composite Sheet of Nine Thumbnail Drawings of Lake District Subjects*

Pencil and stump, on grey paper, 14.1 × 23 cm
Provenance: presented by Sir Hugh Walpole in 1938
The King's School, Canterbury
Illustrated on p. 119

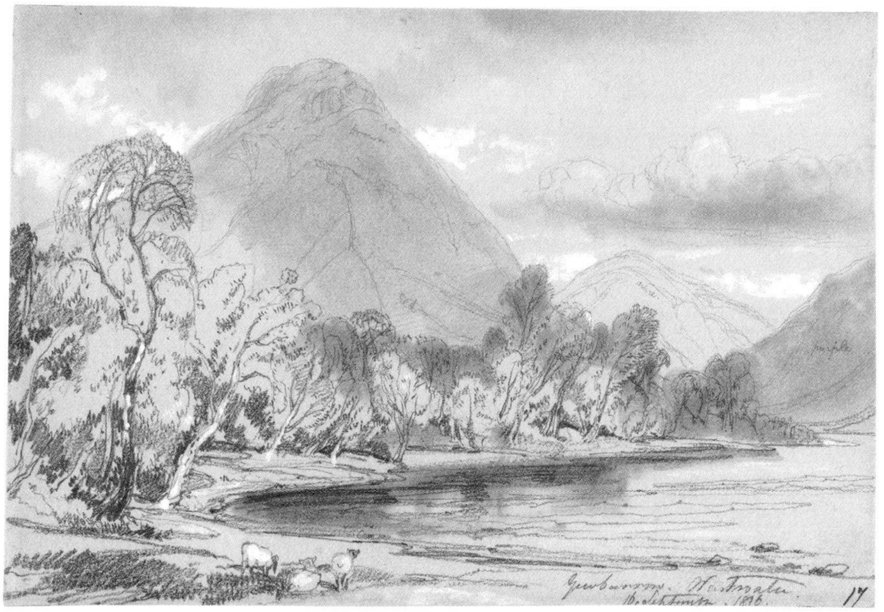

Fig. 30 Yewbarrow, Wastwater, inscribed and dated 'Yewbarrow. Wastwater. / 16 September. 1836.', numbered 17, pencil and stump heightened with white, on blue-grey paper, 17.1 × 25.7 cm (Yale Center for British Art, B1997.7.25).

This recently discovered drawing seems to be unique in Lear's *oeuvre*. Six of the nine sketches are securely identified as views in west Cumberland (see the diagram below), and the likelihood is that the remaining ones are also. Three relate exactly to known surviving sketches (cats. 42–4), while a fourth relates to the only known surviving watercolour of a Lake District subject and a lithograph (see cat. 47 and fig. 31, p. 120). Since three of the thumbnails relate to known sketches, it is likely that the other six provide evidence of the appearance of lost ones. The existence of a sketch of Pikes Crag shows that Lear climbed very high while staying in Wasdale, and that he by no means stayed at low level or kept to recognised roads.

Pikes Crag from Hollow Stones (cat. 43)	A distant View of Wastwater and Wasdale Head	A wooded Stream
Wasdale Hall (cat. 44)	Wasdale Hall from across the Lake	Wastwater and the Screes from Wasdale (see cat. 47 and fig. 31)
Calder Abbey (?)	Wastwater and Wasdale Head (cat. 42)	A House in a wooded Valley

As two of the sketches show Wasdale Hall, it is possible that this drawing may have some connection with the Rawson family, with whom Lear probably stayed. The 1835 edition of *Allison's Northern Tourist's Guide*, which Lear probably read, observed of Wastwater: 'This Lake has lately assumed an air of cheerfulness from the erection of Wastdale Hall, the delightful seat of STANSFIELD RAWSON, Esq., Banker, Huddersfield, Yorkshire, one of the chief ornaments of the neighbourhood' (p. 104). It is likely that a finished drawing of Wasdale Hall dated 1837 remains to be discovered.

46 *Wasdale Head and Great Gable*

Inscribed and dated 'Wastdale. / & Great Gavel. / 15. [altered to 16.] Sept.1836', numbered 20
Pencil and stump heightened with white, on blue-grey paper, 17.2 × 25.3 cm
Provenance: presented by the artist to Ralph Nevill, F.S.A. (d. 1917); by descent to his daughter, Mrs B C Bamber; purchased from Mrs B C Bamber in 1942 (£10 for six drawings)

The British Museum (1942-12-11-3)

Leigh noted: 'Wastdale Head is a very small rural hamlet, consisting of not more than a dozen houses, and a small chapel. It is surrounded by about 400 acres of level land, which is divided into fields by stone walls. There is no inn, but strangers may readily obtain refreshment of the farmers residing there, whose kindness they will, of course, acknowledge by a suitable donation' (p. 103).

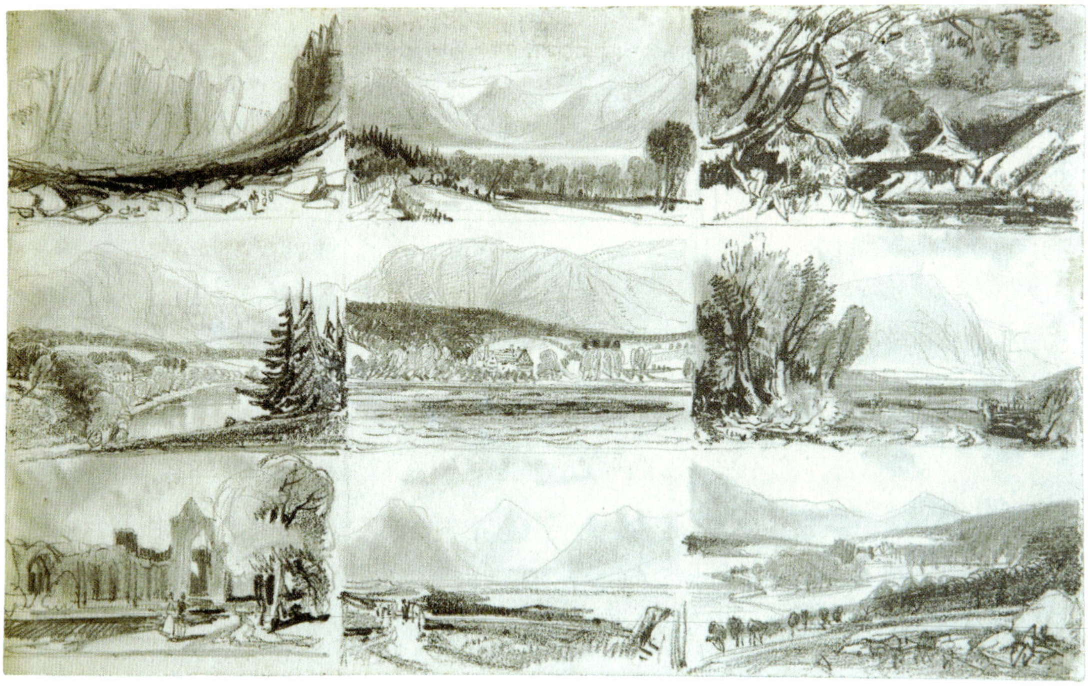

Cat. 45

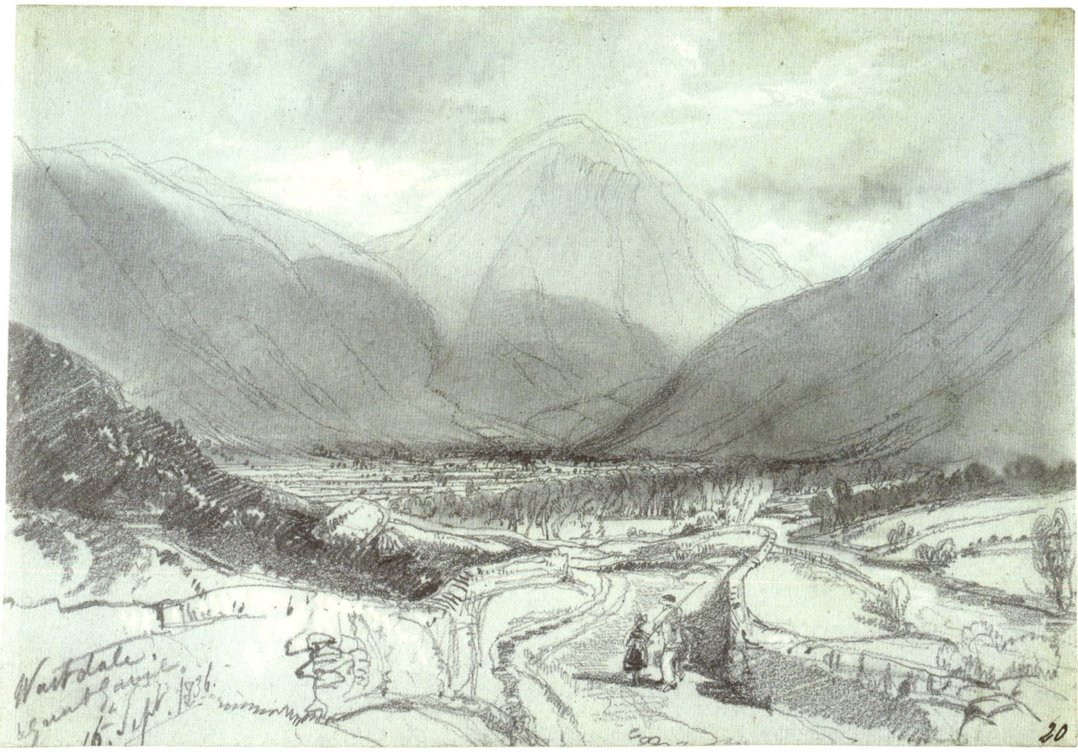

Cat. 46

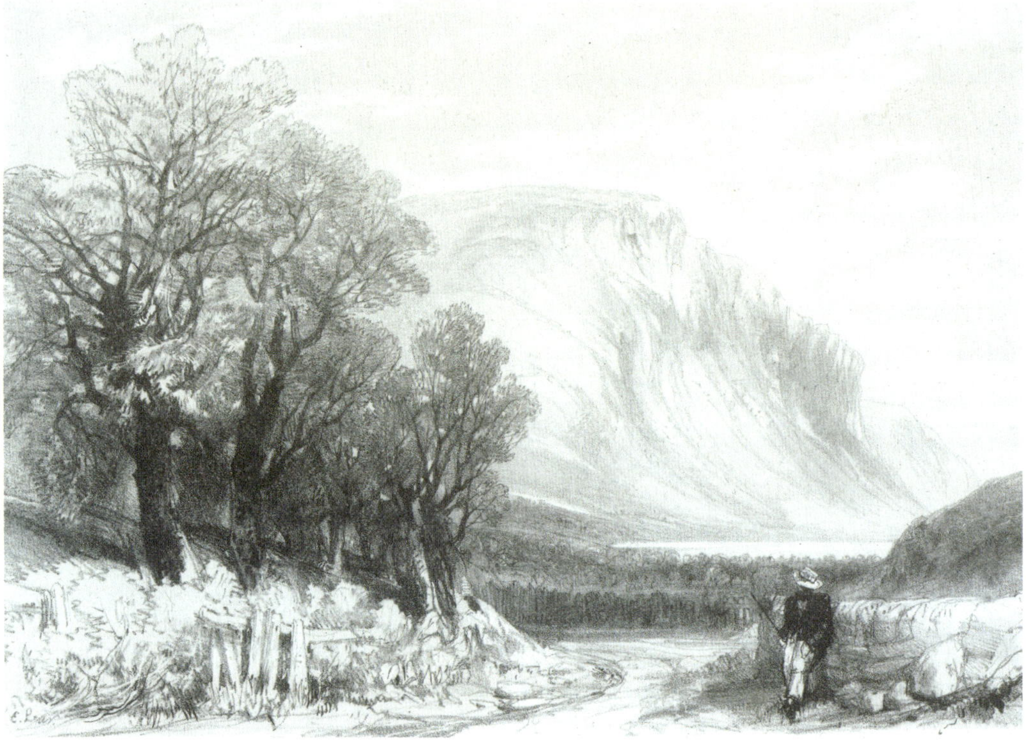

Cat. 47

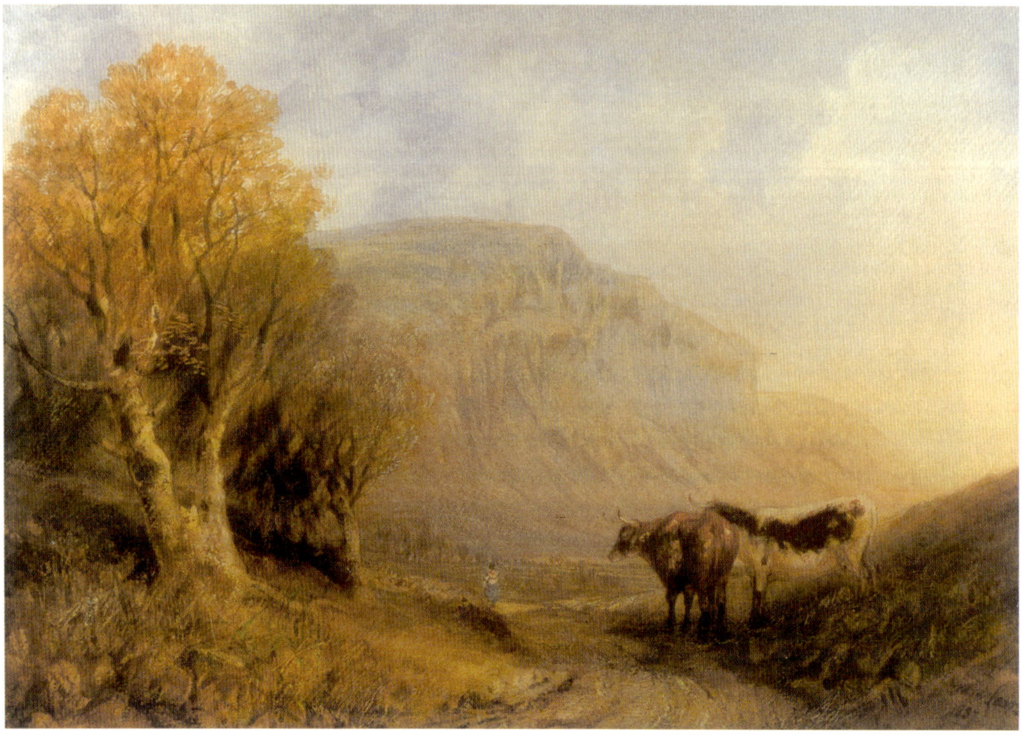

Fig. 31 Wastwater looking towards the south, signed and dated 1837, pen and ink and watercolour, 35 × 58 cm (Private Collection, USA).

47 *Wastwater, looking towards the South*

Signed on the stone, and inscribed (in a later hand) 'Wastwater & the Screes, from Wastdale' (lower right, outside image)
Tinted lithograph, 16.7 × 24.8 cm (image size)
Provenance: presented by E. Rawdon Smith in 1954
The British Museum (1954-11-3-36)

This is the only lithograph that survives which derives from Lear's Lake District tour. It is also, as Michael Twyman has pointed out, a tinted lithograph, using the techniques pioneered by Harding and Hullmandel, which are to be seen in *Sketches at Home and Abroad*, and is a sophisticated exercise in landscape lithography. It is known that Lear liked to work in sets, both as a printmaker and as a watercolourist, so it is surprising that other prints of similar subject matter have not survived. This is the same composition as appears in one of the thumbnail sketches in the composite sheet (cat. 45), and it appears again in the only known commissioned watercolour, which derived from the tour; this is the large Wastwater view in an American private collection (fig. 31, see Noakes 1985, no. 13 (h), col. pl. p. 42).

This was commissioned from Lear by Lord Derby's cousin and brother-in-law, the Rev. James John Hornby (1777–1855), who was Rector of Winwick, Cheshire, and the father of Lear's great friend Robert Hornby. 'Wastwater, looking towards the south' appears to have been Lear's most popular composition. In addition to this lithograph and the watercolour, there was also a finished drawing with this title, signed and dated 1837 (Sotheby's, 18 Mar. 1982, part of lot 8, 2 in the lot).

48 *View to the North-east over Styhead Tarn from the Top of Styhead Pass*

Inscribed and dated 'Saddleback from / Styhead. / 19. Sept. 1836.', and inscribed with colour notes, numbered 31
Pencil and stump heightened with white, on blue-grey paper, 17.7 × 26 cm
Provenance: presented by the artist to the Nevill family; by descent in the Nevill family until sold to H.V. Day (bookseller) of Dorchester, Dorset, before 1958; purchased from H.V. Day by Colnaghi, 29 Dec. 1959 (£13); sold to Dr F.Springell, 28 Mar. 1960 (£21 5s); acquired by the current owner from Dr Springell in 1960
Private Collection
Illustrated on p. 123

Having spent the best part of a week in west Cumberland, Lear headed back east following the old packhorse route over Styhead Pass into Borrowdale. The view in this drawing is looking north-east over Styhead Tarn down into Styhead Gill with the Borrowdale Fells and part of Saddleback/Blencathra on the horizon. At this point he was presumably heading for Keswick, which he had passed through without stopping just over a week earlier.

49 *Scawfell Pikes*

Inscribed and dated (cut), dated 19 Sept. 1836, numbered 32 (cut)
Pencil and stump heightened with white, on blue-grey paper, 17.5 × 25.2 cm
Provenance: presented by the artist to Ralph Nevill, F.S.A. (d. 1917); by descent to his daughter, Mrs B C Bamber; purchased from Mrs B C Bamber in 1942 (£10 for six drawings)

The British Museum (1942-12-11-4)

Previously unidentified, this drawing, from which the inscription, date and number have been tantalisingly cut off along the lower edge, can now be revealed as the sketch for a finished drawing inscribed 'Scawfell Pikes' in an American private collection (fig. 32). The view is taken from the banks of Styhead Gill (the tarn is out of sight over the brow) with Lingmell on the right and Scawfell Pike towards the left. Although the number is cut and cannot be read, in view of the number 31 on cat. 48, it has to be 32.

In Lear's day, the name 'Pikes of Scawfell' was given to the group of summits in the Scawfell group to the east of Mickledore to distinguish them from Scawfell, the mountain that stands alone above Wasdale.

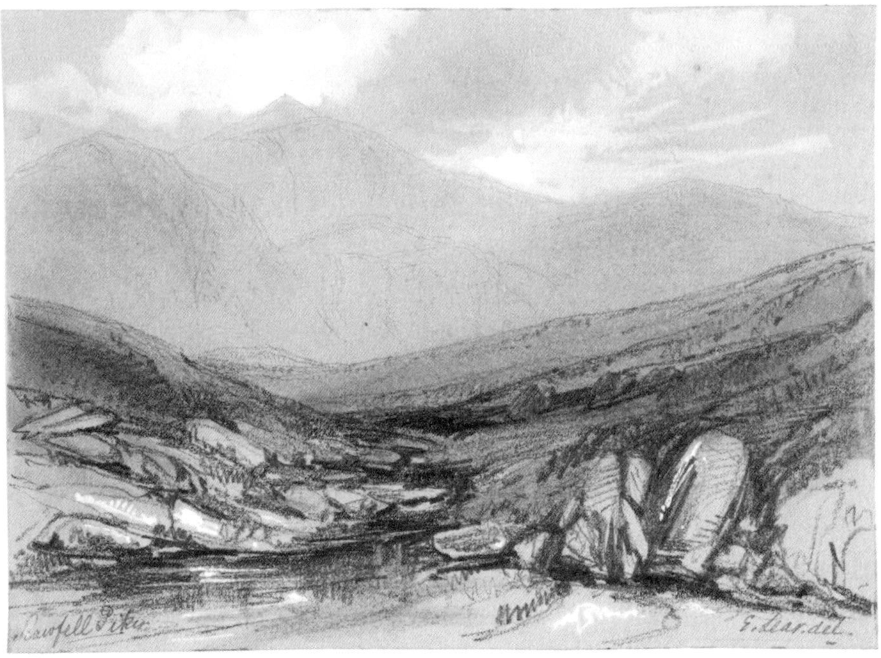

Fig. 32 Scawfell Pikes, signed and inscribed as title, pencil and stump, heightened with white, on blue-grey paper (faded), 12.3 × 17.3 cm (Private Collection, USA).

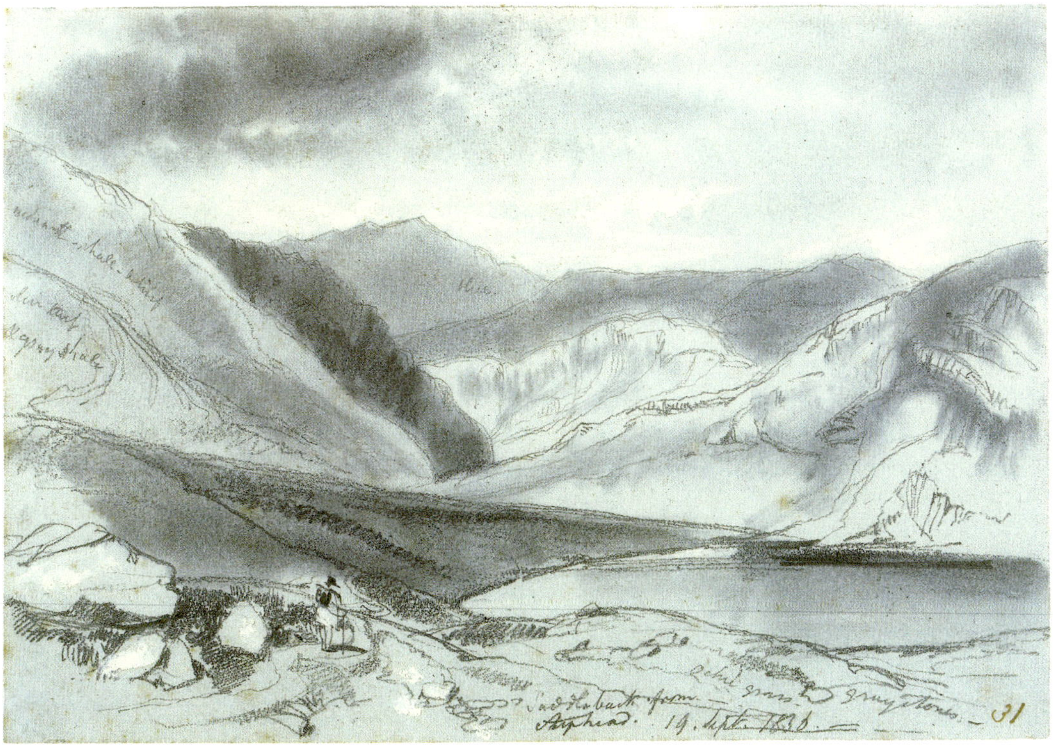

Cat. 48

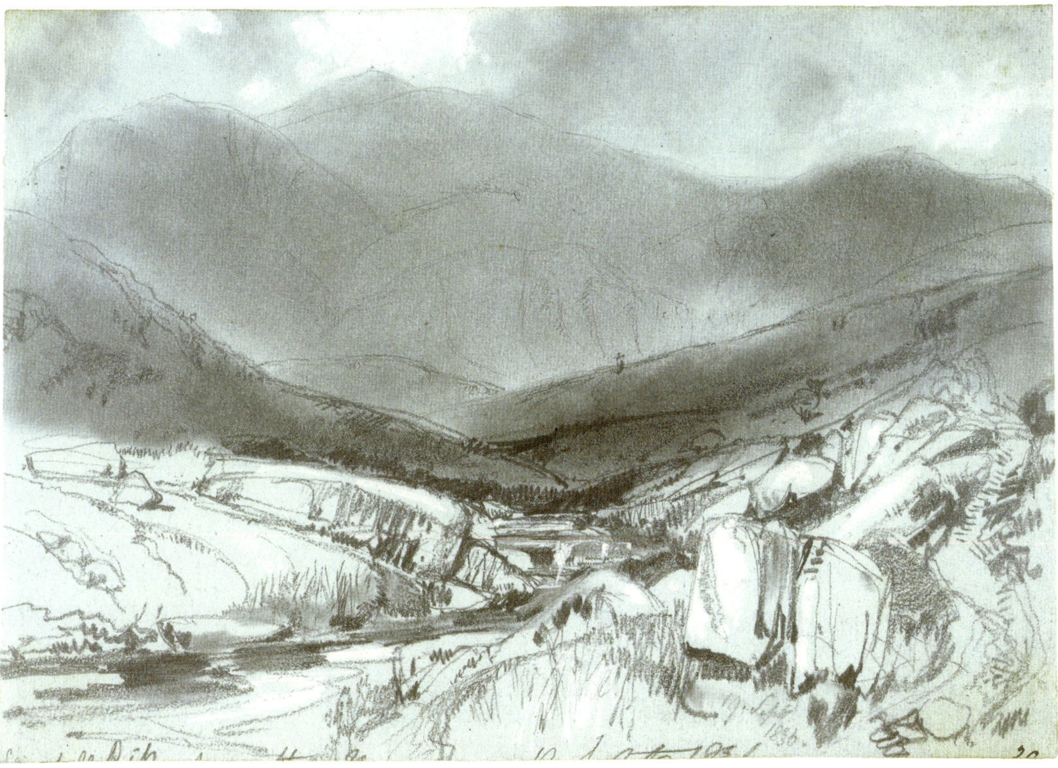

Cat. 49

20–26 September
Keswick, Derwentwater and Bassenthwaite

For the next few days, Lear seems to have based himself in Keswick, exploring, like many tourists before and since, the shores of Derwentwater. Nine drawings are missing from the numerical sequence, although one of these may be the undated and unnumbered view of Derwentwater and Castle Crag (fig. 33).

This last drawing probably derives from this visit to Derwentwater and Borrowdale rather than the one made between 8 and 11 October (see cats. 80 and 81, and fig. 42, p. 153). By the time of Lear's visit, which was before the arrival of the railway, Keswick was already the Lake District's first tourist resort. It is impossible to know where the artist stayed, although it is probable that he favoured either the Queen's Head or the Royal Oak, which were the only two posting houses in Keswick, that is, inns from which coaches could be taken. Despite the number of missing drawings, it is possible to infer that he made a thorough exploration of the shores of Derwentwater; it is hard to believe that, in the course of this, he did not visit Lodore Falls, or that he did not climb Skiddaw. He seems to have reserved his visit to Watendlath until his second trip to Borrowdale in October, since there was a drawing of that subject dated 9 October in the Colnaghi exhibition in 1960. After venturing north out of Keswick along the eastern shore of Bassenthwaite, Lear returned to Keswick and, probably on 25 or 26 September, headed over to the lakes of Buttermere and Crummock Water through the Newlands Valley, the evidence for this being an undated drawing, inscribed 'Newlands Valley' and numbered 50, which was in the 1960 Colnaghi exhibition and in the Spink Annual Watercolour Exhibition in 1977 (current whereabouts unknown).

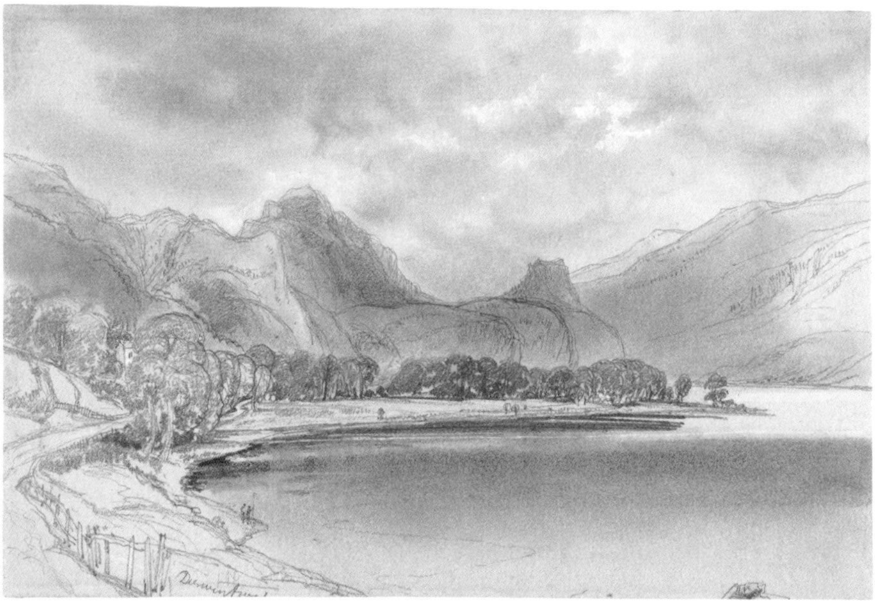

Fig. 33 Derwentwater and Castle Crag from the East Shore of the Lake, inscribed 'Derwentw[cut]', pencil and stump heightened with white, on grey paper, 16.7 × 25.4 cm (Yale Center for British Art, B1997.7.26). This sketch was developed into a finished drawing, signed and dated 1837, now in a private collection.

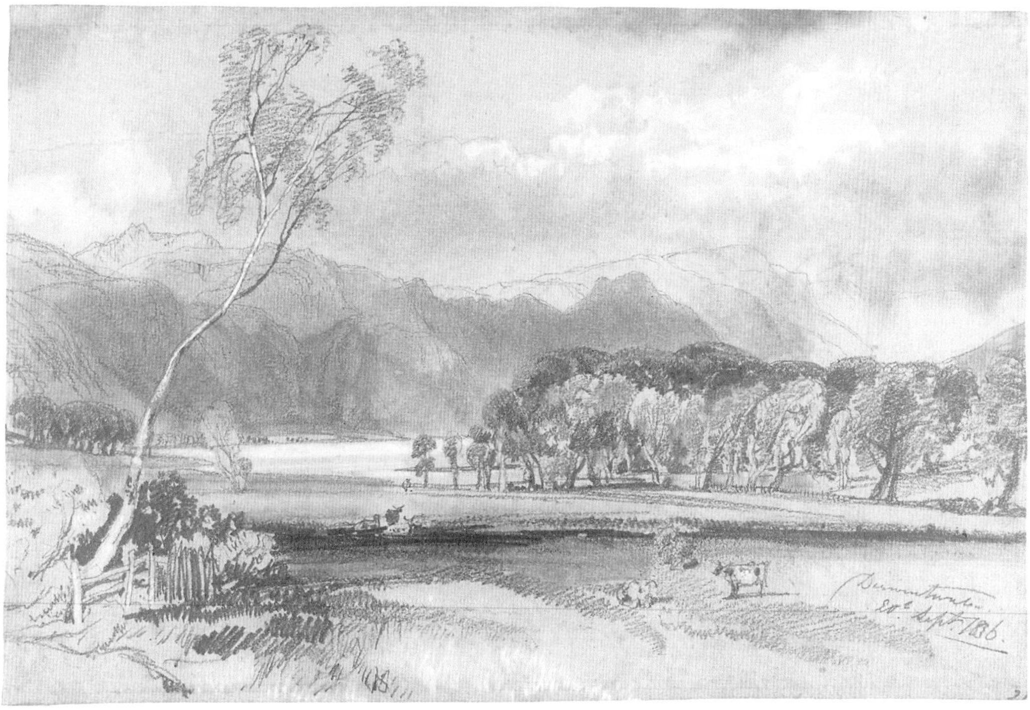

Cat. 50

50 *Derwentwater*

Inscribed and dated 'Derwentwater / 20th Sept.1836.', numbered 34 (cut)
Pencil and stump heightened with white, on grey paper, 16.8 × 25.8 cm
Provenance: bequeathed by the artist to his godson, Allan Nevill; by descent in his family until sold at Christie's, 20 November 2003, part of lot 77, where acquired by current owner

The Wordsworth Trust (2004.119.7)

Drawn on the artist's first full day at Derwentwater, this drawing shows a view south down the lake with Walla Crag on the left; beyond are Falcon Crag, and in the distance High Seat. The number lower right is cut, but enough of it is visible to decipher it as '34'.

51 *Derwentwater*

Inscribed and dated '[Der]went water / Sept.' (cut), numbered 35
Pencil and stump heightened with white, on grey paper, 17 × 25.8 cm
Provenance: bequeathed by the artist to his godson, Allan Nevill; by descent in his family until sold at Christie's, 20 November 2003, part of lot 77, where acquired by current owner

The Wordsworth Trust (2004.119.3)

Illustrated on p. 126

Although the date on this drawing has been cut, it was drawn on 20 or 21 September; the view is looking south down the lake towards Castle Crag, with Lord's Isle (partially hidden behind the tree) and Rampsholme Island to its left. The next two drawings in the numerical sequence, nos. 36 and 37, are both at Yale (figs. 34 and 35).

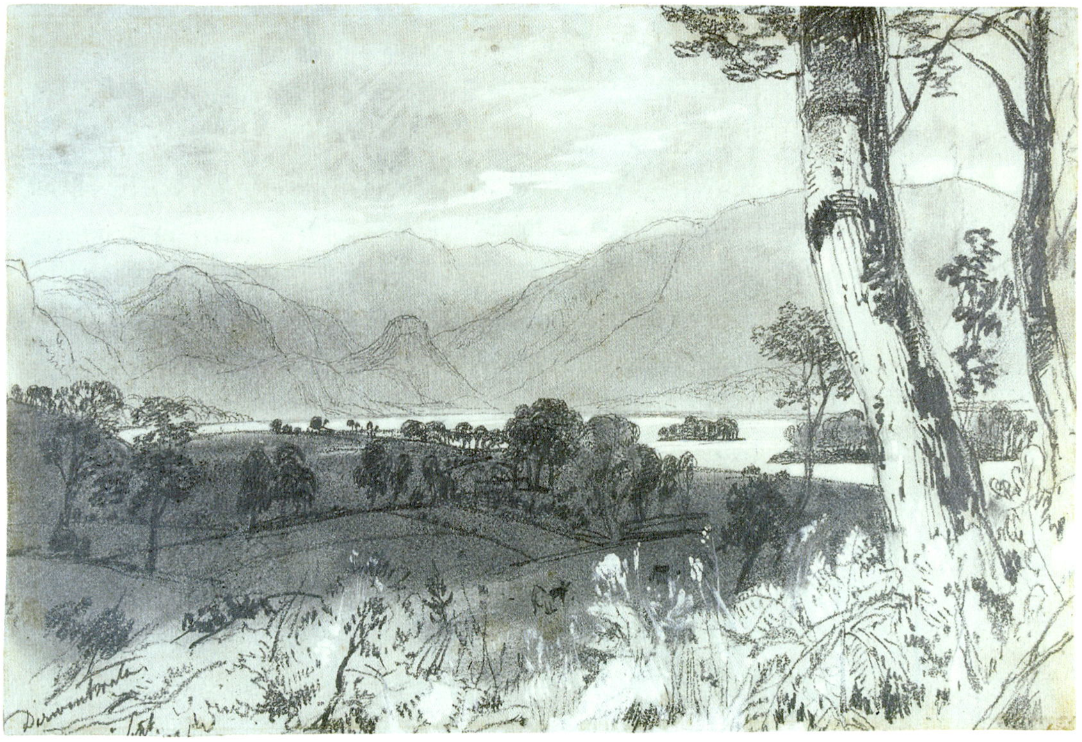

Cat. 51

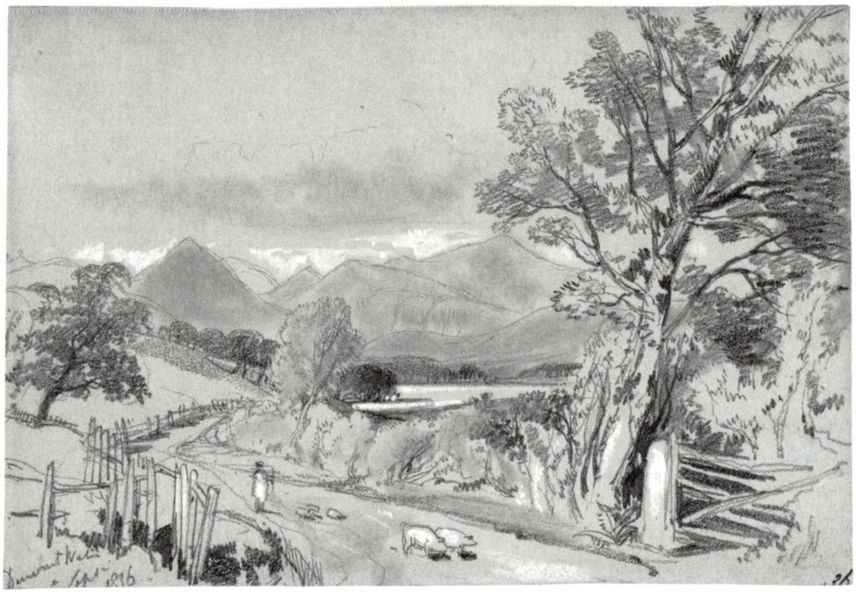

Fig. 34 Derwentwater, inscribed and dated 'Derwent Water / [date cut] Septr / 1836', numbered 36, pencil and stump heightened with white, on blue-grey paper, 17 × 25.5 cm (Yale Center for British Art, B1997.7.27).

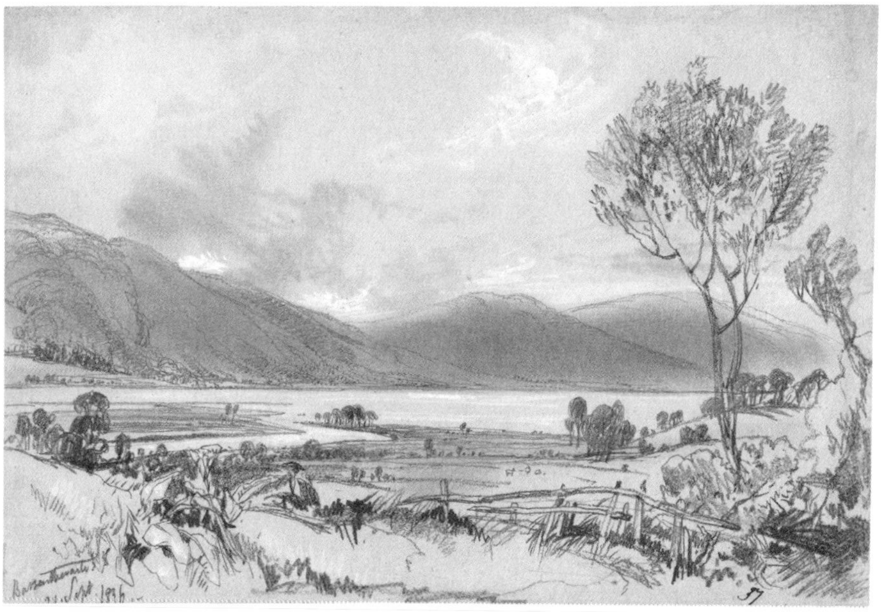

Fig. 35 Bassenthwaite, inscribed and dated 'Bassenthwaite / 21 Sept. / 1836', numbered 37, pencil and stump heightened with white, on blue-grey paper, 17.1 × 25.6 cm (Yale Center for British Art, B1997.7.28).

This shows the southern end of Bassenthwaite with the River Derwent flowing into it from Derwentwater.

52 *Bassenthwaite: View from near Armathwaite*

Inscribed and dated 'Bassenthwaite / 21. Sept. 1836.', numbered 38 (cut)
Pencil and stump heightened with white, on grey paper, 17.2 × 25.3 cm
Provenance: bequeathed by the artist to his godson, Alan Nevill; by descent in his family until sold at Christie's, 20 November 2003, part of lot 77, where acquired by current owner

The Wordsworth Trust (2004.119.6)

Illustrated on p. 128

This view immediately postdates the Yale drawing (fig. 35). Although the number lower right has been cut, enough of it is visible to reveal it as 38 in the numerical sequence. Lear travelled north out of Keswick on the Carlisle road and turned off it to get this view back down Bassenthwaite towards Cat Bells and the Derwent Fells; from this point he seems to have turned back and returned to his base in Keswick. This sketch provided the basis for a finished drawing of the following year (cat. 53).

53 *Bassenthwaite: View from near Armathwaite*

Signed and dated 'E.Lear.del. / 1837'
Pencil, black chalk and stump, on blue-grey paper, 17.2 × 23.9 cm
Provenance: Spink, English Watercolour Drawings, Annual Exhibition, 1981, no. 64, sold to David Mawson (£575); acquired by the current owner from David Mawson

Private Collection

Illustrated on p. 128

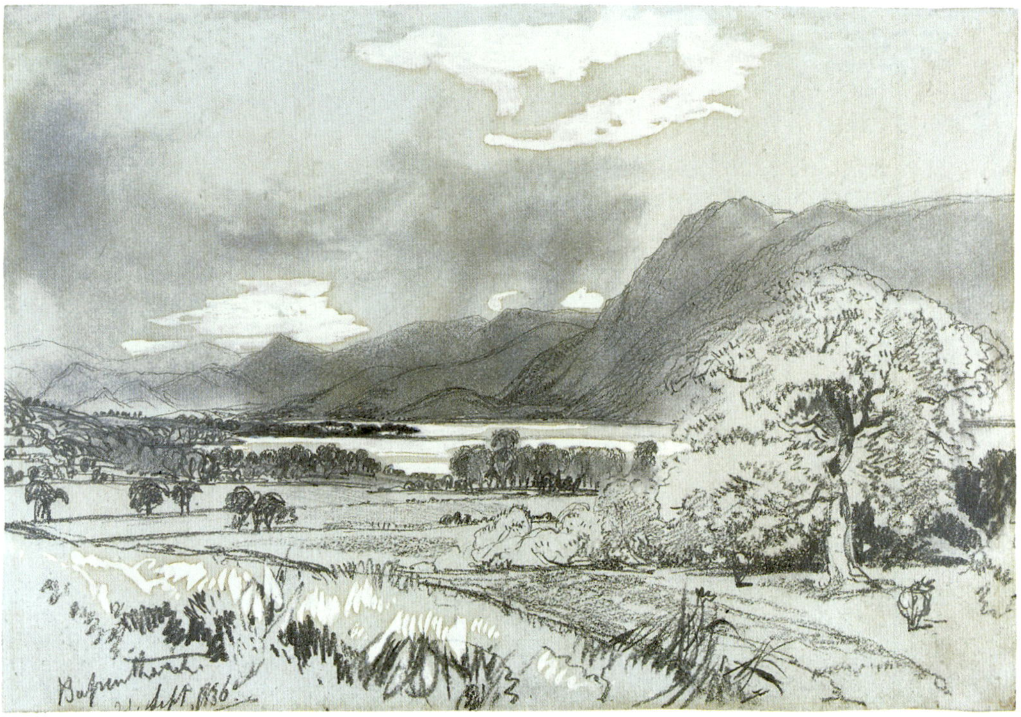

Cat. 52

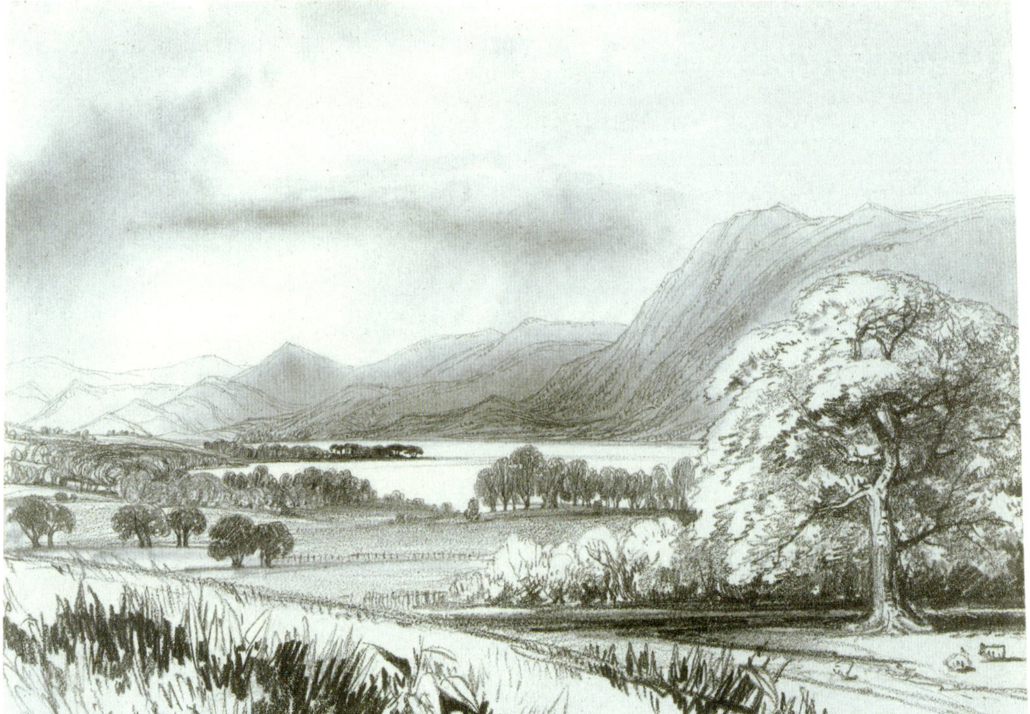

Cat. 53

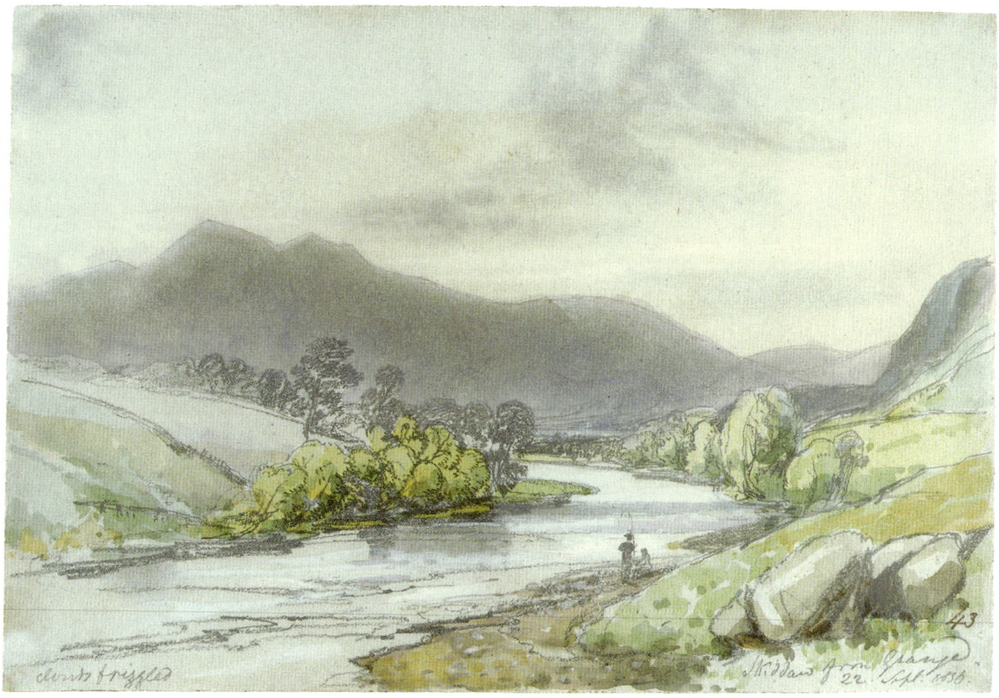

Cat. 54

54 *Skiddaw from Grange*

Inscribed and dated 'Skiddaw from Grange / 22. Sept.1836.', inscribed with notes 'clouds frizzled', numbered 43
Pencil, stump and watercolour heightened with white, on grey paper, 17.7 × 26.2 cm
Provenance: presented by the artist to the Nevill family; by descent in the Nevill family until sold to H.V. Day (bookseller) of Dorchester, Dorset, before 1958; purchased from H.V. Day by Colnaghi, 29 Dec. 1959 (£18); sold to W.W. Spooner, 15 Jan. 1960 (£35); presented by William Spooner to Walter Broughton in 1965, and by descent to the present owner

Private Collection, on loan to the Wordsworth Trust

One of the few drawings in the group to have had watercolour added (another is cat. 56, numbered 47), this is taken from the banks of the Derwent looking north, as it flows towards Derwentwater (out of sight); the bulk of Skiddaw is visible in the distance.

55 *Skiddaw and Derwentwater*

Inscribed and dated 'Derwentwater / 22d. Sept. 1836.', numbered 45
Pencil and stump, on blue-grey paper, 17.1 × 26 cm
Provenance: presented by the artist to the Nevill family; by descent in the Nevill family until sold to H.V. Day (bookseller) of Dorchester, Dorset, before 1958; purchased from H.V. Day by Colnaghi, 29 Dec. 1959 (£13); sold to Dr F.Springell, 28 Mar. 1960 (£21 5s); acquired by the current owner from Dr Springell in 1960

Private Collection

Illustrated on p. 130

This view is taken looking north up Derwentwater from the vicinity of Manesty Park at its south-western end with Skiddaw on the horizon.

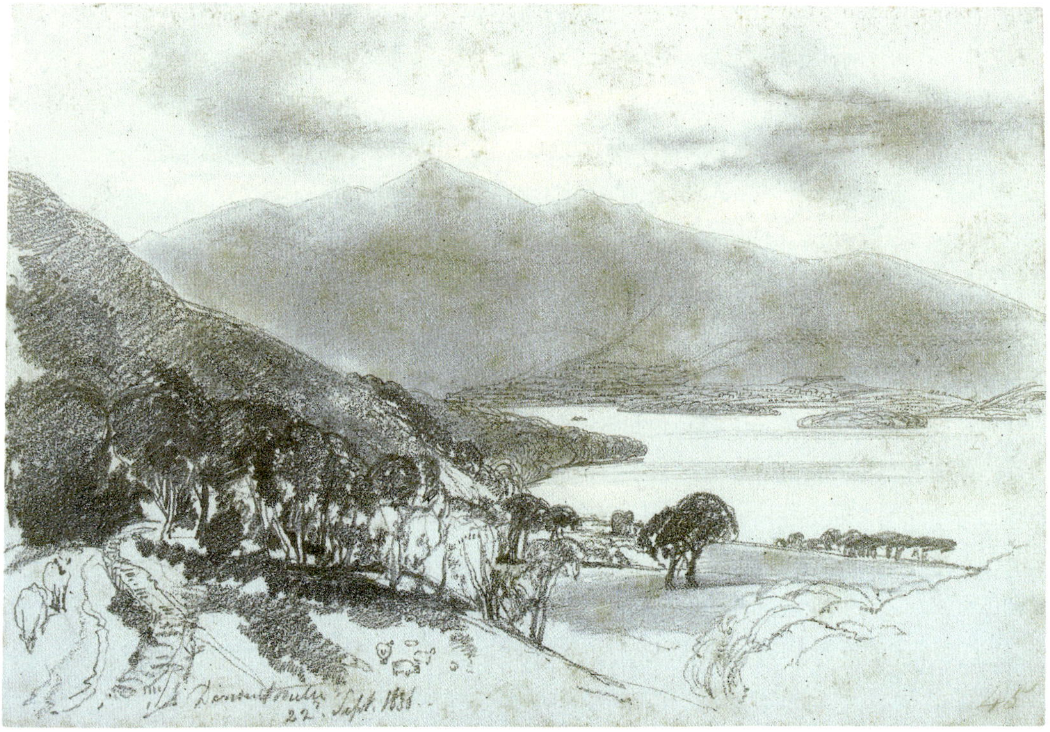

Cat. 55

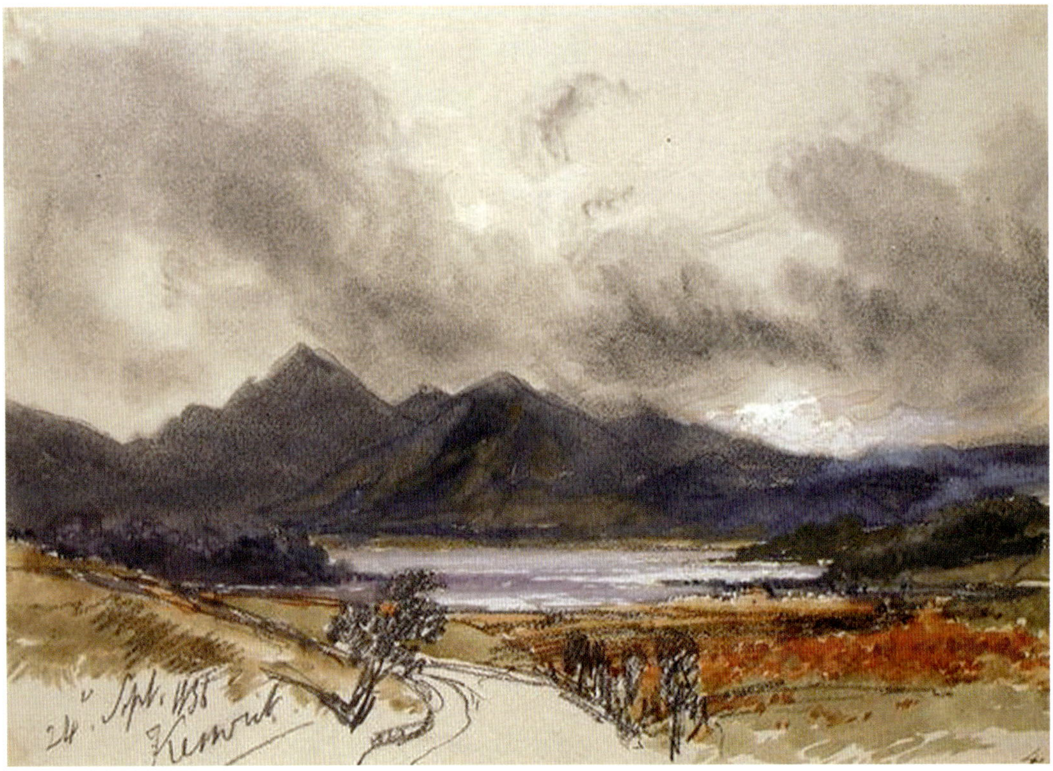

Cat. 56

56 *Derwentwater*

Inscribed and dated '24th. Sept. 1836 / Keswick', numbered 47
Pencil and watercolour heightened with white, on grey paper, 18.1 × 25.6 cm
Provenance: presented by the artist to the Nevill family; by descent in the Nevill family until sold to H.V. Day (bookseller) of Dorchester, Dorset, before 1958; purchased from H.V. Day by Colnaghi, 29 Dec. 1959 (£18); sold to Edward Seago, 6 Jan. 1960 (£35); the Estate of Edward Seago; Christie's, 1 Mar. 1977, lot 74 (£750 to Morton Morris); Spink, Annual Watercolour Exhibition, 1977, no. 59; sold to the current owner in 1978 (£1,125)

Abbot Hall Art Gallery, Kendal, Cumbria

Although this drawing is inscribed 'Keswick', it is not securely identified; it probably shows a view across the northern end of Derwentwater from the old road down into Keswick. The mountains on the far side of the lake include Causey Pike, with Grisedale Pike hidden in cloud.

27–30 September
Buttermere, Crummock, Loweswater and Ennerdale

It is not known for certain when Lear arrived in the Buttermere valley, but the earliest dated drawings were done on 27 September; there are four drawings with that date. His exploration of the north-western lakes was, as one would expect, methodical and thorough. First he travelled down the eastern shore of Buttermere to its southern end; he proceeded back past Buttermere village in order to get a view of Fleetwith Pike and Honister Crag, and then followed the road along the shore of Crummock Water. He probably spent that and the following night at the Scale Hill Inn in Loweswater. Mentioned in most of the contemporary guide books, the Scale Hill was described by Tattersall as 'a neat inn' , and by Wordsworth as 'a roomy Inn, with very good accommodation.' On 28 September, Lear was working in the Loweswater area; there are four drawings in the numerical sequence for this day, two of which survive. On the 29th he headed over to Ennerdale, almost certainly taking the path up Mosedale round the western side of Mellbreak and passing over the top into the Ennerdale Valley via Floutern Tarn. Four drawings survive dated the 29th and numbered 60 to 63, showing that Lear travelled along the eastern side of Ennerdale Water beyond the end of the lake. Sadly, at this point, the numerical sequence runs out; there are seven drawings missing from the sequence, and the next numbered drawing is 71, of the southern end of Buttermere, drawn on the evening of 30 September. The night of the 29th Lear probably spent at the Angler's Inn on Ennerdale Water, before exploring the head of the Ennerdale Valley the following day and heading back to Buttermere, presumably over the Scarth Gap Pass. Given the artist's fondness for waterfalls, it is hard to believe that the missing drawings did not contain one of Scale Force. Until 30 September the weather had been good, and Lear had been able to complete up to six drawings in a day, but at this point the weather must have set in, since only one drawing is missing from the numerical sequence and the next dated and numbered drawing of the Vale of Keswick is number 73, drawn on 4 October. Lear probably headed back to Keswick to sit out the rain, but without other evidence we have no means of knowing where he was between 1 and 3 October.

57 *Honister from near Buttermere*

Inscribed and dated 'Honister / from near / Butter mere / 27th. Sept / 1836.', numbered 51
Pencil and stump, on blue-grey paper, 17.7 × 26.1 cm
Provenance: presented by the artist to the Nevill family; by descent in the Nevill family until sold to H.V. Day (bookseller) of Dorchester, Dorset, before 1958; purchased from H.V. Day by Colnaghi, 29 Dec. 1959 (£13); sold to George Goyder, 31 Dec. 1959 (£25); returned by him, 11 Apr. 1960, sold to Dr Charles Warren, 21 Apr. 1960 (£25); Spink, Annual Watercolour Exhibition, 1974. no. 43 (£220); Anon. Sale; Bonhams, 12 June 2003, lot 614 (£1,500); Abbot and Holder, List 355, no. 193, August 2003, sold to the present owner (£3,250)

Private Collection, on loan to the Wordsworth Trust

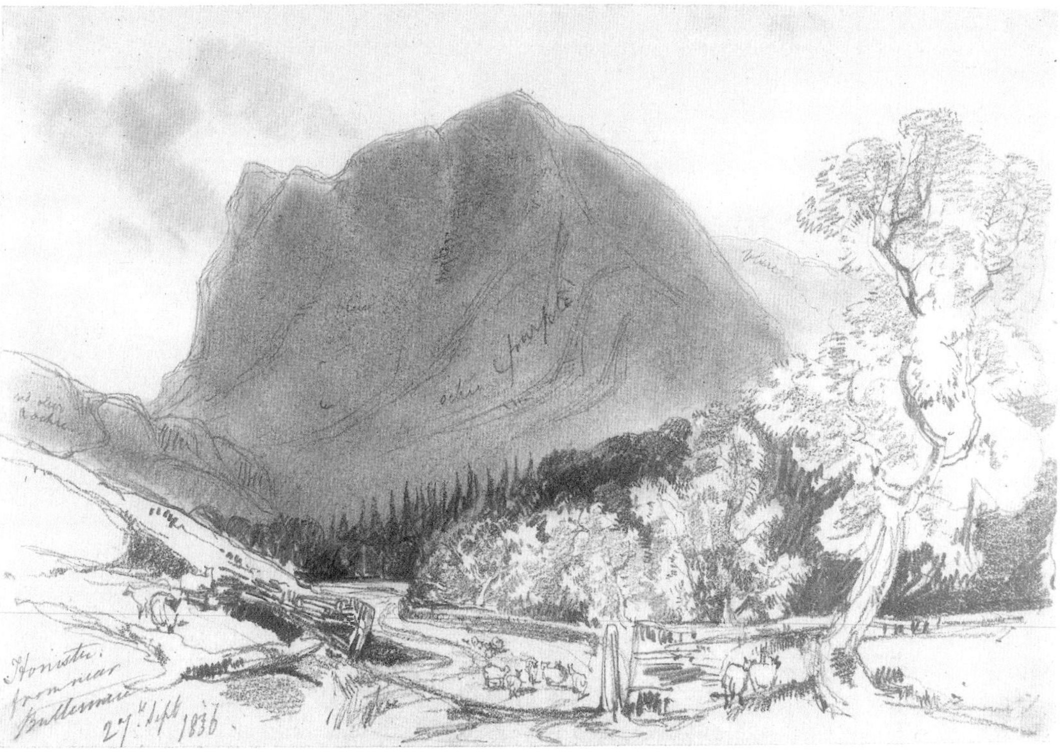

Cat. 57

This is the first of Lear's drawings made in the Vale of Buttermere. After descending from Newlands Hause down into Buttermere village, he turned left and went down to the end of the lake in order to get this view; he did not venture any further up Gatesgarthdale towards Honister Crag, and it was not until 10 October that he returned to the top of Honister Pass and drew the Crag from the other end (cat. 81).

58 *Crummock Water and Mellbreak*

Inscribed and dated 'Crummock 27 Sept. 1836', numbered 52
Pencil and stump heightened with white, on blue-grey paper, 17.2 × 25.6 cm
Provenance: bequeathed by the artist to his godson, Allan Nevill; by descent in his family until sold at Christie's, 20 November 2003, part of lot 77, where acquired by current owner

The Wordsworth Trust (2004.119.2)

Illustrated on p. 134

At this point Lear was travelling along the road from Buttermere towards Cockermouth; this shows a view across the southern end of Crummock Water towards Mellbreak.

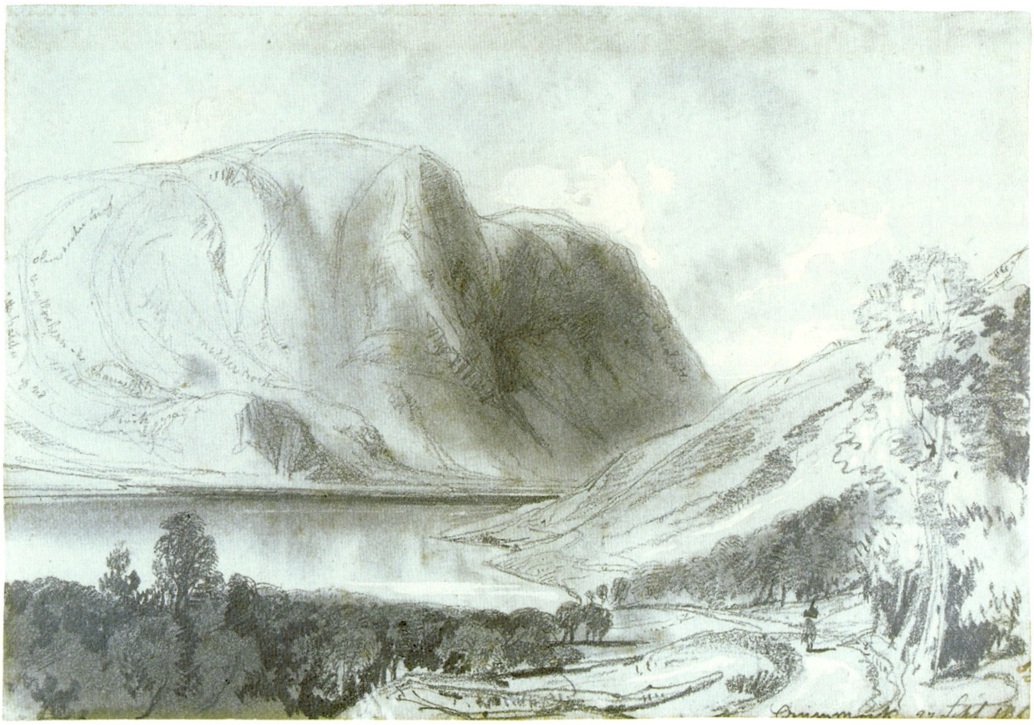

Cat. 58

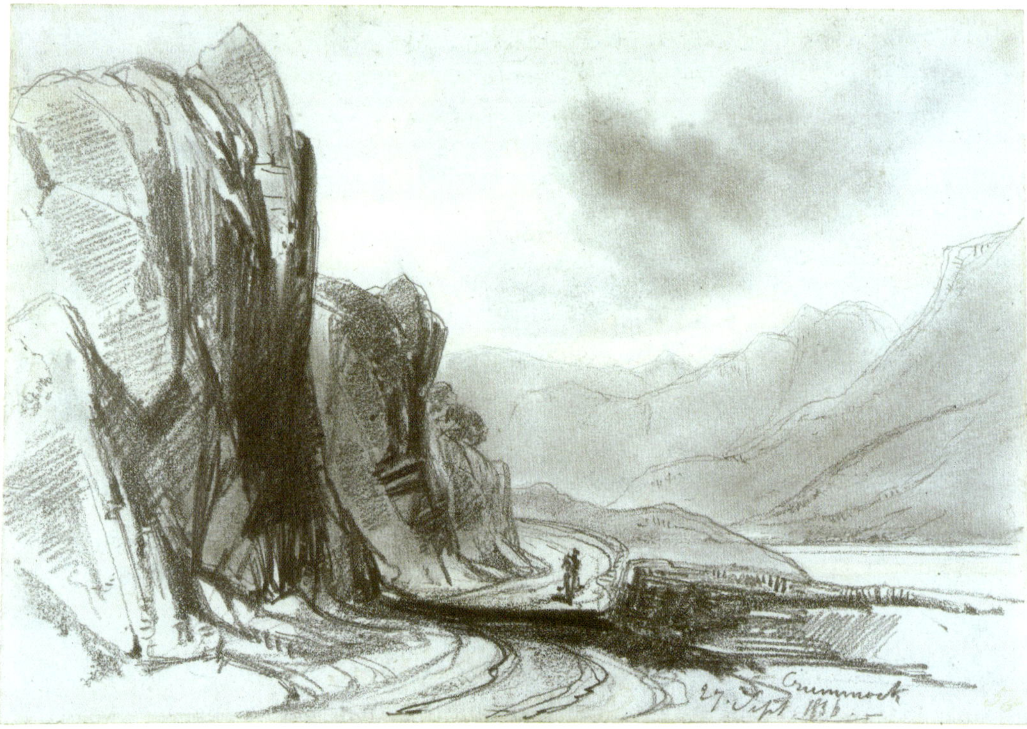

Cat. 59

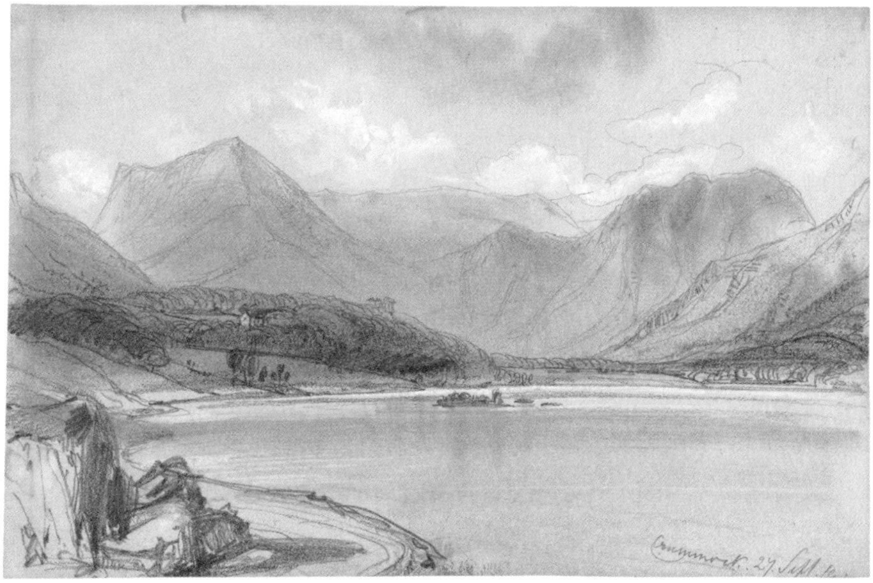

Fig. 36 Crummock Water, with Fleetwith Pike and Haystacks, inscribed and dated 'Crummock. 27. Sept. [1836]', pencil and stump heightened with white, on blue-grey paper, 16.6 × 25.8 cm (Yale Center for British Art, B1997.7.29).

59 *Crummock Water from Hause Point*

Inscribed and dated 'Crummock / 27. Sept. 1836.', numbered 54
Pencil heightened with white, on blue-grey paper, 17.6 × 26 cm
Provenance: presented by the artist to the Nevill family; by descent in the Nevill family until sold to H.V. Day (bookseller) of Dorchester, Dorset, before 1958; purchased from H.V. Day by Colnaghi, 29 Dec. 1959 (£13); sold to Edward Seago, 6 Jan. 1960 (£25); the Estate of Edward Seago; Christie's, 1 Mar. 1977, lot 76 (£300); Anon. Sale; Christie's, 30 June 1981, lot 150 (£400); Spink, Catalogue of English Drawings, Watercolours and Prints, Autumn 1981. no. 101 (£750); purchased by David Mawson, and by descent

Private Collection

As Lear travelled along the shore of Crummock Water, the views to the south over the lake towards Fleetwith Pike and Haystacks began to open up. This is the view that he depicted in an unnumbered drawing at Yale dated 27 Sept (fig. 36).

The Yale drawing is probably number 53 in the numerical sequence, drawn just before this view, which was taken on the road at Hause Point with the lake on the right.

60 *Loweswater*

Inscribed and dated 'Lowes Water. / 28th. Sept. 1836.', numbered 56
Pencil and stump heightened with white, on blue-grey paper, 17.8 × 25.9 cm
Provenance: presented by the artist to the Nevill family; by descent in the Nevill family until sold to H.V. Day (bookseller) of Dorchester, Dorset, before 1958; purchased from H.V. Day by Colnaghi, 29 Dec. 1959 (£13); sold to Cecil Higgins Museum, 18 Jan. 1960 (£25)

Cecil Higgins Art Gallery, Bedford

Illustrated on p. 137

Lear probably spent the night of 27–8 September at the Scale Hill Inn in the village of Loweswater. The following day he explored the environs of the village and lake, travelling along the shore of the lake on the Egremont road. This is a view looking south-east along Loweswater back the way he had come with the imposing bulk of Mellbreak to the right; it was probably from this point that Lear turned back. Another sketch of Lowes Water, which was presumably numbered 57 or 58, formed the basis of the finished drawing of the lake executed the following year (cat. 61).

61 *Loweswater*

Signed and dated 'E.Lear del / 1837'
Pencil, black chalk and stump, on blue-grey paper, 17.4 × 25.7 cm
Provenance: Robert A. Hornby (d. 1857); Anon. Sale; Sotheby's, 18 Mar. 1982, lot 11 (2 in lot) (£680); Spink, English Watercolour Drawings, Annual Exhibition, 1983, no. 19 (£950); John Dayton (d.2003); Anon. Sale; Sotheby's, 30 July 2005, lot 280, purchased by the current owner (£5,200)

The Wordsworth Trust (2006.47.1)

Dated the following year and presumably commissioned by Robert Hornby, Lear's friend and Lord Derby's nephew, this drawing shows a view further along the Egremont road on the shore of Loweswater; it derives from a lost sketch of 28 September, numbered 57 or 58. A sketch of Loweswater was included in the 1960 Colnaghi exhibition, but is now untraced.

62 *Crummock Water looking South*

Inscribed and dated 'Crummock / 28. Sept. 1836', numbered 59
Pencil and stump heightened with white, on blue-grey paper, 17.3 × 24.8 cm
Provenance: presented by the artist to Ralph Nevill, F.S.A. (d. 1917); by descent to his daughter, Mrs B C Bamber; purchased from Mrs B C Bamber in 1942 (£10 for six drawings)

The British Museum (1942-12-11-5)

Illustrated on p. 138

This is the last drawing of the day on 28 September, showing a view looking south-east over Crummock Water towards Rannerdale Knotts; it was drawn in the afternoon before Lear turned back to spend a second night in Loweswater, probably at the Scale Hill Inn.

63 *'From Wandreth Moss'*

Inscribed and dated 'From / Wandreth Moss. / 29. Sept. / 1836.', numbered 60
Pencil and stump heightened with white, on blue-grey paper, 17.5 × 26 cm
Provenance: presented by the artist to the Nevill family; by descent in the Nevill family until sold to H.V. Day (bookseller) of Dorchester, Dorset, before 1958; purchased from H.V. Day by Colnaghi, 29 Dec. 1959 (£13); sold to A.D. Pilkington, 11 Feb. 1960 (£25); bequeathed to Eton College by Alan Pilkington in 1973

The Provost and Fellows of Eton College, Windsor

Illustrated on p. 138

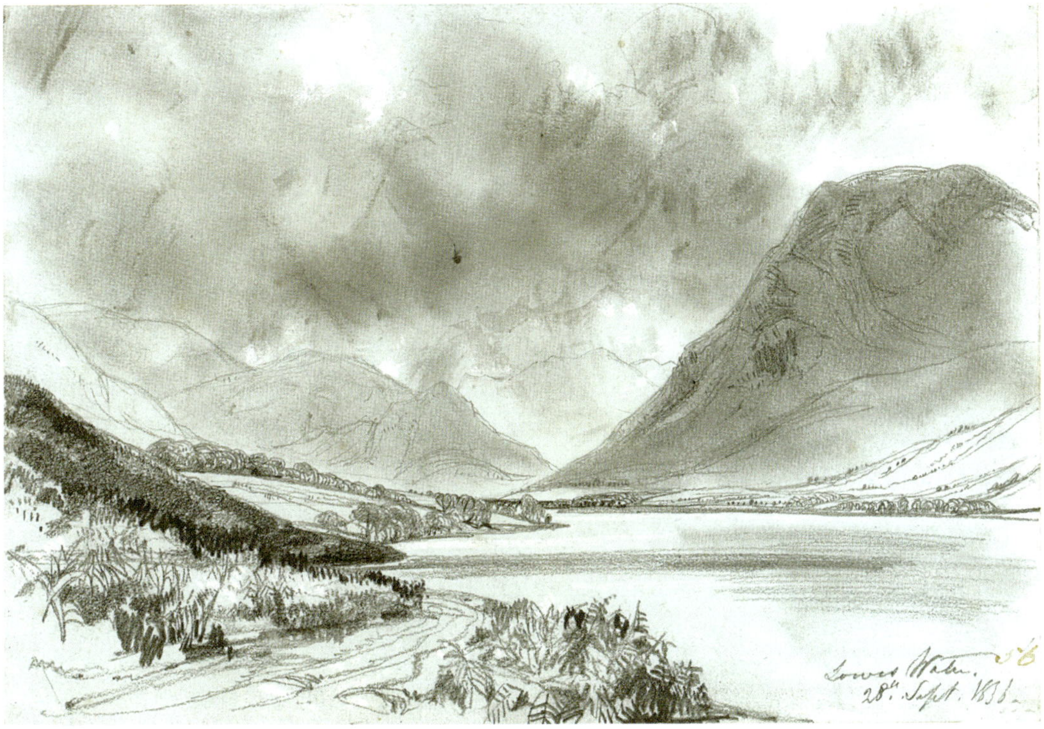

Cat. 60

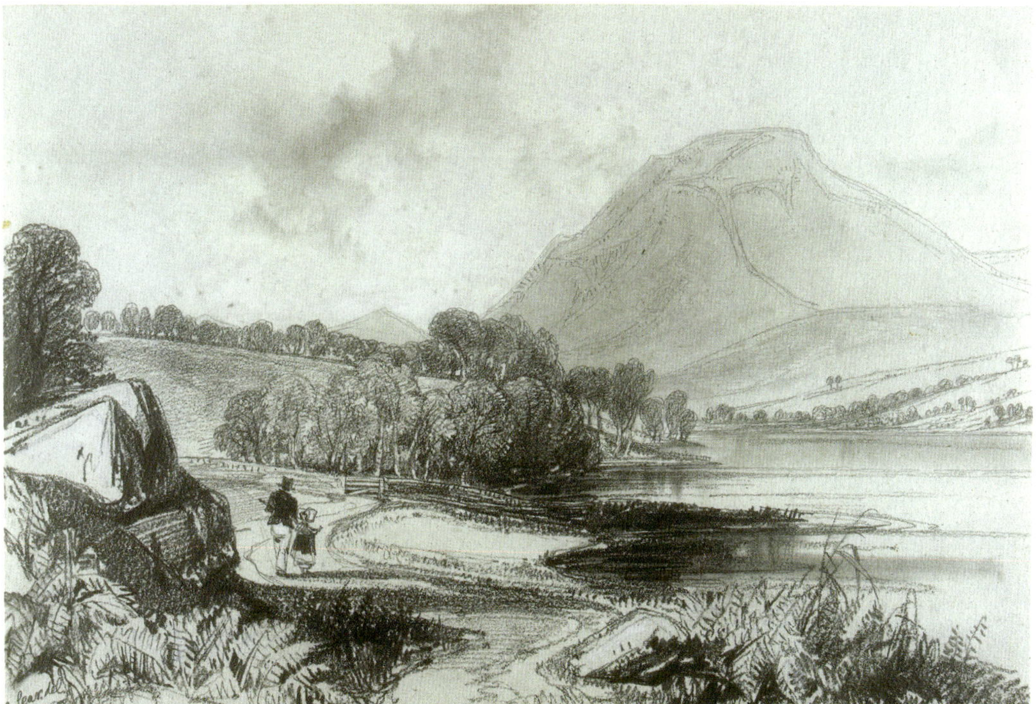

Cat. 61

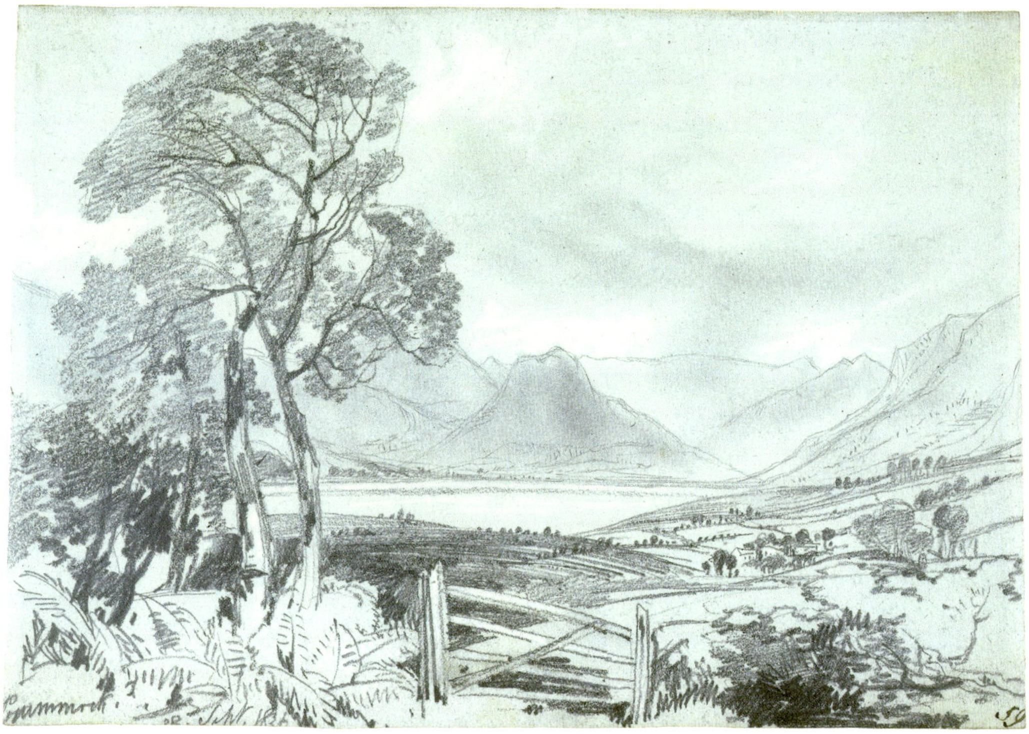

Cat. 62

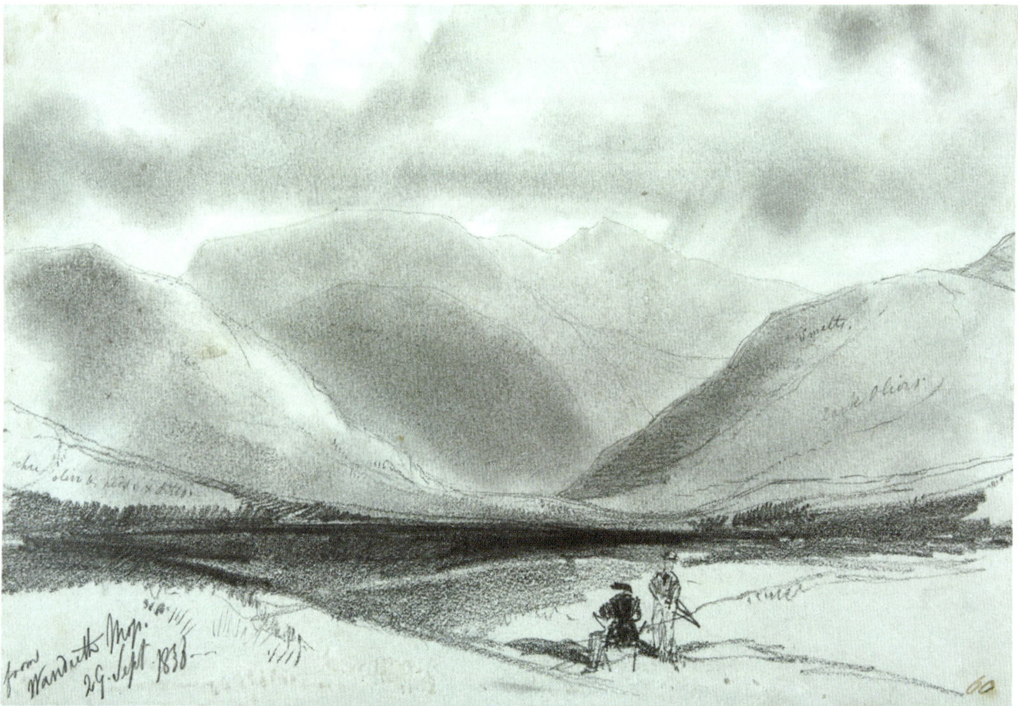

Cat. 63

Despite exhaustive correspondence with local experts and consultation of old maps of the area, the identity of the Wandreth Moss of Lear's inscription remains elusive. Given that it fits into the numerical sequence between numbers 59 and 61, it has to have been drawn somewhere on the journey between Loweswater and Ennerdale. The inscription may be a mishearing or simply a mistake on Lear's part.

64 *Ennerdale Water*

Inscribed and dated 'Ennerdale Water. / 29. Sept. 1836.', numbered 61
Pencil and stump, on blue-grey paper, 17.4 × 25.9 cm
Provenance: presented by the artist to the Nevill family; by descent in the Nevill family until sold to H.V. Day (bookseller) of Dorchester, Dorset, before 1958; purchased from H.V. Day by Colnaghi, 29 Dec. 1959 (£13); sold to Dr F.Springell, 28 Mar. 1960 (£21 5s); acquired by the current owner from Dr Springell in 1960
Private Collection

This is a view looking down onto Ennerdale Water with Bowness Knott on the left. The figure reclining in the foreground, who also appears in the Wandreth Moss drawing standing beside the seated figure and carrying an umbrella, and again in the foreground of cat. 65, is problematic. It is not known whether Lear had a companion for this part of the journey, although certainly it was not his original intention to have one.

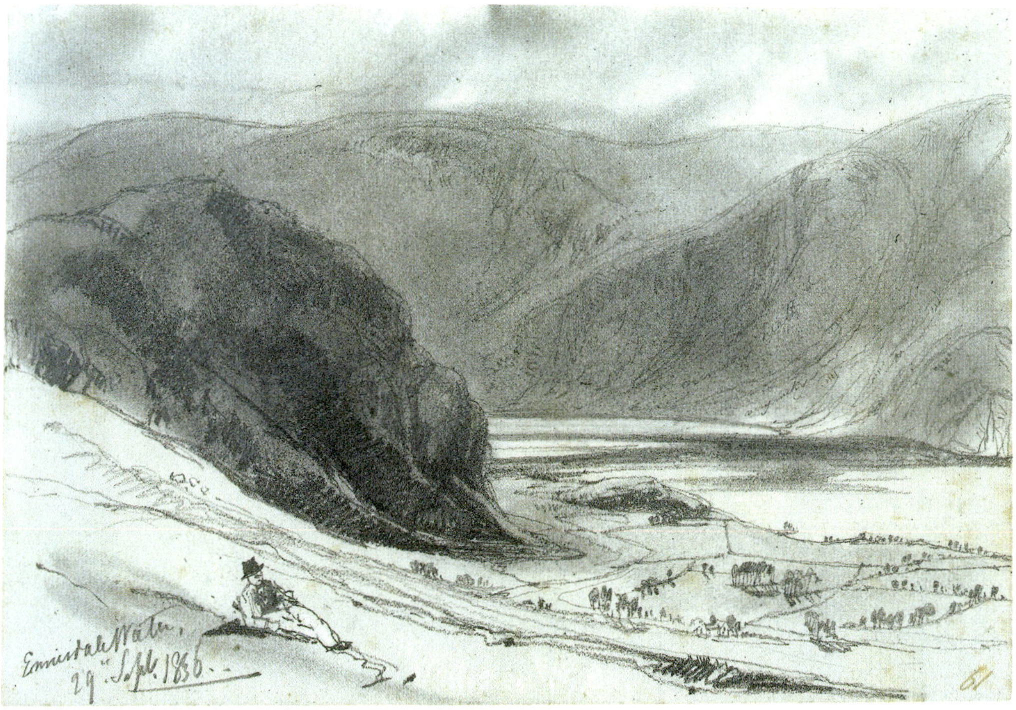

Cat. 64

65 *Ennerdale Water*

Inscribed and dated 'Ennerdale Water / 29. Sept. 1836.', numbered 62
Pencil and stump heightened with white, on blue-grey paper, 17.5 × 26 cm
Provenance: presented by the artist to the Nevill family; by descent in the Nevill family until sold to H.V. Day (bookseller) of Dorchester, Dorset, before 1958; purchased from H.V. Day by Colnaghi, 29 Dec. 1959 (£13); sold to Dr F.Springell, 28 Mar. 1960 (£21 5s); acquired by the current owner from Dr Springell in 1960

Private Collection

The viewpoint for this drawing is the northern shore of Ennerdale Water with Pillar, Steeple and Scoat Fell on the horizon, not far from the site of the Angler's Inn, which is probably where Lear spent the night of 29 September.

66 *Pillar, Ennerdale*

Inscribed and dated 'T'Pillar Ennerdale / 29 Sept. 1836.', numbered 63
Pencil and stump heightened with white, on blue-grey paper, 17.2 × 25.7 cm
Provenance: presented by the artist to the Nevill family; by descent in the Nevill family until sold to H.V. Day (bookseller) of Dorchester, Dorset, before 1958; purchased from H.V. Day by Colnaghi, 29 Dec. 1959 (£13); sold to George Goyder, 31 Dec. 1959 (£25); presented by Dr Charles Warren, probably in 1981

The Wordsworth Trust (GRMDC.B203)

This, the next drawing in the numerical sequence after cat. 65, shows that Lear travelled along the northern shore of Ennerdale Water towards the head of the valley, an area now much disfigured by conifer plantation. He has left the lake behind him and Pillar appears on the right with Pillar Rock clearly visible. The eastern side of the mountain and the head of the valley are in shadow, indicating a time in the late afternoon. The inscription 'T'Pillar' shows Lear's awareness of the local accent.

67 *The Head of Buttermere, with Honister Crag, Fleetwith Pike and Haystacks*

Inscribed and dated '[Bu]ttermere 30th Sept.', numbered 71
Pencil and stump heightened with white, on grey paper, 16.9 × 25.7 cm
Provenance: bequeathed by the artist to his godson, Allan Nevill; by descent in his family until sold at Christie's, 20 November 2003, part of lot 77, where acquired by current owner

The Wordsworth Trust (2004.119.4)

Illustrated on p. 142

After the view of Pillar drawn on the afternoon of the previous day, there are seven drawings missing from the numerical sequence, and this, number 71, drawn in the evening of the next day (the eastern side of Honister Crag is in shadow), is the next drawing to survive. After exploring the head of Ennerdale, Lear probably walked back to Buttermere over Scarth Gap Pass, before spending the night in Buttermere.

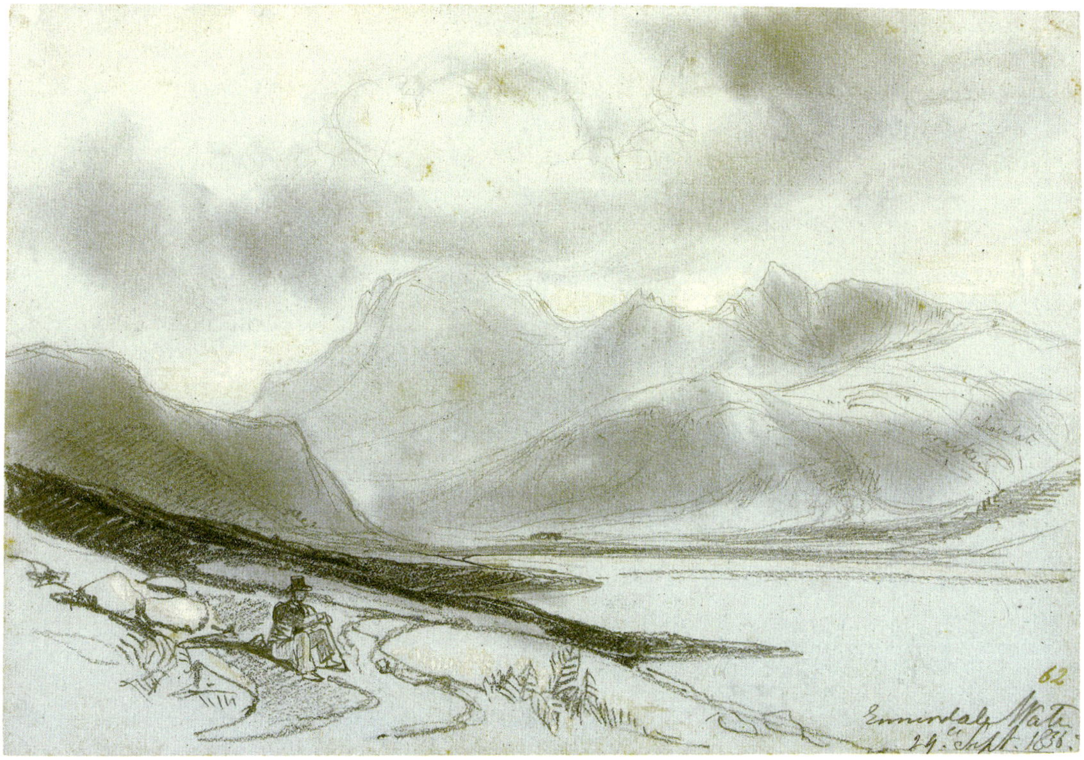

Cat. 65

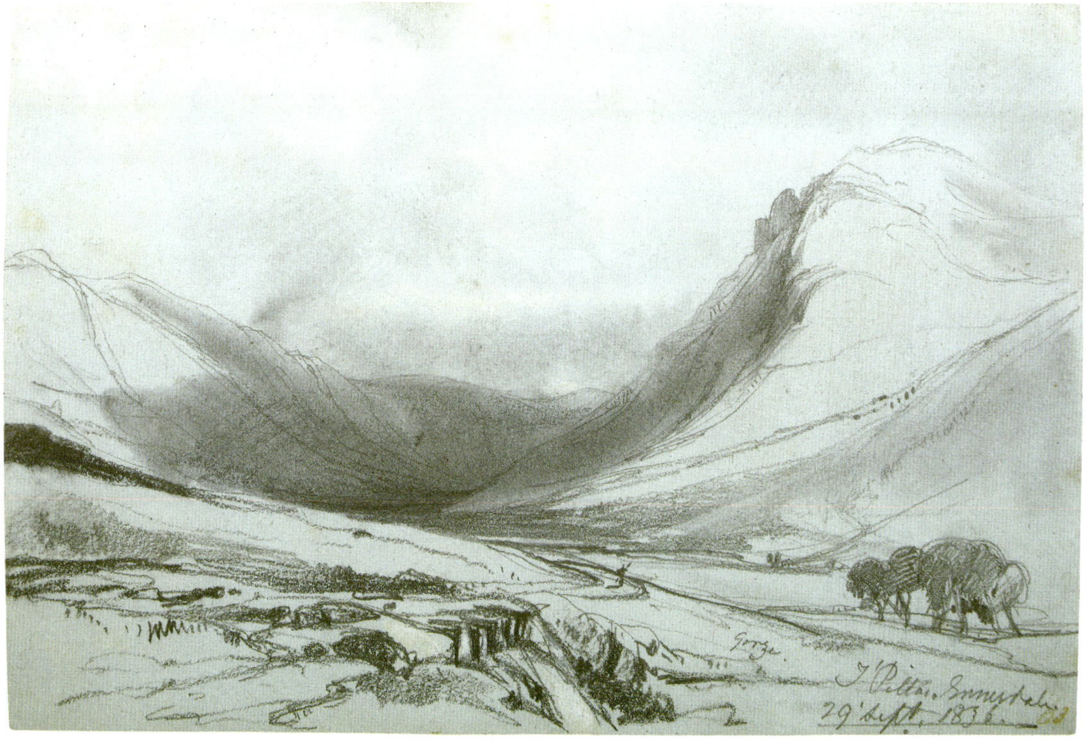

Cat. 66

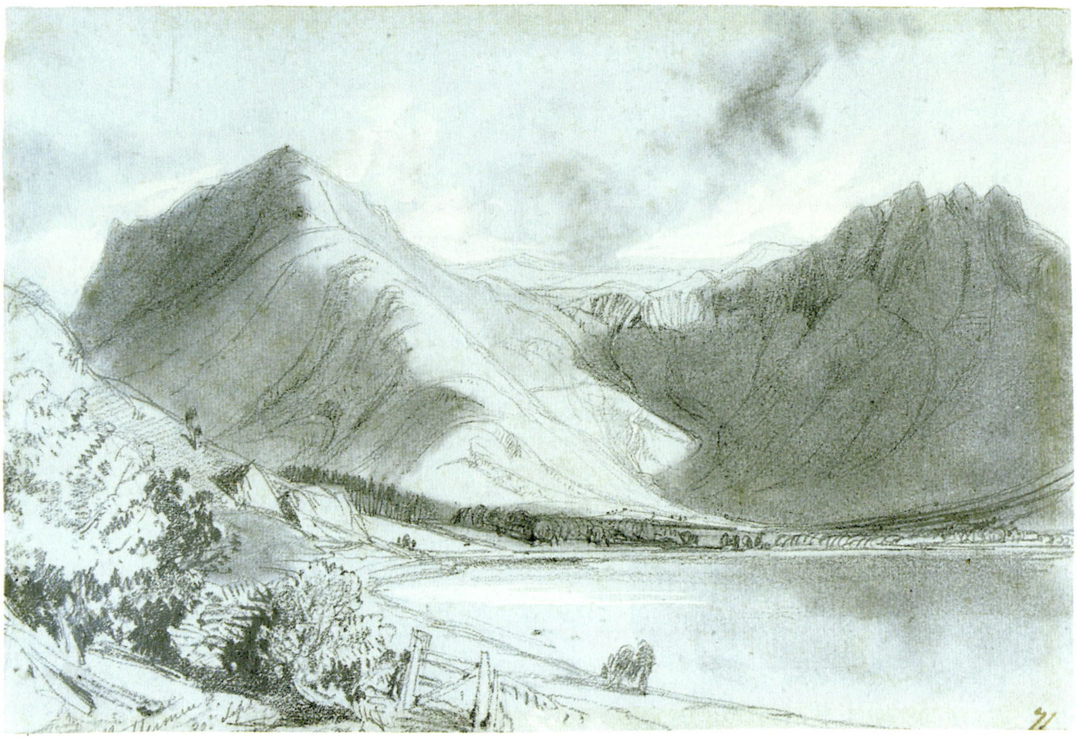

Cat. 67

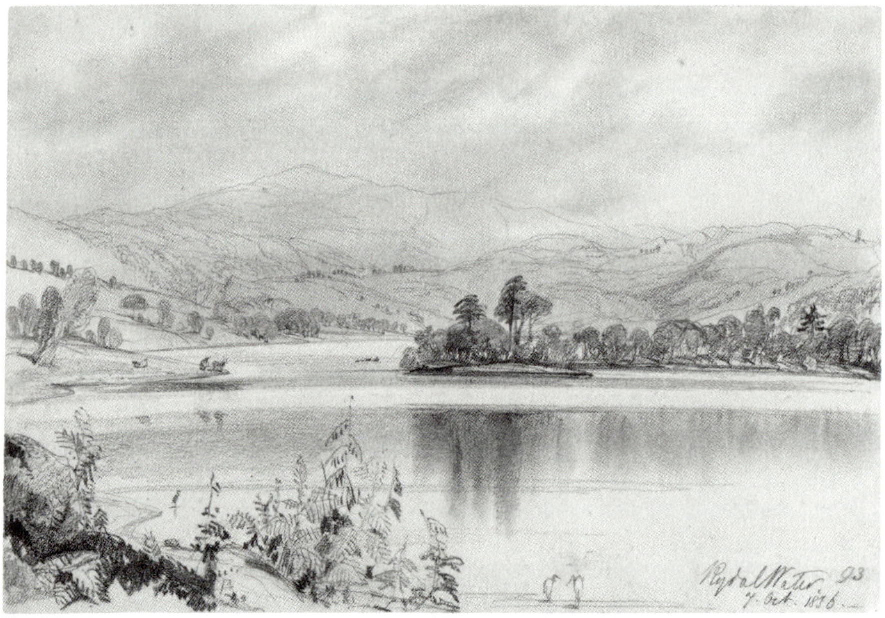

Fig. 37 Rydal Water, inscribed and dated 'Rydal Water. 7. Oct. 1836', numbered 93, pencil and stump, on blue-grey paper, 17.6 × 26 cm (Department of Printing and Graphic Arts, The Houghton Library, Harvard University).

4–7 October
from Keswick south via Thirlmere, Grasmere, Rydal to Ambleside and Windermere

After the intense productivity of the preceding days, only one drawing is missing from the numerical sequence after the drawing of the head of Buttermere drawn on the evening of 30 September, numbered 71, and before the view of the Vale of Keswick, drawn on 4 October, numbered 73. The rain must have prevented Lear's working, but on the 4th it brightened up and he was able to resume his tour. He headed south again, travelling in reverse the route that he had taken the previous month; on this occasion, he proceeded at a more leisurely pace, and must therefore have been on horseback. Lear did not take the most direct route from Keswick, instead travelling via St John's in the Vale and viewing Thirlmere from its north-western corner. At this date, before it became a reservoir in 1894 and the water level was raised by some 80 feet, Thirlmere was still virtually two lakes, divided towards its northern end by a causeway connected by three bridges; these idiosyncratic structures appear in three of Lear's four views of the lake, twice in the distance and once close-up. It is clear from the sequence of drawings, which is complete at this point, that Lear crossed the bridges from the western side, and proceeded south along the eastern shore of the lake towards Dunmail Raise and Grasmere.

Two drawings survive from the following day, 5 October: Skelwith Force, and Grasmere from Red Bank (cats. 73 and 75), numbered 78 and 80. After this there is a large gap in the numerical sequence, until the drawing of Rydal Water from its eastern end, dated 7 October and numbered 93 (fig. 37); the final drawing done that day, numbered 94, is of Windermere looking towards Ambleside, and seems to have been drawn from a boat on the lake. In the absence of letters and surviving drawings, we have no means of knowing where Lear stayed or what he visited. We can assume that he explored the Grasmere area and he must have sketched Rydal Falls, the favourite sketching subject for countless visiting artists; Wordsworth was in residence at Rydal Mount, but there is no evidence that his presence was any attraction to the young artist. The only evidence of subjects sketched comes from a watercolour of the Bridge House at Ambleside, sold at Sotheby's in 1964 and currently untraced (fig. 38, p. 144); this must derive from a now lost on-the-spot sketch.

Lear's base near Ambleside in 1836 is not known; on later visits, probably in 1850 and certainly in 1858, he stayed at Wansfell Holme, a short distance to the south of Waterhead and just off the Bowness to Ambleside road. This house was built in 1840–1 for the Wrigley family, paper manufacturers from Bury, and rented by the Rev. James John Hornby, who paid for alterations to it in 1849; Lear's great friend Robert Hornby, the Rev. James John's son, died there in 1857. Lear stayed at this house on his visit to England in 1858, the first year from which a diary survives; he took the train from London on 27 August 1858 and stayed for a week. The way in which he describes his activities at the house does not suggest that he is visiting it for the first time.

Lear was certainly in England in 1850 and there are big gaps in our knowledge of his whereabouts. The only evidence for a visit to the Lake District that year is a watercolour of Windermere and the Langdale Pikes, dated October 1850, which is at Abbot Hall (fig. 39, p. 144). The Abbot Hall watercolour is inscribed 'Windermere from Wansfell' but the viewpoint is clearly not the summit of a mountain, so the Wansfell of the title is surely the house of that name rather than the hill above it; the watercolour cannot derive from a sketch of 1836, since the house had not at that date been built, and the date of October 1850 on it must refer to an actual visit rather than

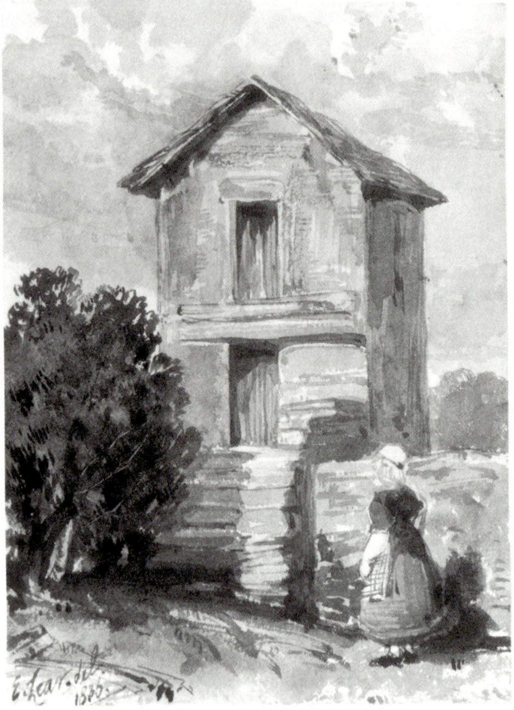

Fig. 38 The Bridge House, Ambleside, signed and dated 1836, 19.1 × 13.3 cm (Sotheby's, 4 Nov. 1964, lot 47). This now untraced work is the only finished watercolour of a Lake District subject signed and dated 1836.

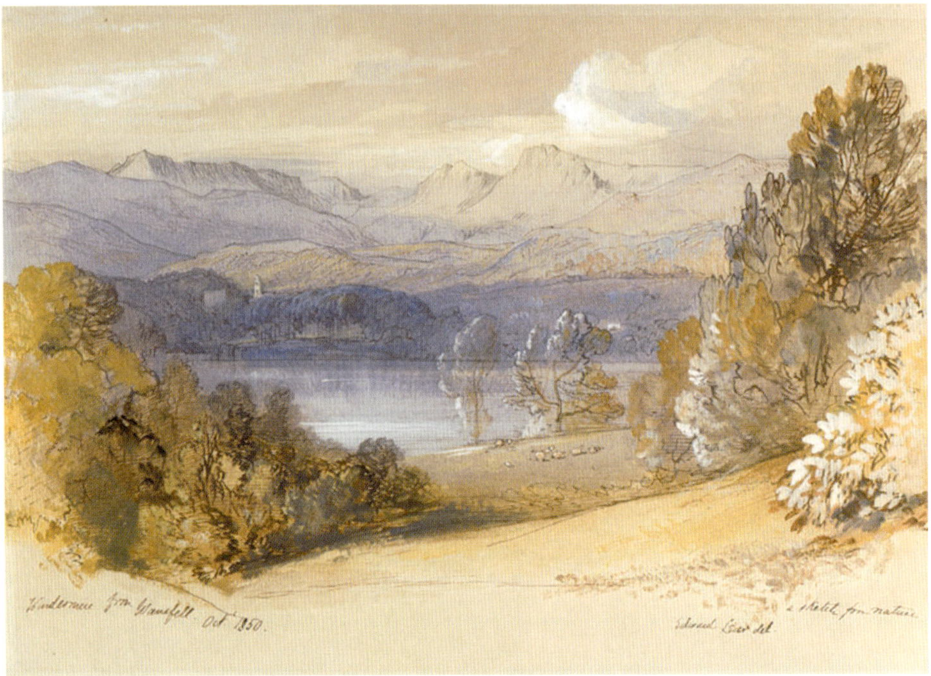

Fig. 39 Windermere from Wansfell, signed, inscribed and dated 'Windermere from Wansfell / Octr. 1850. / a sketch from nature / Edward Lear del.', pen and brown ink and watercolour heightened with white, 25 × 35 cm (Abbot Hall Art Gallery, Kendal, Cumbria).

The tower of the newly built Holy Trinity church at Brathay, consecrated in 1836, stands out above the trees on the other side of the lake, below the Bowfell range in the far distance.

a date of execution. It seems therefore that Lear revisited old haunts during 1850 and that he went back to Windermere and stayed with the Hornby family.

It is possible that other members of the Hornby family were staying near Ambleside in 1836, and this could be the source of Lear's memory in old age of running 'races all over that part of the country' with the future Headmaster and Provost of Eton, J.J. Hornby, then aged ten (see Noakes 1985, p. 95). It is much more likely, however, that this refers to the 1850 visit, since J. J. Hornby would then have been a more appropriate twenty-four, and he was not at Wansfell when Lear stayed there in 1858. The memory of this Hornby house remained very strong, since Lear wrote in a letter of 29 December 1884 to E. Carus Selwyn, Headmaster of Liverpool College: 'do you ever walk as far as the top of Windermere ... to a place called Wansfell? I wonder who has it now:—it used to be the Rev J.J. Hornby's—Uncle of J.J.H of Eton Provost' (MS. Private Collection).

68 *The Vale of Keswick looking towards Bassenthwaite*

Inscribed and dated 'Vale of Keswick. / 4th. October / 1836.', numbered 73
Pencil and stump on blue-grey paper, 16.9 × 25.4 cm
Provenance: presented by the artist to the Nevill family; by descent in the Nevill family until sold to H.V. Day (bookseller) of Dorchester, Dorset, before 1958; purchased from H.V. Day by Colnaghi, 29 Dec. 1959 (£13); sold to Dr F.Springell, 28 Mar. 1960 (£21 5s); acquired by the current owner from Dr Springell in 1960

Private Collection

Crosthwaite Church is visible in the middle distance towards the left; below and to its left can be seen the tower of the Moot Hall with its pyramidal roof. Lear was in Keswick shortly before the building of St John's Church, with its distinctive spire, by Salvin in 1838. A drawing entitled 'The Vale of Keswick and Bassenthwaite Lake', signed and dated 1837, was sold at Sotheby's, 18 November 1971, lot 23; measuring 18 × 25.5 cm, it was probably a finished version of this sketch.

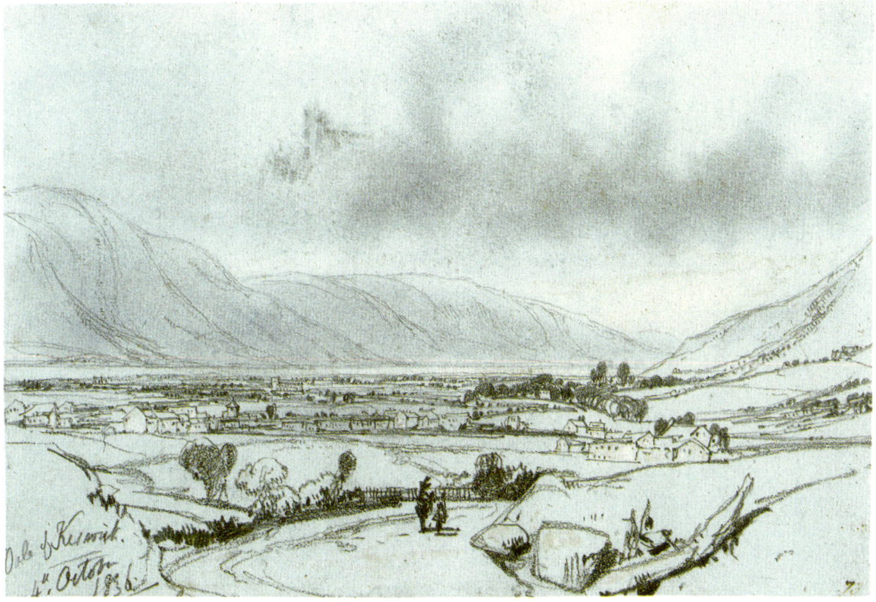

Cat. 68

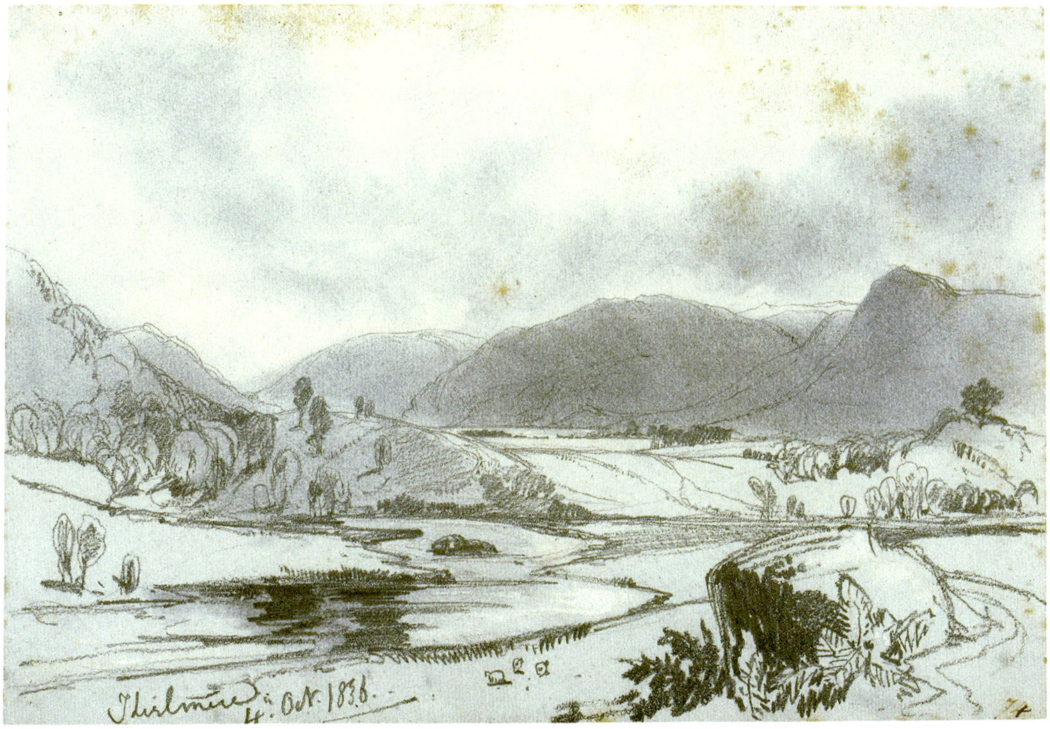

Cat. 69

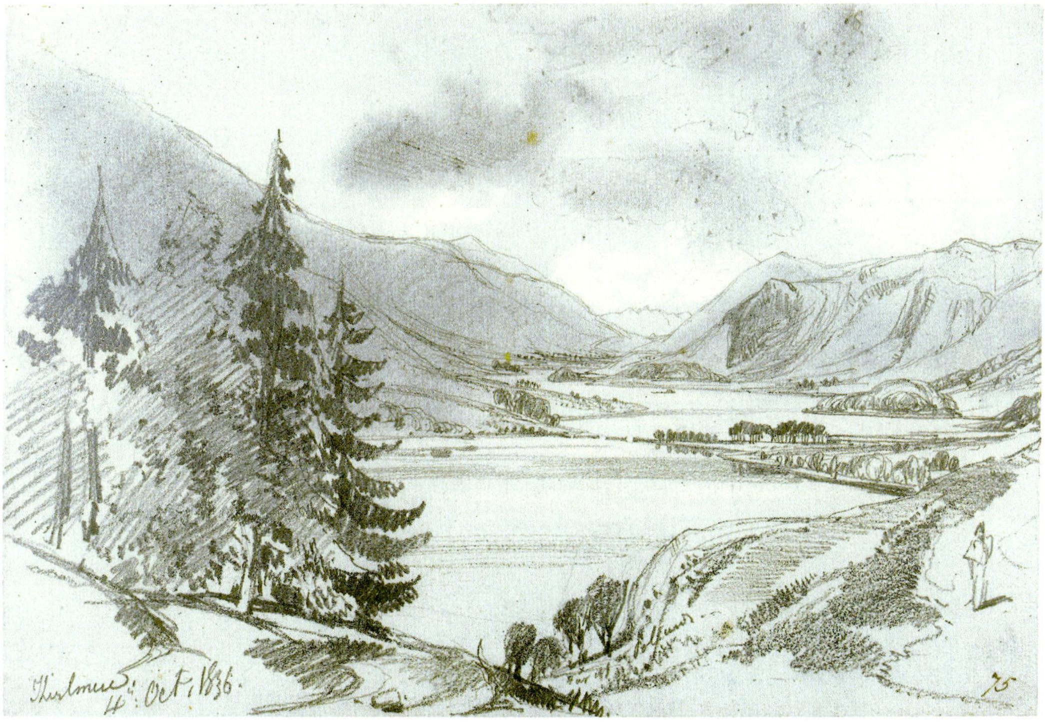

Cat. 70

69 *Thirlmere from the North*

Inscribed and dated 'Thirlmere. / 4th. Oct. 1836.', numbered 74
Pencil and stump on blue-grey paper, 17.4 × 26 cm
Provenance: presented by the artist to the Nevill family; by descent in the Nevill family until sold to H.V. Day (bookseller) of Dorchester, Dorset, before 1958; purchased from H.V. Day by Colnaghi, 29 Dec. 1959 (£13); sold to Dr F.Springell, 28 Mar. 1960 (£21 5s); acquired by the current owner from Dr Springell in 1960
Private Collection

This is drawn above St John's Beck, looking south towards Thirlmere; the three bridges dividing the lake can be seen in the far distance with Raven Crag in shadow on the right.

70 *Thirlmere*

Inscribed and dated 'Thirlmere. / 4th. Oct. 1836.', numbered 75
Pencil and stump on blue-grey paper, 17.5 × 26 cm
Provenance: presented by the artist to the Nevill family; by descent in the Nevill family until sold to H.V. Day (bookseller) of Dorchester, Dorset, before 1958; purchased from H.V. Day by Colnaghi, 29 Dec. 1959 (£13); sold to Mrs Helen Reynolds, 5 Feb. 1960 (£25); by descent to the present owner
Private Collection

This view looks down onto Thirlmere from the slopes of Raven Crag; the viewpoint is similar to the Allom print of 1834 (fig. 40).

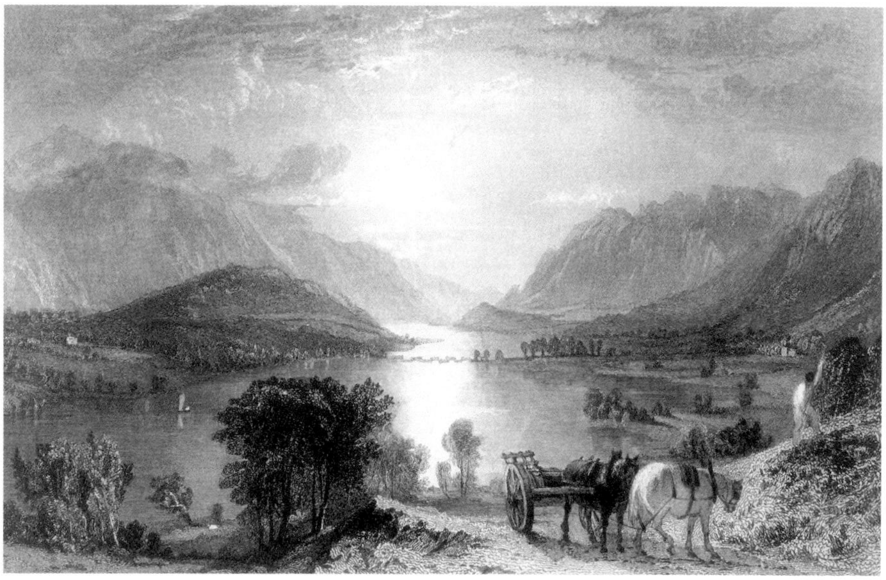

Fig. 40 'Thirlmere & Helvellyn &c., from Raven Crag', engraving after Thomas Allom, 1834, from *Westmorland, Cumberland, Durham, and Northumberland, Illustrated. From Original Drawings by Thomas Allom, George Pickering, &c. with Descriptions by T. Rose*, 1832–5 (The Wordsworth Trust).

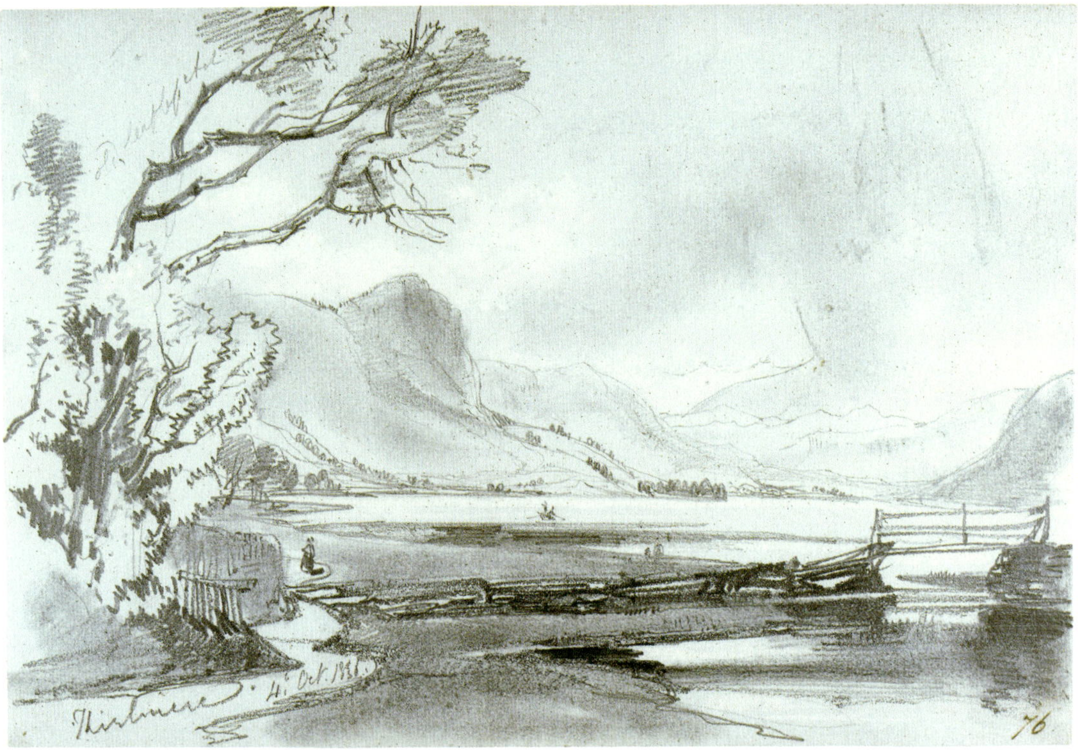

Cat. 71

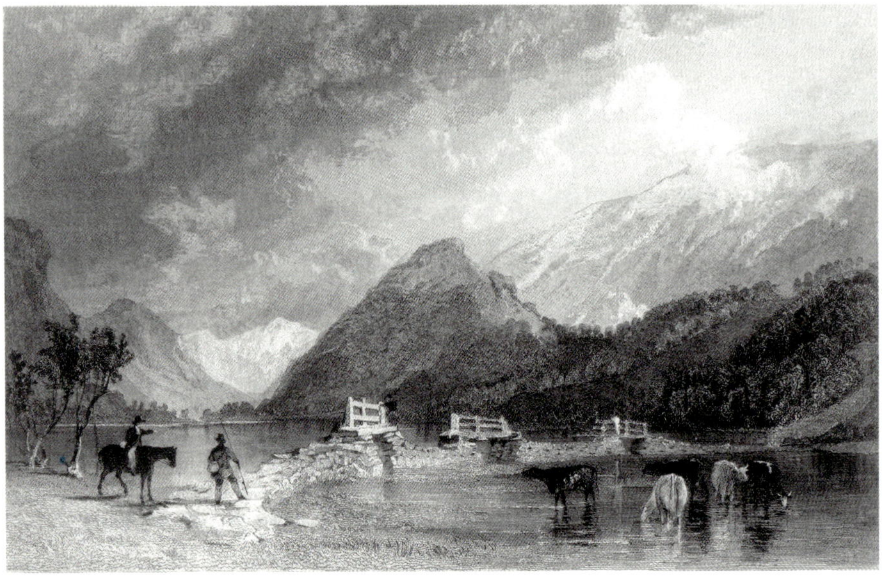

Fig. 41 'Thirlmere Bridge, looking north, Cumberland', engraving after Thomas Allom, 1834, from *Westmorland, Cumberland, Durham, and Northumberland, Illustrated. From Original Drawings by Thomas Allom, George Pickering, &c. with Descriptions by T. Rose*, 1832–5 (The Wordsworth Trust).

71 *Thirlmere*

Inscribed and dated 'Thirlmere. / 4th. Oct. 1836.', numbered 76
Pencil and stump on blue-grey paper, 17.4 × 25.6 cm
Provenance: presented by the artist to the Nevill family; by descent in the Nevill family until sold to H.V. Day (bookseller) of Dorchester, Dorset, before 1958; purchased from H.V. Day by Colnaghi, 29 Dec. 1959 (£13); sold to Dr Charles Warren, 27 Jan. 1960 (£25); presented by him in 1969

Abbot Hall Art Gallery, Kendal, Cumbria

This is drawn on the shore of the lake looking north towards Raven Crag, with one of the three bridges that crossed the lake shown on the right. The Allom print (fig. 41) depicts this unusual crossing point more completely.

72 *Thirlmere from the South*

Inscribed and dated 'Thirlmere. 4th. Oct / 1836.', inscribed with colour notes, numbered 77
Pencil and stump heightened with white, on blue-grey paper, 17.4 × 25.9 cm
Provenance: presented by the artist to the Nevill family; by descent in the Nevill family until sold to H.V. Day (bookseller) of Dorchester, Dorset, before 1958; purchased from H.V. Day by Colnaghi, 29 Dec. 1959 (£13); sold to Dr F.Springell, 28 Mar. 1960 (£21 5s); acquired by the current owner from Dr Springell in 1960

Private Collection

The colour notes lower left, describing the distant Raven Crag, read 'crag nearly black'; the viewpoint of this drawing, the last to be drawn on 4 October, is the road along the shore of the lake, before Lear climbed up over Dunmail Raise and crossed into Westmorland.

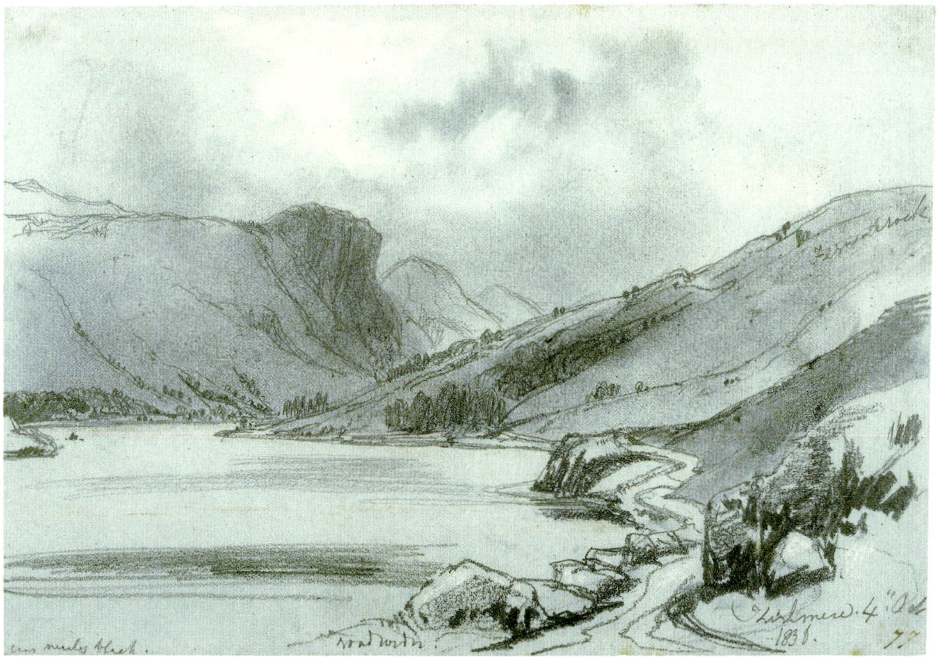

Cat. 72

73 *Skelwith Force*

Inscribed and dated 'Skelwith Force. / 5th. Oct.1836—', numbered 78
Pencil and watercolour heightened with white, on grey paper, 18 × 25.7 cm
Provenance: presented by the artist to the Nevill family; by descent in the Nevill family until sold to H.V. Day (bookseller) of Dorchester, Dorset, before 1958; purchased from H.V. Day by Colnaghi, 29 Dec. 1959 (£13); sold to George Goyder, 31 Dec. 1959 (£35); Spink, Annual Watercolour Exhibition, 1973. no. 13 (£400); acquired by the current owner in 1973

Private Collection

74 *A Waterfall in the Lake District*

Signed and dated 'E.Lear.del. / 1837'
Pencil, black chalk and stump, on blue-grey paper, 17.3 × 25.7 cm
Provenance: Anon. Sale; Sotheby's, 18 Mar. 1982, lot 10 (£1,200 to Morton Morris); purchased from Morton Morris by the current owner in 1982

Abbot Hall Art Gallery, Kendal, Cumbria

Although purchased as a view of Colwith Force, the consensus of informed opinion about Lake District topography is that it is not Colwith. The waterfall that it most closely resembles is Skelwith, but, unless the 1836 sketch from which it derives is rediscovered, an exact identification remains elusive. Another Lear drawing dated 1837 of an unidentified waterfall, presumably in the Lake District, was in the Edward Seago sale at Christie's, 1 Mar. 1977, lot 78.

75 *Grasmere from Red Bank*

Inscribed and dated 'Grasmere. 5. Oct / 1836 (cut).', numbered 80
Pencil and stump heightened with white, on grey paper, 17.1 × 25.6 cm
Provenance: bequeathed by the artist to his godson, Allan Nevill; by descent in his family until sold at Christie's, 20 November 2003, part of lot 77, where acquired by current owner

The Wordsworth Trust (2004.119.1)

Illustrated on p. 152

76 *Windermere*

Inscribed and dated 'Windermere. / 7. Oct.1836.', numbered 94
Pencil and stump, on blue-grey paper, 17.1 × 26 cm
Provenance: presented by the artist to the Nevill family; by descent in the Nevill family until sold to H.V. Day (bookseller) of Dorchester, Dorset, before 1958; purchased from H.V. Day by Colnaghi, 29 Dec. 1959 (£13); sold to Dr F.Springell, 28 Mar. 1960 (£21 5s); acquired by the current owner from Dr Springell in 1960

Private Collection

Illustrated on p. 152

This is the only Lake District sketch which has no foreground and seems to have been drawn from a boat on Windermere, looking north towards the head of the lake, which would explain its rather more sketchy and perfunctory nature.

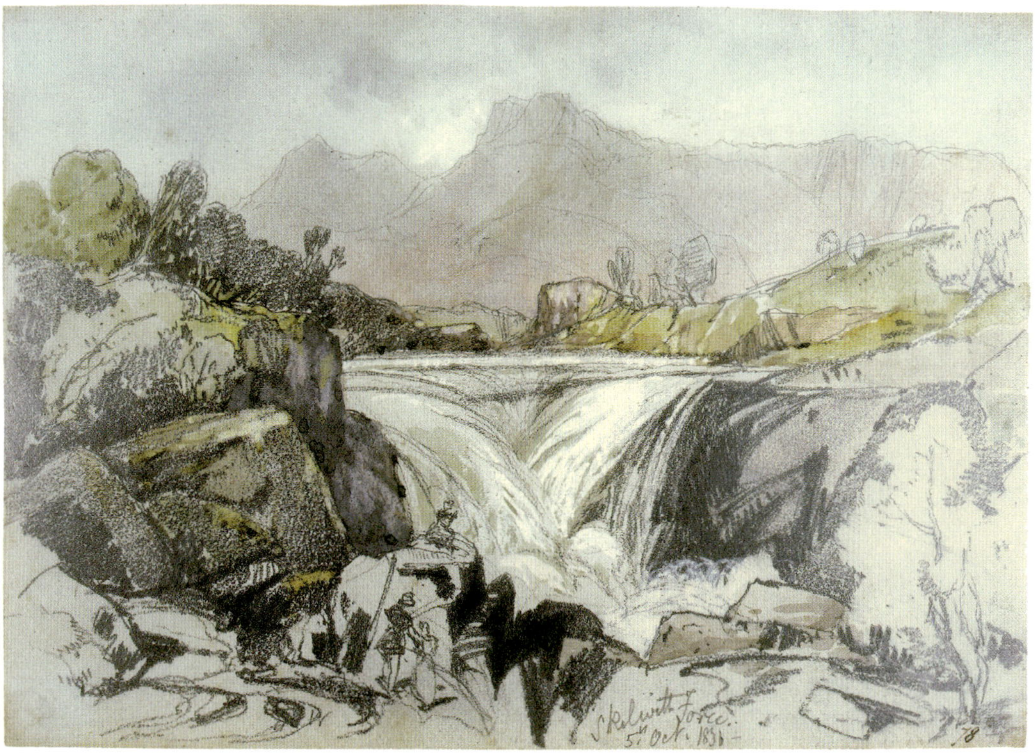

Cat. 73

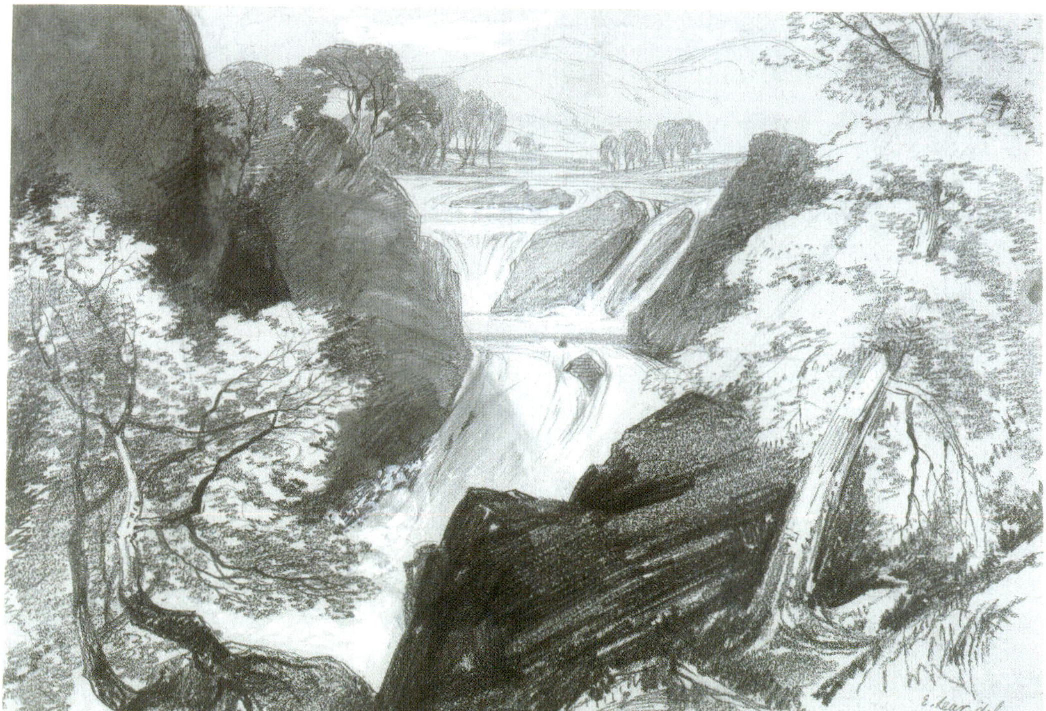

Cat. 74

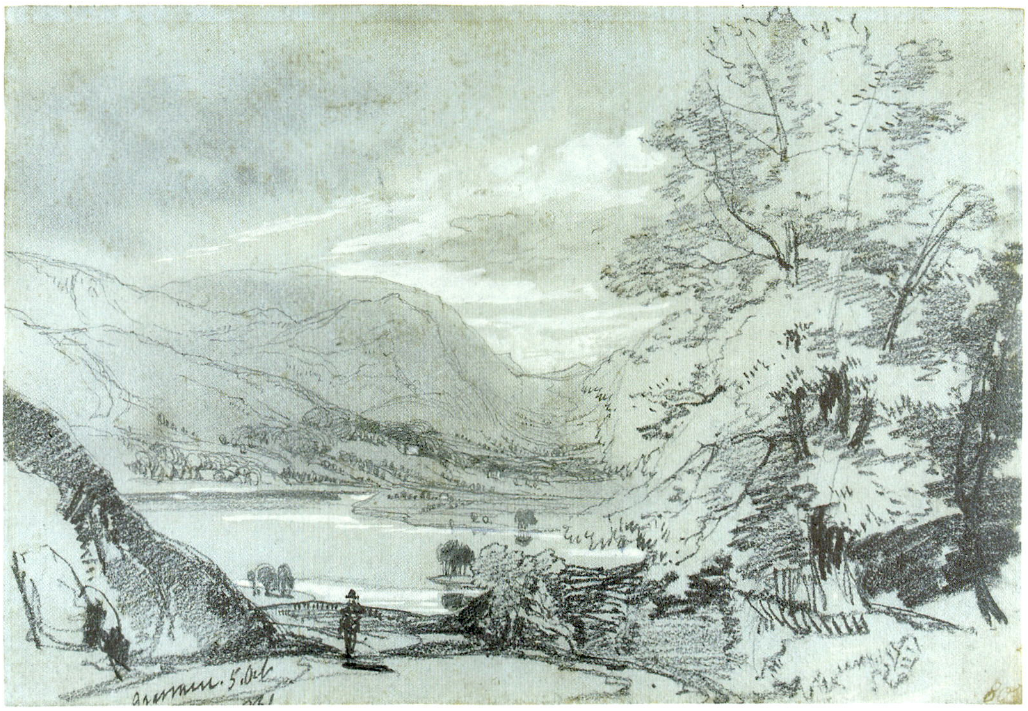

Cat. 75

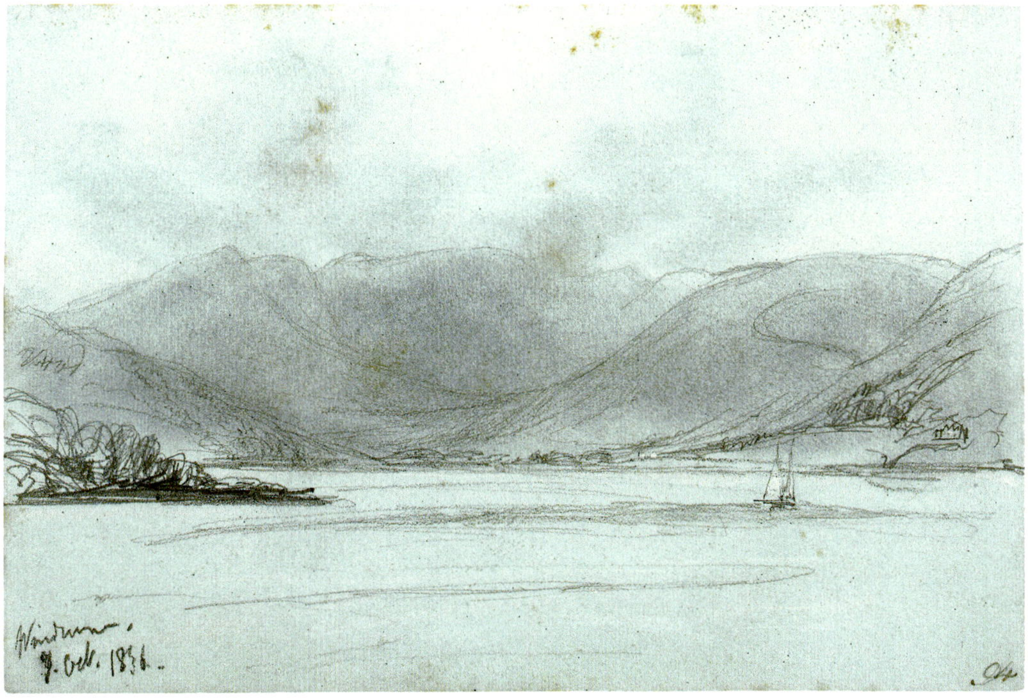

Cat. 76

8–11 October
Langdale and Borrowdale

After spending three days exploring the Grasmere, Rydal and Ambleside areas, Lear headed into Great Langdale following what is now the Cumbria Way. After the view of the head of Windermere, drawn on 7 October and numbered 94, there are two drawings missing from the numerical sequence; one of these is the drawing of Langdale in the Colnaghi exhibition in 1960, sold to J.C. Pierce-Higgins and now untraced. The numerical sequence resumes with number 97, and it is possible to follow Lear through Great Langdale north towards Borrowdale. He seems to have climbed up Stake Gill and crossed Stake Pass down into Borrowdale via the Langstrath Beck. The drawing of Castle Crag from the banks of the Derwent (fig. 42) seems to be the last drawing executed on 8 October, which was a very productive day and saw Lear completing at least six sketches and travelling more than eight miles, indicating that he was probably on horseback.

Lear spent the following two days exploring the Borrowdale area, which he had not covered on his previous visit to Derwentwater, when he passed through the valley on his way from Wasdale to Keswick on 19 September. A currently untraced drawing in the Colnaghi exhibition of 1960, dated 9 October and given the name 'Watendale', is presumably a mistake for Watendlath, showing that Lear visited the small tarn above Borrowdale, which was often a destination for artists. It is hard to believe that he did not also draw the view up the Stonethwaite valley towards Eagle

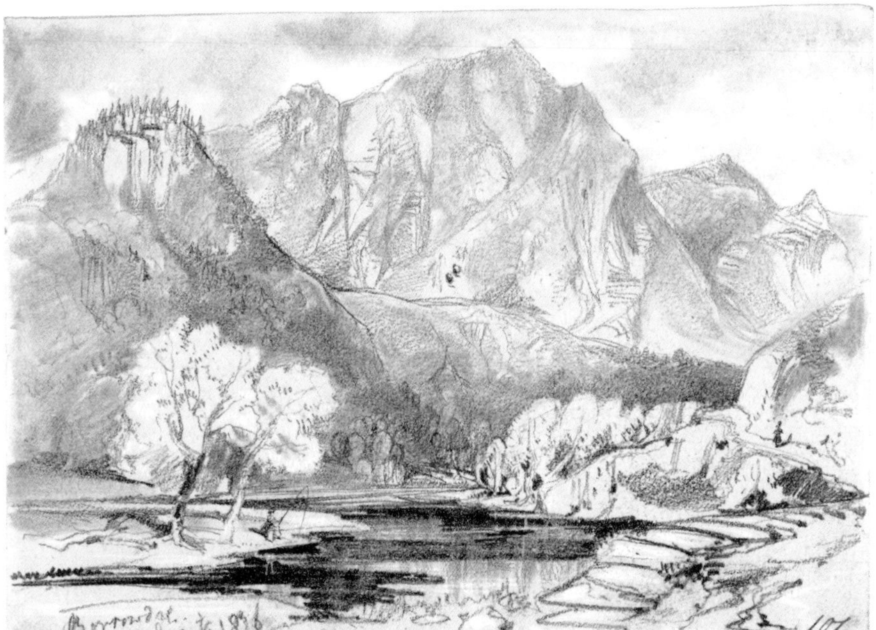

Fig. 42 Castle Crag from the Banks of the Derwent, inscribed and dated 'Borrowdale / 8 Oct. 1836', numbered 101, pencil and stump, on blue-grey paper, 18.4 × 25.7 cm (Huntington Art Collections, 59.55.483).

Crag, as Constable had thirty years earlier. After exploring Borrowdale, Lear headed east to Patterdale and Ullswater. An untraced drawing from the 1960 Colnaghi exhibition dated 11 October and called 'Bleak Tarn' is presumably a mistake for Blea Tarn, and gives a clue as to the route Lear must have taken. This tarn is on the way from Watendlath to Wythburn at the head of Thirlmere. Leigh notes: 'The water of [Watendlath Tarn] is derived from another called BLEA TARN, situated about two miles distant on the heathy mountain between Thirlmere and Borrowdale' (pp. 72–3); the route past this tarn is extremely boggy, and Lear must at this point have been on foot, or at least leading his horse. He probably spent the night of 11 October at the Nag's Head inn at Wythburn; from here he headed over Dunmail Raise, up Raise Beck and then down into Patterdale via Grisedale Tarn and Grisedale.

77 *The Langdale Pikes*

Inscribed and dated 'Gt. Langdale. / 8. Oct. 1836.', numbered 97
Pencil and stump heightened with white, on blue-grey paper, 17.5 × 26.1 cm
Provenance: presented by the artist to the Nevill family; by descent in the Nevill family until sold to H.V. Day (bookseller) of Dorchester, Dorset, before 1958; purchased from H.V. Day by Colnaghi, 29 Dec. 1959 (£13); sold to Dr F.Springell, 28 Mar. 1960 (£21 5s); acquired by the current owner from Dr Springell in 1960

Private Collection

78 *The Crinkle Crags and the Langdale Pikes*

Inscribed and dated 'Langdale. 8. Oct 1836', inscribed with notes, numbered 98
Pencil and stump, on blue-grey paper, 17.5 × 25.9 cm
Provenance: presented by the artist to the Nevill family; by descent in the Nevill family until sold to H.V. Day (bookseller) of Dorchester, Dorset, before 1958; purchased from H.V. Day by Colnaghi, 29 Dec. 1959 (£13); sold to Dr F.Springell, 28 Mar. 1960 (£21 5s); acquired by the current owner from Dr Springell in 1960

Private Collection

79 *Rossett Pike from Mickleden*

Inscribed and dated 'The Stake / 8. Oct. / 1836', numbered 99
Pencil and stump, on blue-grey paper, 17.5 × 25.7 cm
Provenance: presented by the artist to the Nevill family; by descent in the Nevill family until sold to H.V. Day (bookseller) of Dorchester, Dorset, before 1958; purchased from H.V. Day by Colnaghi, 29 Dec. 1959 (£13); sold to Dr Charles Warren, 24 Feb. 1960 (£25); Spink, English Watercolour Drawings, Annual Exhibition, 1977, no. 94 (£450)

Private Collection

Illustrated on p. 156

The inscription is an indication of the route that Lear was about to take, since Stake Gill and Stake Pass are off to the right beyond the middle distance which is in shadow. This view is unchanged today.

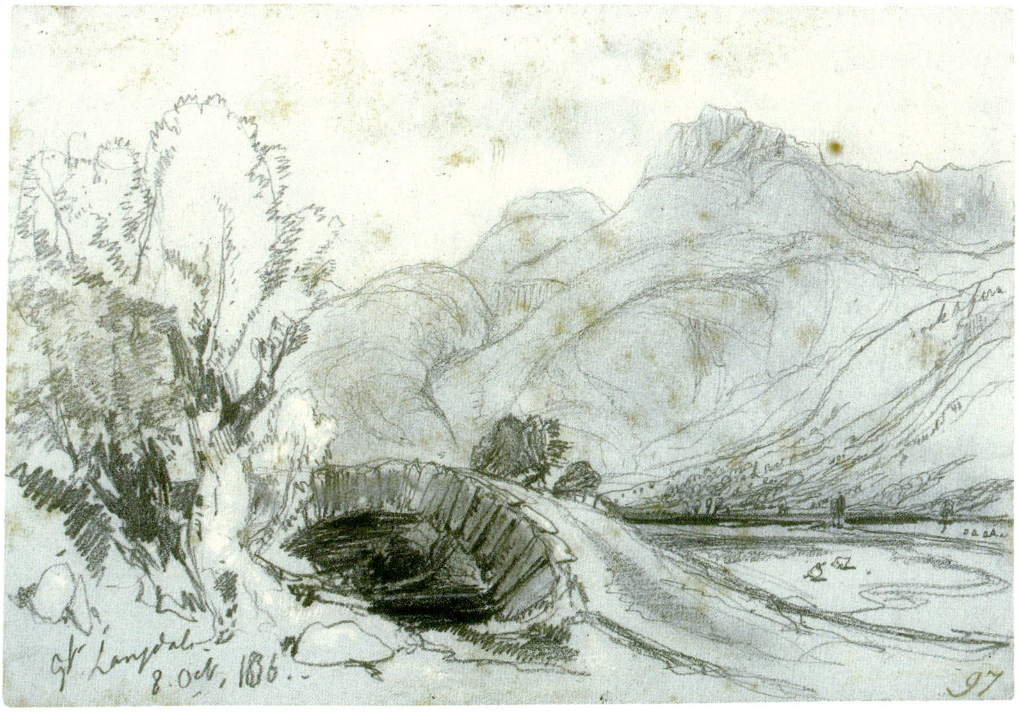

Cat. 77

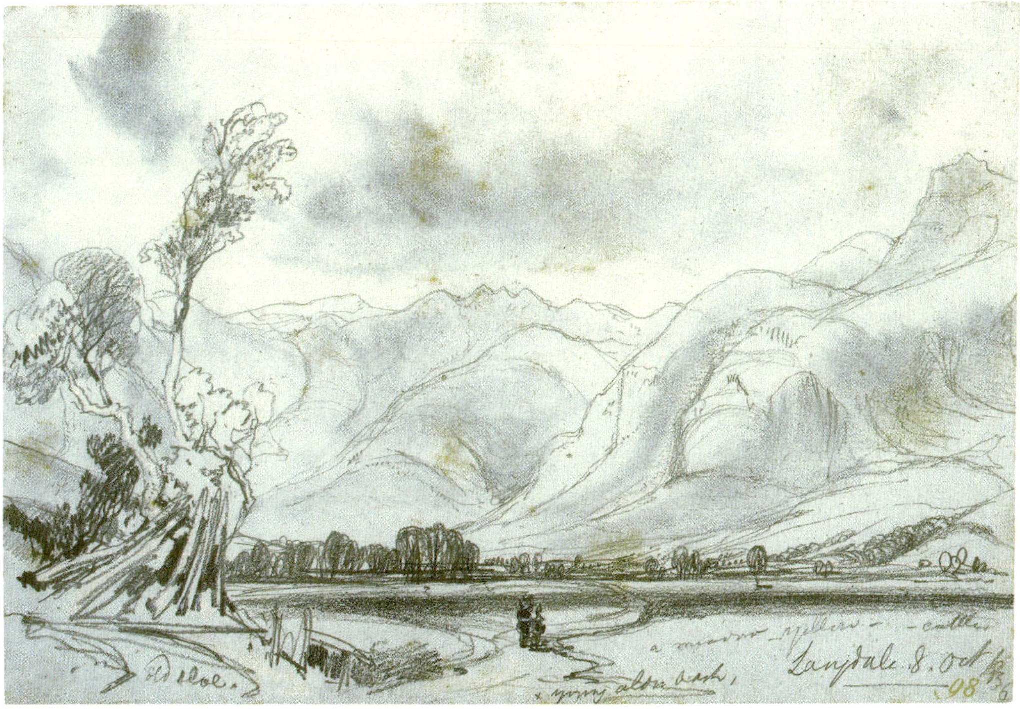

Cat. 78

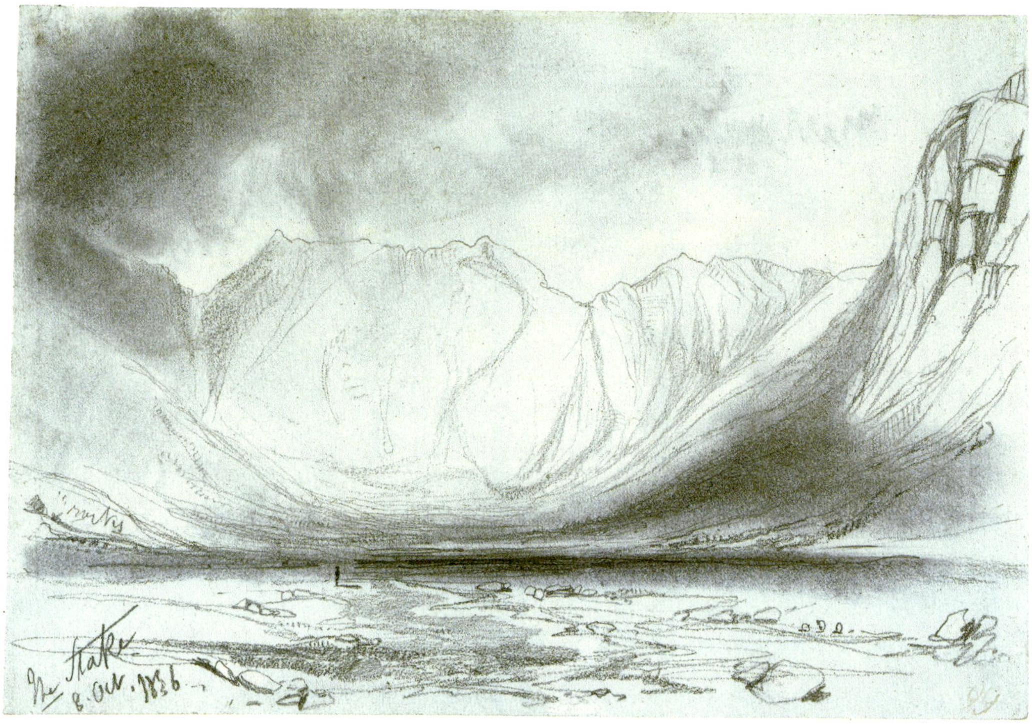

Cat. 79

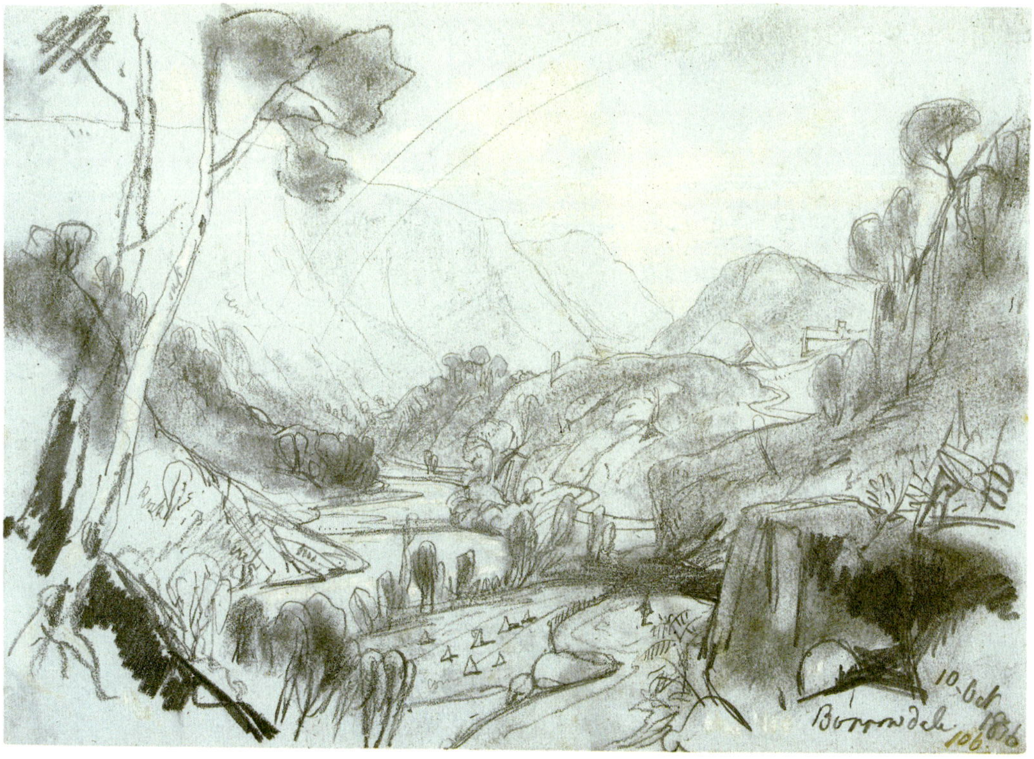

Cat. 80

80 *Borrowdale*

Inscribed and dated '10. Oct / 1836 / Borrowdale', numbered 106
Pencil and stump, on blue-grey paper, 18.1 × 25.6 cm
Provenance: presented by the artist to the Nevill family; by descent in the Nevill family until sold to H.V. Day (bookseller) of Dorchester, Dorset, before 1958; purchased from H.V. Day by Colnaghi, 29 Dec. 1959 (£13); sold to Dr F.Springell, 28 Mar. 1960 (£21 5s); acquired by the current owner from Dr Springell in 1960

Private Collection

The River Derwent can be seen winding north towards Derwentwater, while in the distance on the right the Bowder Stone is visible. The ladder up the side of the stone, and Bowder Stone Cottage, built for a lady resident to provide refreshment to visiting tourists, can be clearly seen.

81 *Honister Crag*

Inscribed and dated 'Honister Crag / 10. Oct. / 1836', numbered 107
Pencil and watercolour heightened with white, on blue-grey paper, 18.4 × 26 cm
Provenance: presented by the artist to the Nevill family; by descent in the Nevill family until sold to H.V. Day (bookseller) of Dorchester, Dorset, before 1958; purchased from H.V. Day by Colnaghi, 29 Dec. 1959 (£18); sold to George Goyder, 31 Dec. 1959 (£35); Anon. Sale: Christie's, 20 November 2003, lot 54 (£3,800), where acquired by present owner

Private Collection

Illustrated on p. 158

Nearly two weeks earlier, Lear had drawn Honister Crag several times in the distance from the other end of Gatesgarthdale and the shores of Buttermere. This view shows a much closer view of the Crag from the top of the pass from Borrowdale. The on-the-spot sketch formed the basis of a smaller pencil drawing drawn for an album (fig. 43, p. 158).

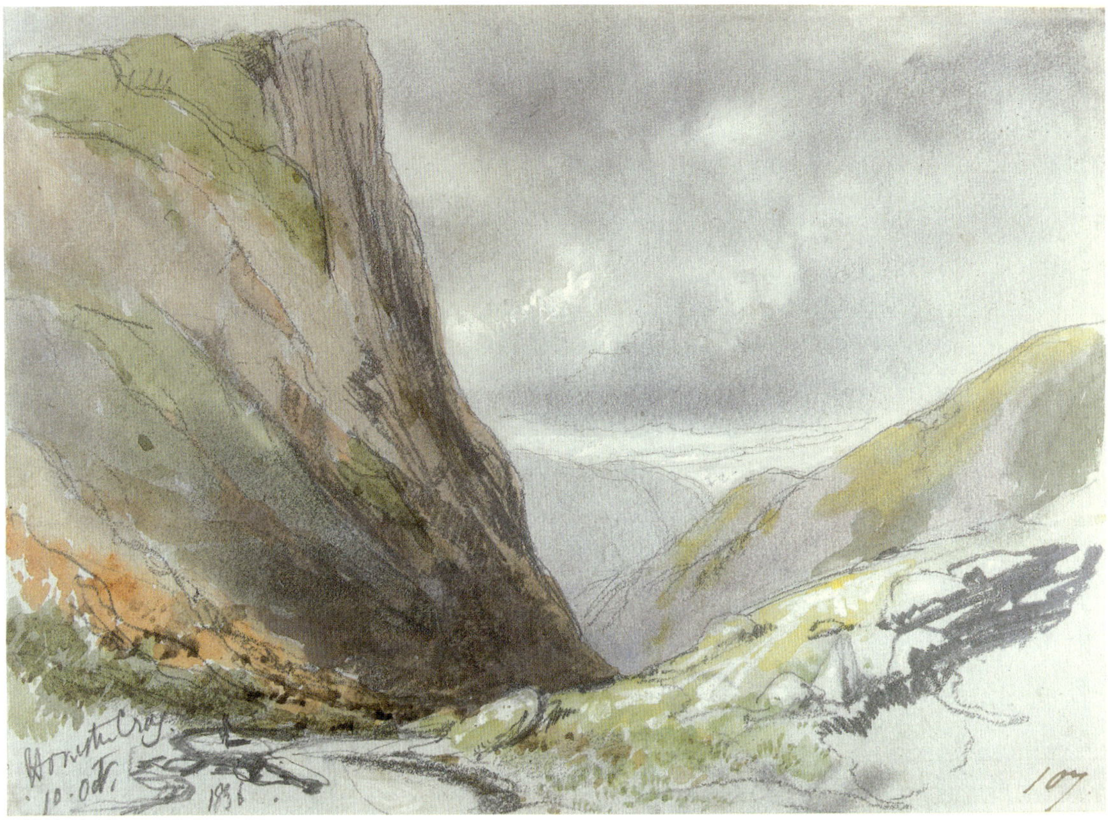

Cat. 81

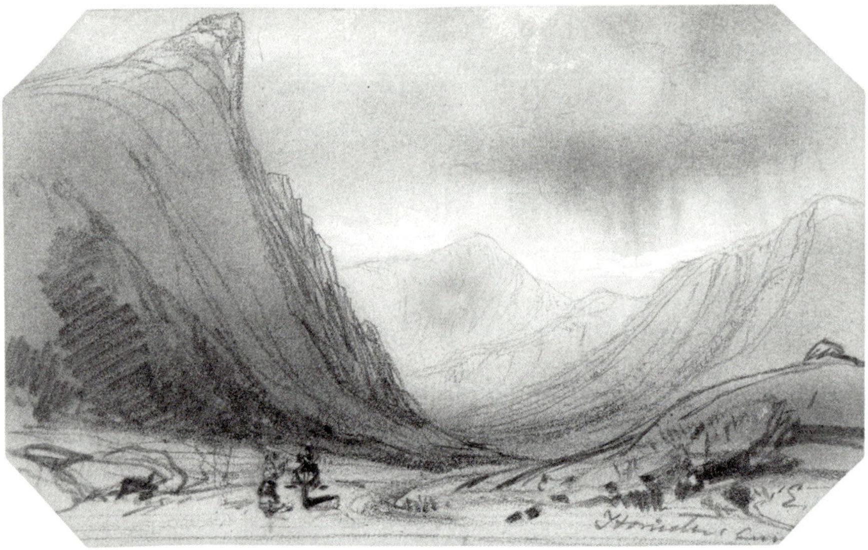

Fig. 43 Honister Crag, Cumberland, signed and inscribed 'E. [Lear] / Honister. Cu[mberland], pencil and stump, on blue-grey paper, corners cut, 10.5 × 17.4 cm (Private Collection, ex-Christie's, 14 Oct. 1966, lot 6).

12–15 October
Ullswater and Helvellyn

Arriving on 12 October, Lear spent the next few days exploring Patterdale, Glenridding and Ullswater; as usual he was systematic in his explorations. He probably stayed at the King's Arms in Patterdale, described by Baines as 'a comfortable inn ... where post horses may be had, and whence a rough carriage road of ten miles conducts, by Brothers-water and over Kirkstone-moor, to Ambleside' (p. 343). Lear did indeed probably head south first, since the first drawing to survive is of Brothers Water at the foot of the Kirkstone Pass (fig. 44), dated 12 October and numbered 111.

The following day Lear appears to have explored Ullswater along its western and northern shores. The goal for tourists then as well as now was Gowbarrow Park and Aira Force, which must surely have been the subject of a lost drawing; three drawings are known which record the journey along the shore of the lake (figs. 45–7, pp. 160–2). After climbing at least part of the way up Helvellyn on 15 October, Lear probably headed south over the Kirkstone Pass to Windermere.

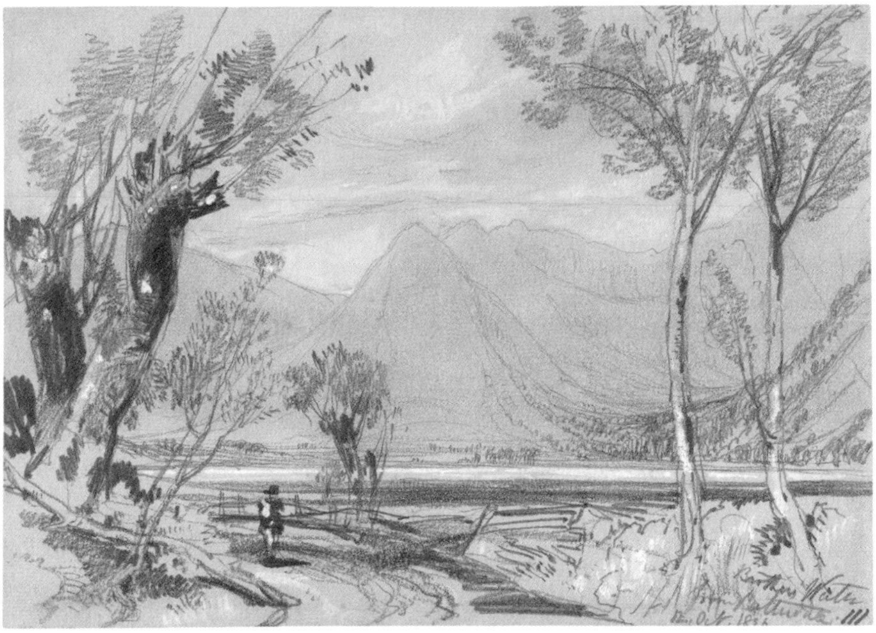

Fig. 44 Brothers Water and Hartsop Dodd, inscribed and dated 'Brothers Water / from Patterdale. / 12.Oct.1836', numbered 111, pencil, stump and black chalk heightened with white, on blue-grey paper, 17.7 × 25.7 cm (Yale Center for British Art, B1997.7.30).

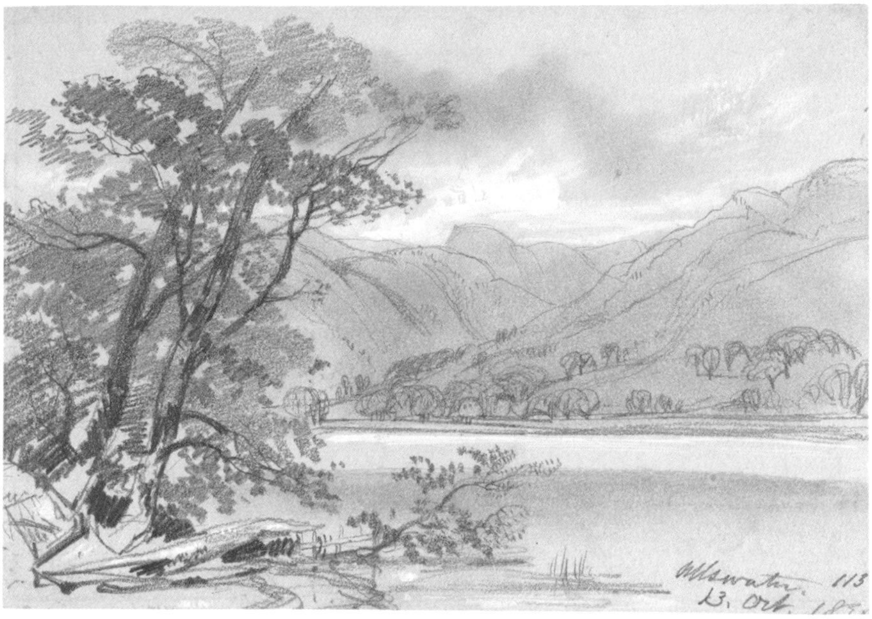

Fig. 45 Ullswater, inscribed and dated 'Ullswater. / 13. Oct.1836', numbered 113, pencil, stump and black chalk heightened with white, on blue-grey paper, 17.1 × 25.3 cm (Yale Center for British Art, B1997.7.31).

82 *Ullswater from Gowbarrow Park*

Signed and dated 'E.Lear.del. 1837'
Pencil, black chalk and stump heightened with white, on blue-grey paper, 17.3 × 25.5 cm
Provenance: Robert A. Hornby (d. 1857); Anon. Sale; Sotheby's, 18 Mar. 1982, lot 11 (2 in lot) (£680); Spink, English Watercolour Drawings, Annual Exhibition, 1983, no. 20 (£950); John Dayton (d.2003); Anon. Sale; Sotheby's, 30 July 2005, lot 281, purchased by the current owner (£7,400)

The Wordsworth Trust (2006.47.3)

Deriving from a sketch dated '14 Oct[ober 1836]' now at Yale, this shows the classic view across Ullswater, which was painted by countless artist visitors to the Lake District.

83 *The Head of Ullswater*

Inscribed and dated 'Ullswater / 14 Oct. 1836', numbered 11[9]
Pencil and stump heightened with white, on grey-blue paper, 17.5 × 24.5 cm
Provenance: presented by the artist to Ralph Nevill, F.S.A. (d. 1917); by descent to his daughter, Mrs B C Bamber; purchased from Mrs B C Bamber in 1942 (£10 for 6 drawings)

The British Museum (1942-12-11-6)

Illustrated on p. 162

This view is taken from the road along the shore of the lake close to Gowbarrow Park; Silver Crag is visible on the left. Although the number has been cut, it is clear from the looping tail that the final digit was a '9'.

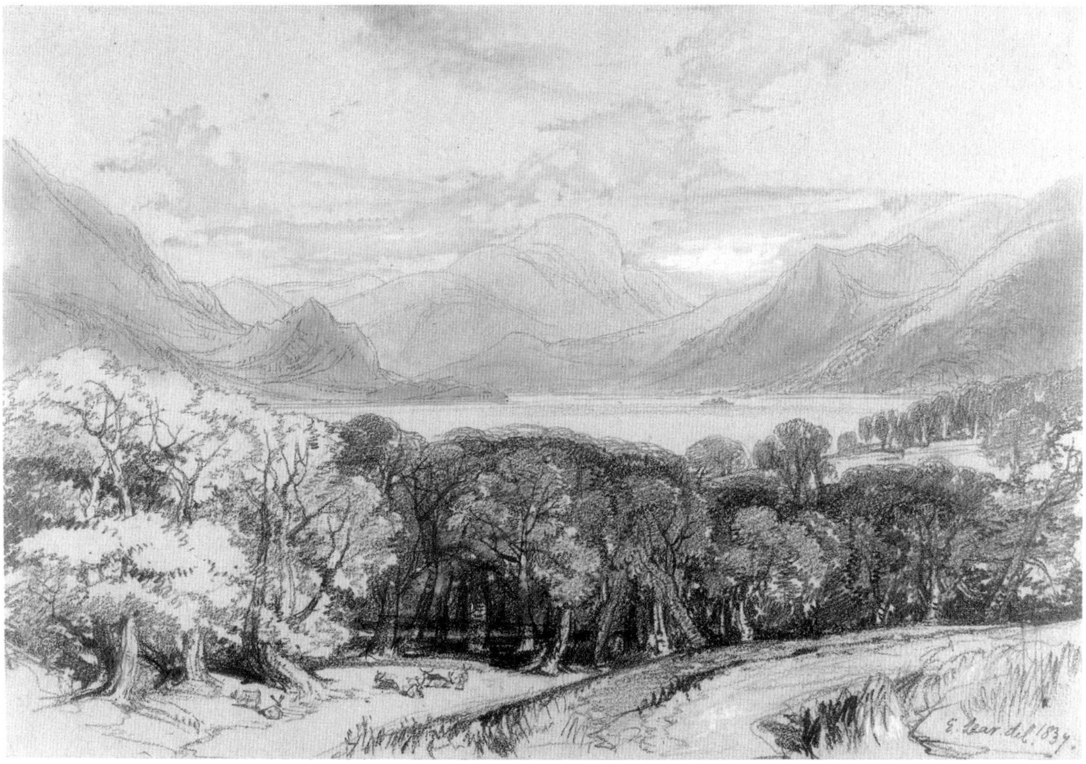

Cat. 82

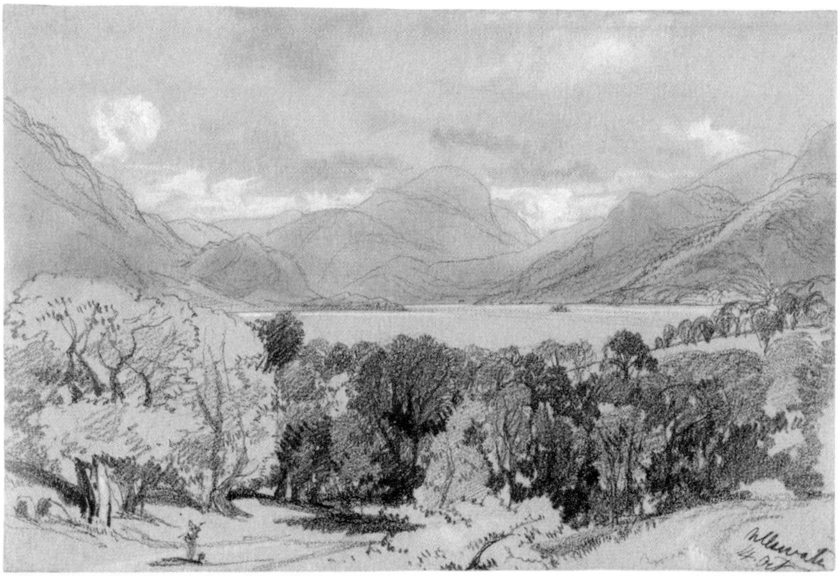

Fig. 46 Ullswater from Gowbarrow Park, inscribed and dated 'Ullswater. / 14. Oct', pencil, stump and black chalk heightened with white, on blue-grey paper, 16.8 x 25.1 cm (Yale Center for British Art, B1997.7.32). This drawing formed the basis for the finished drawing of the following year (see cat. 82).

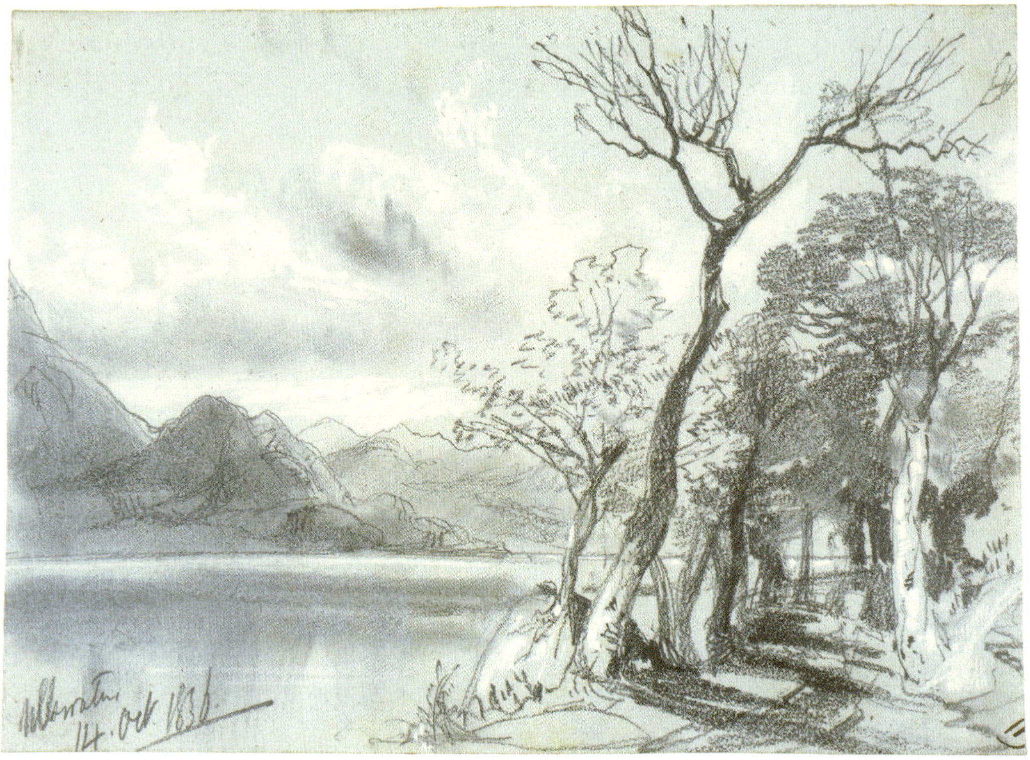

Cat. 83

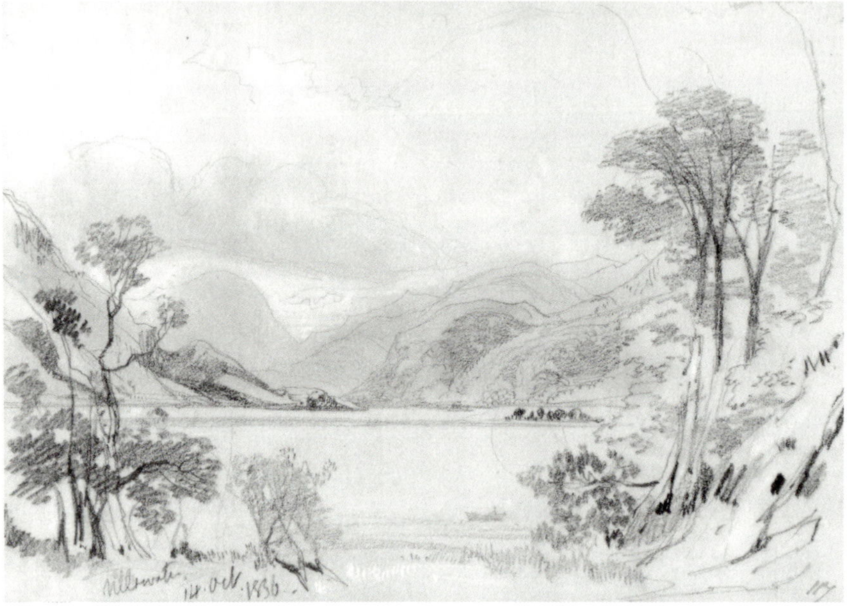

Fig. 47 The Head of Ullswater, inscribed and dated 'Ullswater. / 14.Oct.1836.', numbered 117, pencil and stump heightened with white, on blue-grey paper, 18 × 25.5 cm (Private Collection, ex-Sotheby's, 31 Mar. 1999, lot 148).

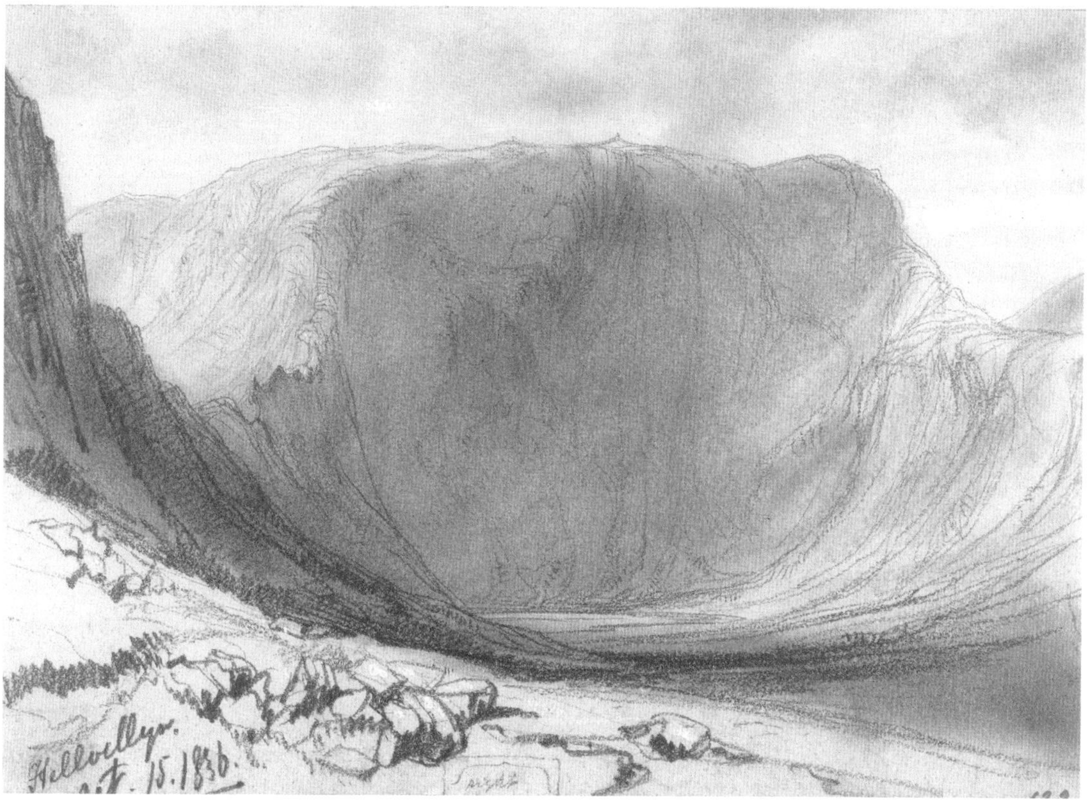

Cat. 84

84 *Helvellyn from the East*

Inscribed and dated 'Helvellyn. / Oct.15.1836.', numbered 122
Pencil and stump heightened with white, on blue-grey paper, 17.5 × 25.4 cm
Provenance: Mrs E.B. Bakhurst; Sotheby's, 6 Nov. 1969, lot 72 (£100 to Gooden & Fox, on behalf of the current owner's family); by descent to the present owner
Private Collection

This somewhat exaggerated view includes Bleaberry Crag and Striding Edge on the left, with Red Tarn in the distance in the centre and Swirral Edge on the right; the cairn on the summit is visible on the skyline.

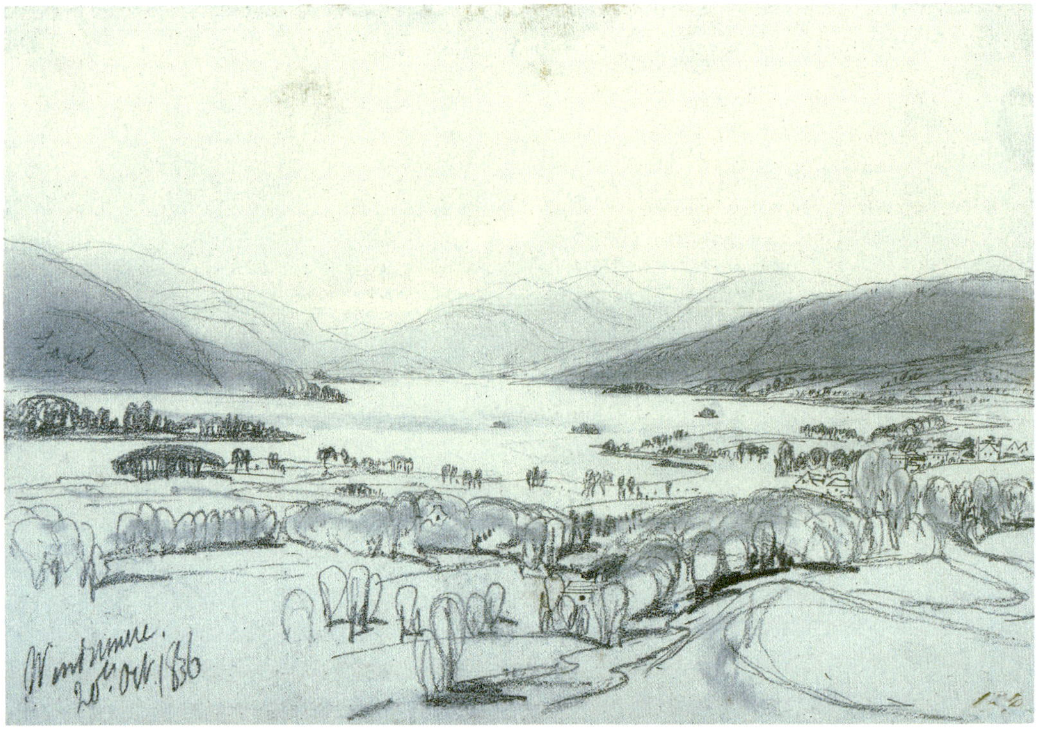

Cat. 85

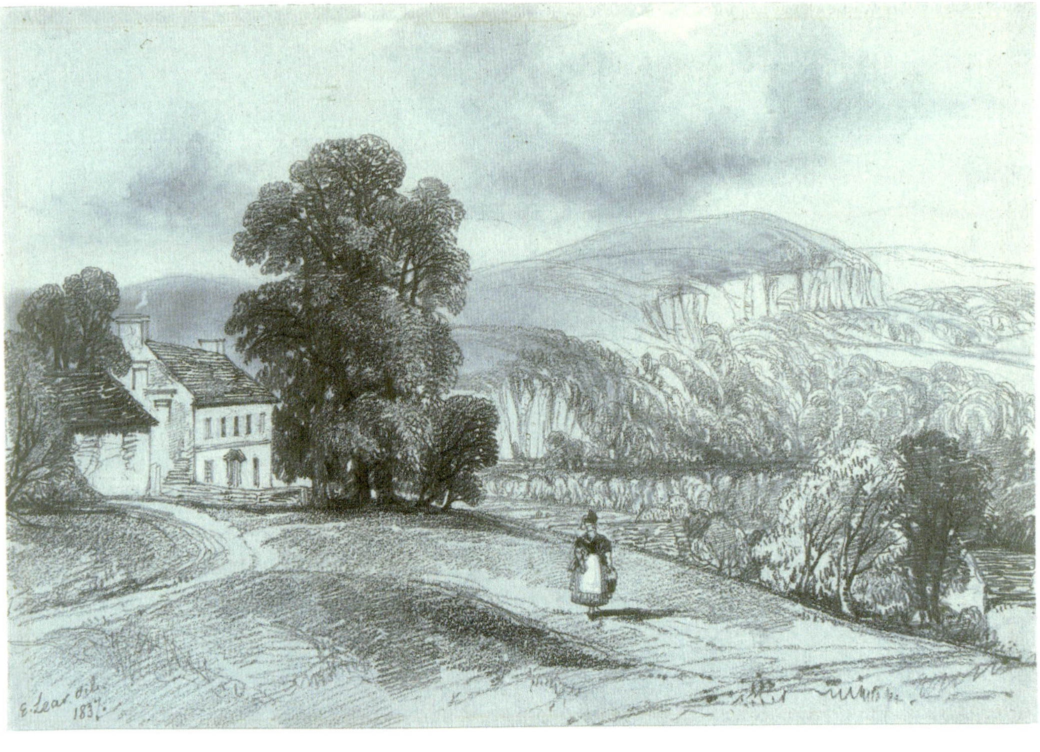

Cat. 86

16–30 October
Back to Knowsley

Only two drawings survive relating to this part of Lear's tour, and there are no letters, so it is impossible to reconstruct with absolute certainty any of his movements for the last two weeks in October 1836. There are, however, a few clues in addition to the drawings. In the letter written from Levens in August (cat. 37), Lear had mentioned his intention to visit the Starkies and the Townleys. At this date, the Starkie family were renting Fell Foot at the southern end of Windermere from the Astley family (the house was demolished in 1907); the elderly James Starkie (b. 1760) would have been Lear's host. The Townleys lived (and still live) at Town Head just to the north of Fell Foot on the eastern shore of Windermere north of Newby Bridge. In 1836, William Townley (1770–1854) was in residence; he was a close friend of Lord Derby, who shared his strong interest in hunting, and would certainly have been a recipient of one of the Earl's letters of introduction, which Lear was carrying. It is probable that Lear visited Town Head and Fell Foot as he headed south down the eastern shore of Windermere after 20 October. In the letter written to John Gould on his return to Knowsley (see Appendix B), Lear wrote, 'I spent a delightful time at Colonel Howard, both going and returning', indicating that he visited Levens Hall on the return journey. It is also clear that he visited Witherslack Hall, as there is a finished drawing of the house which was commissioned by Robert Hornby and is dated 1837 (cat. 86); the sketch of the last week of October 1836 does not survive. Witherslack Hall, situated under Whitbarrow Scar five miles east of the southern end of Windermere, was a hunting lodge belonging to Lord Derby; Lear visited the old house, which is not to be confused with the new Witherslack Hall, which was completed as a Jacobethan mansion in 1874 and stands a few hundred yards to the north. Apart from these clues and the two drawings, all that is known of Lear at this time is that he was back at Knowsley by 30 October. From this evidence, it is possible to suggest an itinerary of visits after Bowness to Town Head, Fell Foot, Witherslack, Levens and back to Knowsley.

85 *Windermere from near Bowness*

Inscribed and dated 'Windermere. / 20th. Oct. / 1836', numbered 124
Pencil and stump, on blue-grey paper, 17.5 × 25.6 cm
Provenance: presented by the artist to the Nevill family; by descent in the Nevill family until sold to H.V. Day (bookseller) of Dorchester, Dorset, before 1958; purchased from H.V. Day by Colnaghi, 29 Dec. 1959 (£13); sold to Dr F.Springell, 28 Mar. 1960 (£21 5s); acquired by the current owner from Dr Springell in 1960
Private Collection

The village of Bowness can be seen to the right, and on the left the end of Belle Isle. Drawn five days after the view of Helvellyn, but numbered only two further on in the numerical sequence, it may be that Lear had been distracted from working by the society he was keeping, or that the weather had prevented outdoor sketching.

86 *Witherslack Hall with Whitbarrow Scar beyond*

Signed and dated 'E. Lear. del. / 1837.', and inscribed on the reverse 'Witherslack'
Pencil and stump heightened with white, on blue-grey paper, 17.3 × 25.6 cm

Provenance: Robert A. Hornby (d. 1857); Anon. Sale (The Property of a Lady); Sotheby's, 18 Mar. 1982, lot 8 (2 in lot) (£520); Dame Kathryn Dugdale (née Stanley) (d. 2004), and by descent in the family

Private Collection

Illustrated on p. 164

This drawing was commissioned by Robert Hornby and presumably derives from a sketch of the previous year. The view looks north past Witherslack Hall towards the limestone cliffs of Whitbarrow Scar. At the time of Lear's visit, Witherslack was a northern outpost of the Derby estates, and the Hall was inhabited by a steward. Later in the century, the new Witherslack Hall was built a few hundred yards to the north (completed in 1874), and the building where Lear stayed is now known as Witherslack Hall Farm.

87 *Sunset at Knowsley*

Inscribed and dated 'Knowsley. Oct 30. 1836'
Watercolour, 11.4 × 17.9 cm
Provenance: the 13th Earl of Derby, and by descent

Lent by The Earl of Derby

88 *A View over the Park, Knowsley*

Inscribed and dated 'Oct. 31. 1836 / Knowsley'
Watercolour, 7.6 × 12.7 cm
Provenance: the 13th Earl of Derby, and by descent

Lent by The Earl of Derby

In the past the final digit of the date on the larger of the two watercolours inscribed 'Knowsley' has been misread as a '1', but it is clearly intended to be a '6'. A visit to Knowsley in October 1831 is not impossible, but there is no evidence that Lear was interested in landscape at this early date, and certainly none that he was using watercolour to sketch it. The watercolour certainly seems stylistically to fit with the other view of Knowsley Park with which it is mounted, and therefore dates from just after Lear's return to Knowsley; it was drawn the same day as he wrote the letter to John Gould (see Appendix B, pp. 228–9).

JAMES DUFFIELD HARDING (1797–1863)

89 'Chudleigh Rocks Devon'
Plate 3 from *Sketches at Home and Abroad*
London: Charles Tilt, 1836
Signed with initials, inscribed and dated Sepr. 1835 on the stone
Lithograph, 38.4 × 28.3 cm (image size)

John Rylands Library, University of Manchester

Illustrated on p. 168

As J.R. Abbey observes:

> This book represents something of a landmark in the history of the lithograph in that it may be said to initiate the series of tinted lithographic views, which, in books and in portfolios, were to dominate the market for many years, reaching

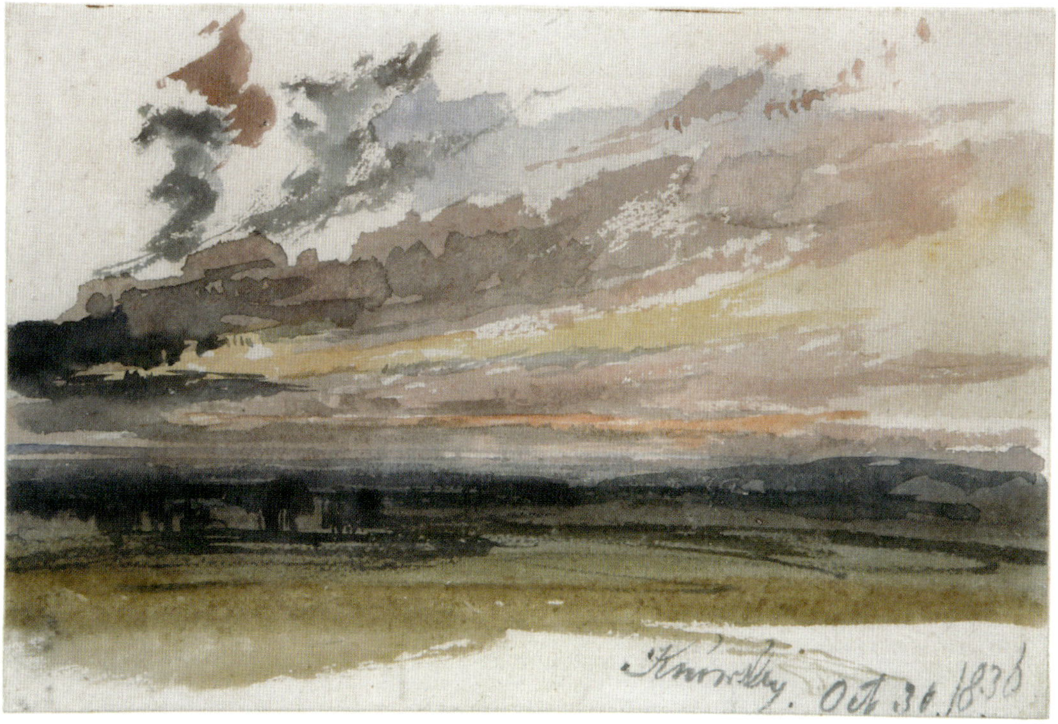

Cat. 87

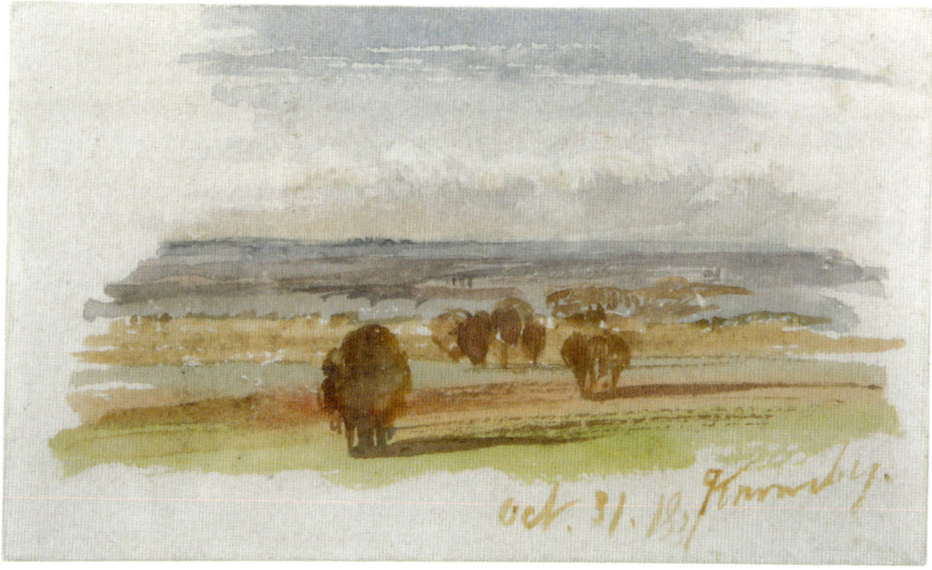

Cat. 88

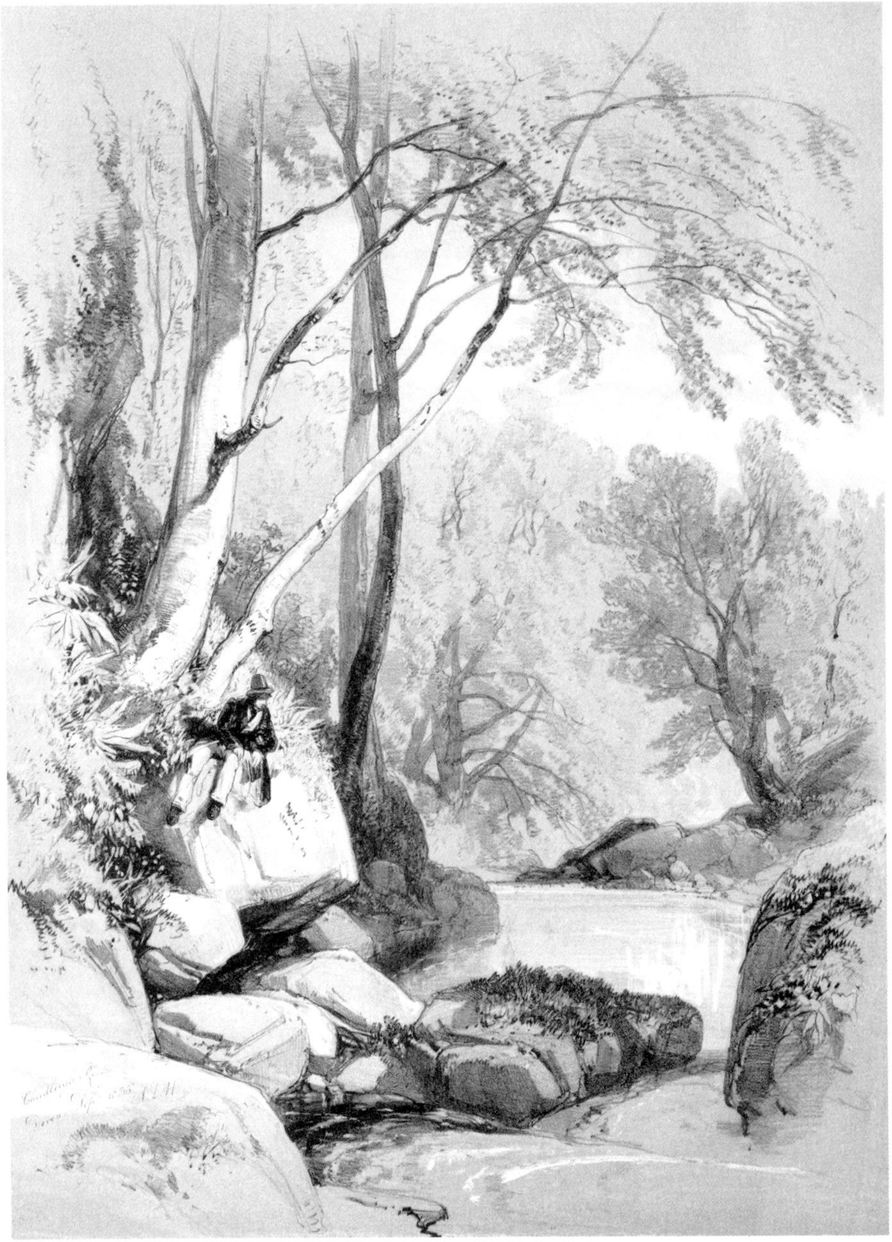

Cat. 89

a peak of ambitious bulk in Roberts's *Holy Land*, 1842–9 ... Tinted lithographs were ... not new, since the style ... had been suggested and put into practice by Senefelder. He, however, had only been able to produce a flat tint, into which the highlights could be scraped ... One important aim was, as in this book, to imitate the effect of original drawings on tinted paper, heightened by Chinese white. The problem remained of how to get a more subtle gradation of tone, and, as part of the same problem, how to draw and preserve in the printing fine-grained tones, especially the lighter ones. Hullmandel directed his efforts ... in this direction, and devised a means of 'facing' his stones which he claimed not only preserved the delicate tones but enabled the artist to retouch.

> Hullmandel never seems to have disclosed the exact nature of his method ... but it seems possible that it may have made use of the same principles as the process which he patented in 1840, and which he called 'Lithotint' ... At all events, Hullmandel's method of facing enabled him to print the delicate tones which he himself, and the other artists associated with him, such as Harding, Prout and Lane, learned to produce on the stone. (Abbey *Travel*, vol. i, p. 36)

This lavish publication, an imperial folio volume, contained fifty plates (actually fifty-eight scenes were depicted, since some of the plates included more than one scene). Most of the views were foreign, and the publication included only nine English scenes; the original drawings were made over a period from September 1824 to October 1835, but the majority of the views were sketched on a journey down the Rhine and through North Italy in the late summer of 1834. The book is open at one of the English sketches, recording a visit to Devon in the summer of 1835, which took place while the book was in production. Lear would certainly have been aware of Harding's ambitious publication, and later tried to emulate it with his own books of lithographs. Lear's own drawing technique remained strongly influenced by the Hullmandel/Harding style until well into the 1840s.

JAMES DUFFIELD HARDING (1797–1863)
90 'Shipwreck – A Study on the Coast of Sussex'
Plate 22 from *Sketches at Home and Abroad*
Signed with initials, inscribed and dated 'Novr 1829' on the stone
Lithograph, 28 × 40 cm (image size)
Provenance: presented by A. Charles Sewter in 1967
Whitworth Art Gallery, University of Manchester (P.21441)

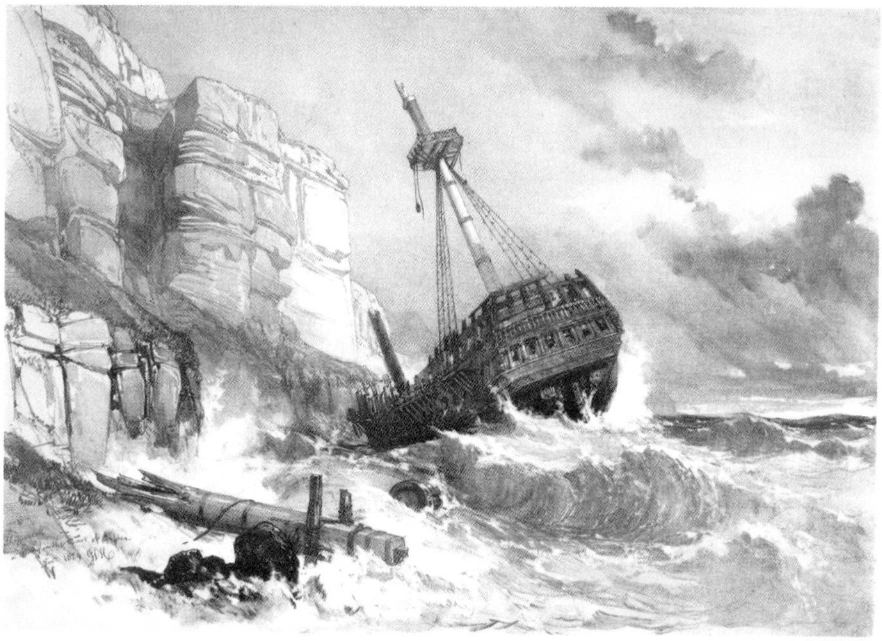

Cat. 90

Although Harding was never a business partner of Hullmandel, both were perfectionists and wanted to get the best out of the lithographic medium. Certainly, they both worked in close collaboration from 1820 onwards, and it is now impossible to determine which advances in the process can be attributed to which practitioner. Hullmandel wrote in a pamphlet in 1829: 'With similar pursuits, and joined by a friendship of several years, Mr Harding and myself have jogged on together through many a failure and disaster, without being disheartened, and any person who has attempted Lithographic printing, well knows that it does not require a slight degree of perseverance and courage to wade through the difficulties which Lithography is at first surrounded with.' Despite this relationship, Harding does not even mention Hullmandel's death in his diary (now in the Courtauld Institute), and did not attend his funeral at Highgate Cemetery in November 1850, a ceremony which Lear did attend.

91 *Letter to Fanny Coombe, from 28 Southampton Row, Bloomsbury, London*

3 January 1837
Autograph letter
The Frederick Warne Archive
Illustrated on pp. 172–3; see pp. 218–20 for full text

In this very informative letter written from his London lodgings Lear describes his journey from Knowsley, where he had spent the Christmas of 1836, to the Greville-Howard's at Elford Hall near Lichfield (they had been Lear's hosts at Levens in August 1836), and back to London. The perils and adventure of travelling by coach in winter are vividly evoked:

> After a dreadful night of cold & snow—2 overturns, & delays innumerable, I reached Colonel Howard's (Elford Hall) near Lichfield on Monday Morning. I passed a very pleasant visit thereat but being anxious to be in London … the destinies propelld me to set off on Tuesday the unlucky 27th.—Such a journey as we had surely never English mortal knew previously! One single bit of luck seemed to bless us,—our getting possession ('twas a mail,) of some snowed up mailbags—from having which with our own, we we [*sic*] forwarded whenever there was a lack of horses, to the prejudice of less fortunate coaches I cannot describe, were I Munchausen himself, half the hideous adventures that befel us!—Conceive miles of a sort of lane between snow walls 10 or 12 feet high—sometimes even actually higher than the mailcoach top:—sometimes drifted again—over which the wretched vehicle was dragged by 8 horses. Conceive encountering wagons—being dragged stern foremost,—having drunken postillions, waiting 2 hours on a heath of 3 foot snow for horses!!—Suffice it to say, (tho' I did not expect it, we reached London about 7 on Thursday morning!

The letter continues with Lear's future plans, which include a trip to Paris to provide drawings for John Gould; although this did take place (in the letter of 19 May – cat. 95 – he refers to 'the thimbles I bought in Paris') the death of his sister Kate later in the month initially delayed it and the change in Lear's fortunes (as described in the letter of 3 March) removed the need to work for Gould in the future. He mentions the work that he has in hand: 'I intended bringing into Sussex some pencil drawings (18 or 20) ordered for sundry Lancashire folks: this however has been set aside by the quantity of Lithography I shall have to do before I go: every eving at Candelight *must* I do it,—& other watercolor dwings will occupy the days. 8 large Lithographs, 20 Landscapes—3 Watercol: drawings—besides other trifling things not to speak of hindrances *are* realities say what one may—& not to be overcome in three weeks hastily.' This passage provides an insight into the numbers of drawings that remain missing from Lear's *oeuvre*, since not even half of the '20 Landscapes' now survive; of the '3 Watercol: drawings', one of them must surely be the Wastwater watercolour, painted for the Rev. J. J. Hornby (fig. 31, p. 120).

92 *Letter to Fanny Coombe, from 36 Great Marlborough Street, London*

11 February 1837
Autograph letter, on mourning paper
The Frederick Warne Archive
Illustrated on pp. 174–5; see pp. 220–1 for full text

This letter is written on mourning paper in honour of Lear's sister, Catherine (Kate), whose recent death is mentioned at the beginning: 'You have heard I dare say of my poor sister Kate's death, which altho' I know it happened seems now more like a dream than a reality. She was the youngest of us all. From the time she grew worse, (about the period of my taking these lodgings,) I was partly in the country with her, & partly here.' In the letter of 3 January, Lear had mentioned a possible trip to France ('I am to go to Paris in three weeks time to make some drawings (Zoological,) for Gould'); this trip was delayed by the illness and death of his sister until late April or early May.

Lear mentions his own health: 'I am strongly advised by the medical folk to go to a climate where less east wind & cold may prevail than in this horrible one—to take precautions ere it be too late', but he is still working away at drawings deriving from the previous summer: 'I am doing views of the Lakes, as a thing which keeps up what little interest I have left in me'. This is the first surviving letter from Lear's new lodgings, 36 Great Marlborough Street, only a few doors away from his friend Charles Hullmandel's Lithographic Establishment at number 49; although he here describes them as 'more comfortable than any I have ever been in', he was to move again by the middle of April.

93 *Letter to Fanny Coombe, from 36 Great Marlborough Street, London*

3 March 1837
Autograph letter, on mourning paper
The Frederick Warne Archive
Illustrated on pp. 176–7; see pp. 221–2 for full text

This short letter on mourning paper begins with a characteristic catalogue of the author's depression: 'until the last week or 10 days I have been as indolent & gloomy as possible, & when the day has been over I have felt too fagged & un-care-about-anything to sit down to write.' The news that then follows is as momentous as it is unexpected:

> And now let me inform you of a 'tide in the affairs' of your humble servant: first promising, lest your Curiosity be overwhelming, that I am neither going to marry the old Duchess of Gloucester, nor turn cannibal, nor become Bishop of Salisbury, but that I am going to put in practice a long nursed dream of

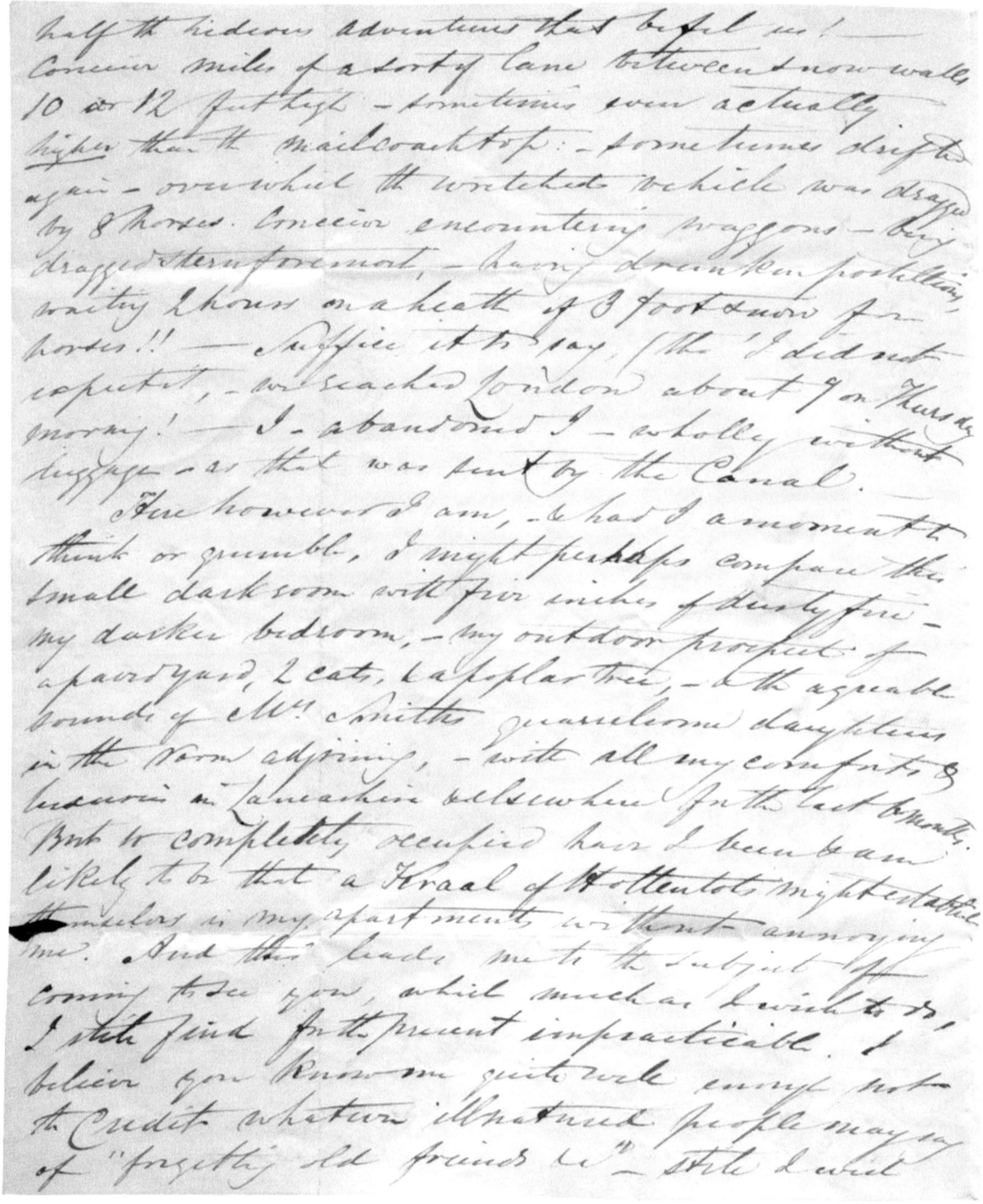

half the hideous adventures that befel us! —
Conceive miles of a sort of lane between snow walls
10 or 12 feet high – sometimes even actually
higher than the mailcoach top: – sometimes drifted
again – over which the wretched vehicle was dragged
by 8 horses. Conceive encountering waggons – being
dragged stern foremost, – having drunken postillions;
waiting 2 hours on a heath of 3 foot snow for
horses!! — Suffice it to say, (tho' I did not
expect it, – we reached London about 7 on Thursday
morning! — I – abandoned I – wholly without
luggage – as that was sent by the Canal.
Here however I am, – & had I a moment to
think or grumble, I might perhaps compare this
small dark room with four inches of dusty fire –
my darker bedroom, – my outdoor prospect of
a paved yard, 2 cats, & a poplar tree, – & the agreeable
sounds of Mrs Smith's quarrelsome daughters
in the room adjoining, – with all my comforts &
luxuries in Lancashire & elsewhere for the last 6 months.
But so completely occupied have I been & am
likely to be that a Kraal of Hottentots might establish
themselves in my apartments without annoying
me. And this leads me to the subject of
coming to see you, which much as I wish to do,
I still find for the present impracticable. I
believe you know me quite well enough not to
credit whatever illnatured people may say
of "forgetting old friends &c" – still I wish

Cat. 91

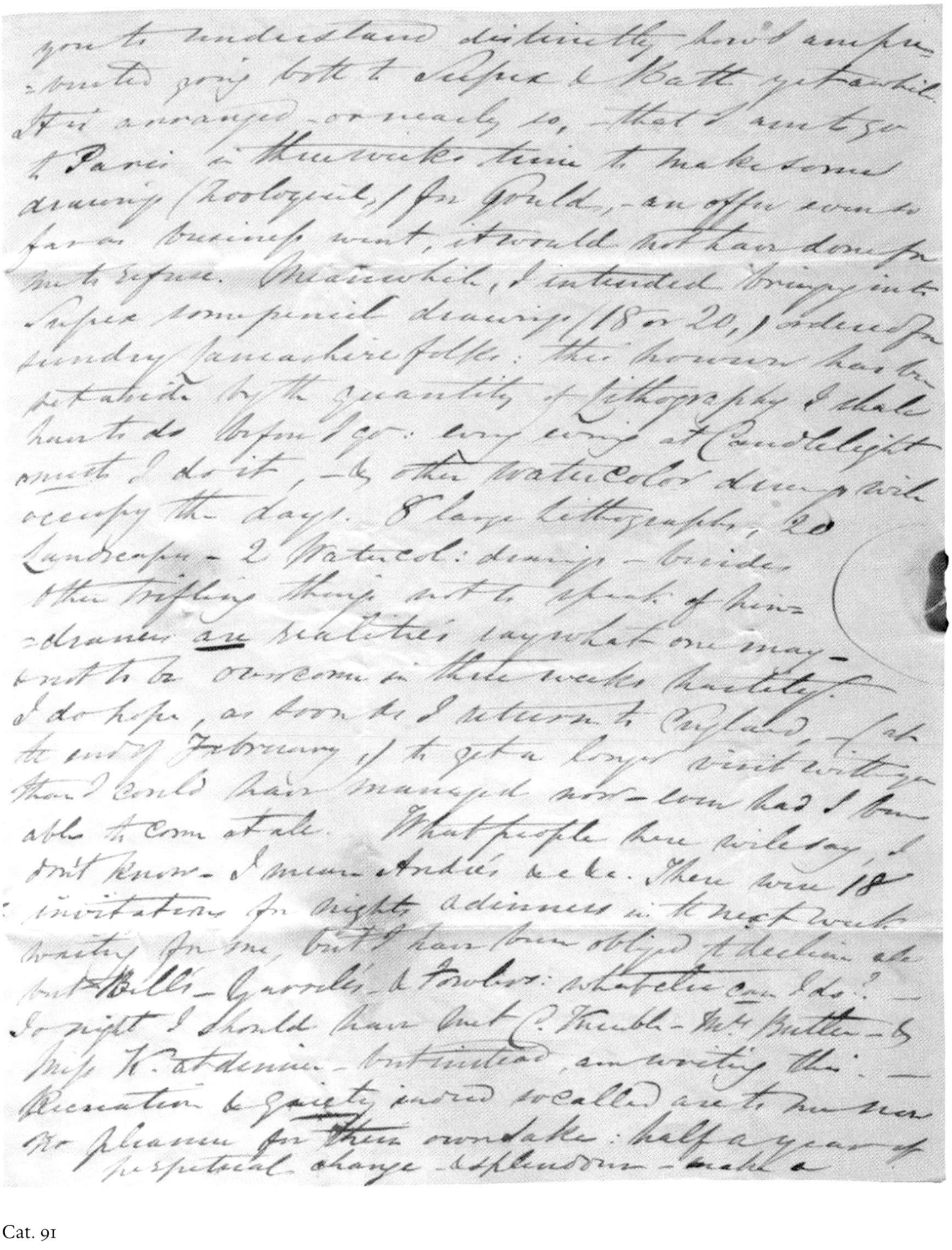

you to understand distinctly how I am pre-
-vented going both to Sussex & Bath yet awhile.
It is arranged—or nearly so,—that I want go
to Paris in three weeks time to make some
drawings (Zoological,) for Gould,—an offer which
far as business went, it would not have done for
me to refuse. Meanwhile, I intended bringing into
Sussex some pencil drawings (18 or 20,) ordered for
sundry Lancashire folks: this however has been
put aside by the quantity of Lithography I shall
have to do before I go: every evening at Candlelight
must I do it,—& other watercolor drawings will
occupy the days. 8 large lithographs, 20
Landscapes—2 Watercol: drawings—besides
other trifling things not to speak of—hin-
-drances are realities say what one may—
& not to be overcome in three weeks hastily.
I do hope, as soon as I return to England, (at
the end of February) to get a longer visit with you
than I could have managed now—even had I been
able to come at all. What people here will say, I
don't know—I mean Andies & c & c. There were 18
invitations for nights, & dinners in the next week
waiting for me, but I have been obliged to decline all
but Bells—Garrods, & Fowlers: what else can I do?—
To night I should have met C. Kemble—Mrs Butler—&
Miss K. at dinner—but instead, am writing this.—
Recreation & gaiety indeed so called are to me never
no pleasure for their own sake: half a year of
perpetual change & splendour—make a

Cat. 91

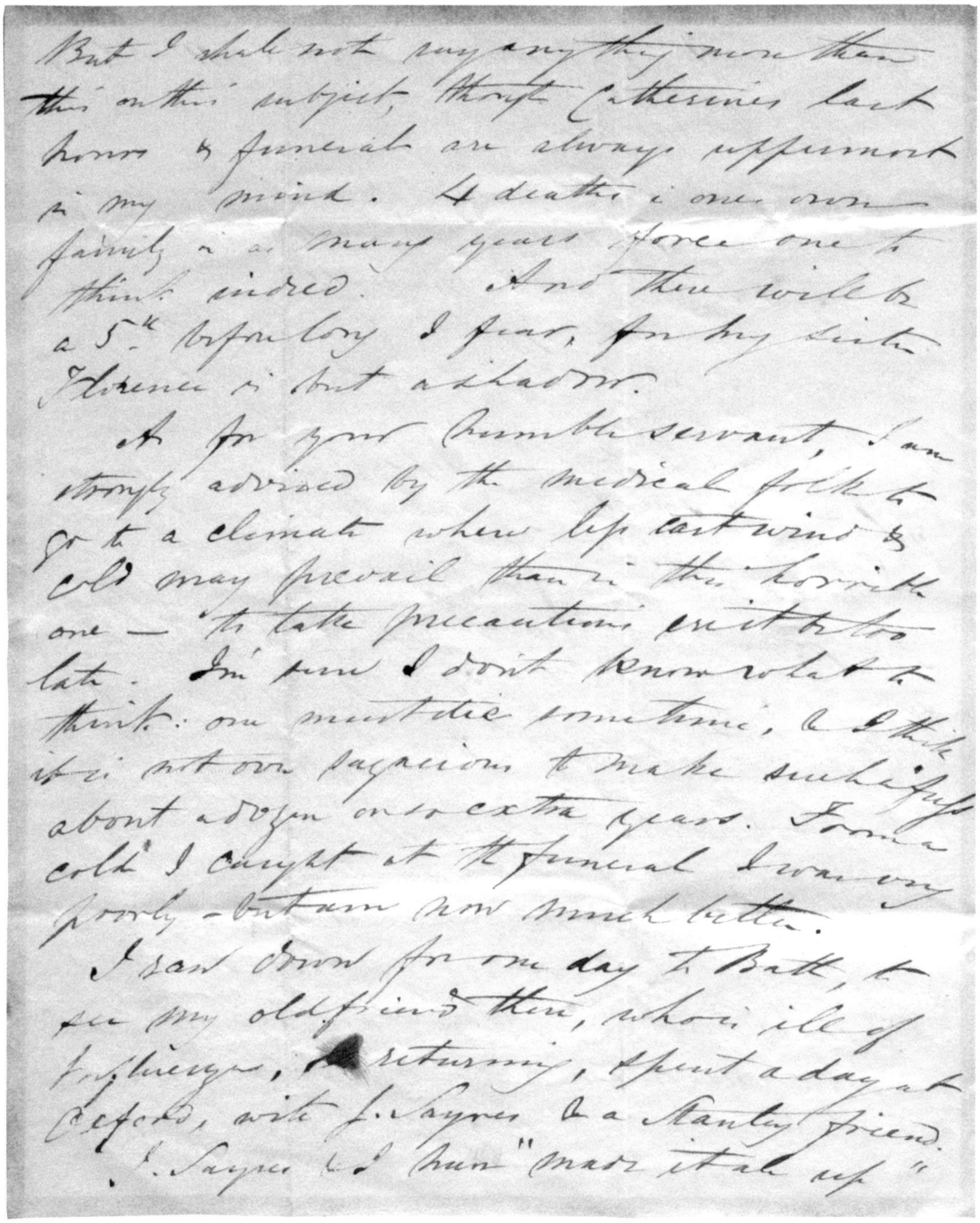
But I shall not say anything more than
this on this subject, though Catherine's last
hours & funeral are always uppermost
in my mind. 4 deaths in our own
family in as many years force one to
think indeed. And there will be
a 5th before long I fear, for my sister
Florence is but a shadow.

As for your humble servant, I am
strongly advised by the medical folk to
go to a climate where less east wind &
cold may prevail than in this horrible
one — & to take precautions ere it be too
late. I'm sure I don't know what to
think: one must die sometime, & I think
it is not over sagacious to make such a fuss
about a dozen or so extra years. From a
cold I caught at the funeral I was very
poorly - but am now much better. I
went down for one day to Bath, to
see my old friend there, who is ill of
Influenza, & returning, spent a day at
Oxford, with J. Sayres & a Stanley friend.
J. Sayres & I then "made it all up"

Cat. 92

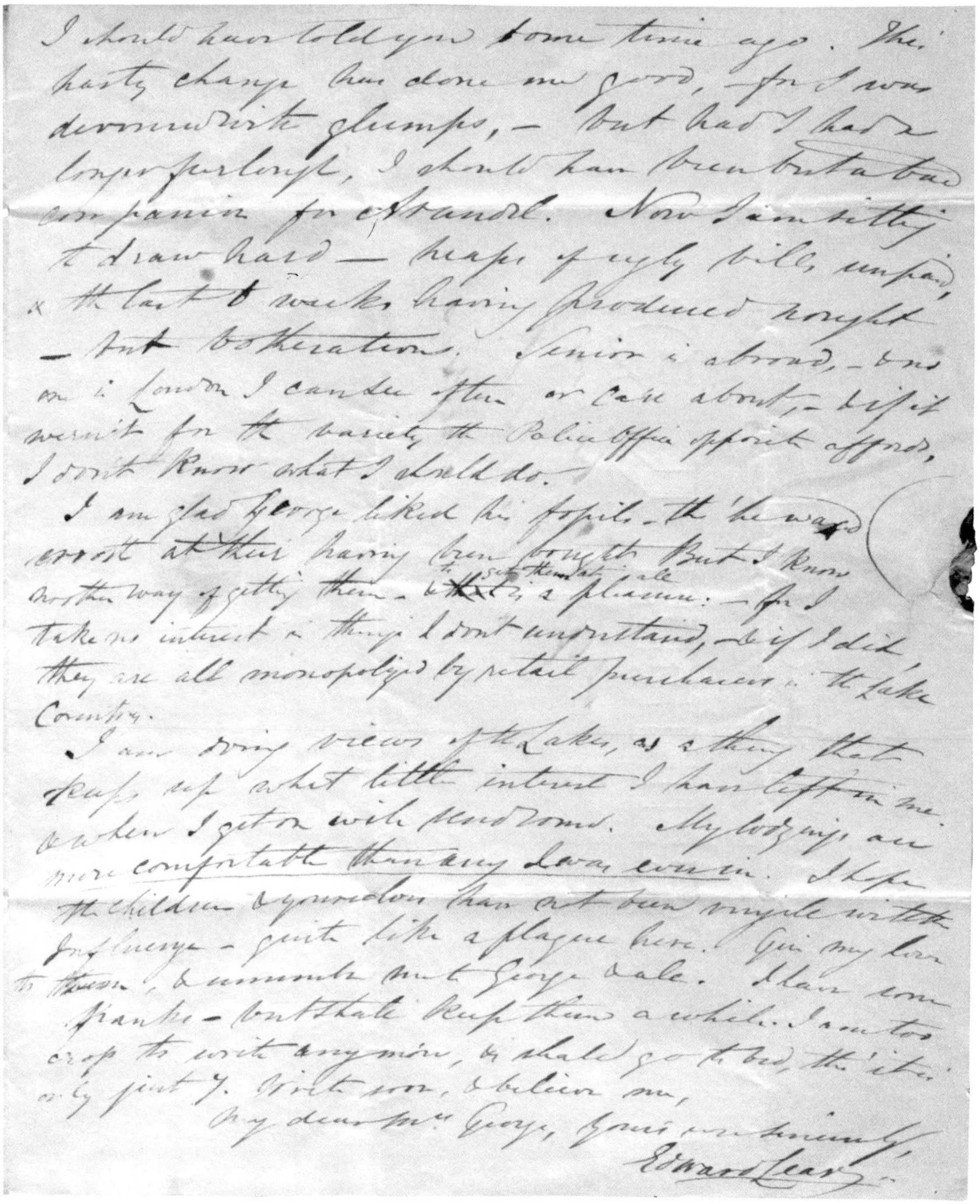
I should have told you some time ago. The
hasty change has done me good, — for I was
devoured with glumps, — but had I had a
longer furlough, I should have been but a bad
companion for a Grandee. Now I am sitting
to draw hard — heaps of ugly bills unpaid,
& the last 6 weeks having produced nought
— but botherations. Senior is abroad, — & no
one in London I can see often or care about, — & if it
were not for the variety the Police Office opposite affords,
I don't know what I should do.
I am glad George liked his fossils — tho' he was
cross at their having been bought. But I know
no other way of getting them — to get them at all is a pleasure: — for I
take no interest in things I don't understand, — & if I did
they are all monopolized by retail purchasers in the Lake
Country.
I am doing views of the Lakes, as a thing that
keeps up what little interest I have left in me.
& when I get on well, I'll send some. My lodgings are
more comfortable than any I was ever in. I hope
the children & yourselves have not been visited with
Influenza — quite like a plague here. Give my love
to them, & remember me to George Dale. I have some
franks — but shall keep them a while. I am too
cross to write any more, & shall go to bed, tho' it is
only just 7. Write soon, & believe me,
My dear Mrs George, Yours most sincerely,
Edward Lear.

Cat. 92

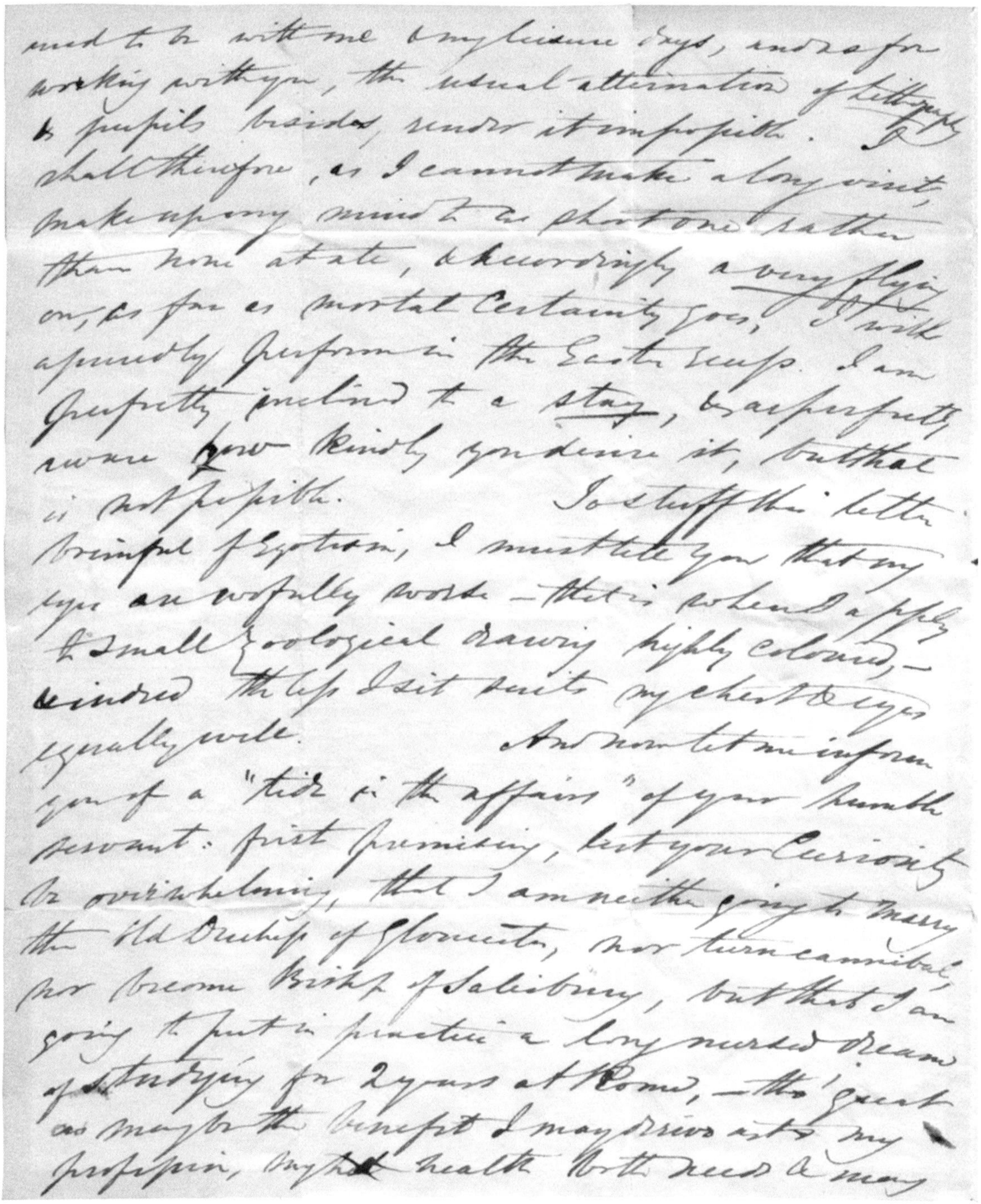

and to be with me & my leisure days, and as for
working with you, the usual alternation of letters
& pupils besides, render it impossible. I
shall therefore, as I cannot make a long visit,
make up my mind to a short one rather
than none at all, & accordingly a very flying
one, as far as mortal certainty goes, I will
assuredly perform in the Easter recess. I am
pretty inclined to a stay, & as perfectly
aware how kindly you desire it, but that
is not possible. To stuff this letter
brimful of Egotism, I must tell you that my
eyes are woefully worse — that is when I apply
to small zoological drawing highly coloured, —
& indeed the less I sit suits my chest & eyes
generally well. And now let me inform
you of a "tide in the affairs" of your humble
servant: first premising, lest your curiosity
be overwhelming, that I am neither going to marry
the old Duchess of Gloucester, nor turn cannibal,
nor become Bishop of Salisbury, but that I am
going to put in practice a long nursed dream
of studying for 2 years at Rome, — tho' great
as may be the benefit I may derive as to my
profession, my health both need & may

Cat. 93

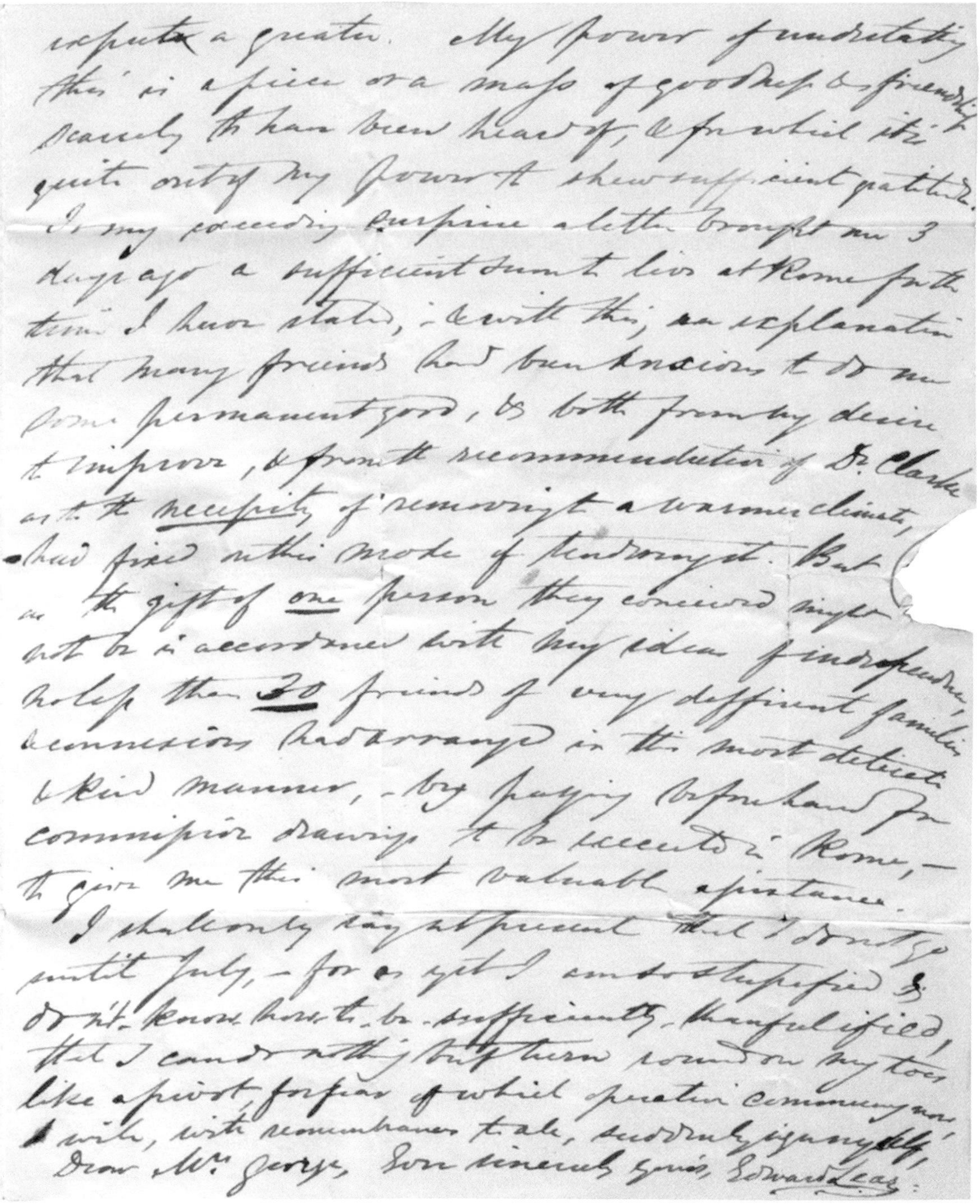
repute a greater. My power of understanding
this is a piece or a mass of goodness & friendship
scarcely to have been heard of, & for which it is
quite out of my power to shew sufficient gratitude.
To my exceeding surprise a letter brought me 3
days ago a sufficient sum to live at Rome for the
term I have stated, – & with this, an explanation
that many friends had been anxious to do me
some permanent good, & both from my desire
to improve, & from the recommendation of Dr Clarke
as to the necessity of removing to a warmer climate,
had fixed on this mode of endeavouring it. But
as the gift of one person they conceived might
not be in accordance with my idea of independence
no less than 30 friends of very different families
& connexions had arranged in the most delicate
& kind manner, – by paying beforehand for
commission drawings to be executed in Rome, –
to give me this most valuable assistance.
I shall only say at present that I do not go
until July, – for as yet I am so stupified &
do not know how to be sufficiently thankful-ified,
that I can do nothing but turn round on my toes
like a pivot, for fear of which operation commencing now
I will, with remembrances to all, suddenly sign myself,
Dear Mr George, Ever sincerely yours, Edward Lear.

Cat. 93

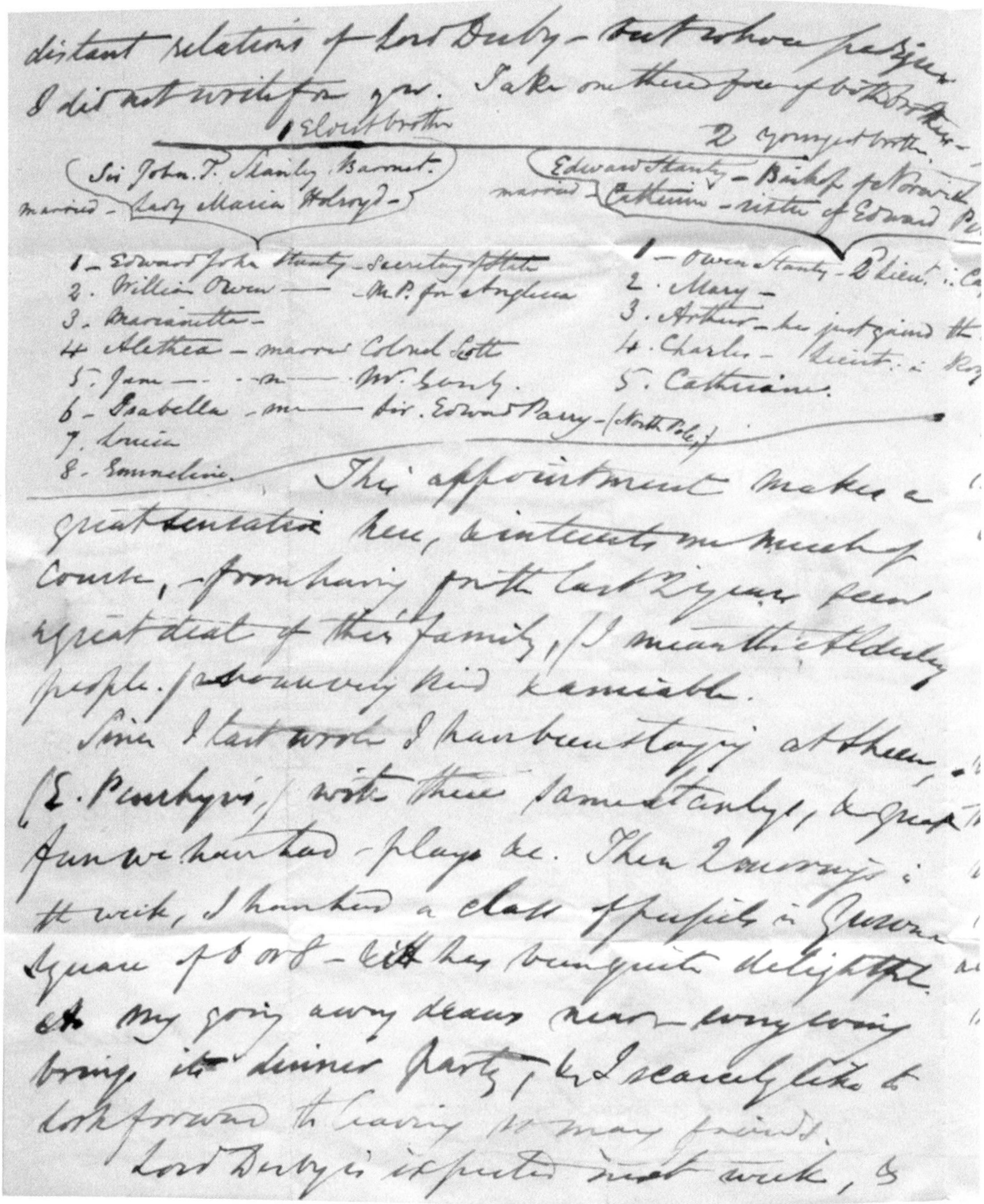
distant relations of Lord Derby – but whose pedigree
I did not write for you. Take on these forms of both brothers –

1 Eldest brother
Sir John T. Stanley Baronet.
married – Lady Maria Holroyd –
1 – Edward John Stanley – Secretary of State
2. William Owen — M.P. for Anglesea
3. Marianne –
4 Alethea – married Colonel Scott
5. Jane — m — Mr. Gordy.
6 – Isabella – m – Sir. Edward Parry – (North Pole)
7. Louisa
8. Emmeline.

2 youngest brother –
Edward Stanley – Bishop of Norwich
married – Catherine – sister of Edward P[illegible]
1 – Owen Stanley – 2d Lieut. in Ca[illegible]
2. Mary –
3. Arthur – he just gained th[illegible]
4. Charles – Lieut. in Ro[illegible]
5. Catherine.

This appointment makes a great sensation here, & interests me much of course, – from having for the last 2 years seen a great deal of this family, – I mean the elderly people. – so very kind & amiable.

Since I last wrote I have been staying at the Ed. Penrhyn's, with these same Stanleys, & great fun we have had – plays &c. Then 2 mornings in the week, I have had a class of pupils in Grosvenor Square of 8 or 9 – it has been quite delightful. As my going away draws near – every evening brings its dinner party, & I scarcely like to look forward to leaving so many friends.

Lord Derby is expected next week, &

Cat. 94

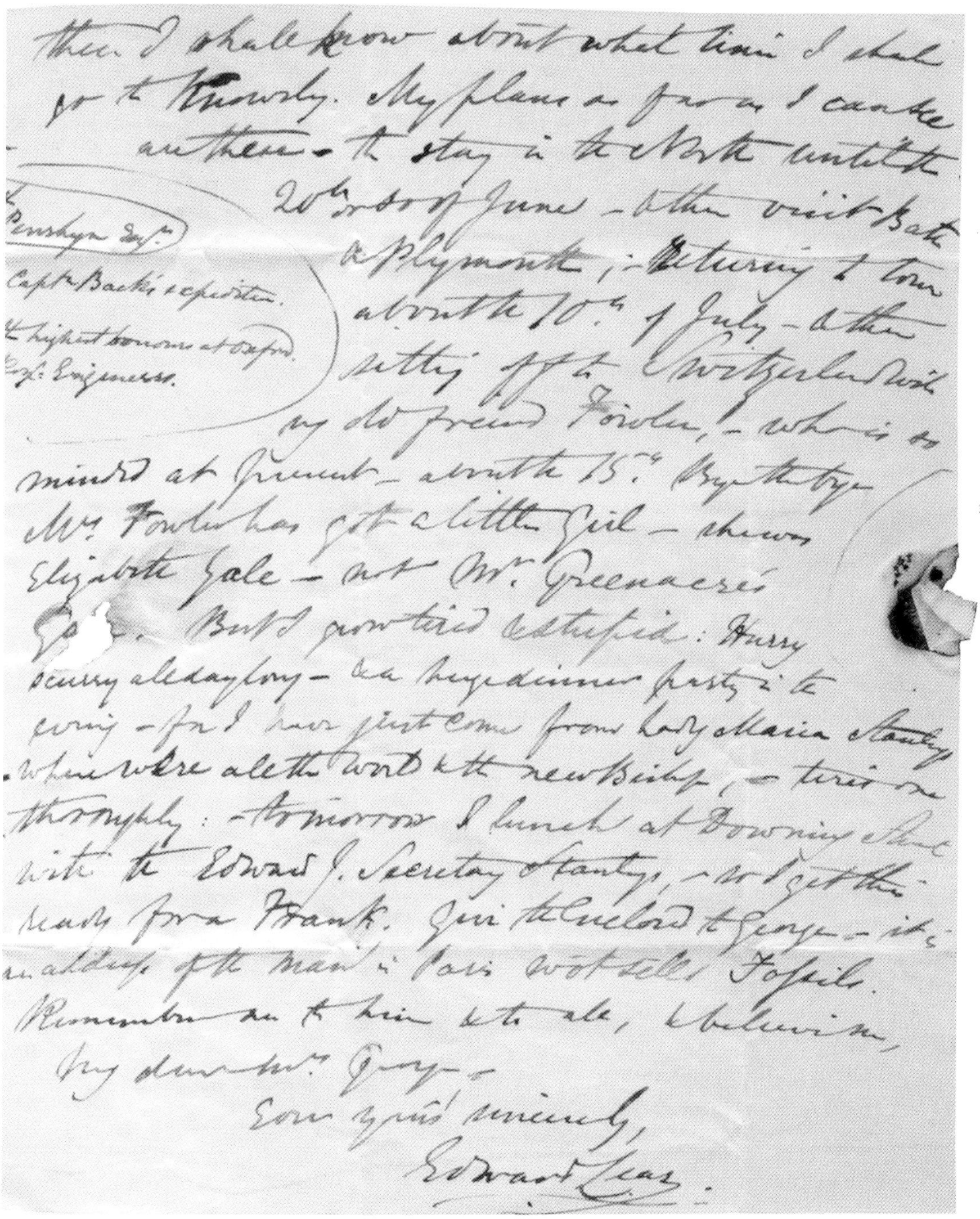
then I shall know about what time I shall
go to Knowsley. My plans as far as I can see
are these — to stay in the North until the
20th or so of June — & then visit Bath
& Plymouth, — returning to town
about the 10th of July — & then
setting off to Switzerland with
my old friend Fowler, — who is so
minded at present — about the 15th. By the bye
Mrs Fowler has got a little girl — she was
Elizabeth Gale — not Mrs Greenacre's
G[irl]. But I grow tired & stupified: Hurry
scurry all day long — & a huge dinner party in the
evening — for I have just come from Lady Maria Stanley's
where were all the world & the new Bishop, — tired me
thoroughly: — tomorrow I lunch at Downing Street
with the Edward J. Secretary Stanleys, — so I get this
ready for a Frank. Give the enclosed to George — it is
an address of the man in Paris wot sells Fossils.
Remember me to him & to all, & believe me,
my dear Mrs Gorge —
Ever yours sincerely,
Edward Lear.

Penrhyn Esqre
Capt Back's expedition.
the highest honours at Oxford.
Esq: Engineers.

Cat. 94

> studying for 2 years at Rome,—tho' great as may be the benefit I may derive as to my profession, my [erased word] health both needs & may expect a greater. My power of undertaking this is a piece or a mass of goodness & friendship scarcely to have been heard of, & for which it is quite out of my power to shew sufficient gratitude. To my exceeding surprise a letter brought me 3 days ago a sufficient sum to live at Rome for the term I have stated,—& with this, an explanation that many friends had been anxious to do me some permanent good, & both from my desire to improve, & from the recommendation of Dr. Clarke as to the *necessity* of removing to a warmer climate,—had fixed on this mode of tendering it. But as the gift of *one* person they conceived might not be in accordance with my idea of independence, no less than 30 friends of very different families & connexions had arranged in this most delicate & kind manner,—by paying beforehand for commission drawings to be executed in Rome,—to give me this most valuable assistance.

The idea of travelling to Rome had probably been discussed when Lear was staying at Knowsley the previous summer, and it seems most likely that the principal movers in this plan were Lord Derby and his nephew Robert Hornby; certainly, Lear later spoke of being sent to Rome by these two alone with no mention of anyone else involved. It seems that crediting thirty friends with this generosity, as in this letter, was Lear's preferred way of explaining the change in his fortunes, and that the conveniently round number was an invention (see Noakes 2006, p. 275 n.43).

94 *Letter to Fanny Coombe, from 21, Sherrard Street, Golden Square, London*

15 April 1837
Autograph letter
The Frederick Warne Archive
Illustrated on pp. 178–9; see pp. 222–3 for full text

Apart from recording Lear's final change of lodgings before leaving for Rome, the main piece of news in this letter is the appointment of his friend the Rev. Edward Stanley as Bishop of Norwich. Stanley, the younger brother of Sir John Stanley of Alderley, had up to this point been Rector of Alderley, and Lear describes himself as 'having for the past 2 years seen a great deal of this family'. The news gives him the opportunity of drawing out the family tree of this branch of the Stanley family. Lear was indeed intimate with the family; he became a particular friend of the Bishop's son, Arthur Penrhyn Stanley (1815–1881), and had accompanied both father and son to Ireland in August 1835 (see cats. 18–26). The younger Stanley went on to become a leading liberal theologian, and was appointed Dean of Westminster in 1864. After hearing of his death, Lear wrote in July 1881: 'Altogether I have not known in my life of fifty odd years among various characters, anyone so thoroughly a real Christian as Arthur was.' (*Later Letters*, p. 218). The friendship between Lear and Arthur Penrhyn Stanley lasted until Stanley's death, and it is a great loss to scholarship that their correspondence has entirely disappeared.

[5]

NORTHERN FAREWELLS
MAY TO JUNE 1837

Lear arrived at Knowsley on 19 May after an overnight coach journey with Lord Derby; it was his last visit to the house before his departure for Rome. He probably stayed about a week (a watercolour of trees in a landscape, inscribed 'Knowsley' and dated 26 May 1837, was sold at Christie's, 14 June 1983, lot 119). From Knowsley, he probably went to the Rectory at Winwick to say goodbye to The Rev. James John Hornby, Lord Derby's brother-in-law and the father of his friend Robert. After this he travelled to the Rectory at Alderley in Cheshire, where he arrived at the latest on 1 June. The drawing of the church at Nether Alderley, and its companion drawn an hour later, date from early the following morning, and are the first two drawings of the day (cats. 96 and 97). The timing noted on them confirms what Lear himself says about his normal daily routine while on a country visit ('I rose at 4 & drew till 6' – Letter of 8 July 1837, cat. 104). It is not known how long Lear stayed at Alderley; his letter of 8 July does not mention the visit, although it does record farewells to the family of Edmund Hornby (presumably at Lancaster). He travelled from the north via Bath to Plymouth, which he records arriving at on 19 June.

95 *Letter to Fanny Coombe, from Knowsley Hall, Lancashire*

19 May 1837
Autograph letter
The Frederick Warne Archive
Illustrated on pp. 183–4; see pp. 224–5 for full text

This letter was written from Knowsley on the day of Lear's arrival there for his final visit before his departure for Italy. He had travelled with Lord Derby and describes the journey: 'at ½ past 4 oclock left London in a chariot drawn by four horses, accompanied by 2 postillions & 2 domestics,—& containing Lord Derby—myself—6 cloaks—one jerboa—3 pigeons—20 or 30 books—some bread & biscuits,—a roast fowl & a bottle of wine. Dinner having been ordered at Dunchurch in Warwickshre at 12—we attacked the last mentioned [agreeables?] at 8,—& at midnight had a delightful dinner, after which I slept perfectly sound until we reached Warrington this morning at 10: we arrived here at qu past 11—& if that is not expedition & comfort—what is?' With the spread of railways around Britain such journeys were soon to become a thing of the past.

Lear is feeling rather lonely in the large house:

> Here I am sitting—in the old red drawing room—with its old gilt mouldings, & its old pictures,—& its red & white striped furniture, & its chiffoniers full of books—& its plate glass recessed windows with fat cushions therein—looking out over the old broad sloping lawn till it is lost in the meadows—then the trees—& then a wide flat country as far as one can see with its extreme edge just dotted with 6 Mills—one raceStand—17 churches—& all Liverpool:—& all this just as placid as if nothing ever did or could happen to disturb it.' His depression leads to a frank admission: 'I don't half like going out of England, now it comes to the point.

Lear's mood of depression is matched by the landscape: 'The country here looks like March:—the Oak & Ash are as bare as they were in January.' Nevertheless, he has his friend Robert Hornby arriving, although it is not until the following Tuesday (23 May). Lear stayed at Knowsley for at least a week, and then probably went to nearby Winwick to say goodbye to the Rev. James Hornby, Robert's elderly father.

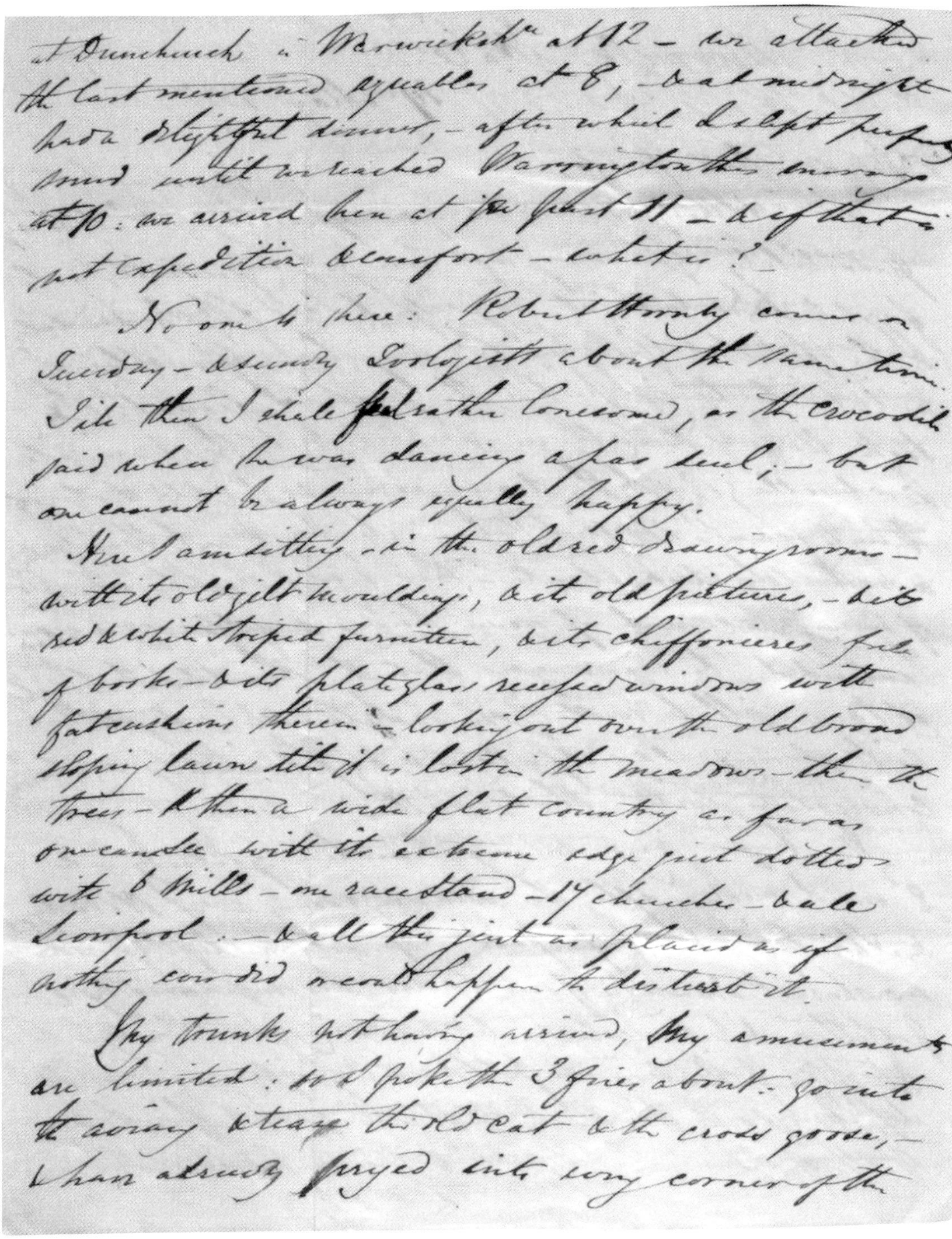
at Dunchurch in Warwickshire at 12 – we attacked
the last mentioned eatables at 8, – & at midnight
had a delightful dinner, – after which I slept perfectly
sound until we reached Warrington the morning
at 10: we arrived here at five past 11 – & if that is
not expedition & comfort – what is? –
No one is here: Robert Hornby comes on
Tuesday – & secondly Zoologists about the same time.
Till then I shall feel rather lonesome, as the crocodile
said when he was dancing a pas seul; – but
one cannot be always equally happy.
Here I am sitting in the old red drawingroom –
with its old gilt mouldings, & its old pictures, – & its
red & white striped furniture, & its chiffonnieres full
of books – & its plate glass recessed windows with
fat cushions therein – looking out over the old broad
sloping lawn till it is lost in the meadows – then the
trees – & then a wide flat country as far as
one can see with the extreme edge just dotted
with 6 Mills – one racestand – 17 churches – & all
Liverpool: – & all this just as placid as if
nothing ever did or could happen to disturb it.
My trunks not having arrived, my amusements
are limited: so I poke the 3 fires about: go into
the aviary & tease the old cat & the cross goose, –
& have already pryed into every corner of the

Cat. 95

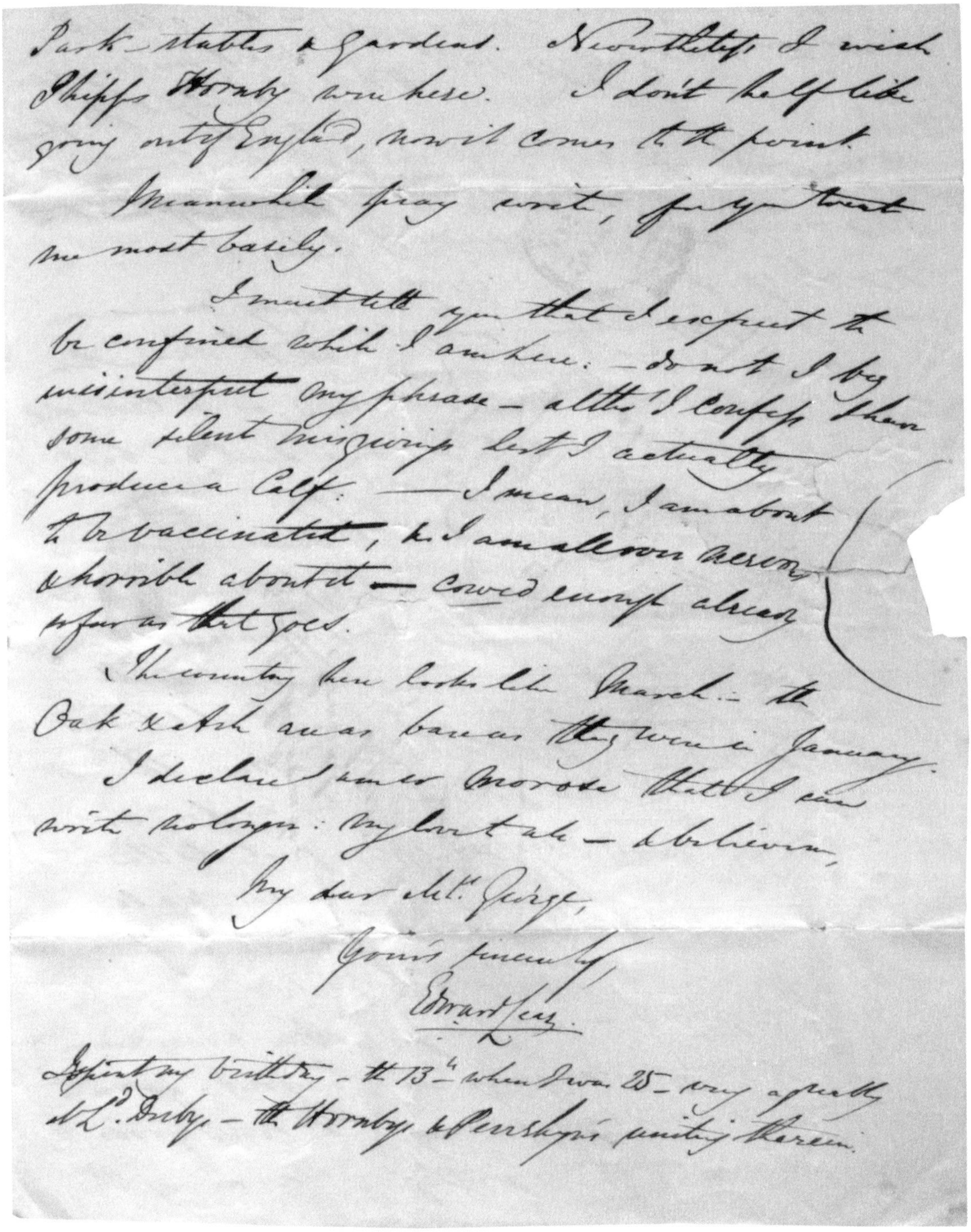
Park – stables & Gardens. Nevertheless, I wish
Phipps Hornby were here. I don't half like
going out of England, now it comes to the point.

Meanwhile pray write, for you treat
me most basely.

I must tell you that I expect to
be confined while I am here: – do not I beg
misinterpret my phrase – altho' I confess I have
some silent misgivings lest I actually
produce a Calf: — I mean, I am about
to be vaccinated, & I am all over nervous
& horrible about it — cowed enough already
so far as that goes.

The country here looks like March: – the
Oak & Ash are as bare as they were in January.

I declare I am so morose that I can
write no longer: my love to all – & believe me,

My dear Mr. George,

Yours sincerely,

Edward Lear.

I spent my birthday – the 13th – when I was 25 – very agreeably
at Ld. Derby's – the Hornbys & Penrhyns uniting therein.

Cat. 95

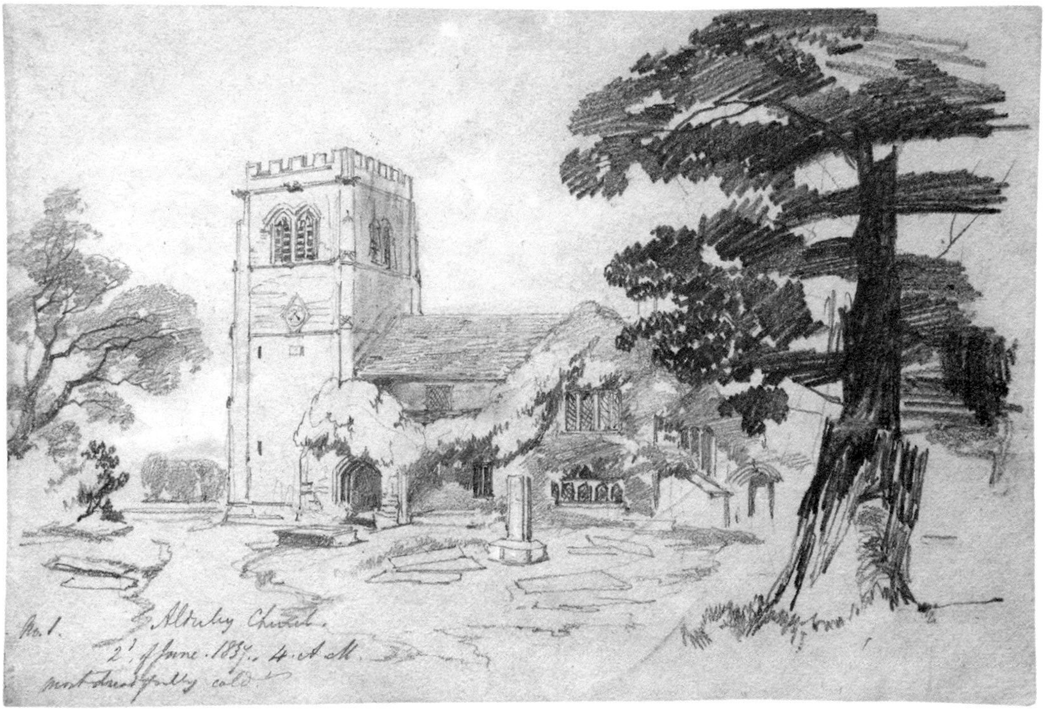

Cat. 96

96 *St Mary's, Nether Alderley, Cheshire*

Inscribed and dated 'No. 1 / Alderley Church. / 2d of June. 1837. 4. AM. / most dreadfully cold'
Pencil and stump, on blue-grey paper, 16.7 × 25.3 cm
Provenance: presented by Sir Hugh Walpole in 1938

The King's School, Canterbury

97 *The Skeleton Oak, Alderley Park, Cheshire*

Inscribed and dated 'Alderley. June 2. 1837. 5.A.M. cold-drizzly. Edward Lear del. / The Skeleton Oak'
Pencil and stump, on blue-grey paper, 25.3 × 16.7 cm
Provenance: presented by Sir Hugh Walpole in 1938

The King's School, Canterbury

Illustrated on p. 186

98 *The Skeleton Oak, Alderley Park, Cheshire*

Signed, inscribed and dated 'Alderley. 1837. / Edward Lear. del.'
Pencil and stump heightened with white, on blue-grey paper, 34.9 × 24.4 cm
Provenance: the Rev. Edward Stanley; A. Hankey (Anon. Sale); Sotheby's, 1 Feb. 1961, lot 45 ('Six Studies of Trees at Alderley', in an album with other drawings) (£40 to Spink); Derek Lockett, from whom purchased via John Baskett Ltd. in 1981 (£2,500, with five others)

Whitworth Art Gallery, University of Manchester (D.1981.1)

Illustrated on p. 187

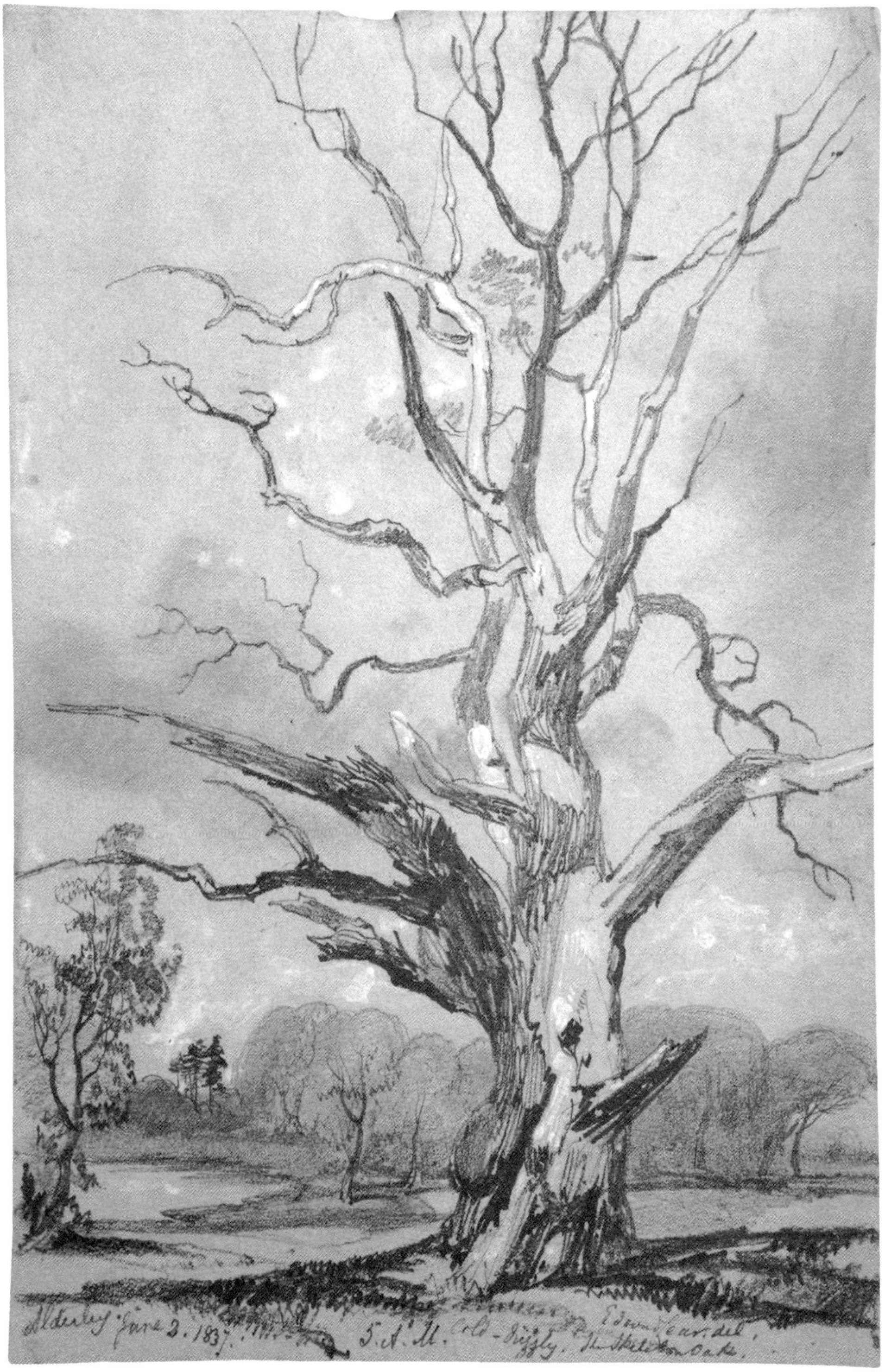
Alderley June 2. 1837.
5 A.M. Cold – drizzly.
Edward Lear. del.
The Skeleton Oak.

Cat. 97

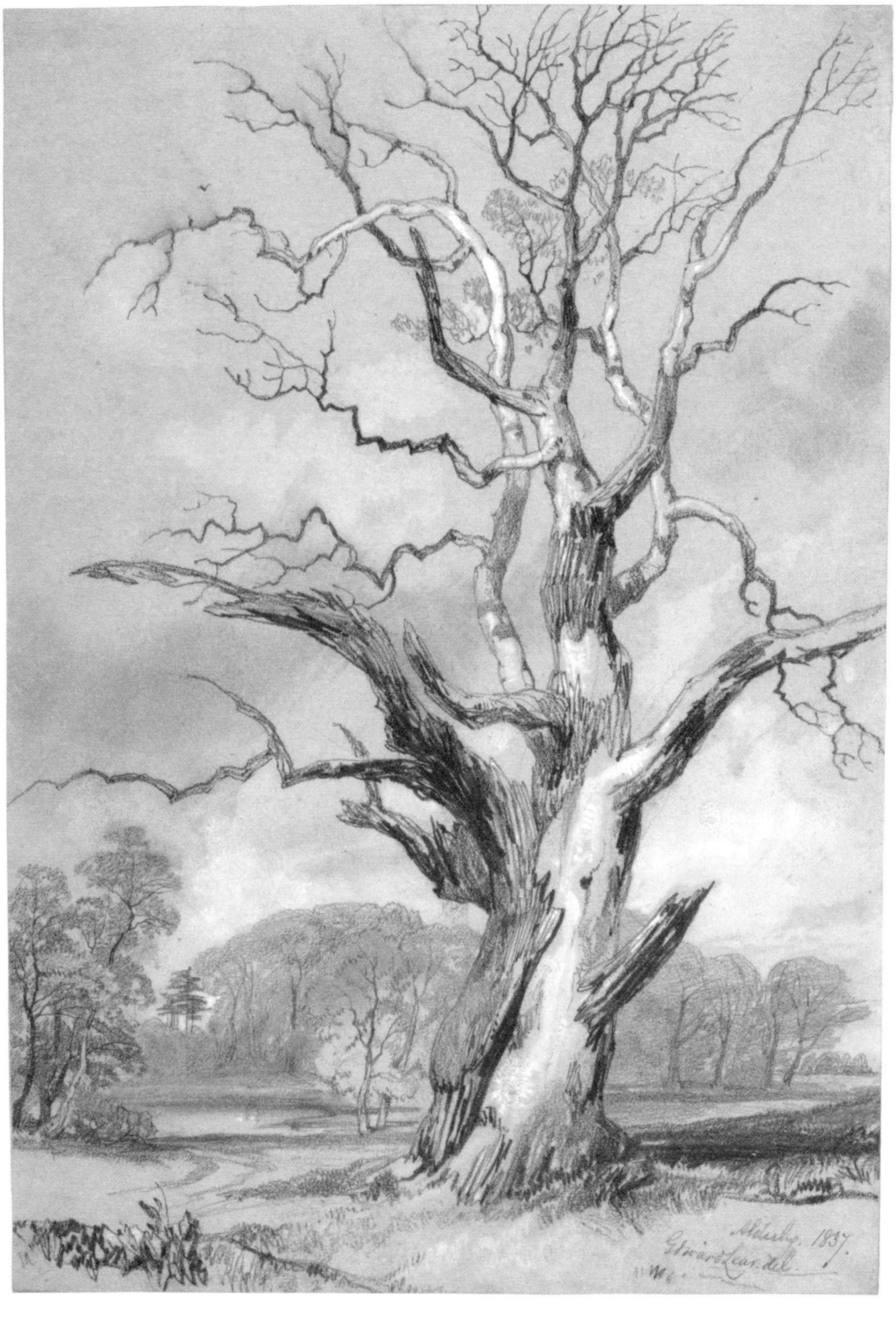

Cat. 98

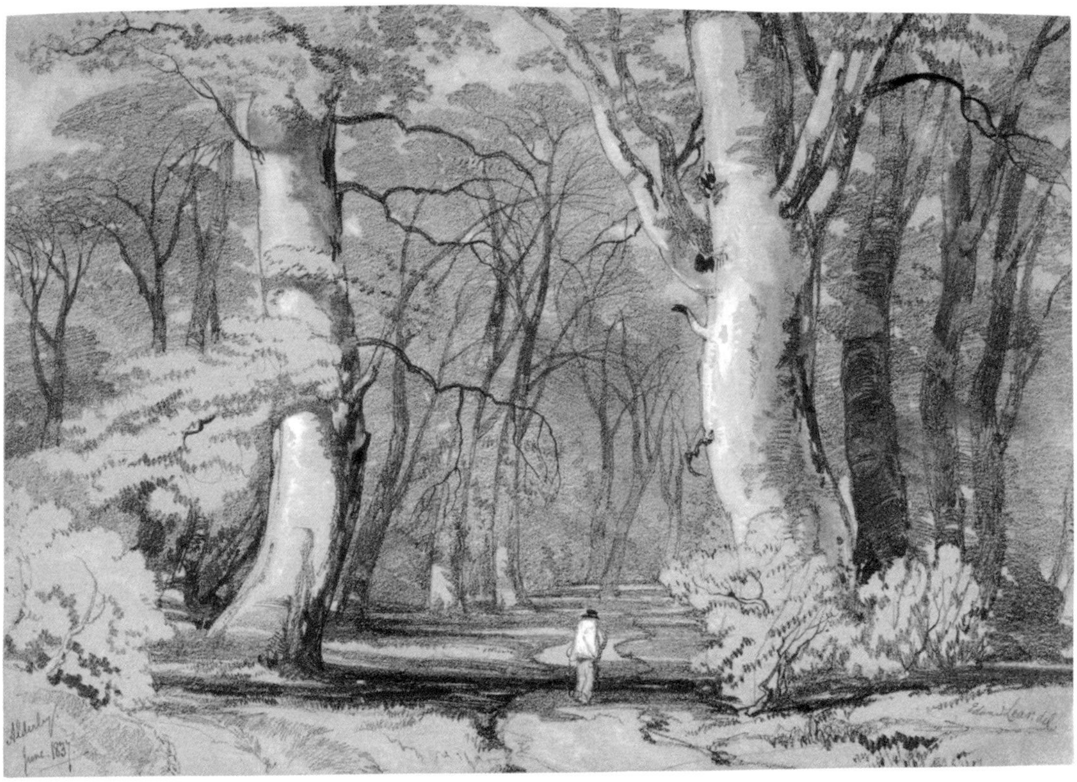

Cat. 99

99 *Study of Beech Trees in Alderley Park, Cheshire*

Signed 'Edward Lear. del.', and inscribed and dated 'Alderley. June. 1837.'
Pencil, black chalk and stump heightened with white, on blue-grey paper, 24.7 × 35.5 cm
Provenance: the Rev. Edward Stanley; A. Hankey (Anon. Sale); Sotheby's, 1 Feb. 1961, lot 45 ('Six Studies of Trees at Alderley', in an album with other drawings) (£40 to Spink); Derek Lockett, from whom purchased via John Baskett Ltd. in 1981 (£2,500, with five others)

Whitworth Art Gallery, University of Manchester (D.1981.2)

100 *Study of Beech Trees in Alderley Park, Cheshire*

Signed 'Edward Lear. del / Alderley.', and dated June 1837
Pencil, black chalk and stump heightened with white, on blue-grey paper, 35.5 × 24.7 cm
Provenance: the Rev. Edward Stanley; A. Hankey (Anon. Sale); Sotheby's, 1 Feb. 1961, lot 45 ('Six Studies of Trees at Alderley', in an album with other drawings) (£40 to Spink); Derek Lockett, from whom purchased via John Baskett Ltd. in 1981 (£2,500, with five others)

Whitworth Art Gallery, University of Manchester (D.1981.3)

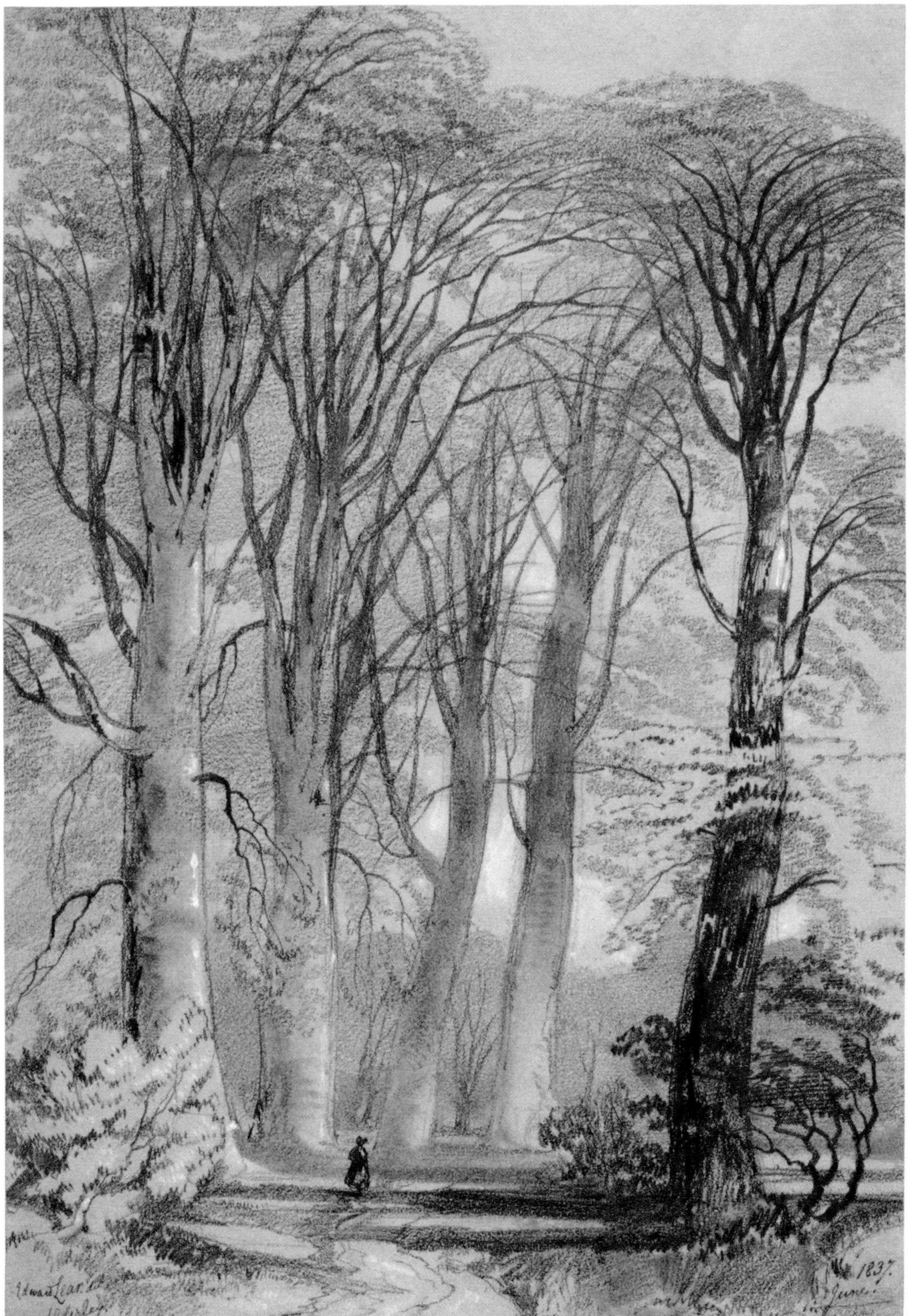

Cat. 100

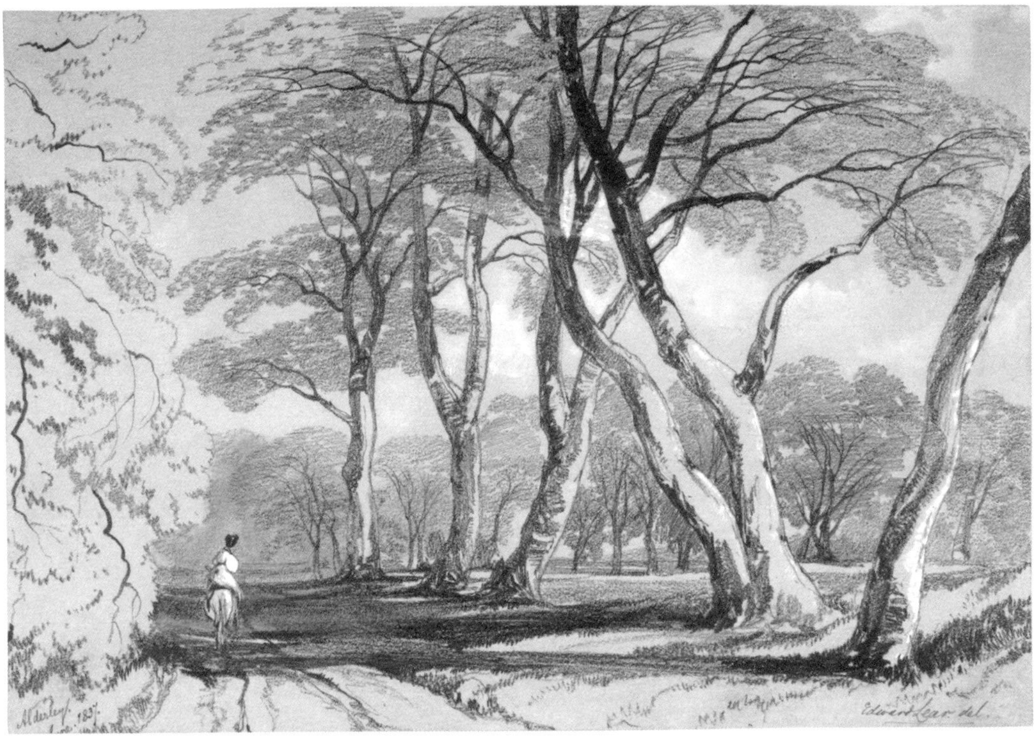

Cat. 101

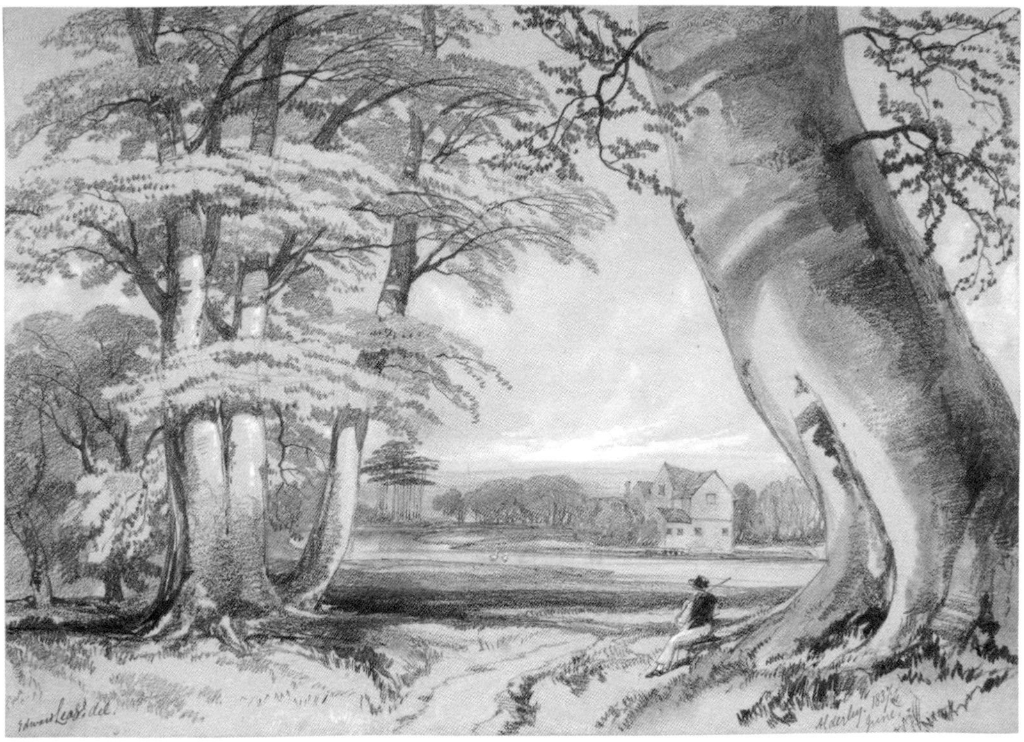

Cat. 102

101 *Study of Beech Trees in Alderley Park, Cheshire*

Signed 'Edward Lear. del.', and inscribed and dated 'Alderley. / June [cut] 1837.'
Pencil, black chalk and stump heightened with white, on blue-grey paper, 24.7 × 35.5 cm
Provenance: the Rev. Edward Stanley; A. Hankey (Anon. Sale); Sotheby's, 1 Feb. 1961, lot 45 ('Six Studies of Trees at Alderley', in an album with other drawings) (£40 to Spink); Derek Lockett, from whom purchased via John Baskett Ltd. in 1981 (£2,500, with five others)

Whitworth Art Gallery, University of Manchester (D.1981.4)

102 *Study of Beech Trees in Alderley Park, Cheshire*

Signed 'Edward Lear. del.', and inscribed and dated 'Alderley. 1837. / June.'
Pencil, black chalk and stump heightened with white, on blue-grey paper, 25.2 × 35.5 cm
Provenance: the Rev. Edward Stanley; A. Hankey (Anon. Sale); Sotheby's, 1 Feb. 1961, lot 45 ('Six Studies of Trees at Alderley', in an album with other drawings) (£40 to Spink); Derek Lockett, from whom purchased via John Baskett Ltd. in 1981 (£2,500, with five others)

Whitworth Art Gallery, University of Manchester (D.1981.5)

103 *Study of Beech Trees in Alderley Park, Cheshire*

Signed 'Edward Lear. del.', and inscribed and dated 'Alderley. June. 1837.'
Pencil, black chalk and stump heightened with white, on blue-grey paper, 34.9 × 25.2 cm
Provenance: the Rev. Edward Stanley; A. Hankey (Anon. Sale); Sotheby's, 1 Feb. 1961, lot 45 ('Six Studies of Trees at Alderley', in an album with other drawings) (£40 to Spink); Derek Lockett, from whom purchased via John Baskett Ltd. in 1981 (£2,500, with five others)

Whitworth Art Gallery, University of Manchester (D.1981.6)

Illustrated on p. 192

The six drawings of trees in Alderley Park, which were drawn for the Stanley family in June 1837 and have stayed together, are a unique survival; for the first of them a preparatory drawing also survives, hinting at how much similar material is now lost. Lear's depiction of trees is clearly indebted to the lithographs of James Duffield Harding (see cats. 6 and 89).

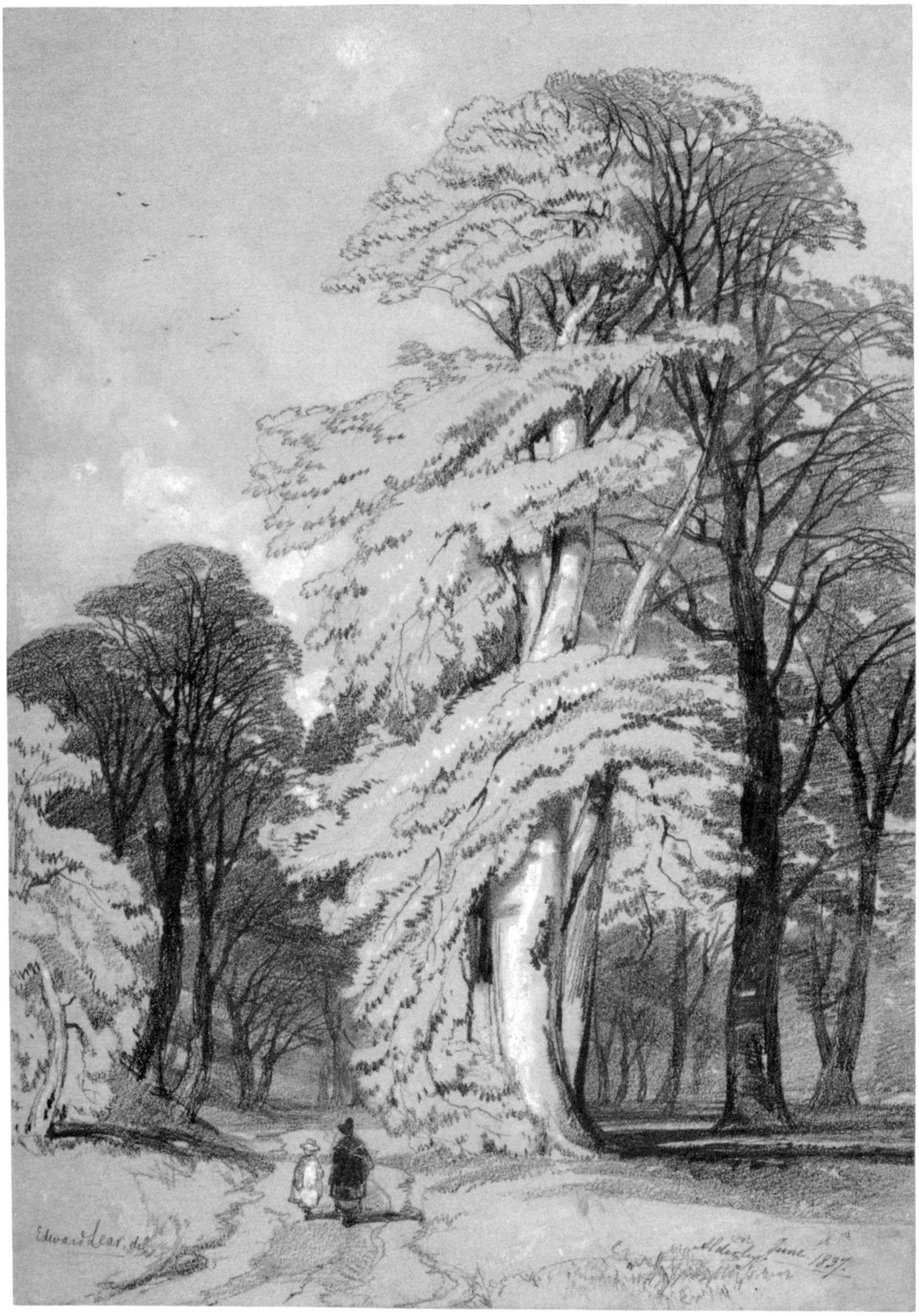

Cat. 103

[6]

VISIT TO PLYMOUTH AND BOVISAND: JUNE TO JULY 1837

Lear's final visit before leaving for Italy was a stay with the family of Phipps Hornby at Bovisand near Plymouth. Captain Phipps Hornby (1785–1867) was a younger brother of Edmund Hornby (Lear's host in Lancaster in August 1836) and of the Rev. James John Hornby, Rector of Winwick; he later became an Admiral and was knighted. His eldest son, also named Phipps (1820–1848), was Lear's particular friend; a younger son, another Rev. James John (1826–1909), later became Provost of Eton. Lear probably knew the Phipps Hornbys from his many visits to Lancashire and seems to have been intimate with all of the family.

Lear arrived in Plymouth on 19 June and probably left on 6 July, making at least part of the return journey to London by boat. The visit is quite fully recorded by the combination of a letter of 8 July mostly written from the Isle of Wight on the return journey to London (cat. 104) and by the contents of an album of drawings in the Victoria & Albert Museum (E.752-788-1939). An inscription, now separately mounted and reading 'The Book of Bovisand / from Edward Lear / To Capn. & Mrs. Hornby / & their family', records the gift of the album of drawings to the Hornbys. The drawings, some of which are dated between 21 June and 6 July, show either figures (presumably members of the Phipps Hornby family), coastal scenes, or views in the Plymouth area.

Apart from hiking expeditions up the Plym on 23 June and the Tamar on 30 June, Lear stayed on the Bovisand side (i.e. the east) of Plymouth Sound, and made expeditions from there. A sheet of studies of parts of buildings, dated 27 June and inscribed with the name of the nearby village of Down Thomas, is strikingly reminiscent of the work of Samuel Prout (fig. 48, p. 194). A drawing dated 2 July shows a view of the River Yealm three miles to the east (fig. 49, p. 194).

Lear clearly decided to return to London at least part of the way by sea, since there is a drawing in the Bovisand album dated 6 July and inscribed 'near the mouth of Dart', which was drawn from a boat. The final part of the letter is written from Lear's London lodgings: '21 Sherrard Street—Golden Sqre. 10th. July. 1837. Here am I in my old Lodgings … I sail on Sunday next by the Antwerp packet.' Lear left England on 16 July.

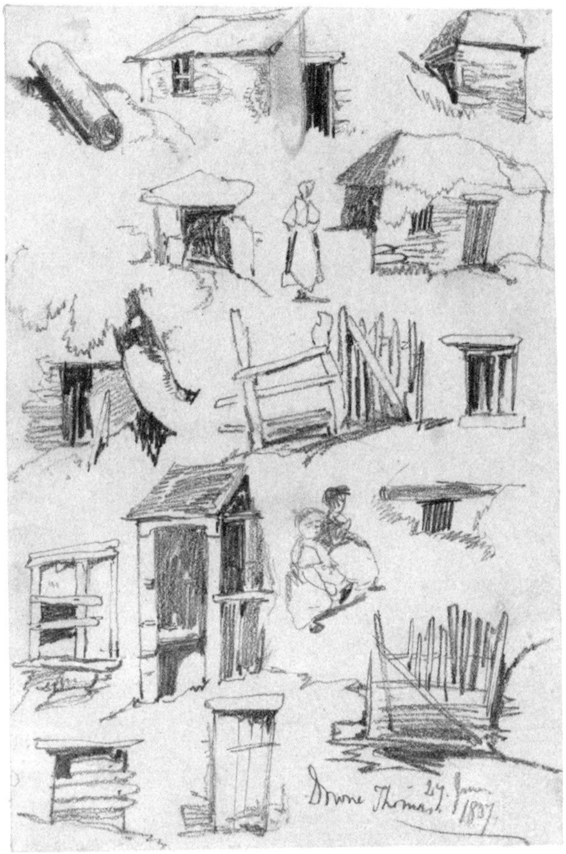

Fig. 48 Sheet of Studies of Buildings at Down Thomas, inscribed and dated 'Downe Thomas. 27. June. 1837.', pencil, 22.7 × 15.3 cm (Victoria & Albert Museum, E.769-1939).

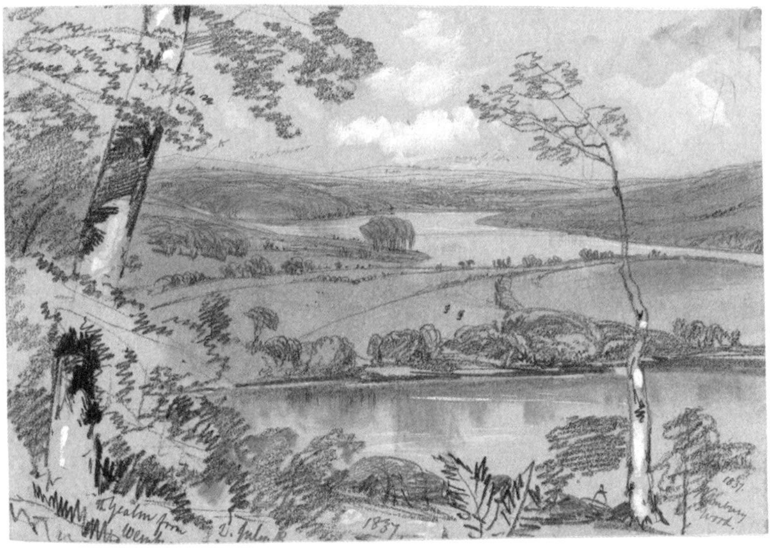

Fig. 49 The Yealm from Wembury Wood, inscribed and dated 'The Yealm from Wemb[ury] / 2. July. 1837' and '1837. / Wembury Wood.', pencil and stump heightened with white, on blue-grey paper, 16.6 × 24.8 cm (Victoria & Albert Museum, E.780-1939).

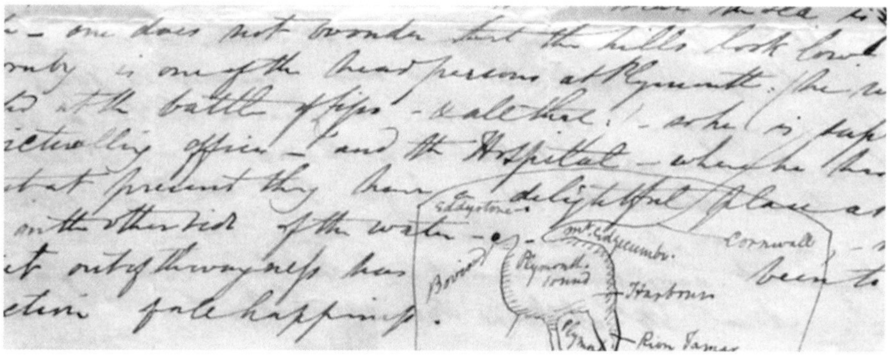

104 *Letter to Fanny Coombe, from Ryde, Isle of Wight and 21, Sherrard Street, Golden Square, London*

8 and 10 July 1837
Autograph letter
The Frederick Warne Archive
Illustrated above (detail) and on p. 196; see pp. 225–7 for full text

Composed over three days, this is the last letter written by Lear before his departure for Italy with Daniel Fowler. The artist recounts his northern farewells, saying that he left Knowsley with 'a great deal of pain' and calling it 'the best home I have ever met with'. He continues: 'I stayed at Winwick—& took leave of Mr. & Mrs. James Hornby ... of the Miss Hornbys ... then of the Edmund Hornbys & others not known to you by name ... And so I came away from Lancashire.'

He then recounts his stay with the Phipps Hornbys at Bovisand near Plymouth:

> which I reached on 19 June. Devonshire is actually nothing more or less than Paradise ... Captain Hornby is one of the head persons at Plymouth: (he was distinguished at the battle of Lissa—& all that—so he is superintendent of all the victualling offices—and the Hospital—where he has a house. But at present they have a delightful place at Bovisand on the other side of the water ... where ... quiet outofthewayness has been to me perfection of all happiness ... [At this point Lear drew a map in the text illustrating the location of Bovisand in relation to Plymouth—see the illustration] ... All the family (11 of them) who were so long my friends at Knowsly—were here—besides Miss Montagu who is all music—not to forget my friend Phipps [Phipps Hornby (1820–1848) was Lear's particular friend; they were later to tour Scotland together in September 1841] who has just got the Engineers at Woolwich. And as a general idea of our days, I rose at 4 & drew till 6—when Phipps & Jamie & I walked or bathe till breakfast. Afterwards in the [sea?] sate indoors with a quiet drawing or musical morning—or dabbled 2 or 3 hours more in the sea—or all sailed about in the wherry—until 4 when Captn. Hornby returned from Plymouth & we dined. After this we usually took a long eving [*sic*] walk—& as often (—& latterly indeed always,) we all adjourned to the rocks with guitars & work—Mrs Hornby in her little pony chair—& there we sate singing to the sea & the moon till late. Charades & all sorts of fun—tea [or?] music—occupied us till Bed. Sometimes a day we spent in a Knapsack walk of 20 miles with Capt. H. up one of the rivers—sometimes pic nics to Mt. Edgcumbe—or lionizing about Plymouth. ... so you see that Bovisand bids fair to take a jump up into Heaven just as it is.'

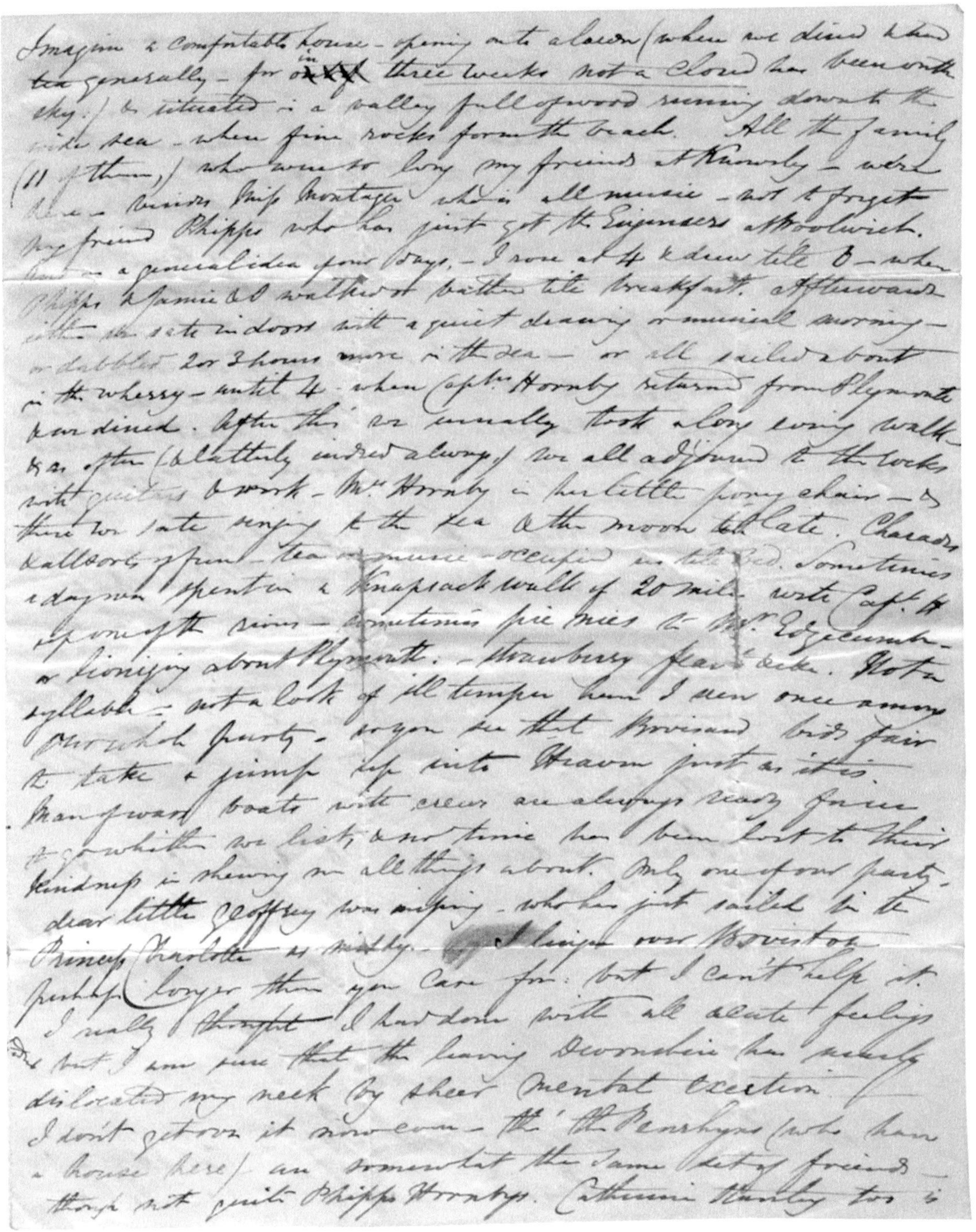
Imagine a comfortable house – opening onto a lawn (where we dined & had
tea generally – for in three weeks not a cloud has been on the
sky.) & situated in a valley full of wood running down to the
wide sea – where fine rocks form the beach. All the family
(11 of them,) who were so long my friends at Knowsley – were
there – besides Miss Montague who is all music – not to forget
my friend Phipps who has just got the Engineers at Woolwich.
Now a general idea of our days, – I rose at 4 & drew till 8 – when
Phipps & Jamie & I walked or bathed till breakfast. Afterwards
either we sate indoors with a quiet drawing or musical morning –
or dabbled 2 or 3 hours more in the sea – or all sailed about
in the wherry – until 4 – when Capt.n Hornby returned from Plymouth
& we dined. After this we usually took a long evening walk
& as often (& latterly indeed always) we all adjourned to the rocks
with guitars & work – M.rs Hornby in her little pony chair – &
there we sate singing to the sea & the moon till late. Charades
& all sorts of fun – tea or music – occupied us till bed. Sometimes
a day was spent in a knapsack walk of 20 miles with Capt. H
& some of the sons – sometimes five miles to M.t Edgecumbe –
or lionizing about Plymouth. – strawberry feasts & c. Not a
syllable – not a look of ill temper have I seen once among
our whole party – so you see that Bovisand bids fair
to take a jump up into Heaven just as it is.
Man of war's boats with crews are always ready for us
to go whither we list, & no time has been lost to their
kindness in shewing us all things about. Only one of our party
dear little Geoffrey was missing – who has just sailed in the
Princess Charlotte as middy. – I linger over Bovisand
perhaps longer than you care for: but I can't help it.
I really thought I had done with all acute feelings
but I am sure that the leaving Devonshire has nearly
dislocated my neck by sheer mental exertion –
I don't get over it now even – tho' the Penrhyns (who have
a house here) are somewhat the same set of friends
though not quite Phipps Hornbys. Catherine Stanley too is

Cat. 104

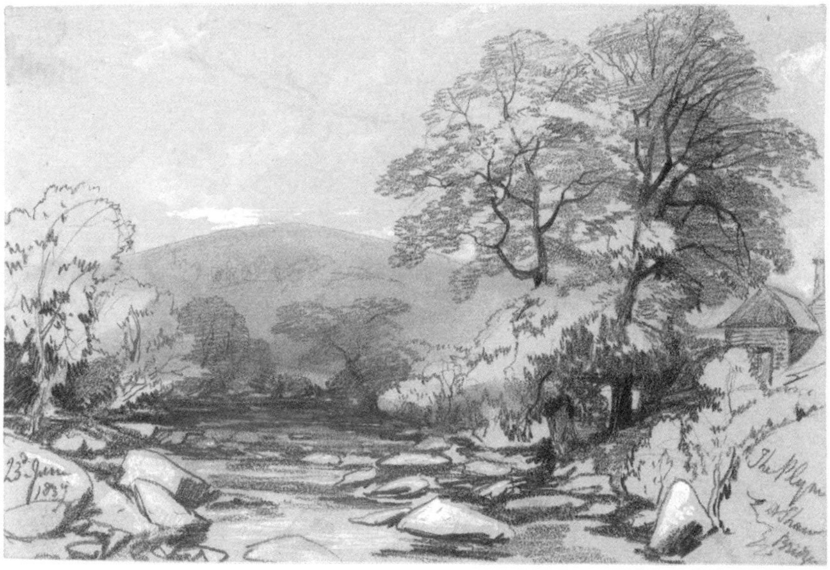

Fig. 50 The Plym at Shaw Bridge, inscribed 'The Plym / at Shaw / Bridge', dated 23d. June 1837, pencil and stump heightened with white, on blue-grey paper, 16.3 × 24.8 cm (Victoria & Albert Museum, E.762-1939)

The Bovisand album contains dated drawings which confirm and augment the letter above. On 23 June there was an expedition up the River Plym; three drawings in the album have this date, including one inscribed 'The Plym at Shaw Bridge' (fig. 50), showing that the party ventured some five miles upstream from Plymouth (a good expedition, but not the twenty miles Lear mentions in the letter). The other hiking expedition was a week later on the 30th, and saw the party heading up the Tamar (see cats. 105 and 106, and figs. 51 and 52, p. 198).

105 *Morwell Rocks on the River Tamar*

Signed 'Edward Lear. del.', and inscribed and dated 'Morwell Rocks. / 30th. June 1837.'
Pencil, black chalk and stump heightened with white, on blue-grey paper, 16 × 24.8 cm
Provenance: Anon. Sale; Christie's South Kensington (Interiors Sale), 22 Mar. 2006, lot 1477 (2 in the lot) purchased on behalf of the W.W. Spooner Trust by Abbot & Holder; presented by the W.W. Spooner Trust to the current owner

The Wordsworth Trust (2007.25.2)

Illustrated on p. 199

106 *Morwell Rocks on the Tamar*

Signed and inscribed 'The Tamar. / Morwell Rocks. / Edwd. Lear. del.', dated '30th. June / 1837'
Pencil, black chalk and stump heightened with white, on blue-grey paper, 16 × 24.8 cm
Provenance: Anon. Sale; Christie's South Kensington (Interiors Sale), 22 Mar. 2006, lot 1477 (2 in the lot) purchased on behalf of the W.W. Spooner Trust by Abbot & Holder; presented by the W.W. Spooner Trust to the current owner

The Wordsworth Trust (2007.25.1)

Illustrated on p. 199

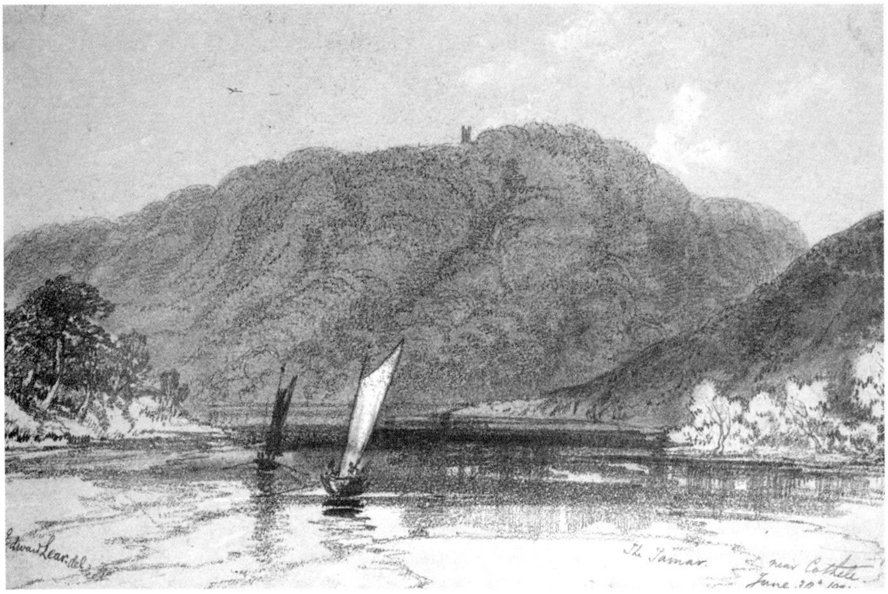

Fig. 51 The Tamar near Cotehele, signed 'Edward Lear. del', and inscribed and dated 'The Tamar. Near Cothele / June 30. 1837.', pencil, black chalk and stump heightened with white, on grey paper, 16.3 × 24.8 cm (Victoria & Albert Museum, E.777-1939).

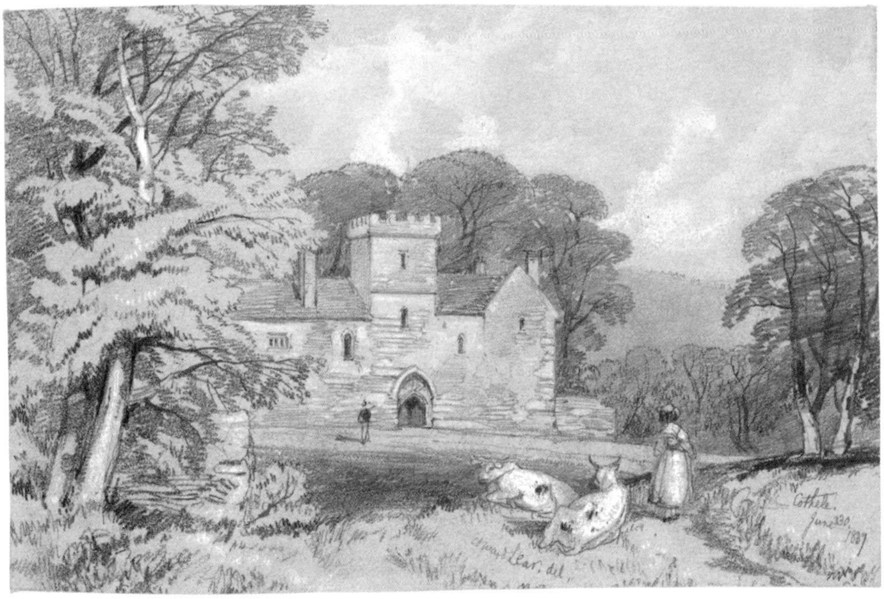

Fig. 52 Cotehele, the Entrance to Cotehele Manor, signed 'Edward Lear del.', and inscribed and dated 'Cothele. / June 30. / 1837', pencil and stump heightened with white, on grey paper, 16.3 × 24.8 cm (Victoria & Albert Museum, E.776-1939).

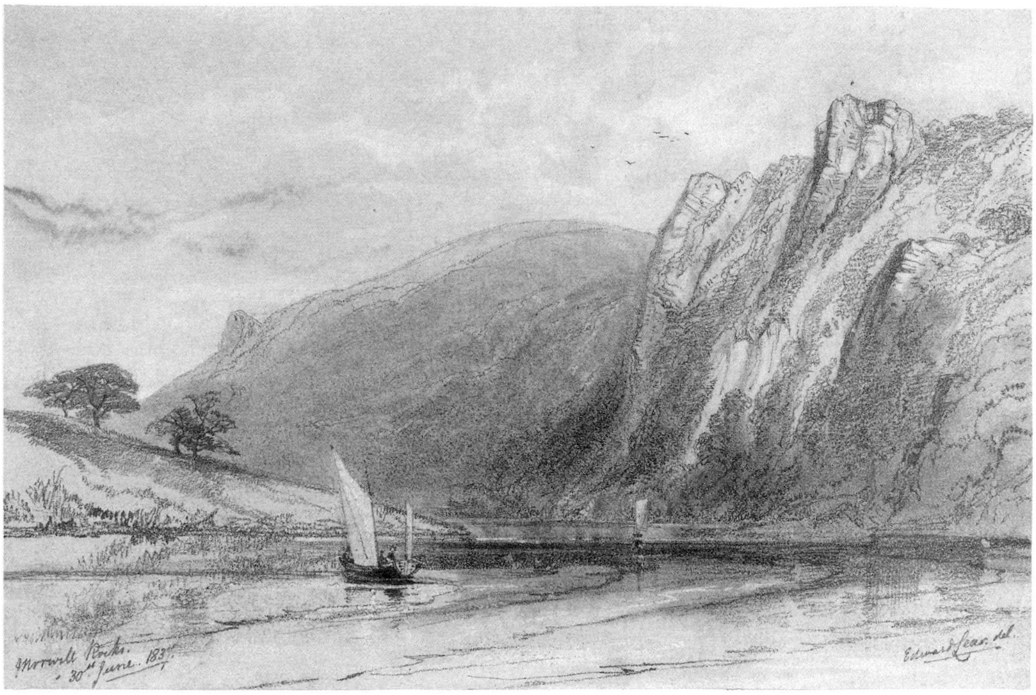

Cat. 105

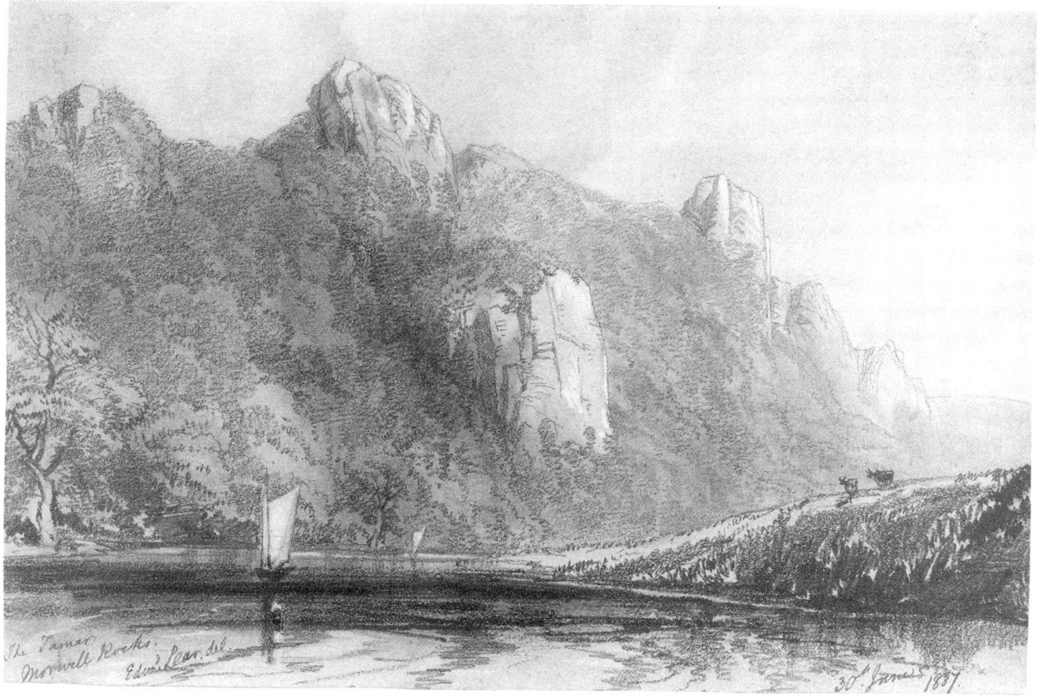

Cat. 106

These two drawings provide a record of an expedition up the River Tamar on 30 June 1837; another similar drawing of the river is in the Bovisand album at the Victoria & Albert Museum (fig. 51, p. 198). Altogether there are five drawings in the album dated 30 June; two of them show groups of ladies with their skirts pulled up for paddling, showing that this was an expedition for all the family, while a third shows the Tudor manor house of Cotehele (fig. 52, p. 198), which was probably the ultimate goal of the day trip.

107 *Oak Trees in the Park at Knowsley*

Signed and dated 'Edward Lear. del. / 1839', and inscribed 'Oak branches (Knowsley) from memory'
Pencil and stump, on brown paper, 26.4 × 38.2 cm
Provenance: by descent in the Hornby family, until presented to Cornish Torbock by Anthony Mason-Hornby in 1969; Cornish Torbock sale; Sothebys, 14 Apr. 1994, lot 243 (£750), sold to the present owner
Private Collection, on long term loan to the Ashmolean Museum, Oxford

Drawn two years after Lear's arrival in Italy, this drawing, showing a distant view of Knowsley Hall from the park, is of little use as a record of the house. As the inscription makes clear, it was drawn from memory, which explains its many inaccuracies: the long eighteenth-century wing is given far too many windows, and the twin towers that flank the entrance to the State Dining Room are greatly exaggerated in height and in the wrong place. Despite this, it provides evidence of the importance of the house in Lear's life. The ink shelf mark lower right, which reads '98H', is an indication of the number of Lear drawings which were once in the possession of the Hornby family and are now widely scattered.

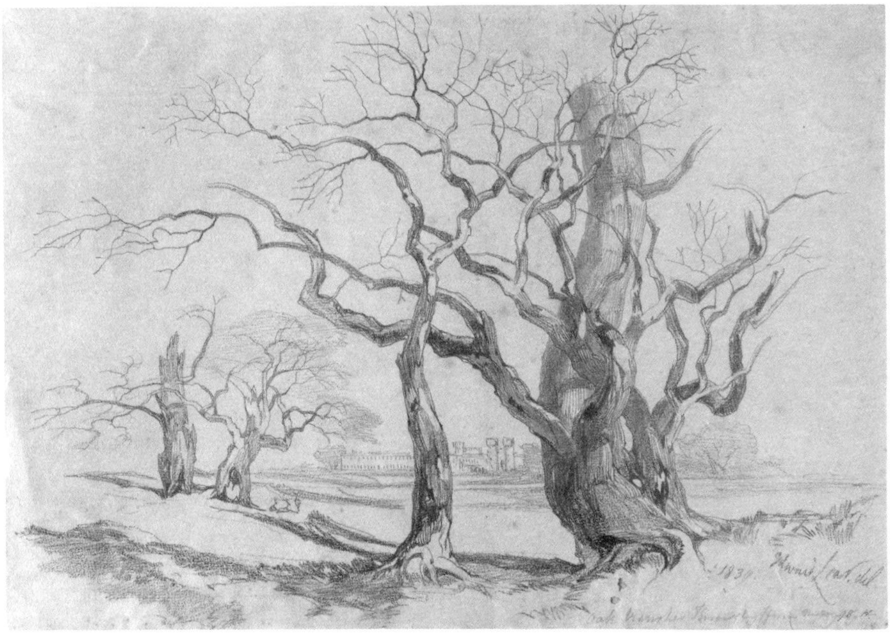

Cat. 107

APPENDIX A

LETTERS

dated between September 1830 and July 1837, to George Coombe and Fanny Coombe (née Drewitt), from the collection of the Frederick Warne Archive

TO FANNY COOMBE, POSTMARKED 21 SEPTEMBER 1830

[1]/2 past five (morning) 38 Upper North Place Gray's Inn Road
Tuesday Septr. 1830

My dear Miss Drewitt

I write to you in the first place because you gave me permission to do so, & secondly—because I some time back heard that you had been staying at Worthing, consequently it is probable you may still be in the land of the living—for, to tell you the truth, I should as soon think of directing to the Moon as to any one else at Peppering—having long since made up my mind to believe the whole settlement has been destroyed by a whirlwind and earthquake, a tortoiseshell tom-cat, or something equally rare, since it is 2 months since I have heard from any of you—It is amazing how I have been wondring at this long silence. If Robert or you could see me looking for every postman—or could hear my perpetual grumbling—every morning & evening—I am sure I should have a note—only just of compassion:– my sister says—I write such long letters that you (if you read them at all,)—are afraid to answer them, but I repel that idea—& fervently suppose that 3 or four letters have been sent by J. Tompkins or some other forgetful Person. Forgive my scrawling—it is hardly light & I am dreadfully pressed for time,—& though I have some news, (egotism)—, I cannot stay to tell it.—I hope you will not be angry at my sending you such a letter, but *really* I am in such a fijit [*sic*]—&, not being able to suppose myself quite forgotten—I intend for the future to set down all silence to the score of that wretched little fat Person, who has lately made so much confusion in Sussex—[picture of a winged figure with a bow and arrow, under which is written (c'est l'amour)]—But now pray—(for I am not so badly off, thank goodness, as to be in want of 8 pence,)—pray send me a note—a scrap just to say you are all well—I shall be delighted.—I hear extraordny reports about Arundel—"I could tear it! "I could tear it!"—&, (although I think I mentioned it before, in case I did not),—give my respects, if you please to Mr. G. Coombe, & say I took his kind letter to Mr. Leadbeter, but they never admit of anyone copying their birds—[erased words] [I] am, however, equally obliged to him—now remember me—though I hope it unnecessary, to dear Robert—& make him write, & *soon*, if you can,—& give my best regards to Eliza & George—with best respects to Mr. & Mrs. Drewitt—& believe me,

always— | Dear Miss Drewitt | Yours very respectfully & gratefully
E. Newwood Lear

Ann desires her best remembrances & Respects.
Of course you have heard of my marriage.

TO GEORGE COOMBE, 19 APRIL 1833 *(cat. 5)*

6 Albany Street Regents
Park
April 19 1833

My dear George

Pour commencer enclosed are the two receipts which you ought to have had long enough ago. Hursts & Nobles—the latter of whom does live in Fleet Street after all Bucklands Reliquae [*sic*] Diluvianae or whatever was the real title of the book—is utterly out of print: Harding & Lepard could not even borrow a stray copy for me to look at it:—thus all your present commission are dispatched—except one about the Salopian Foster, which I will enquire about as soon as I possibly can, since I'm sure you won't be furious at my not having done so before, when I assure you—that excepting yesterday's walk into the City—I have not been farther from my lodgings than Golden Square for the last three weeks nor in any more worthy location. Mr Parker—Lord Stanley—Mr Vigors are all from town so I can't easily get a Frank—consequently this will be a double letter.

Egotism is allowed I believe in correspondence; at least I hope so—for I am going to be very myselfy through the next page—but as you really like, I know, to hear what I am about, I shan't make any stupid apologies. Every thing 10 days ago was completely arranged for our going on the Continent—we were first to visit Paris—then Brussels—Antwerp—Leyden—Utrecht—Amsterdam,—thence sailing to Hamburgh—we were to invade Berlin, Dresden, Leipzig & Munich—& finally (with a possibility of stretching as far as Bernes & the Simplon,) we were to have returned by Strasbourg, Frankfort, Cologne, Metz—Ehrenbreitstein, Dusseldorf & all those other places on the River Rhone. All this was completely fixed on—that is, it was as certain of occurring as anything can be in this weathercock shuttlecock whirligig world of ours,—and now you shall just hear how I first [illegible word] it determine on going. You have often—I dare say—heard me express a wish to get rid of the copies of Parrots which I had still unsold,—the little chance I stood of gaining many fresh subscribers after my regular (& for my age—large,) connexion was well [canvassed?], (unless I could have afforded to employ some one for the purpose) was much against my now disposing of them, and as I was considerably in debt still for their printing, they were always before me like a great nimbus or nightmare or anything else very disagreeable & unavoidable, which prevented my feeling very pleasured in whatever I undertook. To diverge a little—you must be told that John Gould—a man who without any prospects or education, has by dint of a singularly active mind, good talents, & uncontrollable perseverance (not to say impudence backed by no little good luck—risen in the world beyond belief for the last 10 years—John Gould who married a wife—which wife with a little of my instruction commenced lithography, & after publishing the Himalayan Birds—in helping her husband with a magnificent work on the birds of Europe, John Gould, I say, with whom I have always been by circumstances very much allied—as I do all the backgrounds to the European birds besides various touchings up—(for which I get the work gratis), which consequently brings me a good deal to his home—oh—Good heavens—what an unmerciful sentence—aren't you out of breath!—(after all the mountain must bring forth a mouse),—John Gould was on the point of undertaking a journey to the continent this year for the purpose of getting many specimens of Ornithology—of trafficking with the Scientific Institutions & writers of foreign parts, with whom he is already known, & with whom many viva voce transactions are necessary. Now—Gould can't speak French—I can:—& he also wanted a companion—which induced him to offer & [*sic*] payment of the greater part of my expenses if I would go with him, but I had other fish to fry—& although it was a tempting offer. & although Gould has always behaved ~~with~~ in the most handsome & grateful manner to me—I refused—so there for the time the matter ended. This was in February —:—now in March it came to his ears—that I wanted to get rid of my Parrots,—for which I asked £70—so he came to me—& after sundry negociations—offered me £50—in money—on condition that I would continentalize with him—& to pay my expenses there & back entirely, for whatever length of journey he might go to.—Now, putting the blessing of pocketing 50 pounds—(which for the same affair I should scarcely ever get offered again to me)—the delight of seeing so much of the world for nothing—together with some circumstances which had just occurred to make me glad to leave England about the time we proposed doing so, putting all this together,—after mature thinking & advising with Mr Bell on the subject—I accepted his offer—was paid my £50—& determined thoroughly on going on the 10th of May next—the day he had fixed on for sailing.—But there's many a slip betwixt the cup & lip. on yesterday week—Mrs Eliza Gould—for no reason at all apparent—either to herself or her medical advisers—was taken with a premature labour (her 4th child in 3 years)—(at 4 months,) in so dangerous a manner as to give no hopes of her life:—she continued actually—*being confined*—till the day before yesterday—but she is of course though alive still in imminent danger:—add to this (have you got this horrid Influenza down with you?)—Gould himself—her father & brother—her child—the nurse & one servant—have been all confined to bed (except G who sat up though very ill,)—& you will have a pleasing idea of human comfort. The plan of going abroad is postponed, if it can take place till the 20th of June—& Mrs G is for a long while incapable of lithography & all its etcetera.—I—(its an ill wind &c—) have in the mean time been engaged to go on with this European Ornithology—(he had engaged me before about another work he is publishing)—so I am up to my neck in hurry—& work from 5 AM—till 7 P.M without cessation:—my lute & my flute are locked up—& you can represent me to Mrs. George—as perfect a packhorse as she could possibly desire—Here is the history of my continentalisms—all of which however are as yet entirely undecided.

Don't be in a passion—I must cross—If we do not—& I see no chance of the contrary—go to France in May—I go to the North—Newcastle & Lancashire for the purpose of collecting a grievous 40£ which I might write for for ever & a day—most possibly I shall go about the same time I first intended to foreignize.—I particularly wish to be able to put by the £40 I also receive on "my coming of age"—without touching it:—its rather ridiculous too—saving at 21—but I intend to begin—& when I have saved 500£ which will be about the year 1875. I shall purchase & settle in a small cottage on the left hand side of Bunhill Road:—I was there the other day—& think that Geraniums & silkworms in the windows will make it look very rural & pleasing.

Now I have told you my plans as far as I can see them myself—which is obscurely enough by the bye:—I do so at the risk of being boring & troublesome, because you know very well that I feel all the interest I am capable of feeling towards your family—& I should wish to be thought of at least as well as possibility will allow. Did Mr Drewitt get the [graffs?] safe which I sent?—don't forget to tell me. Any noose (news)—as the rope said to the executioner?—Peter's wife lays all day long on a *sofa*—& *sofar* as I know is not yet confined:—I very much wish you would write as soon as you can possibly find leisure—I am not so blue tho' as I might expect—considering I have got no spirits at all scarcely:—however my chief annoyance is the unpleasantly slow growth of my whiskers—& do say for I really want to hear about you all—when they are coming up to this loathsome place?—Please Heaven I can perform my promise of getting those tickets—for Mr Parker's Aunt has just managed to die like a booby—& so he has left London—I should think he'll come back tho' if not I must try elsewhere—Is there anything else to say?—I think not—so now for windings up. Tell me what the new dot is like & all about here & kiss them both for Uncle Edward. Remember me to Mrs George—& all at Peppering—& above all write soon—Yours very sincerely

E Lear

I shall write again before I go
61 Albany St.
Regents Park Friday 19—April

There is no occasion, if you please, to tell Mrs Street any of my proceedings: you know none of my sisters are confidantes of mine

TO GEORGE COOMBE, 4 MARCH 1834

28 Southampton Row.
Russell Square. 4 March.

My dear George—I'm convinced I am thoroughly cracked;—
I've waited a week 'ere your parcel I packed
In order to send it down free of post, yester
-day, by the hand of my Argyleshire sister,—
To save you an eightpence,—& all this in one of my
Violent fits of unnatural economy:—
Mr. Curtis's note you must know after all
Was the primary cause of my sending at all,—
So what was my horror in reaching to day
To my bookcase—to find an [illegible] full—
Which there fore has been thrust for these 3 weeks away
To find the said note lying staring there still!
I declare I'd as soon have encountered a dragon! I
Felt quite dismayed with an impromptu agony.
So now,—after thinking and reasoning & posing
I've made up my mind to the act of enclosing—
The entomological gentleman's letter,—
With a hope that my memory may shortly grow better.

Please the fugs!—. Well; to call a new topic;—to day,
I've [seen?] *Miss* & Miss *Margaret Watkins*; they stay
Number 9 Woburn Place—but that's nothing to you—
~~Only~~ Though it fills very nicely a distich or two:—
Miss Margaret Watkins was dressed in pea-green
—as fine a young lady as never was seen;—
And I never remember.—(except a great Dutchman

Who at Rotterdam sat at end of a barge—
You might travel through Europe, yet scarcely see such man,)
To have seen any creature one quarter so large.

James Winchworth Esqr.—of the Royal Berks corps—
Rides often by here—on a long tailed gray horse—
And for fear I should make such another bad rhyme,
I'll conclude—& I dare say you'll think it's high time.—
Remember me pray to all yours—& the dear
Little dollies, write soon,—ever yours,
Edward Lear

TO FANNY COOMBE, 19 OR 20 JUNE 1835[1] *(cat. 12)*

Good Heavens! this last sentence has upset me into a violent laughter—though I don't see much joke in the reality.—

Do tell George that I have poked into all the Cutler's shops within a mile of Egg's at Piccadilly & at last found the man next door. I have told them to send to Mr. Bethell's after Monday—thinking Mr. B. might be at Hampton till then. Is not this all I could Do?—Enclosed is a C[illegible]—& two Franks for Eliza's collection.

I must go to Lord de Tableys I believe—for a few days after leaving Knowsley—but I shall write a long epistle on Thursday or Friday to George. Lord D—I must say—has behaved with very great kindness: two or 3 things while he was in town were particularly marked:- such as at the Gardens & Zoological Meetings—shaking hands with me before all the great bodies—& in calling & sitting for a long half hour at 28 Southampton Row. These attentions—little in themselves—have a great effect when coming from people of rank—to us small fry of artists—& it is very praiseworthy of noblemen to make use of such means to bring young beasts forward one step in life. I must tell you & George about an opportune misunderstanding when Lord D called—thro' his dreadful deafness. "My Lord—" said I—"I hope your head is better"—for he had had a bad headache the day before. "Oh!"—replied he—"I have found a remedy for that. I have taken out all the little birds & put in one Cockatoo & three large Red Macaws."—Can you imagine a difficulty in keeping a countenance?—I screwed mine all sorts of ways—& providentially caught up the clue of his ideas which were plainly in his aviary. Fowler has brought back—without *exception* the *finest sketches* I ever saw from any artist's portfolio: some are beyond wonderful. He is dreadfully marked poor fellow—with the smallpox—but his expression of countenance not the least changed.

I hope George will like the crab: the fossils for Mr. Bale tell him are sent to day.

Kiss the three littlenesses for me. I am glad to hear they are all so well: Ann told me all about them. Remembrances to Robert & all. tell Robt. I shall either [erased word] send [erased word] part of the money I borrowed in the Autumn Is this a letter or not?—Believe me

My dear Mrs George— | Most sincerely yours,
Edward Lear.

1. Daniel Fowler returned from the Continent on 17 or 18 June 1835, so the letter must date from shortly after this.

TO FANNY COOMBE, 19 JUNE 1835

June 19. 1835. 28 Southampton Row

My dear Mrs. George –

Oh dear!—oh! Law!—oh! Dear one!—I am writing under an accumulation of violent feelings. You must know I have just produced a party—& although to persons of your experience—(I was almost going to say—age,) parties of 20 are trifles—yet to a bachelor as ignorant as I am they are absolutely no such thing. I know you don't like bachelor parties: & indeed this winter I have very much avoided them: yet in my situation there are some connexions which render them partly necessary—partly pleasant, & between old cronies—& people to whom one is under an obligation of some sort, one is obliged once a year to be civil. If it had not been for W.W.W. I must certainly have quite died yesterday: he has a peculiar genius for marketing, & the manner in which he provided my lobsters & beef was quite merciful & skilful. But Hark—!—I had asked only Senior & [Grecuny?]—Hullmandel Holm—R.Gale—& Kempton thinking that 8 were sufficient & more than that even:—picture my awful state of mind early yesterday morning in rushed Daniel Fowler red hot from Rome.—of *course* if he could be split into 10—he must all come. Presently before 7 in the evening—a letter from Mr Hullmandel that a friend had come from a far country to see him—& he must either give up me—or bring him. Of *course*, unhappy wretch that I was—I was obliged to say—Come thou also.—Five minutes after—my friend Bernard Senior writes that his only Brother in England comes up for a night—may he take the great liberty of bringing him?—I own my blood curdled at this last volunteer, & for one moment I felt my brains sensibly affected by ~~the thought~~ anticipations of my own gigantic hospitality: But this ended like the last—Of *course*—he must come. Conceive—for they can't be described—the momentous cogitations with my landlady which ensued—the cleanings—the hurryings—the widening of table & multiplication of dishes,—& above all—add the misery of an Irish servant who almost always misunderstands whatever you say—I only thank St. Peter that I am speaking of the Past!—The Gales very kindly—as usual—sent me in some very old fine Arrack for Punch—of *course* I had no punch bowl—but I borrowed one from them. Yet when the multitude were just coming—up rushed Jane with a face of horror—Plase—serr _ "Messes Smith has found out all her ladles—bootter ladles & all have been *smished*."—Misfortune helps Genius I suppose—for a sudden fit of the muse came upon me & I instantly sent round the following pathetic stanzas.

My dear Mrs. Gale—from my leaving the cradle
Till now I have never such agony known
What use *is* a Punch bowl without any ladle,—
Be it Ivory—Silver—Wood—China—or bone?—
My landlady rushes & foams in a flurry –
Her Ladles for Punch & her Ladles for Soup
Besides all her Ladles for Butter & Curry
Are all, ~~of them~~ she vows—"smished" in one family Group.

Then dear Mrs. Gale—have a little Compassion
—If it's only a Ladle full—Send me in one!—
And Ill ever proclaim you in my estimation—
The most *"Ladle-like"* personage under the sun!—

TO GEORGE COOMBE, 24 JUNE 1835 *(cat. 14)*

Knowsley Hall. 24th. June. 1835.

My dear George

I keep my promise of writing early to you—though possibly there would be a better chance of amusing you if I waited longer before I did so. It is about seven o'clock—the rain is coming down in torrents, and the vast pancake of landscape from here to Liverpool is all in a beastly gray mist. All this, (besides nearly 4 mortal hours to breakfast,) will doubtless produce a vivacious sort of spittle.

I started on Saturday at 5 in the eving outside the Tartar coach—outside, I repeat:- not only—*not inside*,—but shoved to the last extreme edge of the seat behind the box by 2 middle sized & one Teasdalish creature, until I was flat as a biffin—& my feet—from having no ~~sole~~ rest to their soles—very troublesome. Nevertheless—the night was lovely—the hay smelt beautifully, & I soon managed pretty well. My companions—brutes as they were fell asleep—& I sung aloud to the delight of Coachy who was rather drunk.—Made a good supper in Bedfordshire—& at 8 next morning reached Birmingham—perfectly frozen, to make a beastly breakfast of far gone eggs—& high beef. All Sunday was a lovely day—& barring that the Coach was stopped there several half hours by the wheels' catching fire, (if which Catastrophe had occurred I should have preferred being off than to being on—if only for the sake of taking a sketch of the Combustion,) the journey was gotten over pleasantly enough. The delays had caused us to get to Prescot about 8—so as no one was waiting for my luggage—I ordered it to be brought immediately to the Hall, & I walked over myself. The trees—oh! the trees!—"what once be thought wise Giants—now seemed dwarfs."—Positively there is not a tree in the whole park fit to draw—though there is promising timber enough:—after Parham & Arundel I see nothing but Gooseberry bushes, & wonder how I could think as I did formerly. I entered by the back of the house & having seen the Housekeeper—a new one since I was here—I was shewn my *rooms*. The sitting room is a perfect jewel of a room.—square—(about the size of your bedroom—2 windows & a west aspect—in the great front of the house. a Grand piano book case—sofa—fire—&c—with lots of Orthodox furniture make it very comfortable. The bedroom joins this—& is also a jewel. Having dressed,—not knowing what I was to be done with, I asked the servant for some dinner—& was accordingly told that supper would be presently in the housekeepers room;—thither, (adapting myself to circumstances) I went & soon made a good meal. Of course—as I saw how matters were going to be—I took *all* the pains in the world to make myself pleasant—& all things were going on swimmingly—when, lo!—a messenger from Lord D. begged me to come immediately to him. To my surprise his Lordship was in the Passage, where he gave me a regular *shake* of the hand, & apologized for my having been put where I was. "I intended of course," quoth he—"that you should have been *one of us*—& not dine with the servants."—Pray—he continued—finish your supper & then come & join us in the drawing room. Ergo I finished my supper—& then to the eminent opening of eyes of the good people assembled—my modesty was obliged to desire that one of them would forthwith worrie [*sic*] me to the presence chamber. I swear it required a little philosophy not to laugh.—In the drawing room were Miss Hornby—the Hon. Mrs. Hornby—Mr Robert Hornby—& the Earl himself of all of whom more anon. (En passant—I may observe, that the Hornby family are a legion in themselves: they are all related more or less to the Stanleys—are a any old &

wealthy set of Lancashire Aristocracy, & are some of them tenants for a term at the Hall at almost all times in the year. Here follows a plan of the Drawing rooms—&c. Everything of course is of the first style of furniture—& although the Drawing rooms are not near high enough for their large size—yet [plan of house showing first Lord Derby's room, Library, Great Hall, two Drawing Rooms, Picture Gallery, Great Blue Drawing Room, and Dining Room 45 feet high] the Dining room is one of the finest I ever saw.—Oh! there is such a picture of Rembrandt in it!—The little dots I have made in the plan of the Dining room—are where the servants stand at dinner.

Exit here to bed—& slept soundly.

At 10. every morning a bell rings for prayers, & down to the library we go—the establishment muster in the hall. After this breakfast ensued in the in the enormous dining room—a good one you may guess. Lord Derby was then taken very unwell with one of his giddy fits & he was obliged to lie down. Having waited til 12—I went round the Aviaries with Thompson the keeper, & find them incredibly altered & improved.—I should say it is by far the most beautiful ~~sort of~~ thing of the sort extant. I then returned to luncheon with Mr R. Hornby—an exceedingly gentlemanly man—with whom I talked til 3. I then sketchd till 5—but not knowing what Lord D wanted, I did not do much. At ½ past six a huge bell is rung for dressing—at 7—another for dinner, & into the huge Dining room away we marched—I repeating to myself all the time—"Plaze—zur—there's some [illegible word] at the bottom."—I behaved myself however—very decently during dinner, & devoured some of the good things with great complacency.—Coffee follows in the drawing room—& then tea. Lord Derby plays at Patience with Miss or Mrs. Hornby—& then bed. Yesterday I did little also—Lord D walking about with me nearly all day. Today is filthily wet—& after breakfast I must ask Lord D to let me have a bird or two in doors—as I cannot draw in the Aviary—& I want to do 4 every week for him. Really his extreme kindness is quite extraordinary—he takes opportunities continually of shewing it—& is without partiality—a perfect Gentleman in every respect.

I have some idea I shall not stay long—for I hear them talking of some Races—which will bring down an immense party. In that case I shall go immediately to town—& give up Wales entirely—as my money will be short instead of long:—the expenses of coming down—have been hideous:—&c &c well I brought lots things—as a clean shirt—stockings—& the deuce knows what are indispensable every day. There—now I have told you all I can at present. If I run down to Sussex in the Autumn I shall have lots to say. (Perhaps I may do so—as Robt. Gale says he should like to go—& besides—I think my stay here will make me burst to have some fun.)—I long to have a good laugh. I don't know at what though—Alack!—

Tell Mrs. George—I shall have quantities of etiquettical minutiae from the fountainhead. N.B. I don't half enjoy my peaches—because I am obliged to *peel* them.—The connexion—the change of air—& the tone of society one sees are the bright side of the matter. The darks I don't bother you with. Now I beg & implore you & Fanny to concoct me a long letter next week. Consider I have no creature of my own grade of society to speak to—& without my saying more—believe that I *shall be heartily* glad of some symptoms of old acquaintance in the shape of a letter. Did you like your Peregrines?—c—~~En~~ *Seal up your letter to me & address* it to me: *then* enclose it ~~the one~~ in a half sheet addressed thus. Rt. Hon: Earl of Derby.

Knowsley Hall. | Prescot. | Lancashire.

How on earth is the Hay doing at Peppering?

Kiss the children for me—& remember me to all.

Dear George | Sincerely yours

Edward Lear.

TO GEORGE COOMBE, 20 JULY 1835 *(cat. 15)*

Knowsley Hall. 20th. July. Monday. 1835.

Another!—Another!!—& Another!!!—the rattling & bustle is very superlative:—at the moment I am writing no less than 3 carriages & 4—four carriages & 2—2 Phaetons with white ponies—1 Gig—& 3 Grooms with single horses are congregated before the awful door:—surely out of all the contents there must be something good at the dinner party—I am sick of splendour—vomiting with excess of pomp—longing for a little porter out of a pewter pot—& some bread & cheese eaten with my fingers:—in short—My dear Mrs. George & George—you may perceive that I am suffering with a dreadful attack of black bile—i:e: disgust & melancholy as odious as you can imagine.—How can it be otherwise?—as soon as one gets to like one Sett of people—away they go—& a perpetual change keeps one in a froze.—Would I live so!—St Peter!—

I have been passing a most delightful week at Tabley Hall—Lord de Tabley's—Everybody ought to see Lady de Tabley before they die—she is a most glorious creature:—& not less delightful than beautiful—in fact, I never felt more at home in my life—so kind & unaffected were the whole family & guests. One day we—(the Parkers, de Tableys—& I,) went to Lord Stamfords', a fine old place—& lionized all about it,—another was spent in a similar excursion to Sir Philip Egerton's,—whose Lady is *preterpluperfection*, (she used to be called "the pride of Cheshire",) & whose house is little inferior. Another of my white days was a gipsey party to Beeston Castle—sublime old ruins—from whose towers 300 feet high one might break ones neck really with satisfaction—the lovely rides you may very well conclude I enjoyed—but above all I put the glorious Raspberry beds, at Tabley Hall!—How I did stuff & cramm—they called me "raspberry Lear".—Every evening at this lovely house—we had lots of music: Lady de T. & I duett wonderfully—& I only marvel at my not being hired as nurse to the baby—who was always quietted by my playing the Accordion.—

Well I came back to a dinner party of 20 here on Saturday—noise & splendour enough—beggaring all description—but no Ladies but Lady & Miss Shelley—whose ugliness may heaven forget—I can't.—Sunday—a [erased word] fine day—but small party & I very unwell—& to day as I told you just now a great influx of people.—Thank you for your letter—Mrs. George—it was a very acceptable one, & also thank Robert for the Franks:—I am sorry to hear of his health suffering so.—The dressing bell is going to ring—the noise of children—the hurrying of valets—the bustling of ladies maids—the orderings of housekeepers—the stumping & squawking of Sir J. Shelley—the giggling of Miss [Shelley]—& the Volubilities of My Lady—the barking of six dogs, & the reports of the honorable Capt. Stanleys detonator all compel me to say goodbye for the present.

Sunday 21. I write at luncheon time—sick unto death. Mr & Ly. Charlotte Penrhyn & an indefinite number of Children—the bride & bridegroom Ldy. Ellinor & Mr Hopwood—several Messrs [Jeffes?]—several Messrs. Stanley—several Messrs. Mostyn & Wilbraham, were the contents of the Cavalcade of yesterday.—(There go

4 of them in the Poney Phaetons.) The dinner nearly killed me—today's *will* I think *quite*. By an additional horror too—Miss Shelley has done me out of my corner place by C. Stanley where I could not possibly carve anything—& I was shoved up to the middle of the table both yesterday & at breakfast to day—till I was so miserable as to expect apoplexy continually.—Mr. Penrhyn upset a deck of truffles—if it had been me I should have burst instantly. The salvation of the dinner was that Miss Hornby came—but alas! She is gone this morning—so are most of the gentlemen to a clergy meeting.

Goodbye—I am too wretched to add anything but that I am now going to stick my head in a bush of fern ever so far off where there is nobody to bother me.

Your's ever [truly?]

Edward Lear

Pray tell little Fanny & Marion never to envy a fine life

There were 8 Edwards at dinner the other day.
Between 20 & 30 servants to wait at dinner.-

Lawk! I forgot to say that at Lord de Tabley's was a nice man—Rev. somebody Allan: he used to stay with Cartwright, & knows Turney (how's Miss H——n?) & other people: Rabbit slaughter began 2 days ago. 138 were demolished in one morning. "Great fun" as Lady Shelley says. I think something will happen early next month very surprising.—There's a mystery for George: I know he likes one. A great fool at Liverpool whom I ordered to get some fossils—has sent a lot of Derbyshire spar!—

TO GEORGE COOMBE, 24 JULY 1835 *(cat. 16)*

Knowsley Hall. Friday. 24 July 1835

My dear George

Though I only just sent off a letter yesterday I commence another—as I shan't finish it all at once, & am [then?] not know how long it may be before one is able to write a whole one. What lovely weather for a whole week!—I don't know how you are off—but it is the first *warmth* I have felt these 5 weeks: it *always* rains at Manchester—poor devils—& *generally* here.—Spite of the heat—cricket is all the fashion, or rather rage at Knowsley just now: morning, noon, & night—bats & balls have no sinecure. After breakfast,—the green,—for there is an immense lawn before the house, is covered with the most odd gamesters—Sir J. Shelley—Miss S.—Lady Ellinor H. & all the children male & female play away till I should think their brains nearly fry: it is very amusing to see,—notwithstanding Miss Shelley might have made a little less noise I think:—After luncheon—out the males rush again, & then there is a match general—grooms—riders—footmen—& aristocrats all in a bundle:—not that I saw perceive [*sic*] the unfortunate grooms do anything but become fags—(isn't that the word?—)—catching & throwing the ball. I fear the game is carried on on rather an exclusive principle—since Sir John—the Stanleys—Hopwoods. & Penrhyns are always at the wickets when I look out of window.—It is now half after 2 at midday—& the sun quite broiling over the misty distance: you don't think how pretty the scene is, & how lively the voices make it.

The day I wrote to you the Molyneux's were expected to dinner were they not?. I do hate strangers—let on [be?] that I had a dreadful toothache—I was quite miserable: can you conceive anything more horrid than my being obliged to sit in a seat opposite 2 boiled fowls?—2 live tigers would have been a farce to it—I could eat nothing—drink nothing—do nothing but perspire with horror at those 2 boiled fowls!—How I watched every body's plate! How I chuckled at every fresh call for venison & mutton! I thought I should have brought my soul up when the Viscountess Molyneux look distinctly 3 times at the boiled fowls—but it proved only a fowl look & no more—At last they were cleared off, & if the wretched light from the window opposite my visage did not quite distort my expression—surely I must have given tokens of immense joy!—I went to bed soon—for I eschew all the Sefton people rather. All to day I have been drawing an insane partridge who will sit still on no account whatever—little beast,—& now I am so hot as to be utterly incapable of any activity [erased word] in the world.—Hark!—what a screaming—they are crying Fire—I declare—Fire! fire! fire!—Engines!—Water. God bless us—the noise increases & all the cricketters are rushing toward the out buildings across the lawn: I smell smoke—a chimney on fire I dare say—must go & see—variety is delightful.—The great bell is set aringing—more than a chimney I fear!—for the confusion increases rapidly & the smoke too.

4. O'clock. I date from Knowsley now—but before you get my letter I sadly fear Knowsley Hall will have ceased to be. The house has taken fire behind the kitchen & above it—from the overheating of some flue, & in spite of every exertion—the flames spread dreadfully. I write this in a [rest?] for a few minutes,—having had more hard work in this last hour & a half than for the last 3 months. The engines are playing—but can do little execution—the fire is so central—they are unroofing the house—Water—water is the universal cry—the dignities are done away with—we are all in shirts & trowsers & perspiration—the grand staircase is covered with human beings—to & fro—jugs—tubs—buckets—vessels—everything that can carry water. The fire has entirely destroyed the painted Chamber—& Mr Stanley's room is already reached—featherbeds are rolling down the stairs—curtains—clothes—books—furniture are being tossed from windows—the heat is dreadful—the women are losing their presence of mind—they won't keep their right side of the staircase—twice the old upper housemaid has rushed into my arms & deluged me with water—a feather bed has precipitated at a cook—& the fat butler has rolled over 4 bricklayers & 2 grooms—Awful state of violence—they are tearing away the carpets—but the pictures are destroyed in the painted chamber—Down comes Belshazzar—for in another half hour the fire must reach the great dining room:—ladders—shrieks—men—women—engines—water—soot—falling tiles—wet blankets flames—smoke—its excessively horrible. The alarm bell still rings & the peasantry flock in from all quarters—but to very little purpose.

5., O'clock. The fire has been quite subdued on the inside by the plan of breaking away some windows thro' which the water has played effectively. I am quite knocked up with working in the hot [room?] & have been violently sick—& [then?] fainted. The scene now is all before the house—& worthy any painters looking at. On the top of the engine—among the half naked—covered with soot—stands Captn. Stanley.—A crowd work on the house—& at the windows: a mob surround the engine filling it with water.—a long line of a 100 people or more convey filled & empty buckets from & to the horse ponds. Grooms—Ladies—Lord Derby & the Lord knows who—all take a part. Lady Charlotte Penrhyn & her beautiful daughters—3 footmen—10 housemaids—& the fat coachman are all drawing buckets at the tank—The French Governess & Sir John Shelley are tubbing it—the Rev. F. Hopwood—Lady Ellinor & 20 Gardeners command a regiment of watering pots. Lady Shelley keeps joking about with a leaky washing bucket. Some right honorable children who can do nothing else are sounding the alarm bell. All the country is coming—but the fire gives [two illegible words] every moment.

6 o'clock. All is safe.—they still pump—but there is no further danger. Had all this occurred in the night—everything must have been lost.—Lord D. is dreadfully shaken by it—tho' he has every possible [firmness?] at the time. The drawing room & dining room are such a scene as has never been seen before in Knowsley:—Yet in this most clockwork of establishments even now everything is beginning to go on as usual: the 4 Butlers are actually carrying in the plate & trays—though the dining room floor is covered with beds & books—I have counterordered the carriage—as I don't think it decent to ride thro' all the confusion:—so now goodbye. I am going to a dinner party at Mr Ashton's, tho' I am much more fit for bed.

Saturday. 25.th July. 1835.

We sat down 15 to dinner at Huyton—but there was nothing particular: good music afterwards came away early. This morning the workmen are all busy at the late place of fire—but that is all to keep yesterday's disturbance in memory.- Lady—Sir—John, and Miss Shelley depart to day:—Lady Ellinor & Mr. Hopwood on Monday:—after that a new set are coming—Hornbys—Gilpins—Lilfords Burns—&c &c. Have just got a letter from Robert. We were talking at breakfast about hypochondriacal whims Lord D. mentioned a gentleman but I'll keep all the stories till I come, which I hope to do in the Autumn.- Must go & draw a Kangaroo. Goodbye—Love to all.

Your's ever sincerely,
Edward Lear

Lady C. Penrhyn is [illegible word ending '-ly'] like Fanny: her way of speaking & manner particularly. Of course she is a very nice person

TO FANNY COOMBE, 6 AUGUST 1835 *(cat. 17)*

Hotel! Beaumaris !! Anglesea!!! North Wales !!!!!!!!!
Thursday 6th August 1835

My dear Mrs George—

When you have recovered the amazement you will be in at my commencement—I will thank you for your last letter which I got about the time my fiery epistle reached you I imagine. I am really in apoplexies of gratitude for the number of letters you write me, & believe you to be so good a person—that you would certainly have invented christianity had you only lived soon enough.—I shall not remark on the news—as I have but little time before breakfast—but I will only say that I have not heard McNeale—tho' a great deal of time—his church is so crowded that you must go—I should think overnight from all I hear.—Well, let me see:—what did I tell you of last—for I give you I think pretty nearly a journal: on Tuesday the 28th July a Mr Gilpin landscape gardener, & an architect [Mr Beeson?] joined us:—both very pleasant & clever Gilpin is 75 years old but looks 50—walks literally all day—has one eye—& wears six waistcoats.—the week went away very easily—Lady Ellinor & her spouse have gone but Lady Charlotte still remains with her darling children cherubim. On Saturday the first of August came Colonel Hornby—delightful man:—in person he is Miss Fisher in coat & trowsers—but good looking in the face—& the nicest drollest little man in the world.—Well one day Capt Stanly Mr Penrhyn asked Lord D. if he was going to Puffin Island—a Rocky isle near Anglesea—whither he goes yearly generally at the Puffin time—those birds breeding there by millions. Lord D said it was nearly too late—but for the last 10 days the subject was never allowed to rest—till his Lordship was finally coaxed into fixing the jaunt for the 4th Tuesday—I who could not see any pleasure in shooting parties refused when Ld. D. offered my being one of them—but hearing that Beaumaris was to be to stay for a day or two—I altered & went. Up we all got on Tuesday & breakfasted at 8:—at 9 we 5 Ld. D. Col. H Capt S. Mr. Penrhyn & myself rolled away in the four horse carriage—2 keepers—& a valet & footman following with luggage in a chariot & a gig. Of course the Lord Lieutenant's cavalcade made a deviation at Liverpool. & a crowd came to the quay. Very merry & jolly we were: bounce we went into a little boat & were soon on board the Lewellyn Steamer. Oh! What a glorious day it was! Not a cloud! But you can only imagine the fun from one of our Peppering parties. No stiffness or humbug—I thought of George & I on our Midhurst trip. When ones merry ones soon set off in a giggle—very shortly Colonel Hornby who is the oddest creature in the world—came to us & said he had discovered a mermaid or a devil in the shape of a most queer woman on board: I shall never forget her certainly but you will one day see my sketches of the creature :—we called her "the dejected"—& the day passed in fits of laughter—duetts—& fun: at luncheon time a most lovely bucket came forth: every sort of wine & delicacy &c &c. As for the scenery as you approach Wales—it is beyond expression! The inn we went to is opposite Penmanmawr—& delightful it is. Before dinner we went all over Sir R Bulkeley's park—then a glorious dinner—singing—then Sir R Bulkeley came in & I wished him out:—then (the breakfast is coming so I must be short) singing—then a walk with Col H & Capt S. on the beach by moonlight till 1.——Wednesday—a mizzly dizzly day—& I almost unable to move for a headache—off we went tho' at 11 in a sailing boat to Puffin Land—the birds were gone: adjourned to rabbit shooting—sketched ashtrees & made love to Welsh washerwomen while it rained. lunched. came home at 6—all wet through & I very well again I dined alone—refused Sir R Bulkeley's dinner party, after walked to Beaumaris Bridge—the Menai I mean—beyond all glorious. eat hearty supper after 10 miles walk & then sang with accordion & flute till 2 in the morning on the beach.

This morning is again lovely up & roaming about & just time in life to write this. There—there comes the grilled trout & the cocoa—there comes my Lord [cut in page] there the [hole in page]:—so goodbye—we return at 10 o'clock to filthy Liverpool.

We are all praying for the "dejecto" again. Goodbye—love to George & all.

Yours sincerely

Edward Lear

Lord D. has just asked for a "raw egg".

TO FANNY COOMBE, 17 MARCH 1836

28 Southampton Row. Bloomsbury
17th March 1836.

My dear Mrs George—

I have been going to write these 5 days but have been always prevented,—but this morning George's letter has compelled me to shear off some minutes of my breakfast to reply. When I got your last (with George's Fossil Book, which I am much obliged for, & will take every care of, & which I will return as soon as Sir P. Egerton comes to town) I had made up my mind that you & all Arundel with no exceptions whatever had been washed away in a rising of the Arun. I am delighted to hear the contrary, & that you were pleased with the rubbish I sent: pray, tell [illegible word] I will look every where for Laura's [arms?], tho' I have kept it for so long a time that I think it can scarcely have kept good. Mrs. André tells me She, (Laura—not Mrs A.) grows just like you. You are perfectly welcome to the box—which , if it is the one I allude to, has seen some odd changes, but as I had 2 of the sort & painted, I cannot be certain which of the 2 it is. Howbeit—one of those 2 & may be that one—was an ancient property of Ann's—given her by some one who I suppose had it from Adam:—it went, as a clothes box, with one of my brothers to the South pole—came back—passed some time as my sister's painting box, changed its situation in life & became one of a set of boxes [and?] [by?] a benevolent society for [sending?] the distress of lying in women,—was used for some years as a "Blacking"—box & shoe case" by Ann & myself in our Grays Inn Road vicissitudes—for 2 more has kept my bills & letters in Southampton Row—& lastly has transplanted its square body into your own family where I hope it will remain, until you see fit to [vary?] its monotonous existence as a romantic utensil by filling it full of Carraway Comfits & sending it to the Emperor of China. So much for the box:—to go on answering your letter concerning the Dukes—it only exemplifies my prophecy that the peace of Arundel will be always very equivocally founded. I am glad you both—(for this letter is for you & George too,) see Woodland often: I shall be very vexed if he ever gets Arundelled—tho' I hope & think he will not. You recommend W. Watkins to me as a successor to W.W.W.—a plan I would gladly catch at were he not so stout: it must be a very thin man to live in these rooms as there are only a few weasel like corners not filled up.

And now to touch upon George's blue letter of just now's post it accords wonderfully with the state of things here. The winds blew—(they blew since a fortnight past,) & I am blue with a dreadful cold & cough of 3 weeks standing, & everything is smoky & misty & blue, except the sky, which has long been chocolate. Incessant rain has made London like an omelette to walk in, & I have been in a rage ever since the 5th of February - & shall be till the 1st of May. At last you have got into your new house: I am very glad of it—as there must have been a great deal of fatigue. Please, when I come, put me in a Buggy room: I always like bugs—& they never incommode me: fleas are horrible—which 28 Southampton Row abounds in,—& if I could exchange—or get a hybrid [brand?] I should be very glad. It seems an age since I was with you for any time—but it is not at this present time actually possible for me to leave town. Gould who is about to visit the Americas, & who has engaged to finish his book on European birds before he goes has made me enter into a written agreement that I will do a certain number of birds before I work for anyone else: & as he has always employed me & paid me well, I am bound, (particularly as I have done scarcely anything for him in the winter,) to pay some attention to him. Besides this I have a pupil who of course is just now a tie. The weather is not yet of course decent,—but in the *earlier* part of the spring I do not see how I *can* get away. We cannot however see a day before us with certainty,—& all I can say at present, is that I thank you for your kindness, & will come as soon as I can do so for even a short time. I should like to have been at little Dudley's christening—but when did you intend that to have taken place?—The children too must be growing so—& Fanny will be coming out soon.

Pray then—where is John Sayres now?—I shall be glad to write to, see, or hear from him. Now I have forgotten Charlesworth. I was sitting working in Mr Gray's room at the British museum lately when a very young looking man came in, & while he was speaking to Gray—I heard the name of Charlesworth mentioned. "Do you know Mr C." said I?—"I be he"—quoth he. He is not above 20 much—& very geological in his tastes. He has got to box a *long* while ago, & was going to send to you the other day when I saw him again.

I am now going to ask, (tho' I should have done it before,) about Curtis's work. I scarcely like to speak of it, but you can't but tell me your opinion you know—& then I can act upon it. I have delayed sending the one number which was already [near?] me to Mr C. until I could hear again from you. I believe Mr C. to be the sort of person—that if you did continue the numbers now,—he will *not* as you expect supply you with the volumes when finished,—& this risk involves your having an imperfect work—which of course you could not sell for so good a price. He—Mr. C.—makes great pieces of work about the losses he has had from subscribers discontinuing & I observe—(why I don't know—has printed George's name as a *new* subscriber at the commencement of the present vol.—Now—you will just see I have only made a suggestion—& I shall be glad if you will write to me what I am to do*—What shall be done.

I think now that all the Business is got over. Of News there is not much. The Chimpanzee was reported dead, but is recovering. 4 Cameleopards are purchased for the Zoo: Soc: & are at Malta: they come in June. The New Museum is in Leicester Square. Give my love to Mr Drewitt, & say that I should have sent down a 3d. vol of Audubon but my friend [V?] Audubon has gone to Italy, & I shall not have it till he returns. As for Robert—on the most moderate calculation I have written 5000000 letters to him, & I conclude he will send me a volume shortly.

Poor Lady De Tabley has had a sad fall & miscarriage.—Mrs. Ball—(so much for the year of the Comet!!) who married on the other side of 40—& had been married 4 years—is going to be confined!—Gracious—St Peter—there is 11 o'clock! Love to children—Remember me to all friends—& let me conclude this Megatherium of a letter by putting my name as yours ever sincerely,

Edward Lear

*—Pray do not repeat what I have written of Curtis, as I only judge from hearsay
Is George particular as to only the fossils he himself found being drawn—or—may they be foreign fossils—or only British.

TO FANNY COOMBE, 24 AUGUST 1836 *(cat. 37)*

Levens Hall. Milnthorpe. Westmoreland.
12 oclock. P.M. 24 th. Aug. 1836.—

My dear Mrs George—

I am already half asleep—but as I have delayed scrawling day after day—(from Lord Derby being away from Knowsley (grouse shooting)—& my not caring to expose you to the expense of unfranked letters,) I am resolved to indite 6 lines, (however stupid, since there are a "batch of Peers"—Bandons, Bagots, Talbots, & Barnard, coming to morrow—& surely I shall get a Frank from one of them.

Behold now! I left Knowsly on a sketching tour—but as Lord Derby—Ld. Stanley—four or five Hornbys &c &c—all thrust (in the moment of my going,) letters into my hand to different friends,—my life is one of extreme gaiety—& vastly little improvement. I forget when I wrote you last:—however, I can't help repeating—that I never remember passing so happy a consecutive 6 weeks as I did this year at Knowsley: the breaking up of the party was a regret to all,—& knowing that I could not meet with better fun—or better friends elsewhere—I did not set out with all the alacrity with which a tourist ought to begin his journey. Nevertheless—from that time till now—I have been happiness personified—for a more exquisite country than Westmoreland I never dreamed of—& as the people I have seen already are agreeable, I don't grumble: what is beyond, who knows!

To give you a brief Egotism: those lovely days about the 10th of August—I spent at Lancaster—with the Edmund Hornbys—a delightful family. Mrs. Hornby—the mountains of Westmoreland—the Castle—& the Lunatic Asylum—are all balanced in my mind—you might see them all at once—& each was perfection in its way. I regretted leaving Lancaster—as I grow "at home" so soon—thence however I came to this place Levens—perhaps the finest existing specimen of an antique house. From Henry the 8th's time downward not a thing has been altered about it:—except the Gardens—which are James the 2ds.—& perfectly wonderful in their way: Consider no shrub—no plant ever allowed to grow without cultivation! avenues—[oriels?]—squares—walks of yew trees—centuries old—30 or 40 feet high—cut into cows—bottles—hats—& every possible shape—unaltered by an inch since 1680!! Imagine turf between walls of high beech trees—all magically shorn quite even—& looking like fable & nonsense!! Then the house itself—every wall & room covered with oak—carved [massively?] a foot deep—the chimnies 8 feet wide,—no grates—only peat burning—the windows recessed—with little cut panes—arms painted on all,——the ceilings fretted—the floors solid oak—chairs tables—buffets—all carved oak,—the chairs highbacked—the sofas of damask or tapestry with pointlace hangings of Cardinal Wolsey's date,—the hall hung profusely with armour—the very staircase scattered with jackboots—gauntlets—& spears of 1400—the bedrooms courious little oaky nooks—gloomy with little windows & crimson tapestry—& approached up turrets by stone stairs——!!—only imagine this! For the reality is far beyond what I can describe. On the whole it is the most perfect piece of antiquity extant,—& if you add to this,—that the people are admirable—& the park & country round exquisite—you won't wonder I am pleased.—But my eyes fail me: I must conclude:—from Levens I went to Kendal—Nature's slopbasin—where it always rains—& while there saw the Hinds—& din'd there on Sunday—Thence I came to Milnthorpe & Dallam Tower—lovely seats—but beyond a letter's description—& today I have returned here for some festivities to morrow. On Friday I go to Mr Webster's, & then to Underley—Whittington & Kirby Lonsdale:—after this (for I have not yet seen the Lakes,) with Lord Stanley's letters—to Messrs. Bradylls—Townleys—Starkies—& Col: Boltons on Windermere—so I shall stand a chance of seeing some society. But I will write before then. I expect to return to Knowsley in September.

I am worn out—for I get up at 5—walk all day—& [dine?] at 7, I am generally done for by 12. So give my love to George—& hoping hes better & that the children are all well & yourself—good night.

Believe me—Dear Mrs George— | Yours sleepy & sincerely,
Edward Lear

Mrs [Ovrington?] asked quite lovingly after Mr. Drewitt.——I wish you could see the wood in this country! Ash trees! I thought there would be fossils—but find none.

TO GEORGE COOMBE, 6 SEPTEMBER 1835 *(cat. 40)*

Whittington Hall: Kirkby Lonsdale.
6th. Septr. 1836

Dear George—I have so little opportunity of writing now a days, that I fear you have thought me dead: as it is I shall perhaps only send a scrawl, as the length of my letter will depend on the accuracy of time in which the bell for breakfast is rung:- after that I shall seal & send—as to delay further might be not to send till October. For aught I know—you & Mrs George may have written me 7 letters each—since Lord Derby forwards all mail from Knowsley to Kendal—where I have not been this fortnight—but go thither today:—pray the fates there may be a budget!—This information I put in lest you may imagine, by my not answering any letter you may have sent—that they have been lost.

Do you know I have now been a month in the Lake Country—& have seen nothing of a Lake at all!—The fact is—water is an unpleasantly too superfluous [as any?] here to seek for more:—almost all this time I have only made studies of rain—[series of three cross hatching lines] crosswise—or in whatsoever wise it falls. Day after day—incessant torrents flood the land, & although today (the 6th.) was appointed by the moon & the prophets of the atmosphere for a clearing—yet I perceive a mass of clouds rolling up from Ingleborough, which will give them all the lie. In Consequence of this wet season, I have been paying a succession of visits—pleasures & palaces, one after another—& just enough of fair sunshine, to get a ramble now & then in this most lovely of all counties. Wales is in my opinion—far below Westmoreland,—the foliage—the forms of the hills, here are all superior.—I believe I told Mrs George how I staid at Lancaster on leaving Knowsley—how I saw the prison & the Lunatic Asylum—& other sundries: how dancing, music, & dining made the time very short:—also how I enjoyed myself at Colonel Howard's—that curious old hall—where ghosts are as common as mice,—& you sit among armour & starched ruffs till you find even your own limbs growing stiff & mouldy:—also how I went to the Wet City of Kendal, where it always rains—& the little dear babies are born with fins—webbed feet—& umbrellas under their arms:—after which—I think—I had not imparted any of my very important doings. I spent another week at Col: Howards after this—for they had heard I was growing mouldy at Nature's slopbasin (Kendal,) & kindly sent for me. There was then a large party—Lords Talbot, Bandon Pagets &c &c. staying there,—& I can assure you it was one of the finest sights I ever saw—the old tapestry hall set out as a dinner table:—but there is little to say—one day passing happily just like its predecessor sitting drawing or at music if wet—riding or walking in parties if fine: plenty of merriments, & kindness without end—but this looks stupid on paper.

Followed this—a visit to Ellerhow—where there were Mr Webster's good natured family: this—tho' very handsome—was not a palace—& as it was rather dull, & the children not nice ones—I lusted more than once after the Flesh pots of Egypt: Some exquisite scrambles I got nevertheless over the hills—& really the Bay of Morecambe is more lovely than anything I ever saw!—I omit parties to see Cartmel Abbey—Lord Burlingtons &c &c. I then went to Dalton—a most outoftheway [*sic*] town in the Peninsula of Furness—hoping to get some sketching at the noble ruins of Furness Abbey—Lord bless you! it poured deluges from 5 in the morning till 8 at night—& I played the philosopher for two days in an old Inn where the people scarcely spoke

English—till I was tired. So then I set off with a note from Lord Derby—to the finest house in these parts——Mr Bradyll's—whose family are Saxon, & so old, that Adam is supposed to have been brought up in it. Conceive any place so lovely!—Enormous sycamores & ash bury it—great rocks shelter it from cold—& all this slopes down to the sea—where the Bay spreads on each side & on one hand Helvellyn—the other far in the distance Pile Castle & the Isle of Man!—the landscape however was my least pleasure: for the 3 Miss Bradylls are 20 degrees beyond perfection—& what with all sorts of singing & music with them, their father, & Brother, & Admiral Sotheran,—a band of 2 accordions—flute—harp—guitar & piano—we minded not the rain a tittle. Oh! dear! oh dear!—that splendid priory,—how sorry I was to leave it!—But I did, &—(still in the rain,) I came to Ingmire Hall—Underley Hall—& now Whittington hall: of all which I may say—they are exquisite mansions full of pleasant society in a lovely country:—the valley of the Lune below Ingleborough being extremely beautiful. Of Underley, I may add, that Mr Nowell its proprietor is a rich possessor of East Indn. property, and the valuable splendour there beats credibility!—& such living! curries! pilaus! champagnes!—Dear me! At this place & here & elsewhere—nothing can be more friendly or hospitable, & I assure you that I leave each batch of new friends with regret. I go today to sloppy Kendal!—& shall call on Mrs. André in my way:—N.B. as I have lately travelled in a Coach & four with 2 outriders I hope you will get some ready against I come. I would have given anything the other day for some of the children instead of certain impracticable little vipers I had to deal with—Here there are some nice little ducks, & Mrs Green is a most delightful woman.—Tomorrow I go to my last visit,—Col: Bolton's of Stoors, I believe the finest seat in the Lakes:—N.B. also—I have *refused*—(don't stare,) to go to Lord Lonsdale's—(Lowther Castle,) as this sort of life is all very fine—but very improper. I expect to meet a very gay party—Lowthers & Littledales at Storrs—& from *there*—I intend taking walks from different Inns all over the Lakes: that's if the weather is tolerant—if not—I shall toddle back to Knowsly.

All the world here are crazy about a great Will trial—Marsden ?—Tatham v: Wright. Do you see it in the papers? There goes the bell!—

Now pray write—if you haven't written—for by this time I conclude & hope you are quite set up again—& if it makes your head ache—let Mrs George send a line—to say an earthquake has not swallowed you all up. Remember me to her & to all the little ones, & all friends, & believe me,

Dear George, | Yours sincerely,
Edward Lear.

N.B. I shan't forget your Geology when I get to Keswick If Mrs. George didn't believe in Ghosts *here*—she would be excommunicated: all Westmorland abounds with them, & they are as Common as Thrushes.

TO FANNY COOMBE, 3 JANUARY 1837 *(cat. 91)*

28 Southampton Row. Bloomsbury
3d. January. 1837.

My dear Mrs George,

Tired of waiting for my luggage,—still frozen up in a filthy Leicestershire canal,—I write to give an account of myself, tho' I have delayed doing so hoping to have written with a box I intend forwarding to George when my things come. I left

Knowsley after a very nice Xmas dinner on the night of the 25th:—quite a *voluntary quittal* I beg to say, as I was much pressed to remain, & indeed have now received an invitation to come when I please without being asked. After a dreadful night of cold & snow—2 overturns, & delays innumerable, I reached Colonel Howard's (Elford Hall) near Lichfield on Monday Morning. I passed a very pleasant visit thereat but being anxious to be in London, & knowing that Gould, (who has had the scarlet fever in his family,) was much in want of me to draw for him,—the destinies propelld me to set off on Tuesday the unlucky 27th.—Such a journey as we had surely never English mortal knew previously! One single bit of luck seemed to bless us,—our getting possession ('twas a mail,) of some snowed up mailbags—from having which with our own, we we [*sic*] forwarded whenever there was a lack of horses, to the prejudice of less fortunate coaches I cannot describe, were I Munchausen himself, half the hideous adventures that befel us!—Conceive miles of a sort of lane between snow walls 10 or 12 feet high—sometimes even actually higher than the mailcoach top:- sometimes drifted again—over which the wretched vehicle was dragged by 8 horses. Conceive encountering wagons—being dragged stern foremost,—having drunken postillions, waiting 2 hours on a heath of 3 foot snow for horses!!—Suffice it to say, (tho' I did not expect it, we reached London about 7 on Thursday morning!—I—abandoned I—wholly without luggage—as that was sent by the Canal.

Here however I am,—& had I a moment to think or grumble, I might perhaps compare this small dark room with five inches of dusty fire—my darker bedroom,—my outdoor prospect of a paved yard, 2 cats, & a poplar tree,—& the agreeable sounds of Mrs. Smiths quarrelsome daughters in the room adjoining,—with all my comforts & luxuries in Lancashire & elsewhere for the last 6 months. But so completely occupied have I been & am likely to be that a Kraal of Hottentots might establish themselves in my apartments without annoying me. And this leads me to the subject of coming to see you, which much as I wish to do, I still find for the present impracticable. I believe you know me quite well enough not to credit whatever ill natured people may say of "forgetting old friends &c "—still I wish you to understand distinctly how I am prevented going both to Sussex & Bath yet awhile. It is arranged—or nearly so,—that I am to go to Paris in three weeks time to make some drawings (Zoological,) for Gould,—an offer even so far as business went, it would have not have done for me to refuse. Meanwhile, I intended bringing into Sussex some pencil drawings (18 or 20) ordered for sundry Lancashire folks: this however has been set aside by the quantity of Lithography I shall have to do before I go: every eving at Candelight *must* I do it,—& other watercolor dwings will occupy the days. 8 large Lithographs, 20 Landscapes—3 Watercol: drawings—besides other trifling things not to speak of hindrances *are* realities say what one may—& not to be overcome in three weeks hastily. I do hope, as soon as I return to England,—(at the end of February,) to get a longer visit with you than I could have managed now—even had I been able to come at all. What people here will say, I don't know—I mean Andres &c &c. There are 18 invitations for nights & dinners in the next week waiting for me, but I have been obliged to decline all but [Bills?]—[Garricks?]—& Fowlers: what else *can* I do?—To night I should have met C. [Kemble?]—Mrs. Butler—& Miss K. at dinner—but instead am writing this.—Recreation & gaiety indeed so called are to me now no pleasure for their own sake: half a year of perpetual change—& splendour—make a little quiet, (if one could get it,) very desirable. For a 12 month I have lived in a whirlwind—surely there must be rest somewhere.

My sister Ann comes here tomorrow. Kate is worse & unlikely to recover. I find a great many changes & death among my acquaintance in half a year

I regret much writing this, but I cannot avoid it: George I am sure looks forward to my coming & will be vexed at hearing I cannot start.

I was about taking lodgings elsewhere, but under the present circumstances have put up with them. I have been leeching & sitting up with my old friend Hullmandel who is very ill, & am too fagged to write more. Give my love to the children & George, & all,

& believe me, | My dear Mrs. George,

Yours ever sincerely, Edward Lear.

Write soon—for I shant know if you get this the roads are so bad. Such a fuss has been made about my 2 missing letters! As you shall see when we meet

TO FANNY COOMBE, 11 FEBRUARY 1837[1] *(cat. 92)*

36. Great Marlboro' Street. 11. Feby. 1837

My dear Mrs George—

I ought to have replied to a joint composition of yours & George's long before this, but I have been so unsettled & unwell that I have not applied to any thing. [Even?] now I shall only muster capabilities for a short letter: I don't in the least remember when I wrote last, so upset have I been of late,—& tis likely enough I may say again what I have said before.

You have heard I dare say of my poor sister Kate's death, which altho' I know it happened seems now more like a dream than a reality. She was the youngest of us all. From the time she grew worse, (about the period of my taking these lodgings,) I was partly in the country with her, & partly here. I do not know when I have been so unhinged & miserable. I wonder if people who ridicule Christianity ever saw a religious person's deathbed: it is at least something I should think to be able to die happily. But I shall not say any thing more than this on this subject, though Catherine's last hours & funeral are always uppermost in my mind. 4 deaths in ones own family in as many years force one to think indeed. And there will be a 5th. Before long I fear, for my sister Florence is but a shadow.

As for your humble servant, I am strongly advised by the medical folk to go to a climate where less east wind & cold may prevail than in this horrible one—to take precautions ere it be too late. I'm sure I don't know what to think: one must die some time, & I think it is not over sagacious to make such a fuss about a dozen or so extra years. From a cold I caught at the funeral I was very poorly—but am now much better.

I ran down for one day to Bath, to see my old friend there, who is ill of Influenza, & returning, spent a day at Oxford, with [J. Sayres?] & a Stanley friend. [J. Sayres?] & I have "made it all up" I should have told you some time ago. This hasty change has done me good,—for I was devoured with glumps,—but had I had a longer furlough, I should have been but a bad companion for Arundel. Now I am sitting to draw hard—heaps of ugly bills unpaid, & the last 6 weeks having produced nought—but botheration. Senior is abroad,—& no one in London I can see often or care about,—& if it weren't for the variety the Police Office opposite affords, I don't know what I should do.

1. On mourning paper.

I am glad George liked his fossils—tho' he waxd wroth at their having been bought. But I know no other way of getting them—& ~~that~~ to get them at all is a pleasure:—for I take no interest in things I don't understand,—& if I did, they are all monopolized by retail purchases in the Lake Country.

I am doing views of the Lakes, as a thing that keeps up what little interest I have left in me. & when I get on will send some. My lodgings are *more comfortable than any I have ever been in*. I hope the children & yourselves have not been very ill with the Influenza—quite like a plague here. Give my love to them., & remember me to George & all. I have some Franks—but shall keep them a while. I am too cross to write any more, & shall go to bed, tho' it is only just 7. Write soon, & believe me,

My dear Mrs. George, Yours ever sincerely

Edward Lear.

TO FANNY COOMBE, 3 MARCH 1837[1] *(cat. 93)*

36. Great Marlboro' St. 3d. March. 1837.

My dear Mrs. George

A most shameful fortnight has elapsed since I received your letter, which the more needed an earlier answer from being so kind a one. But I don't know how it is, until the last week or 10 days I have been as indolent & gloomy as possible, & when the day has been over I have felt too fagged & un-care-about-anything to sit down to write. My good friends the Hornbys have however been in town lately, & their quiet & rational society has done me a vast deal of good: alas! They go tomorrow—& leave a wretched East wind in their place: so that I shall cough out my lamentations loudly.

I was very sorry to hear such an account as you gave of all of you, & I hope by this time you are recovered. You speak of the baby having had convulsions, which, from my not understanding these things perhaps appears more alarming than it really is: I thought children so affected did not usually recover. You & George must have been in sad anxiety.

My coming to you for any length of time seems an Utopian scheme: it is not as it used to be with me & my leisure days, and as for working with you, the usual alternation of Littlepeople & pupils besides, renders it impossible. I shall therefore, as I cannot make a long visit, make up my mind to a short one rather than none at all, & accordingly a *very flying* one, as far as mortal certainty goes, I will assuredly perform in the Easter recess. I am perfectly inclined to a *stay*, & as perfectly aware how kindly you desire it, but that is not possible.

To stuff this letter brimful of egotism, I must tell you that my eyes are wofully worse—that is when I apply to small zoological drawing highly coloured,—& indeed the less I sit suits my chest & eyes equally well. And now let me inform you of a "tide in the affairs" of your humble servant: first promising, lest your Curiosity be overwhelming, that I am neither going to marry the old Duchess of Gloucester, nor turn cannibal, nor become Bishop of Salisbury, but that I am going to put in practice a long nursed dream of studying for 2 years at Rome,—tho' great as may be the benefit I may derive as to my profession, my [erased word] health both needs & may expect a greater. My power of undertaking this is a piece or a mass of goodness & friendship scarcely to have been heard of, & for which it is quite out of my power to shew sufficient gratitude. To my exceeding surprise a letter brought me 3 days

1. On mourning paper.

ago a sufficient sum to live at Rome for the term I have stated,—& with this, an explanation that many friends had been anxious to do me some permanent good, & both from my desire to improve, & from the recommendation of Dr. Clarke as to the *necessity* of removing to a warmer climate,—had fixed on this mode of tendering it. But as the gift of *one* person they conceived might not be in accordance with my idea of independence, no less than *30* friends of very different families & connexions had arranged in this most delicate & kind manner,—by paying beforehand for commission drawings to be executed in Rome,—to give me this most valuable assistance.

I shall only say at present that I do not go until July,—for as yet I am so stupefied & don't-know-how-to-be-sufficiently-thankfulified, that I can do nothing but turn round on my toes like a pivot, for fear of which operation commencing now, I will, with remembrances to all, suddenly sign myself, Dear Mrs. George, Ever sincerely yours,

Edward Lear

TO FANNY COOMBE, 15 APRIL 1837 *(cat. 94)*

21 Sherrard Street. Golden Square
Saturday Evening. 15th.

My dear Mrs. George—

I have got very comfortable lodgings at the above address during my stay in town, which is very uncertain,—& occupied thoroughly you may conclude. Thank you for your letter of the 9th. I was much grieved to hear little Dudley had had more illness: you do not say what it arose from—so I conclude [erased] suppose teething. Your dinner I was glad to hear proved so agreeable. —Without further dwelling on your letter—(for I have but little time or intellect being sadly sleepy,) I will tell you what little novelty one may collect. The first, & greatest, is—(what the papers have scarcely yet announced, so I beg you will pay all respect to my ministerial knowledge,)—the preferment of my friend Rev. Edward Stanley to the Bishopric of Norwich:—these Stanleys are the Alderley Stanleys—distant relations of Lord Derby—but whose pedigree I did not write for you. Take one therefore of both brothers –

1 Eldest brother
Sir John T. Stanley. Baronet. married Lady Maria Holroyd

1 —Edward John Stanley—Secretary of State
2. William Owen—M.P. for Anglesea
3. Marianetta
4 Alethea—married Colonel Scott
5. Jane m.—Mr [Ganly?]
6 - Isabella—m.—Sir Edward Parry—(North Pole,)
7. Louisa
8. Emmaline

2 youngest brother
Edward Stanley—Bishop of Norwich married Catherine—sister of Edward Penrhyn Esqr

1 - Owen Stanley -2d Lieut. Capt. Bank's expedition
2. Mary -
3. Arthur - has just gained the highest honours at Oxford.
4. Charles—Lieut. in Royl. Engineers.
5. Catherine.

This appointment makes a great sensation here, & interests me much of course,—from having for the last 2 years seen a great deal of this family, (I mean the Alderley people.) who are very kind & amiable.

Since I last wrote I have been staying at Sheen, (E. Penrhyn's,) with these same Stanleys, & great fun we have had—plays &c. Then 2 mornings in the week, I have had a class of pupils in Grosvenor Square of 6 or 8—& it has been quite delightful. As my going away draws near—every eving [*sic*] brings its dinner party—, & I scarcely like to look forward to leaving so many friends.

Lord Derby is expected next week, & then I shall know about what time I shall go to Knowsley. My plans as far as I can see are these—to stay in the North until the 20th or so of June - & then visit Bath & Plymouth,—returning to town about the 10th of July—& then setting off to Switzerland with my old friend Fowler,—who is so minded at present—about the 15th. Bye the bye Mrs Fowler has got a little Girl—she was Elizabeth Gale—not Mr. Greenacre's [Gale?] [hole in page]. But I grow tired & stupid: Hurry scurry all day long—& a huge dinner party in the eving [*sic*]—for I have just come from Lady Maria Stanley's—where were all the world & the new Bishop.—tires one thoroughly: tomorrow I lunch at Downing Street with the Edward J. Secretary Stanleys, so I get this ready for a Frank. Give the enclosed to George—it's an address of the man in Paris wot sells Fossils.

Remember me to him & to all, & believe me,
My dear Mrs. George—
Ever yours sincerely,
Edward Lear.

TO FANNY COOMBE, 18 APRIL 1837[1]

My dear Mrs George—

I did not get a Frank on Sunday, so [stop?] to send this to day. How dreadfully wintry it continues! I have got another pupil—which makes 7—shewing how one would get on if one stayed.

I saw Fowler's baby yesterday—a nice little thing:—he & I purpose going together as far as Coblentz:—Lord Derby has not come yet: I shall most likely go back with him: but when & how I cannot tell. Ann, who is at Bath, writes that the country is covered with snow—& that she has scarcely been out these 3 weeks. My love to all the children & to George. I hope Dudley practises his walking well. Good bye—

Believe me ever.
Sincerely yours,
Edward Lear.

21 Sherrard St.
Golden Square—Tuesday Morning [18 April 1837]

1. Franked by Thomas Greene.

TO FANNY COOMBE, 19 MAY 1837 *(cat. 95)*

Knowsley Hall—
19. May. 1837.

My dear Mrs George

Although I wrote to you yesterday, there is a possibility you may not have got my note, as I forgot to ~~send~~ take it myself to Lord Skelmersdales, & the porter at Grosvenor Sqre may have been oblivious anent its being put in the post. I lunched with & took leave of the Lathom people, but they were all in a bustle going to the drawing room, so I could not ask them to frank it just then. As for my letter's contents, or rather discontents—they were highly abusive of you on account of never having written,—& also intended to warn you that the thimbles I bought at Paris will be with you on Saturday—together with [sundry?] exculpatory & explanatory sentences connected with that matter.

We had a very merry luncheon yesterday—a 2d one I mean—after the Drawing room,—of Hornby, & Stanleys, & at ½ past 4 oclock left London in a chariot drawn by four horses, accompanied by 2 postillions & 2 domestics,—& containing Lord Derby—myself—6 cloaks—one jerboa—3 pigeons—20 or 30 books—some bread & biscuits,—a roast fowl & a bottle of wine. Dinner having been ordered at Dunchurch in Warwickshre at 12—we attacked the last mentioned [?]ables at 8,—& at midnight had a delightful dinner, after which I slept perfectly sound until we reached Warrington this morning at 10: we arrived here at qu past 11—& if that is not expedition & comfort—what is?

No one is here: Robert Hornby comes on Tuesday—& secondly Zoologists about the same time. Till then I shall feel rather Concerned, as the crocodile said when he was dancing a pas seul,—but one cannot be always equally happy.

Here I am sitting—in the old red drawing room with its old gilt mouldings, & its old pictures,—& its red & white striped furniture, & its chiffoniers full of books—& its plate glass recessed windows with fat cushions therein—looking out over the old broad sloping lawn till it is lost in the meadows—then the trees—& then a wide flat country as far as one can see with its extreme edge just dotted with 6 Mills—one raceStand—17 churches—& all Liverpool:—& all this just as placid as if nothing ever did or could happen to disturb it.

My trunks not having arrived, My amusements are limited: so I poke the 3 fires about: go into the aviary & tease the old cat & the cross goose,—& have already pryed into every corner of the Park—stables & gardens. Nevertheless I wish Phipps Hornby were here. I don't half like going out of England, now it comes to the point.

Meanwhile pray write, for you treat me most basely.

I must tell you that I expect to be confined while I am here:—do not I beg misinterpret my phrase—altho' I confess I have some silent misgivings lest I actually produce a calf:—I mean, I am about to be vaccinated, so I am all over nervous & horrible about it—*cowed* enough already as far as that goes.

The country here looks like March:- the Oak & Ash are as bare as they were in January.

I declare I am so morose that I can write no longer: my love to all—& believe me,

My dear Mrs George, | Yours sincerely,
Edward Lear.

I spent my birthday—the 13th—when I was 25—very agreeably at Ld. Derbys—the Hornbys & Penrhyns uniting therein.

TO FANNY COOMBE, 8 & 10 JULY 1837 *(cat. 104)*

(Ryde—Isle of Wight. 8th July 1837.)

My dear Mrs George-

Look whence I am writing this!—from a high window I can see over the beautiful green sea—Portsmouth opposite—and Chichester spire (!) in the distance!—I had thought sometimes of staying tomorrow with you—(for I leave here today),)—but when I considered that seeing you for one day only, would hardly compensate for another goodbye—I gave it up: particularly as from the sort of farewell visits I have been lately paying my nerves are not too strong. I reproach myself for not having written more—(your last letter I received only a few days back at Plymouth—but I don't know how it is—spite of getting up at 4 in the morning—days seem to roll by like minutes and nothing is done: and sometimes I have not liked to send melancholy letters. You must not think I am melancholy from *this* epistle,—that is not as I *used* to be: I am sad enough at times—& did I give way to being so might be much worse:—but I have much to be very thankful for—& a great deal to hope, as I find that looking forward is the best policy on all accounts. It is often a great comfort to me that of the early *friends* I made—I have lost none,—for the change of *acquaintance* only goes for nothing. And I don't doubt that George, you, & I—shall eat a dinner together (if we are all alive,) in 1870. (Let me ask while I think of it if you have received the Bombay ducks at Peppering:—I will see about them at the Gardens tomorrow.)—Before me lie 2 of your letters, one of the 25th of May tells me of George having the gout—& abuses me about the thimbles—whose price I never told you of: I cannot quite remember it now—but I know it was 3 shillings more than you told me to give: I beg however that this debt may go towards buying the greens & potatoes for our dinner in 1870. Your 2d. letter is dated—shocking!—10th of June!—There is little in it to answer, tho' as a whole—a great deal to be thanked for. What can W.W.W. mean by his strange ways?—As for Mrs. Hall—"I hope she'll be happy"—but it is a stretch of hope certainly. An old boatman at Plymouth says sometimes—"there's nothing like a family Groupe [*sic*]"—& certainly Mrs. Atkins' ménage that is to be—will be a fine illustration. I am very glad the children have got the poney: how is Robert's head now? & does he go to Geneva? And now let me go back to Knowsley—to leave which cost me a great deal of pain. We were very quiet while there—the same daily routine of early walks—constant drawing,—riding,—& sitting down in the eving [*sic*] to dine by the sunset on the old quiet terrace & distant trees. I have been very happy at different times in many places as you know very well: but having had a longer duration of comfort in Lancashire I shall always look back to it as the best home I have ever met with. I stayed at Winwick—& took leave of Mr. & Mrs. James Hornby—& of poor Mrs Latouche who at 84 is now fast going:—of the Miss Hornbys—a (—my friend Robert—) Mr Atherley's "hypochondria", whose malady shows itself—(spite of a spinal complaint which keeps him ever a sufferer,) in working 6 hours of every day in doing kindnesses for other people.) then of the Edmund Hornbys & others not known to you by name.—Lady Ellinor had another little girl before I left so I did not see her. Lord Derby wrote a kind note before I set off—in preference to a verbal 'goodbye'. It would make me very wretched did I think I should not see him again—but as he is in better health than he has been of late—I trust he will live many years.—And so I came away from Lancashire. I have no pleasure in looking back to Bath—where I stayed 2 days—so I skip that part gladly—& go on to Plymouth—which I reached on the 19th of June. Devonshire is actually nothing more or less than Paradise: at first Plymouth Sound —& Mount Edgcumbe of which one hears so much—disappoints one *horribly*:—but when one becomes accustomed to know that the sea is [erased number] 7 miles wide—one does not wonder that the hills look low. Captain Hornby is one of the head persons at Plymouth: (he was distinguished at the battle of Lissa—& all that— so he is superintendent of all the victualling offices—and the Hospital—where he has a house. But at present they have a delightful place at Bovisand on the other side of the water—[little sketch map showing location of Bovisand, Plymouth Sound, Plymouth, the River Tamar etc.]—where [erased word] quiet outofthewayness has been to me perfection of all happiness.

Imagine a comfortable house—opening onto a lawn (where we dined & had tea generally—for in ~~out of~~ three weeks not a cloud has been in the sky.) & situated in a valley full of wood running down to the wide sea—where fine rocks form the beach. All the family (11 of them) who were so long my friends at Knowsly—were here—besides Miss Montagu who is all music—not to forget my friend Phipps who has just got the Engineers at Woolwich. And as a general idea of our days,—I rose at 4 & drew till 6—when Phipps & Jamie & I walked or bathe till breakfast. Afterwards in the sea sate indoors with a quiet drawing or musical morning—or dabbled 2 or 3 hours more in the sea—or all sailed about in the wherry—until 4 when Captn. Hornby returned from Plymouth & we dined. After this we usually took a long eving [*sic*] walk—& as often (—& latterly indeed always,) we all adjourned to the rocks with guitars & work—Mrs Hornby in her little pony chair—& there we sate singing to the sea & the moon till late. Charades & all sorts of fun—tea or music—occupied us till Bed. Sometimes a day we spent in a Knapsack walk of 20 miles with Capt. H. up one of the rivers—sometimes pic nics to Mt. Edgcumbe—or lionizing about Plymouth.—strawberry feast &c &c. Not a syllable—not a look of ill temper have I seen once among our whole party—so you see that Bovisand bids fair to take a jump up into Heaven just as it is. Man of war boats with crews are always ready for us to go whither we list, & no time has been lost to their kindness in shewing me all things about. Only one of our party—dear little Geoffrey was missing—who has just sailed in the Princess Charlotte as middy.—I linger over Boviston [*sic*] perhaps longer than you care for: but I can't help it. I really thought I had done with all acute feelings but I am sure that the leaving Devonshire has nearly dislocated my neck by sheer mental exertion. I don't get over it now ever—tho' the Penrhyns (who have a house here) are somewhat the same set of friends—though not quite Phipps Hornbys. Catherine Hornby too is staying here—& one gets letters from all people now & then. I have many anecdotes of our young queen—through the Bp. of Norwich—(ArchBp. of Canterbury) &c. Did you hear that when the King died—it being necessary for her to answer the Queen Dowger's note on that matter—the ArchBp. suggested that her letter should have been directed—to the Q. *Dowager* & not to the *Queen* as she had done. "No" said Victoria—"I will not be the first so to style my Aunt."—And she sent it off as it was! I cannot relate many other traits equally good & which I know to be true: but it is evident from the testimony of several who have had good reason for knowing—that her tact—spirit—reasonableness—& business like manner—are quite beyond what were expected from so young a person. On the Mayor presenting his address—her attendant Officers had not come to her—so she said to Lady C. Jenkinson—"Come—Kate—we'll go to them alone"—which she did much to the confusion of the Citizen. Perhaps these things are in print but having heard them direct from Kensington I thought they would amuse you. I shall write no more at present, but send this from London—when I shall be aware of the day I sail on—

21 Sherrard Street—Golden Sqre. 10th. July. 1837. Here am I in my old Lodgings—too busy to think or move. The Ducks—I find are sent off:—I sail on Sunday next by the Antwerp packet. If you write—not earlier than the first week in August,——

address Edward Lear Esqre.
Poste Restante.
Coblenz. sur le Rhin

APPENDIX B

LETTER

to John Gould from Knowsley Hall, in the collection of the Department of Printing and Graphic Arts, The Houghton Library, Harvard University.

This letter was written the day after returning from his Lake District tour. Until the rediscovery of the two letters in the Frederick Warne Archive, this was the only surviving letter by Lear that referred to the tour.

Knowsley Hall 31. Oct. 1836
hail—snow—frost—& desolation.

Dear Gould

I got you letter last eving [*sic*], as I was about to write to you: thank you for it:—I wanted to know how you were going on. As for your replying I never expect that, as I know how busy you are always.

Your accounting for Capn. Coxon's death is sad enough: but I was much surprised at the circumstances under which it occurred. For Mr. Bennett's—I don't remember ever to have been more shocked: even now I have heard no particulars. Indepently [*sic*] of his being a good principled & kind hearted man, he was a wonder—inasmuch as he was of the very first who were scientific for science's sake. You especially must feel his loss very much,—& so must Rees. You are very just in your remarks—: sudden deaths make a greater impression than others on us, tho' we ought to know & feel the uncertainty of life continually.

To your numerous enquiries, I must answer rather briefly, for I have so bad a cold as to be half blind: add to which so bad a cough & sore throat, that if they don't go I shall be in town much sooner than I expected. I left Knowsley, (only half my work done,) on the 12 August for a sketching tour, & really it is impossible to tell you *how*, & *how enormously* I have enjoyed the whole Autumn. The counties of Cumberland & Westmd [*sic*] are superb indeed, & tho' the weather has been miserable, yet I have contrived to walk pretty well over the whole ground, & to sketch a good deal beside. I hope too, I have improved somewhat—(hard if I haven't after slaving as I have done) but you will judge when I get back.

I spent a delightful time at Col: Howard, both going & returning—also at some other subscribers of yours – Messrs. Stanniforth, Bradyll,—&c &c.

I could not go on to Scotland. Bye the bye—on coming here, I found a letter from Lizars, ordering drawings for a British Ornithology—!!!!!!!!!—but I have written to say I can't set about it *at present*. To say truth, I had rather not at all, for my eyes are so sadly worse, that no bird under an Ostrich shall I soon be able to see to do.

I am staying to finish what I had promised Lord Derby I would do before I went away, & shall, I imagine, be home by the end of November, ~~&~~ when I shall ~~then~~ be most happy to set about anything you please. 3 parts of yours are coming to night I believe. How are going on with the Zoo: Soc?—Not very well: I guess:—but I now am more in the dark as to their politics than ever.

Remember me to Mr. Rees:—I am going to send him a scrawl. And to V. Audubon also if you see him. Mr. Hullmandel I have written to.

Nothing particularly new here that I remember:—Weasel headed Armadillo, &c &c. I should like to, (but doubt if I can,) to [erased word] bring up the drawings of the last 2 summers with me.

I have been most extremely well all thro' my excursion—& am now otherwise for the first time. Am glad to hear Mrs Gould and the children are well:—you don't say if you have been out of town anywhere. Remember me to Mrs Gould if you please, & believe me,

Dear Gould, | Ever yours sincerely,
Edward Lear

This place is colder than Kamschatka!

APPENDIX C

THE PROBLEM OF THE JULY LAKE DISTRICT DRAWINGS

In the absence of hard evidence, and with the lack of letters and journals from the early years, earlier Lear biographers have been able to make sweeping statements with impunity. Angus Davidson, in his 1938 book *Edward Lear – Landscape Painter and Nonsense Poet (1812–1888)*, wrote: 'The parrots finished and published, Lear went to Knowsley, and though he and Ann kept on the rooms in London he spent most of the next four years at Lord Derby's house in Lancashire. … He had been, two or three times, during those years, to the Lakes' (p. 25). With the discovery, or as Vivien Noakes more recently put it, the rediscovery, of some of Lear's letters to the Drewitt family in the archive of Frederick Warne, it is possible to see that this statement is overstated and inaccurate. There is currently evidence for only one visit to the Lake District.

The myth of the multiple visits to the Lake District has proved to something of a persistently flogged dead horse. The letters in the Frederick Warne Archive (Appendix A) are tantalising just as much for what they omit as for what they contain. Importantly, they include two crucial letters written from his tour of north Lancashire, Cumberland and Westmorland in the late summer of 1836. The exact dates of this tour after leaving Knowsley are still unknown as Lear himself made contradictory statements about it. In the first letter from the tour, written from Levens Hall on 24 August (cat. 37), he wrote: 'those lovely days about the 10th of August – I spent at Lancaster'. In a letter written to John Gould from Knowsley on 31 October, he is more categoric, writing: 'I left Knowsley … on the 12 August for a sketching tour' (Appendix B). In the second of the two letters written on the tour, composed at Whittington Hall near Kirkby Lonsdale on 6 September 1836 (cat. 40), Lear wrote: 'I have now been a month in the Lake Country – & have seen nothing of a Lake at all', and later in the same letter: 'I expect to meet a very gay party … at Stoors – & from there – I intend taking walks from different Inns all over the Lakes.' The implication of the first statement is that he is visiting the Lakes for the first time, and of the second that this is a course of action that he has not adopted before.

In spite of the clear evidence of these statements, various drawings of Lake District subjects with July dates ascribed to Lear exist in both public and private collections. Some have been included in exhibitions either on Lear or on the Lake District, and have thus muddied the waters:

1. *Windermere Lake from the Road from Kendal to Bowness*, inscribed, annotated and dated 10 July, pencil and watercolour (fig. 53). This watercolour was included in the Gooden & Fox Exhibition, *Edward Lear 1812–1888 – A Loan Exhibition*, 1968, no. 35 and plate VII, and later included in *The Discovery of the Lake District*, Victoria & Albert Museum, 1984, no. 178, illustrated page 63, and Noakes 1991 repr. p. 42. Formerly in the collection of the Clonterbrook Trust, now Private Collection.

2. *Ullswater: A View of the Lake*, inscribed, annotated and dated 18 July, pencil and watercolour. Included in the Gooden & Fox Exhibition, *Edward Lear 1812–1888 – A Loan Exhibition*, 1968, no. 36. Formerly in the collection of the Clonterbrook Trust, now Private Collection.

3. *Grasmere*, inscribed and dated on the reverse 'Grasmere Lake / July 12 / 1836' (apparently transcribed from an old mount), pencil, squared for enlargement. Ex-Manning Gallery. Wordsworth Trust, purchased from Derek Lockett in 1986.

4. *Coniston Water*. Inscribed and dated 11 July, pencil. The Wordsworth Trust. This is one of a group of eight drawings of Lake District subjects, dated between 11 and 12 July (no year), which were sold at Sotheby's, 5 April 1973, lots 6, 7, and 7A; none of the others seem to have appeared on the market since (at least not with an attribution to Lear). A comparison with 'Windermere Lake from the Road from Kendal to Bowness' (No. 1 in this list, and fig. 53) was cited in support of the drawings' idenfication as Lear. The fact that none of the eight drawings were illustrated in the catalogue and that the prices achieved for them were quite low (a little over £36 on average each, considerably less than the going rate) suggests that neither Sotheby's nor the buyers had much faith in the attribution.

5. *On the River Brathay, near Ambleside*. Inscribed and dated 11 July, pencil. Department of Printing and Graphic Arts, the Houghton Library, Harvard University, purchased from the Manning Gallery in 1966. Mentioned in Peter Levi, *Edward Lear – A Biography*, 1995, p. 50.

6. *Langdale Pikes as seen above Skelwith Force*. Inscribed and dated 21 July, pencil. Abbot Hall Art Gallery, purchased in 1967.

Lear is known not to have been in the Lake District in any July from 1833 onwards (in 1833, he was probably on the Continent with John Gould; in 1834, he was in London, and in 1835 and 1836 he was at Knowsley). In addition, all of these drawings are stylistically quite unlike any definitely known to have been produced by Lear in the years up to 1837. Numbers 1 and 2 are by the same artist, and numbers 5 and 6 are by the same artist; both hands are unidentified. The remaining two drawings are by other hands. All six have been mistakenly ascribed to Lear through a combination of ignorance, enthusiasm and wishful thinking, of which both dealers and collectors have been willing victims.

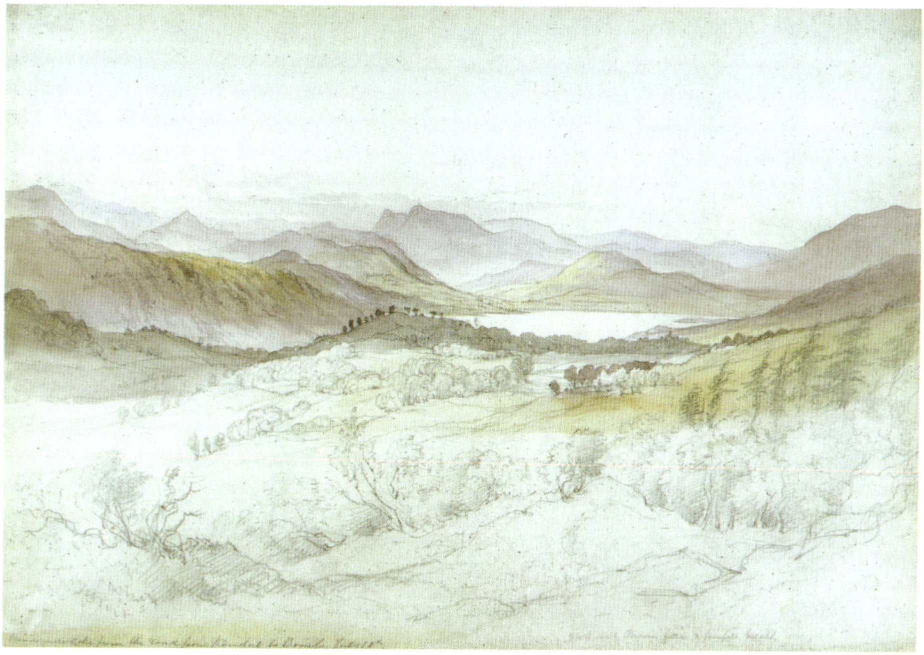

Fig. 53 Unknown English artist, formerly attributed to Edward Lear, *Windermere Lake from the Road from Kendal to Bowness*, inscribed as title and dated 10 July, and further inscribed with notes, pencil and watercolour, 27.5 × 36.3 cm (Private Collection).

APPENDIX D
THE HORNBY FAMILY

Lear's friendships made through his relationship with the 13th Earl of Derby (1775–1851) were very important in his life, and none more so at this time than the ones he made with various members of the Hornby family, who were closely connected with the Derby family by marriage. The 12th Earl's sister Lucy was married in 1772 to the Rev. Geoffrey Hornby (1750–1812), Rector of Winwick in Cheshire from 1781 until his death. There were six sons and five daughters from this marriage, and Lear knew, stayed with, and formed friendships with many of them and their children. The eldest son Edmund (1773–1857) married his cousin Charlotte, daughter of the 12th Lord Derby; it was their eldest son Edmund George (1799–1865), with whom Lear stayed in Lancaster in August 1836. The second son James John (1777–1855) was Rector of Winwick from his father's death in 1812 until his own in 1855; he was the patron who employed Pugin to add a chancel to the medieval church at Winwick in 1847–8 and who commissioned the only known watercolour of a Lake District subject from Lear (fig. 31, p. 120). His son Robert Atherton Hornby (1805–1857) was Lear's particular friend. It was he who, with his uncle the 13th Earl of Derby, concocted the plan of providing Lear with a sum of money sufficient to pay for his trip to Rome (see cat. 93). Lear first met Robert Hornby in June 1835, and, when he heard of his death in 1857, he wrote to his sister Ann: 'he was my oldest & kindest friend in the world ... and I cannot replace him'. Robert stayed at Winwick and from the 1840s the family rented the large house Wansfell Holme to the south of Ambleside each summer. Sadly, no letters survive recording his friendship with Lear.

The fourth son of Geoffrey and Lady Lucy Stanley was Phipps Hornby (1785–1867), later to become Admiral Sir Phipps Hornby. Lear stayed with him and his family near Plymouth in June 1837; the letter recording this stay is cat. 104. Lear was friendly with several of Phipps Hornby's children, including the eldest, another Phipps (1820–1848), with whom Lear made a tour of Scotland in 1841, and another Rev. James John Hornby (1826–1909), who later became Headmaster of Eton from 1864 and then Provost from 1884 until his death. In 1884, Lear wrote, 'He & I – (the Provost) – used to run races all over that part of the country – & perhaps you don't know that I know every corner of Westmorland; Scawfell Pikes is my cousin, and Skiddaw is my mother in law' (Noakes 1985, p. 95). This considerably later recollection needs to be taken with something of a pinch of salt, but is probably not a total invention; it seems likely that Lear is recalling a visit to Wansfell Holme in 1850, since James John would have been far too young in 1836 (see pp. 143 and 145).

The youngest four of Geoffrey and Lucy's six daughters remained unmarried, but the second, like her eldest brother's wife also called Charlotte, married her cousin the 13th Earl of Derby in 1798. The 13th Earl (1775–1851) was Lear's most important and munificent patron during these years. The Hornby and the Stanley families were thus closely interlinked by marriage over two generations, relationships of which the young Lear would have been well aware. While the artist's relationship with the 13th Earl remained one of patron and employee, Lear's dealings with the younger members of both families in several cases blossomed into serious friendship. Although nothing now survives recording their friendships, Lear's relations with Robert Hornby and Phipps Hornby were of great importance in his life and career.

APPENDIX E
LEAR'S LONDON LODGINGS

Lear's first London lodgings, which he shared with his sister Ann, probably from late 1827, were at 38, Upper North Place, Gray's Inn Road. In April 1832 brother and sister separated and Lear moved into bachelor lodgings at 61, Albany Street, Regent's Park, where he stayed until the end of January 1834. By the middle of February 1834, he was at 28, Southampton Row, Russell Square, where he stayed until January or February 1837. On 3 January 1837, he wrote from Southampton Row: 'I was about taking lodgings elsewhere, but under the present circumstances have put up with them'; on 11 February, he wrote from his new lodgings at 36, Great Marlborough Street: 'My lodgings are *more comfortable than any I have ever been in*', suggesting that his move there is recent, since it is obviously fresh in his mind. This move meant that he was only a few doors down from his friend Charles Hullmandel at no. 49. He was still there on 3 March, but by 15 April had moved to his final set of London lodgings, at 21, Sherrard Street, Golden Square; in a letter dated that day, he mentions these lodgings in the first sentence, implying that he had only just moved in. This raises the intriguing possibility that for a short period he was lodging in the same house as the young Charles Darwin, who moved into 36, Great Marlborough Street, on 14 March 1837. Darwin, who had recently returned from his voyage in the Beagle, echoed Lear's sentiments in a letter of 28 March mentioning his 'nice comfortable lodgings' (*The Correspondence of Charles Darwin*, ed. Frederick Burkhardt and Sydney Smith (Cambridge: 1985), vol. ii, p. 13). It appears, however, that the two young men did not know each other.

BIBLIOGRAPHY

Abbey, J.R., *Scenery of Great Britain and Ireland in Aquatint and Lithography 1770–1860 from the Library of J.R. Abbey – A Bibliographical Catalogue*, London, 1952

—*Travel in Aquatint and Lithography 1770–1860 from the Library of J.R. Abbey – A Bibliographical Catalogue*, 2 vols, London, 1956–7

Allison's Northern Tourist's Guide to the Lakes, of Cumberland, Westmorland, and Lancashire; wherein the Mountains, Lakes, and Scenery are correctly described; and the Stages and favourite Excursions distinctly pointed out, Penrith, 1835 (5th edition of Shaw's Guide, first published in 1812)

Baines, Edward, *A Companion to the Lakes of Cumberland, Westmoreland and Lancashire; in a Descriptive Account of a Family Tour, and Excursions on Horseback and on Foot. With a new, copious, and correct Itinerary*, 3rd edition, London, 1834

Drummond, Maldwin, *After You, Mr Lear: In the wake of Edward Lear in Italy. The story of a voyage to rediscover the ways of Edward Lear, artist and author, through his paintings, diaries and letters*, Rendlesham, 2007

Fisher, Clemency (ed.), *A Passion for Natural History: The Life and Legacy of the 13th Earl of Derby*, exhibition catalogue, National Museums & Galleries on Merseyside, Liverpool, 2002

Hall, Mr and Mrs S.C. (Samuel Carter), *Ireland: Its Scenery, Character, &c.*, 3 vols, London, 1841–3

Hullmandel, Charles, *The Art of Drawing on Stone*, London, 1824

—*On Some important Improvements in Lithographic Printing*, London, 1827

Hyman, Susan, *Edward Lear's Birds*, London, 1980

Jackson, Christine E., *Bird Illustrators: Some Artists in Early Lithography*, London, 1975

Lear, Edward, *Illustrations of the Family of Psittacidae, or Parrots*, London, 1830–2

—*Letters of Edward Lear to Chichester Fortescue Lord Carlingford and Frances Countess Waldegrave*, ed. Lady Strachey, London, 1907

—*Later Letters of Edward Lear to Chichester Fortescue (Lord Carlingford), Lady Waldegrave and Others*, ed. Lady Strachey, London, 1911

—*Selected Letters*, ed. Vivien Noakes, Oxford, 1988

Leigh, Samuel, *Leigh's Guide to the Lakes and Mountains of Cumberland, Westmoreland, and Lancashire. Illustrated with a map of the country, and maps of Windermere, Derwent Water, Borrowdale, Ullswater, Grasmere, Rydal Water, and Langdale*, 3rd edition, London, 1835

Library of the Fine Arts, 'A View of the Present State of Lithography in England', 1, April 1831, 201–16.

Morrell, Jack and Arnold Thackray (ed.), *Gentlemen of Science: Early Correspondence of the British Association for the Advancement of Science*, London, 1984

Noakes, Vivien, *Edward Lear: The life of a wanderer*, Stroud, 2006 (1st edition, 1968; reprinted, 1979; revised and enlarged edition, 2004)

—*Edward Lear 1812–1888*, exhibition catalogue, Royal Academy, London, 1985

—*The Painter Edward Lear*, Newton Abbott, 1991

Proceedings of the Fifth Meeting of the British Association for the Advancement of Science, held in Dublin, during the Week from the 10th to the 15th of August 1835, Inclusive. With an Alphabetical List of Members enrolled in Dublin, Dublin, 1835

Reade, Brian, *Edward Lear's Parrots*, London, 1949 (reprinted as *An essay on Edward Lear's Illustrations of the family of Psittacidae or Parrots*, 1978)

—*Edward Lear 1812–1888: An Exhibition of Oil Paintings, Water-Colours and Drawings, Books and Prints, Manuscripts, Photographs and Records*, exhibition catalogue, Arts Council of Great Britain, London, 1958

Ritchie, Leitch, *Ireland – Picturesque and Romantic* (*Heath's Picturesque Annual, for 1837. Ireland*), London, 1837

Ruskin, John, *The Works of John Ruskin* (Library Edition), ed. E.T. Cook and A. Wedderburn, 39 vols, London, 1903–12

Sauer, Gordon C., *John Gould The Bird Man: A Chronology and Bibliography*, London, 1982

Smith, Frances K., *Daniel Fowler of Amherst Island 1810–1894*, exhibition catalogue, Agnes Etherington Art Centre, Kingston, Ontario, 1979

Stanley, Arthur Penrhyn, *The Life and Correspondence of Arthur Penrhyn Stanley, D.D. Late Dean of Westminster*, ed. Rowland E. Prothero, 2 vols, London, 1893

Tattersall, George, *The Lakes of England*, London, 1836

Twyman, Michael, 'The tinted Lithograph', *Journal of the Printing Historical Society*, 1 (1965), 39–56

—*Lithography, 1800–1850: The Techniques of Drawing on Stone in England and France and their Application in Works of Topography*, London, 1970

—*Directory of London Lithographic Printers, 1800–1850*, London, 1976

—'Charles Joseph Hullmandel: Lithographic Printer Extraordinary', in P. Gilmour (ed.), *Lasting Impressions – Lithography as Art*, London, 1988, 42–90, 362–7

—*Images en couleur: Godefroy Engelmann, Charles Hullmandel et les Débuts de la Chromolithographie*, exhibition catalogue, Musée de l'Imprimerie, Lyon, and Panama Musées, Paris, 2007

Williams, W.S., 'On Lithography', *Transactions of the Society for the Encouragement of Arts, Manufactures, and Commerce*, London, 1847–8, 226–50

Wordsworth, William, *A Guide through the District of the Lakes in the North of England, with a Description of the Scenery, &c. for the Use of Tourists and Residents, Fifth edition, with considerable additions*, Kendal and London, 1835

IMAGE CREDITS

Cats. 56, 71, 74: Courtesy of Abbot Hall Art Gallery, Kendal, Cumbria
Cat. 107: Ashmolean Museum, Oxford
Cats. 7, 8, 9, 10, 33, 34, 46, 47, 49, 62, 83: © The Trustees of the British Museum
Cat. 60: Trustees, Cecil Higgins Art Gallery, Bedford, England
Cat. 63: Reproduced by permission of the Provost & Fellows of Eton College
Cat. 89: Reproduced by courtesy of the University Librarian and Director, The John Rylands University Library, The University of Manchester
Cats. 90, 98, 99, 100, 101, 102, 103: The Whitworth Art Gallery, The University of Manchester
Cats. 5, 12, 14, 15, 16, 17, 37, 40, 91, 92, 93, 94, 95, 104: Reproduced by kind permission of Frederick Warne & Co.
Cat 6: The Bodleian Library, University of Oxford, Bodl. 1701 c.32, Plate XXIV

Figs. 15, 19: Photograph courtesy of Cumbria Record Office and Local Studies Library, Barrow
Fig. 24: © A. Taylor
Fig. 32: © 2008 Museum of Art, RISD Private Collection, Providence; photography courtesy of Museum of Art, Rhode Island School of Design; Photography by Erik Gould
Figs. 4, 5: Licence granted courtesy of the Rt. Hon. The Earl of Derby 2009
Fig. 21: © Christie's Images Ltd 2009
Fig. 12: Houghton Library, b MS Typ 55.14 (46)
Fig. 37: Houghton Library, Typ Dr 805.L513.36W Sz 2
Figs. 11, 42: Courtesy of the Huntington Library, Art Collections, and Botanical Gardens, San Marino, California
Frontispiece: © National Portrait Gallery, London
Figs. 28, 38, 47: Courtesy of Sotheby's
Figs. 29, 48, 49, 50, 51, 52: V&A Images/Victoria and Albert Museum
Figs. 6, 7, 14, 16, 22, 25, 30, 33, 34, 35, 36, 44, 45, 46: Yale Center for British Art, Gift of Donald C. Gallup, 1934, 1939 Grad.

INDEX